Religious Liberty
and
Human Rights
in Nations and in Religions

edited by
Leonard Swidler

ECUMENICAL PRESS
Philadelphia
HIPPOCRENE BOOKS
New York

Published with the assistance of the
Jacob Blaustein Institute for the Advancement of Human Rights

Library of Congress Catalog Card Number: 86-80618

ISBN: 0-931214-06-8

Printed and bound in the United States of America

Published by Ecumenical Press, Temple University (022-38),
Philadelphia, PA 19122

Co-published by Hippocrene Books, Inc., 171 Madison Avenue,
New York, NY 10016

CONTENTS

WITHIN RELIGIONS

APPENDIXES

PREFACE

In 1971 an Institute honoring the name and memory of Jacob Blaustein was founded to encourage projects in interreligious understanding and other human-rights causes with which he was closely identified as a prominent leader of the American Jewish Committee. Analyzing and combatting religious intolerance has always been a central purpose of the American Jewish Committee and its Jacob Blaustein Institute for the Advancement of Human Rights. One effective way to further this objective, the Institute decided in 1981, is to promote understanding of the United Nations' Declaration on the Elimination of All Forms of Intolerance and of Discrimination Based on Religion or Belief, which was adopted by the U.N. General Assembly on November 25 of that year.

Since its founding, the Institute, in association with leading academic institutions and human-rights organizations, has sponsored a number of significant colloquia in the area of religion and human rights. The first was in 1974 at McGill University in Montreal, Canada. The papers, discussion, and recommendations of this colloquium were published in 1978 in *Essays on Human Rights: Contemporary Issues and Perspectives*. In 1982 the Institute cooperated with Columbia University in a follow-up colloquium on the relationship between religion and human rights, with the participation of scholars from various countries, religions, and intellectual disciplines. The colloquium papers are the basis of a volume in preparation, tentatively titled, "Studies in Religion and Human Rights."

The present volume is the product of the latest Jacob Blaustein Institute collaboration in this field—in this instance, with Professor Leonard Swidler of Temple University's Religion Department and editor of its important *Journal of Ecumenical Studies*. He has brought together in this volume the written and oral presentations at an international colloquium assembled under his leadership in Haverford, Pennsylvania, November 3-8, 1985, to inquire into the problem of religious intolerance as it has been, and currently is being, manifested in conflicts within nations, between nations, and within religions.

The colloquium was privileged to have among its participants Mme. Elizabeth Odio-Benito, whom the UN Subcommission on Prevention of Discrimination and Protection of Minorities had assigned to report to it the results of a study it asked her to conduct on the root causes of religious intolerance, its current dimensions, and the educational and other means that can be brought to bear in combatting it. In formulating its Final Statement, comprising both general principles and action-oriented recommendations, the colloquium benefitted greatly from her presentation, which included information on the findings of a U.N. Seminar on the subject of religious intolerance, held in Geneva, Switzerland, in December, 1984.

The Final Statement endorsed generally the recommendations of this U.N. Seminar, which called on nations to provide in their constitutions and laws guarantees consistent with the provisions of the 1981 U.N. Declaration and other relevant human-rights documents, to designate national institutions charged with promoting religious tolerance, and to provide guidelines to public officials on showing respect for different religions or beliefs. The Final Statement also recommended that school teachers be educated in issues of religious freedom; that religious groups foster a spirit of tolerance toward other religions and beliefs, as well as within their own ranks; that the mass media play a major role in educating society in a spirit of tolerance in matters of religion or belief; and that interreligious dialogue, taking into account the 1981 U.N. Declaration, be pursued actively.

The present volume enriches existing writing on the complex and critical question of religious freedom and tolerance from international, national, and intrareligious perspectives. The principles and recommendations in the colloquium's Final Statement, reproduced at the end of this volume, constitute a clarion call to both religious believers and nonbelievers everywhere to unite in promoting religious liberty and tolerance.

The Jacob Blaustein Institute is pleased to cosponsor this volume and wishes to express deep appreciation to the editor, Professor Leonard Swidler.

Sidney Liskofsky
Director, The Jacob Blaustein Institute for the Advancement of
Human Rights of the American Jewish Committee, New York, NY

HUMAN RIGHTS AND RELIGIOUS LIBERTY
—FROM THE PAST TO THE FUTURE

Leonard Swidler

A human right, including religious liberty, is a claim to be able and allowed to perform an action because one is a human being—not because one is a citizen, or is permitted in law, or has a grant from the king or the pope, or for any other reason. Human rights, or at least the recognition thereof, are a relatively recent development in Western Civilization, that has been universalized. However, their roots reach back into Greco-Roman and Judeo-Christian cultures. Not every human being, of course, enjoyed the political freedom of citizens in the Greek states or the legal rights and juridical equality of Roman citizens in the Roman Republic and Empire, but these elements were essential in the foundation of the edifice of human rights that was slowly taking place. To these was added the notion of the inviolable dignity of every human being by the Judeo-Christian tradition. Nevertheless, it took a long time for these, and other, elements to develop into the notion of human rights of the modern period. This is not, however, surprising for human beings are historical beings, not only individually but also corporately. Our human reality is not something given once and for all, but it has developed—and will continue to develop.

One of the most basic of human rights is that of religious liberty, for religion is perhaps the most comprehensive of all human activities. Religion can be described, perhaps somewhat over-briefly, as "an explanation of the meaning of life and how to live accordingly," and it almost always entails the four C's: Creed, Code of action, Cult, and Community structure. Since religion is so comprehensive, it also, however, often tends toward absolutism and authoritarianism. Thus, in the ancient world where each nation had its own gods who rode into battle with them, the defeated nations often had to give up their own and accept their victors' gods.

It was here especially that the Romans made progress in religious liberty: they usually allowed nations they defeated to keep their religion and gods; the vanquished merely had to add the Roman gods to their own. The Romans even went so far as to make an exception for the Jews in this requirement, for theirs was an ancient religion. Not so, however, for that Jewish offshoot, Christianity. It suffered frequent persecution from the time of Nero on. This oppression brought Christian writers to lay claim to religious liberty already in the second century of the Christian era. Perhaps its clearest expression came from Tertullian in his A.D. 212 appeal to the Roman Proconsul Scapula:

> It is a fundamental human right, a privilege of nature, that all human beings should worship according to their own convictions; one human person's religion neither harms nor helps another. It is not

vii

proper to force religion. It must be undertaken freely, not under
pressure.[1]

In a way, the high point of religious liberty was reached publicly with its
universal declaration for the whole Roman Empire in the Edict of Milan (A.D.
313) by Emperor Constantine: "We should therefore give both to Christianity
and to all others free facility to follow the religion which they may desire."[2]
This moment of freedom was, however, short-lived, for in A.D. 380 the Edict
of Thessalonica was issued by Emperor Theodosius, stating that, "It is our will
that all the peoples who are ruled by the administration of Our Clemency shall
practice that religion which the divine Peter the Apostle transmitted to the
Romans."[3] For well over a millennium the clarion call for religious liberty by
Constantine, Tertullian, and other pre-Constantinian Christian writers was muted
by the insistence that the state enforce the teaching of the only true religion,
Christianity.

Just outside the Roman Empire, however, in the eighth century, the upper
classes of the Tartar Kingdom of the Khazars (in southern Russia from the sixth
to the thirteenth centuries) converted to Judaism and permitted religious freedom to Christians and Muslims as well. In the West, though, it was not until the
sixteenth-century Protestant Reformation that the call for religious liberty was
widely heard again, and then only from the Radical Reformers—who often paid
for their actions with their lives at the hands of both Protestants and Catholics.
Eventually, nevertheless, the "Protestants" established religious liberty—William
the Silent, though with some restrictions, in the Netherlands; Roger Williams in
Rhode Island; and William Penn in Pennsylvania—as did the Catholic Lord Baltimore in Maryland. Soon thereafter the liberating ideas of the Enlightenment
began to make themselves evident in the development of the notion of human
rights—religious liberty among them. Thus, religious liberty found political expression in the Bill of Rights of the colony of Virginia in 1776 ("that religion
. . . can be directed only by reason and conviction, not by force or violence; and
therefore all men are equally entitled to the free exercise of religion, according
to the dictates of conscience"), and eventually in 1791 in the U.S. Constitution's
Bill of Rights and the 1789 *Declaration des droits des hommes* of the French
Revolution. Resistance to this breakthrough was intense on all fronts; nevertheless, the principle continued to spread in country after country.

Then, in 1919, the President of the United States, Woodrow Wilson, drafted
the Covenant of the League of Nations in person, using his own typewriter. One
of Wilson's proposals was to include an article on religious liberty in the Covenant, but it was scuttled as soon as Japan sought to link it with racial equality

---

[1]Tertullian, "Ad Scapulam," *Patrologia Latina*, I, 699.
[2]Constantine, "De mortibus persecutorem," ibid., VII, 267.
[3]Colman Barry, ed., *Readings in Church History* (Westminster, MD: Newman Books,
1960), I, p. 142.

and the equality of states. The next milestone in the internationalizing of religious liberty, as well as the notion of human rights in general, was also set down by an American president, Franklin D. Roosevelt, when he delivered his famous address to Congress on January 6, 1941, on the "Four Freedoms." In it he outlined the four essential freedoms upon which the whole world should be founded: freedom of speech and expression, freedom of religion, freedom from want, and freedom from fear. "Roosevelt was explicit in stressing that these freedoms were to be secured everywhere in the world, that is to say, on a universal basis. He made it clear that traditional freedoms of speech and of worship should go hand in hand with such wider human rights as economic and social welfare and peace and security for all peoples and persons."[4] (It is quite amazing how Roosevelt anticipated—and influenced?—the development of the so-called three generations of human rights: first generation, civil and political rights; second generation, social and economic rights; third generation, rights of world development and peace.)

Here was an immediate vision for the framing of the United Nations Charter in San Francisco in 1945. Article 1 of the U.N. Charter stated that among the purposes of the United Nations is: "To achieve international cooperation . . . in promoting and encouraging respect for human rights and for fundamental freedoms for all without distinction as to race, sex, language or *religion*" (emphasis added). Article 55 repeated: "The United Nations shall promote: . . . universal respect for, and observance of, human rights and fundamental freedoms for all without distinction as to race, sex, language or religion." Important as this move was, many felt a "bill of human rights" needed to be spelled out, and it was—in the 1948 Universal Declaration of Human Rights. Included in its thirty articles was Art. 18 on religious liberty:

> Everyone has the right of freedom of thought, conscience and religion; this right includes freedom to change his religion or belief, and freedom, either alone or in community with others and in public or private, to manifest his religion or belief in teaching, practice, worship and observance.

Various regional organizations, such as the Council of Europe and the Organization of American States, issued declarations on human rights, including religious liberty, and several subsequent U.N. documents—in focusing on specific human-rights matters, such as the elimination of racism—included references to "the right to freedom of thought, conscience and religion" (Declaration on the Elimination of All Forms of Racial Discrimination, Art. 5, d, vii). In 1959, the U.N. Special Rapporteur Arcot Krishnaswami submitted his *Study of Discrimination in the Matters of Religious Rights and Practices*. In its wake a specific Declaration against religious discrimination (as occurred on racism in 1963) was

---

[4]Theo C. van Boven, "Religious Liberty in the Context of Human Rights," *The Ecumenical Review* 37 (July, 1985): 347.

to be passed quickly, in turn to be followed by an internationally legally binding Covenant or Convention (as, for example, the "International Covenant on Economic, Social and Cultural Rights," and the "International Covenant on Civil and Political Rights," in 1966). However, the U.N. political scene shifted dramatically and greatly postponed the passage of the Declaration, which finally came after long and heroic efforts by a few dedicated persons[5] on November 25, 1981.

It is clear, then, that—since human beings are by nature historical beings—what human rights are and what it means to be fully human will evolve, both in terms of basic capabilities and in terms of a growing recognition of what in fact exists. Basically, everything human flows from the essential human structure, that is, being an animal who can think abstractly and make free decisions. Through these abilities humanity has gradually, through history, come to the contemporary position where claims are made in favor of "human rights," that is, things which are due to all humans specifically because they are human. This position, however, was not always and everywhere held; it was, for the most part, hardly even conceived until recently. It is only slightly over 100 years ago, for example, that slavery was still widely accepted—even vigorously defended and practiced by high Christian church leaders (not to speak of Jewish, Muslim, Christian, etc. slavetraders). This radical violation of "human rights" has today been largely eliminated, not only *de facto* but also *de jure*. No thinker or public leader today would contemplate justifying slavery, at least in its directly named form of the past (see the Universal Declaration of Human Rights, Art. 4). Here is a glaringly obvious example of the historical evolution of the understanding of what it means to be fully human in terms of *recognition* of what was always the case, that is, that human beings are by nature radically free.

However, the human right to private property (Universal Declaration, Art. 17), which was first publicly acknowledged in eighteenth-century Europe, would have been unthinkable without the requisite previous development in control over matter. The same is true of the twentieth-century claim to the right to work (Universal Declaration, Art. 23):

> The development of this new control over nature—first over external nature and increasingly also over human nature . . . has made possible entirely new dimensions of human self-development, and its apparently illimitable expansion leads to the expectation, at least in the developed countries, that it can release a sufficient potential so that everyone can participate in them—and consequently has a right to participate therein.[6]

---

[5]Sidney Liskofsky, "The UN Declaration on the Elimination of Religious Intolerance and Discrimination: Historical and Legal Perspectives" (typescript, April, 1984, 93 pp., available from the Jacob Blaustein Institute for the Advancement of Human Rights, 165 East 56th St., New York, NY 10022), pp. 37 ff.

[6]Johannes Schwartländer, ed., *Modernes Freiheitsethos und christlicher Glaube* (Munich: Kaiser; Mainz: Grünewald, 1981), p. 11.

Here are clear examples of the historical evolution of the understanding of what it means to be fully human in terms of the expansion of the basic *capabilities* of humanity. (Of course, claim of and/or general acknowledgement of a human right—unfortunately as humanity painfully knows—does not automatically guarantee its realization, but it is the indispensable first step thereto.)

What fundamentally has been acknowledged in the twentieth century as the foundation of being human is that human beings ought to be autonomous in their decisions—such decisions being directed by their own reason and limited only by the same rights of others: "All human beings are born free and equal in dignity and rights. They are endowed with reason and conscience and should act toward one another in a spirit of brotherhood" (Universal Declaration, Art. 1). This autonomy in the ethical sphere, which Thomas Aquinas recognized already in the thirteenth century,[7] expanded into the social and political spheres in the eighteenth century—well capsulated in the slogan of the French Revolution: Liberty, Equality, Fraternity (contemporary consciousness of sexist language would lead to such a substitute for "Fraternity" as "Solidarity"). In the term "Liberty" are understood all the personal and civil rights; in "Equality" are understood the political rights of participation in public decision-making; in "Solidarity" are understood (in an expanded, twentieth-century sense) the social rights.

The great religious communities of the world, though frequently resistant in the past, and too often still in the present, have likewise often and in a variety of ways expressed a growing awareness of and commitment to many of the same notions of what it means to be fully human. One such joint, global-level expression reflecting the thought and *engagement* of leaders of all the major world religions (over 1,000 persons, including 219 full delegates) was issued by the World Conference on Religion and Peace, at Kyoto, Japan, in October, 1970:

> As we sat down together facing the overriding issues of peace we discovered that the things which unite us are more important than the things which divide us. We found that we share:
>
>> A conviction of the fundamental unity of the human family, and the equality and dignity of all human beings;
>>
>> A sense of the sacredness of the individual person and his conscience;
>>
>> A sense of the value of human community;
>>
>> A realization that might is not right; that human power is not self-sufficient and absolute;
>>
>> A belief that love, compassion, selflessness, and the force of inner truthfulness and of the spirit have ultimately greater power than hate, enmity, and self-interest;
>>
>> A sense of obligation to stand on the side of the poor and the

---

[7]*Summa Theologiae*, I-II, Q. 91, a. 2: "Inter cetera autem rationalis creatura excellentiori quondam modo divinae providentiae subiacet, inquantum et ipsa fit providentiae particeps, sibi ipsi et aliis providens."

oppressed as against the rich and the oppressors; and
A profound hope that good will finally prevail.[8]

Clearly, however, the full exercise of religious liberty and other fundamental human rights is not everywhere a reality—hence the need for the 1981 U.N. Declaration on the Elimination of All Forms of Intolerance and of Discrimination Based on Religion or Belief" and the commissioning by the U.N. Subcommission on Prevention of Discrimination and Protection of Minorities in 1983 of a study to be carried out in light of the Declaration. This study by a Special Rapporteur, Professor Elizabeth Odio-Benito of Costa Rica, is scheduled to be submitted late in 1986. It is to look into (a) the "current manifestations of intolerance and discrimination on the grounds of religion or belief," (b) the "root causes" of such intolerance, and (c) remedial actions to be recommended, especially in the field of education; it should (d) highlight the "human rights principles . . . and the universal spiritual principles underlying all the major world religions"; and it should show (e) "appreciation of the different ways in which these universal principles are manifested in different religions and different cultures."

In studying religious intolerance it is important to recognize that, although all religious intolerance is intolerance between or among religions and beliefs, it takes three major forms:

(1) *Between nations:* History is full of the stories of human destruction resulting at least partly from religious intolerance between nations: the "Crusades" (against Jews, Orthodox Christians, and Muslims) from the eleventh to the fifteenth centuries, the sixteenth-century "Wars of Religion," the "Thirty Years War" in the seventeenth century, the wars from the eighth to the nineteenth centuries between Islam and Christendom, etc. Unfortunately, we are not free from such international human destruction resulting from religious intolerance even today; recall the constant conflict between Muslim Pakistan and (predominantly) Hindu India, the Shiite-Sunni battles between Iran and its neighbors, the Christian-Muslim struggles of the Greeks and Turks, etc.

(2) *Within nations:* This usually takes the form of a dominant religion or belief using government and other instruments to oppress the other religions or beliefs, for example, Hindus and Sikhs in the Punjab, Northern Ireland, Sri Lanka, the Philippines, Lebanon, etc. (This is not to claim that religious hostility is the sole or even necessarily most important factor in these and other conflicts, but that it is at least one very important element.) Then there is the human destruction resulting from religious oppression within nations which does not reach the level of riots and war but is, nevertheless, penetratingly corrosive of human life and spirit.

(3) *Within religions:* Beyond the above is the repression of human rights

---

[8]Homer A. Jack, ed., *Religion for Peace* (New Delhi: Gandhi Press Foundation, 1973), p. ix.

that takes place on a massive scale within many religions; that, too, is a kind of religious intolerance which is deeply destructive of full human life.

For some time, scholarly and other remedial efforts have been directed at each of these areas of the problem of religious intolerance. There is a growing honesty in historical scholarship which more and more eschews apologetics and tries to come as close as possible to telling the stories of religious intolerance *"wie es eigentlich gewesen war."* The same is true to some extent for current manifestations of religious intolerance, with various institutions such as the U.N. Human Rights Commission being established, replicated, and supplemented on a whole range of levels throughout the world; some of these agencies work on an international basis, some on a national or regional one. Most of these efforts, however, are directed mainly at the legal level, which, though extremely important, is not the sole level on which problems of religious intolerance must be attacked.

Further, religious intolerance as the violation of human rights within various religions is beginning to be worked on systematically, for example, through the formation of such organizations as the Association for the Rights of Catholics in the Church, with its Charter of the Rights of Catholics in the Church,[9] which is based on the U.N. Declaration of Human Rights.

Though much has been accomplished, much more remains to be done. The work to be done can be divided into four broad categories, one historical and three contemporary:

(1) *Historical research* is needed to ferret out the role religious intolerance and discrimination—between nations, within nations, and within religions—has played in human destruction in the past ("whoever does not know the past is condemned to repeat it").

(2) We need descriptions of current manifestations of religious intolerance, analyses of their root causes, and recommendations for remedial action in cases *within nations*. This area has been the focus of the bulk of the work of human-rights institutions in the past. It is extremely important and must be continued and extended, but it should not be done isolated from or to the neglect of work to eliminate religious intolerance between nations and within religions. All three are interrelated and reinforce each other for good or ill.

(3) Obviously, *international* human destruction resulting at least partly from religious intolerance—for example, the Hindu-Muslim conflict between India and Pakistan and the Jewish-Muslim conflict between Israel and surrounding Islam—cannot be stopped simply by eliminating religious intolerance in the legal sense within the various countries in question. Moreover, religious intolerance between religions, such as in Northern Ireland or Sri Lanka, will not be eliminable solely by juridical means, important though they are. In order to

---

[9]The Charter and further information about the Association for the Rights of Catholics in the Church (ARCC) can be obtained by writing Dr. Leonard Swidler, Religion Dept. (022-28), Philadelphia, PA 19122.

attain and maintain true religious tolerance in the above cases and throughout the world, we need to go beyond the study and advocacy of religious tolerance as such and move to *interreligious dialogue*. Only thus can we get at the roots of religious intolerance and do so in a positive way that will have a real chance of promoting fundamental change.

For example, Christian Antisemitism will never be thoroughly uprooted simply by attacking it directly. Whenever a weakness occurs in Western society, Antisemitism will reappear—unless it has been uprooted at its source, unless Christians and Jews have met each other over an extended period of time in dialogue *qua* Christians and Jews. Only thus, reports the Harvard social psychologist Gordon W. Allport, can the bases of prejudice be destroyed.[10] Then the recurring crises in society will have no ground from which to bring forth Antisemitism. Hence, the promotion of interreligious, interideological dialogue, with clear linkages with religious freedom and human rights, should have the highest priority in the present and future.

(4) A further truly creative, but also very delicate, area of work to be done is that of religious freedom and human rights *within the various religions*. It is simply not true that a religion is a totally voluntary institution that one can leave at will if one's rights are being violated—for example, the attempt to leave Islam can be fatal. Moreover, even where such withdrawal is legally possible, the human destruction resulting from such wrenching withdrawals, or from the persistent oppression if for any reason one is unable or unwilling to withdraw, is withering of human life and spirit.

Moreover, it is true that:

> [T]he way each religion and belief teaches its own members to treat fellow members who think differently than they do will tend to carry over in the treatment of members of other religions and beliefs. Hence it is imperative that all religions and beliefs school their members to accord all others, both within and outside of their ranks, the full human integrity, dignity, and religious liberty they claim for themselves.[11]

Stated otherwise: *"The first and oldest aspect of religious liberty is the right which a group claims for itself to practice its faith without interference from others . . . Only later—and often half-heartedly—is freedom of conscience extended to other groups who differ in belief and practice."*[12] It is only after a great struggle, which in most religious communities has barely begun, that the highest stage of religious liberty emerges—*"when a religious group, dedicated to*

[10]Gordon W. Allport, *The Nature of Prejudice* (Cambridge, MA: Addison-Wesley Publishing Co., 1954).

[11]Final Statement of the Conference; see p. 245, below.

[12]Robert Gordis, "Judaism and Religious Liberty," in Franklin H. Littell, ed., *Religious Liberty in the Crossfire of Creeds* (Philadelphia: Ecumenical Press, 1978), p. 26 (emphasis in original).

its belief and tradition, is willing to grant freedom of thought and action to dissi-dents within its own ranks."[13]

It cannot be overemphasized that religious liberty, like all human freedom, is a whole cloth; unfreedom in one area will distort, if not destroy, freedom else-where. None will be completely free unless all are free. The unity of humanity has always been true, but it is becoming ever more intensely so with each new technological advancement—and the coming of those new advancements is accel-erating exponentially.

This book is the result of a project which began to study religious liberty *within nations, between nations,* and *within religions*—and their interconnection. With unlimited financial, human, and temporal resources, all nations and reli-gions could have been studied thoroughly, but, as is always the case, more mod-est resources were at hand; therefore, six nations from the first, second, and third worlds (the U.S.A., the U.S.S.R., Yugoslavia, Egypt, the Sudan, and South Korea) were selected for study of the violation of religious liberty *within nations* by experts, both for their own sakes and to serve as replicable models for others to follow for other nations. A similar choice was made of one example of the violation of human rights because of religious intolerance *between nations,* namely, Muslim Pakistan and (largely) Hindu India. Lastly, education for human rights *within* five major world *religions* was focused on by an expert of each.

The results were most stimulating and encouraging, as can be discerned in the following essays and most of all by the creative and courageous Final State-ment. Though most of the sixteen participating scholars (from fourteen coun-tries on four continents and from five different religions) had never met each other before, they quickly learned to understand and trust each other.[14] This doubtless was true because they all are not only critical-thinking scholars and committed members of their respective religions, but they are all open human beings as well, who are experienced in true dialogue.[15] This combination of all three elements—and especially the last one—is unfortunately rare. All the partici-pants were aware of this and therefore had no illusions about how easily or quickly their mutual broad agreement would be matched by a broad spectrum of their communities. Nevertheless, this deep agreement of critical, open, com-mitted scholars—both women and men, from such diverse cultures and religions —sets the goal that must now be translated to the mass level.

This project was cosponsored by the *Journal of Ecumenical Studies,* the

---

[13]Ibid.

[14]The interchanges in response to each paper presented were extremely stimulating, and in a number of instances insights gleaned from these discussions were incorporated into the final, revised manuscripts published here. In the case of the commentary by Professor Abe on Professor Talbi's paper, the response was made available in written form and is such that it merits being published here.

[15]See "The Dialogue Decalogue" in the appendix, pp. 251-255, below.

Religion Department of Temple University, and the Jacob Blaustein Institute for the Advancement of Human Rights. Special gratitude is due to the latter both for contributing significantly to the human resources for the project and for providing the necessary funding.

Leonard Swidler (Roman Catholic) has been a Professor of Catholic Thought and Interreligious Dialogue in the Dept. of Religion at Temple University since 1966, following six years at Duquesne University, Pittsburgh, in history and theology. He co-founded the *Journal of Ecumenical Studies* in 1964 with his wife, Arlene Anderson Swidler, and has been its editor since that time. He holds a B.A. from St. Norbert's College, an M.A. from Marquette University, an S.T.L. from the University of Tübingen, and a Ph.D. (1961) in history from the University of Wisconsin. Long involved in interreligious/interideological dialogue on both the grassroots level and the academic level, he has published over 100 popular and scholarly articles, and nearly thirty books, including *Freedom in the Church* (Pflaum Press, 1969), *Women in Judaism* (Scarecrow Press, 1976), *Biblical Affirmations of Women* (Westminster Press, 1979), *From Holocaust to Dialogue: A Jewish-Christian Dialogue between Americans and Germans* (Ecumenical Press, 1981), *Authority in the Church and the Schillebeeckx Case* (Crossroad, 1982), and *Buddhism Made Plain* (with Antony Fernando) (Orbis Books, 1984).

KEYNOTE ADDRESS

Elizabeth Odio-Benito

A preoccupation common to us all justifies our presence in this meeting. I am surely not mistaken in asserting that we find ourselves here in response to our shared concern for the full exercise of and respect for the fundamental rights of all human beings at this historic moment in which we are living. It is within that broad context that the specific field of action against intolerance and discrimination because of religious conviction or belief is to be placed and within which the full scope of our study, aspirations, and struggle should occur.

Freedom of thought, of conscience, and of religion or belief is, as we know, proclaimed and recognized by the most important legal instruments of the international community. Starting with the fundamental principles of the Charter of the United Nations regarding the proper dignity and equality shared by all persons, and ending with the "Declaration on the Elimination of All Forms of Intolerance and Discrimination Based on Religion or Beliefs," adopted by the General Assembly of the United Nations, November 25, 1981, the peoples forming the international community have legally organized and pledged to fight against all forms of intolerance and discrimination violating the fundamental right of the human being to live according to the dictates of his or her faith and conscience. This Declaration of November 25, 1981, was preceded by similar declarations and conventions in an attempt to prevent and eliminate forms of discrimination and intolerance based on race and sex.

This background leads us to reflect briefly on the atrocious reality—only too real and verifiable by simple observation of daily occurrences and a careful reading of history—of the widespread existence of intolerance and discrimination among peoples and nations. These manifestations of intolerance, discrimination, and oppression occur, sometimes in isolation, and sometimes in combination because of race, sex, religion, or belief. We cannot, however, look for the origin of, and therefore the possible solutions to, such serious problems exclusively within the legal norms that apply internally and internationally among states. The profound reasons for such attitudes and behavior of the human being must be sought in the social and cultural spheres.

Norms, judgments, prejudices, superstitions, myths, and archetypes whereby we model our behavior in society and which are culturally transmitted from generation to generation, as well as anachronistic and unjust economic structures that result in regional majorities of human beings sunk into misery and ignorance —all allow the germination of dogmatism, intolerance, and discrimination, and with it persecution and armed aggression. These norms, judgments, and prejudices, which give rise to deepfelt feelings and to the transformation of unfocused emotions into sharp feelings that condition our ideas about equality among human beings as well as tolerance and respect for the ideas and feelings of others,

1

are, as I pointed out, a product of societal forces. This means that in order to eliminate discrimination and intolerance in all its forms there must necessarily occur a change in attitude of the human being which will be a product of the needed social changes and psychic transformations of individuals.

In a reflection of such a general nature that I allow myself to make on discrimination, it is pertinent to remember that the idea of superiority of one group over another and the consequences of such an idea have not disappeared. It is just important to take into account that equality among all human beings means the absence of discrimination. Equality, however, is not uniformity. A regime of absolute respect for human rights must reconcile unity with diversity, interdependence with liberty. The equal dignity owed to all seeks the respect for the differences in the identity of each person. It is in the absolute respect for the right to be different that we find authentic equality and the only possibility of the full enjoyment of human rights without racial, sexual, or religious discrimination.

Having made these general considerations on discrimination as the violation of the right to be different, it behooves us to concentrate on the specific field we are dealing with in this Conference, that is, religious freedom and human rights, in the international community, within the nations, and within religions. The Jacob Blaustein Institute for the Advancement of Human Rights, the *Journal of Ecumenical Studies*, and the Religion Department of Temple University have joined efforts to make this Conference possible. It is a most generous effort made for which all of us, myself in particular, feel most thankful. These institutions have created a space which will allow us, for several days, to reflect and exchange ideas and experiences on how we can efficiently contribute to identifying the manifestations of intolerance and discrimination due to religion or belief, isolating their root causes, and projecting how we can collaborate in the prevention and elimination of such violations of human rights. This enormous effort by the institutions sponsoring this meeting is an encouragement and a stimulus of invaluable importance for those of us who find ourselves working on these matters from different points of view.

In my personal case, it grants me the opportunity to hear the outstanding professors who will participate in the discussions to enrich my knowledge and add to the information I need in my work as Special Rapporteur of the Subcommission on the Prevention of Discrimination and the Protection of Minorities of the United Nations. The preoccupation of the Subcommission with the existence of discrimination and intolerance in matters of religion and belief determined in the 1950's that Professor Arcot Krishnaswami be designated Special Rapporteur to undertake the study of these manifestations.

The brilliant report presented by Mr. Krishnaswami in 1959 describes the road leading to the development of the freedom of thought, the freedom of conscience and religion, and the principles of tolerance inherent in almost all the religious traditions of the world; it shows the gradual evolution of the concept in local legislation and its final acceptance by the international community. The

study defines the nature and essential elements of the right to freedom of
thought, conscience, and religion, and it discusses the condition of the religions
in relation to the state. The study includes a summary of the tendencies observed
and the conclusions Mr. Krishnaswami reached as Special Rapporteur, as well as
a series of recommendations for action on this matter. Taking the report as a
basis, the Subcommission prepared a project on the principles relative to discrimination in matters of belief, conscience, and religion, which was transmitted to
the Commission on Human Rights.

In 1962, when the Commission was considering the principles submitted by
the Subcommission, the General Assembly asked the Commission to develop a
Declaration and also a legal Convention on the elimination of all forms of religious intolerance in order to present them for the consideration and approval of
the General Assembly. It took twenty years of intensive and exhaustive debates
on all the aspects of the problem for the General Assembly to adopt in 1981 just
the "Declaration on the Elimination of All Forms of Intolerance and Discrimination Based on Religion or Belief."

It cannot be denied that the adoption of the Declaration represents an
advance of enormous importance along the difficult road toward abolishing
discriminatory practices and intolerant attitudes in regard to the human right of
religious liberty in all its aspects. With this Declaration, the General Assembly
has reminded the nations of the world that it is among the superior interests of
humanity to put an immediate end to the persecutions and manifestations of
religious prejudice. However, the length of the process before its adoption and
the discussions and compromises that preceded its approval on November 25,
1981, prove how delicate a subject it is. The discussion and the analysis of the
right to religious freedom can be held only within the scope of full liberty and
equality afforded to the dignity and the rights of all human beings. To admit
that the exercise of freedom in matters of religions and belief finds its most
adequate place in a clearly defined separation of what is religious and what is
political is a question that touches very closely all the institutions and structures
of the political dimension of the states, as well as the self-understanding of many
religions. This explains, in my opinion, why the road travelled to the adoption of
the Declaration has been so arduous, and it shows why it will also take a very
long time to adopt a Convention on this matter in the future.

The praiseworthy preoccupation of the Subcommission on the Prevention
of Discrimination and the Protection of Minorities with this subject did not stop
with the conclusion of the study by Professor Krishnaswami or with the adoption of the 1981 Declaration. Based on this Declaration, it was decided in 1983
to undertake a new study on the current dimensions of the problem of discrimination because of religion or belief, on its root causes, and on the possible
measures that could be adopted to prevent and eliminate such discrimination
and intolerance. The generosity and confidence of my former fellow members of
the Subcommission led to my designation to undertake such a study. The work
done since then is explained in the 1984 preliminary report and the 1985 report

on the progress of the work, which I submitted to the Subcommission during its
sessions in the years mentioned.

The reticence and fear with which the governments of the states comprising
the United Nations approach this type of study has been reflected in my study
since the very beginning. The sad proof of this is that by the 10th of May of
this year, 1985, the closing date for the reception of replies prior to my 1985
progress report, only twenty-two countries had replied to the questionnaire prepared by myself and sent on September 28, 1984, by the Centre for Human
Rights. Those twenty-two countries are: Argentina, Barbados, Burkina Faso,
Burundi, Chad, Chile, Cyprus, Denmark, Honduras, Iraq, Jordan, Mexico, Peru,
Qatar, the United Kingdom of Great Britain and Northern Ireland, the Arab
Republic of Syria, the Dominican Republic, the German Democratic Republic,
the Islamic Republic of Pakistan, the Socialist Republic of Czechoslovakia,
Thailand, and Tonga. I also received a reply from the Holy See. After writing the
1985 progress report, I received replies from another eleven countries: Austria,
Cape Verde, Ecuador, Colombia, Guatemala, Italy, Morocco, Portugal, Rhuanda,
Sudan, and Surinam.

Besides noting the small number of countries that have replied, I must add
that the information contained in their replies is meager, fragmented, and inadequate for determining the present dimensions of the problem of discrimination
and religious intolerance in our time, as well as their causes and possible measures
to combat such violations of human rights. Without any doubt, it can be said
that the data included in the replies is markedly insufficient. To give only two
examples, let me read the replies of the governments of Tonga and the Arab
Republic of Syria, which illustrate my present concern with the lack of information forthcoming from countries. The following can be read in Tonga's reply:

> . . . Tonga guarantees to its people liberty of thought, conscience
> and religion in general. There is at present no legal limitation to the
> freedom to make manifest a belief in a religion or credo nor as far as
> the right of any person to have and hold a religious or other convic-
> tion.

The Arab Republic of Syria replied in the following manner:

> . . . The problem of intolerance and discrimination due to religion
> or to belief does not exist in Syria. Our laws do not make any dis-
> tinction among citizens in this respect, and all citizens are treated
> equally by all departments of the Government and in what respects
> to the appointment to public and private positions. As a consequence
> we have no need to adopt measures to foster mutual tolerance and
> respect, given that such principles are promoted fundamentally by
> public morality and social and religious doctrine.

As far as intergovernmental organizations are concerned, the information
received up to now also cannot be called satisfactory. With the sole exception of
the reply sent by the United National Organization for Education, Science and

Culture (UNESCO), the rest of the replies are frankly insufficient. The same situation is true of the regional intergovernmental organizations. Regarding the nongovernmental organizations, only twelve have replied to the questionnaire, but the information provided is of great value.

In addition to the problems I have indicated, I must add another that has earned my deepest concern: I am referring to the collaboration that the Centre for Human Rights of the United Nations should provide toward the preparation of the study. For reasons peculiar to the Centre, a functionary who does not possess the prerequisites for such activity was appointed to act as my advisor in my work. Because of this, I limited my expectations of help simply to having information forwarded to me regularly as it came in, with the corresponding translations. However, due to the irregular and deficient way the documentation was forwarded, I expressly asked the Director of the Centre in May of this year, 1985, during my consultation visit to the Centre, that the problems be corrected. Far from being corrected as I asked, the problems have become remarkably worse, so that not even the documents which I specifically asked for, such as the lists with the names of countries and of the nongovernmental organizations, were sent. I have expressed my concerns to the Director of the Centre, Mr. Kurt Herndl, in various communications which I have sent, and to which I have not yet received any reply.

The lack of assistance on the part of the Centre for Human Rights—which to date has not even informed me whether any decision or resolution on the subject of my study was taken at the last session of the Subcommission (August, 1985) —added to the lack of collaboration from the governments will prevent me from making a profound and well-documented study on the current dimensions of intolerance and discrimination because of religion and belief. If the problem is not corrected soon—which does not seem possible—I will be forced to present a final report of my work next year (1986) which will not be a proper response to what I was asked to do.

This final report would have to analyze almost exclusively the possible measures to be taken to implement the Declaration or, in other words, the measures to be taken to prevent, combat, and eliminate intolerance and discrimination based on religion and belief. These measures would be those that the United Nations could adopt in the area of international law, as well as in its respective internal legal systems, and the measures that could be adopted on the part of its competent dependencies (administrative, legislative, and judicial), to prevent and combat intolerance and discrimination. These measures should also be taken appropriately by intergovernmental organizations and, of course, by individual states—and be followed up carefully by nongovernmental organizations.

Within the scope of this study which has been entrusted to me and which I have explained in brief, the Conference on Religious Liberty inaugurated today has a very particular meaning for me. First, as I pointed out, it allows me the exceptional opportunity to learn from the distinguished participants, to broaden my insights, and to obtain more trustworthy information on the problems of religious freedom within the international community, within nations, and within religions. Also, this Conference is evident proof that, at the margin of political problems which limit the action of governments and in many ways condition it, there are institutions and men and women all over the world dedicated to the struggle for the full respect of the fundamental rights of the human being.

If the efforts of the United Nations to prevent and eradicate intolerance and discrimination among and within countries and between individual human beings can draw a much needed support from such undertakings as this one—held under the sponsorship of the Jacob Blaustein Institute for the Advancement of Human Rights, the *Journal of Ecumenical Studies*, and the Religion Department of Temple University—we will be advancing toward finding solutions to the serious problems that worry us so.

What we must not allow under any circumstances is for us to be overcome with pessimism and discouragement. We must continue to investigate, to propose ideas, and to exert efforts toward the search for understanding, tolerance, and the respect for the right to be different, because—as I said before—the denial of such respect is the basis of all discrimination.

To my thanks to all of you for the support of the study that I undertake for the United Nations expressed by your presence, I wish to add my recognition to Professor Leonard Swidler for his tireless efforts to make this Conference possible, and for the invitation with which I was honored when I was asked to direct these words to you as the opening statement of the Conference. Its success will be, without doubt, an important contribution to the strengthening of peace and human solidarity.

Elizabeth Odio-Benito (Roman Catholic) is the Special Rapporteur for the United Nations Subcommission on the Prevention of Discrimination and the Protection of Minorities. Her home is San José, Costa Rica, where she is a lawyer and a Professor of the Faculty of Law of the University of Costa Rica. She served as the Minister of Justice of Costa Rica from 1978 to 1982. She was a member of the U.N. Subcommission for Human Rights, 1981-83, and (since 1983) of the Board of Trustees of the U.N. Voluntary Fund for Victims of Torture. She is director of the research project about religious liberties for the Interamerican Institute of Human Rights, and has written numerous articles and essays on human-rights issues and the juridical conditions of women.

RELIGIOUS LIBERTY IN THE U.S.A.

Franklin H. Littell

Because toleration and religious liberty are so often confused in such discussions, it is necessary to emphasize some of the theoretical and historical factors which make the American situation unusual.

The Background in European Christendom

The style of lowgrade religion from which the people of the new American republic took their departure at the opening of the nineteenth century can be documented both from the records of persecution and spiritual indolence in the American colonial period and from descriptions of religion at that time in the home country.

During the time when religious life in America was a peninsula of Europe, as it were, the religious dialectic oscillated for nearly 200 years between persecution and indifference. The First Great Awakening (c. 1730) was the first major renewal in a complacent and frequently persecutive Protestant establishment, during which nearly 100 congregations in New England alone broke away to become voluntary congregations, with voluntary support, covenant, and membership standards. This was the beginning of a series of revivals of religion, accompanied by mass evangelism, which has to this day given American Protestantism its characteristic style and structures. Mass evangelism has also saved it from the plight of European Christendom, where official statistics of 84% (Hamburg) to 94% (Denmark) to 99.2% (Italy) church affiliation are in fact but a facade for wholesale disaffection and alienation from both churches and Christianity.

The spiritual condition of the establishment in England before the Wesleyan revivals has been described many times by historians, most recently by Peter Gay:

> Guided by supple politicians, the Hanoverians used the Anglican church as a reliable political adjunct. The twenty-six bishops, who sat in the House of Lords, could be counted on to vote as they were told: in 1733, in some crucial divisions, Walpole was saved by twenty-four episcopal votes. The government's favorite device was known as 'translation'; it was nearly infallible. A promising cleric, usually a complaisant and articulate orator, would be first appointed to one of the least desirable bishoprics—to Bristol (worth £450 a year) or Llandaff (worth £500). Then, if he had behaved himself by voting right and talking well, he could move up to middle-range sees like Lincoln or Exeter, which carried between £1,000 and £1,400 a year.

7

Finally he might aspire to one of the sees endowed with great prestige, munificent funds, and lucrative patronage: the archibishop of
Canterbury drew £7,000 and the bishop of Durham £5,000 a year,
to say nothing of the clerical sinecures in their gift.

These were the professional soldiers of Christianity, living without
care, without thought, and without trouble—asleep at their posts
while philosophies quietly invaded their domains.[1]

The Evangelical awakening in England and America must be understood
against that background of complacent *Kulturreligion*. We may note in passing
that similar conditions of lowgrade religion in Tsarist Russia opened the way for
the Marxist victory in the early winter of 1917, and in the Germany of the
1920's for the Nazi triumph in the spring of 1933.

The American Experiment

The breakthrough to voluntary religion and secular government, which was
effected in the thirteen former colonies in the years 1785-1834, was the first
time in recorded history that governments voluntarily abandoned the use of
religion as a mechanism of social and political control. Since the human mind
ran not to the contrary, religious and military and economic and educational
structures had intertwined as part of the way in which ruling castes maintained
themselves in control of peoples. There had been a few edicts of toleration
before, issued on the pragmatic basis that persecution was counter-productive,
but with religious establishments still receiving political preference and support.
But religious liberty was a new thing, and it is still rarely found on the face of
the globe.

As a definitive statement issued from a religious liberty conference in Los
Angeles in November, 1984, put the matter:

> The most dearly won of liberties is Religious Liberty. It is also a
> human right, and on the world map the right most rarely out of
> jeopardy.

> Religious Liberty was a fundamental human right before any govern-
> ment of record acknowledged its inviolability, and it is a fundamen-
> tal human right whether a specific regime persecutes, tolerates, or
> protects.

> The free exercise of religion belongs to communities and individuals
> alike, embracing the right to practice, the right to profess, the right
> to propagate, and the right to convert.

---

[1]Peter Gay, *The Enlightenment: An Interpretation—The Rise of Modern Paganism* (New
York: Alfred A. Knopf, 1966), pp. 343, 345.

> *Persecution* is often counter-productive and always immoral. *Toleration* may be granted by a wise government for pragmatic reasons. But *Religious Liberty* derives from a Source more ultimate than any transitory, temporal power.[2]

The process by which America became a pluralistic society conveys certain significant lessons about the nature of coercive religion and religious liberty. One lesson is that voluntary religion works to the benefit of organized religion. Another lesson is that new methods and institutions must be invented if religion no longer can lean upon the prop of government.

When the colonial state-churches were dismantled, church membership fell to the percentage of true adherents—just as it would in England or Spain, Sweden or Italy today, if voluntary religion were risked. The statistics for voluntary membership in America, following the disestablishments, are as follows:

1800 —	c.	7.0%
1850 —		17.5%
1900 —		37.5%
1926 —		49.+%
1980 —		79.+%

Church attendance and giving have made a comparable percentage growth. By 1907, the American Catholic Church was the largest single supporter of the Vatican's world enterprises. By 1938, three-fourths of all the missionaries in the world were supplied by the American Protestant free churches. American Jewry is the largest in the world—and by all odds the most intellectually and spiritually vigorous and financially philanthropic of all the *galut* communities.

In 1776, of the 3,800,000 population in the colonies there were but 20,000 Roman Catholics and about 5,000 Jews. Protestantism brought the people back to the churches from which they had taken a walk and also produced great new denominations—especially branches of the Methodist, Baptist, and Disciple or Christian movements. The great Catholic immigrations of the nineteenth and twentieth centuries also produced characteristically American institutions, of which the school system has been the most important. With the great Jewish immigrations, especially those fleeing exploitation and persecution in Tsarist Russia and Russian Poland, characteristically American Jewish institutions also developed—including defense and educational agencies and, above all, the philanthropic networks that developed out of the simple mutual-aid societies of the first years.

Today the eleven largest Protestant denominations encompass eighty-three percent of all Protestants. The Roman Catholic Church, claiming 53,000,000 adherents, is the largest single denomination. The Jewish community, with a low birth rate and relatively static in recent decades, nevertheless gains about as many

---

[2]Mimeographed conference report in possession of writer.

congregational adherents from the gentile community as are lost to the churches. All three of the great faith communities face each other in strength—as equals at law and in a liberty never before found in human history. The challenge for such great communities, of equal legal status and unparalleled strength, is to relate to each other in ways also new in human history through interreligious dialogue and growing cooperation.

Nor is the significant religious pluralism in America confined to the familiar trio. The Greek Orthodox Church is large, with about 4,000,000 adherents. There is even one state of the fifty where the largest religious membership is outside the Western Judaeo-Christian tradition entirely: in Hawaii the largest religious denomination is Buddhist. Since the great World Congress of Religions in Chicago in 1893, there have come to be Buddhist and Hindu congregations in all of our major cities. The Baha'i faith is known in all metropolitan areas and major university towns. Since World War II there has been a striking growth in the number of Muslims, variously estimated at between 1,000,000 and 2,000,000 adherents.

The social effect of this variety of options is felt in many ways. Studies in Michigan and Ohio, for instance, have shown that our population mobility is matched by religious mobility: Protestants who move tend to choose their local church on a functional rather than denominational basis. Another symbolic fact: at the end of World War II, ninety percent of the Air Force Protestant chaplains came from six large denominations; today, there are Air Force chaplains from seventy-seven different sponsoring bodies.

Most Americans now accept voluntary religion and religious pluralism, with separation of the political from the religious covenants, as a good thing. By 1960, it was possible to elect the first non-Protestant President. The populist religion which is so vocal today is only in part a regression to Protestant nativism: it seems rather to be aligned with the reshuffling of religious and political boundaries that has become evident among both Jews and Christians in America since 1967.

From Legal Establishment to Social Establishment

Most vestiges of the old Protestant establishments have disappeared. Nevertheless, until thirty years ago there were still Protestant preachers conducting general Protestant services in chapels at a number of Eastern state universities, their salaries and work paid by taxpayers' money. And it was just over twenty years ago that proscribed Protestant prayers and Protestant Bible readings were eliminated from the public schools—a step that some citizens, including the incumbent President, evidently find hard to accept.

During this time of transition from political establishment through disestablishment to the acceptance of pluralism, the constitutional definitions of the American religious situation also changed. The incumbent Attorney General, Mr.

Edwin Meese, evidently finds it hard to understand the Constitution as a living and changing entity. But it has proven to be viable and adaptable to date, making it the oldest continuing written constitution in the world. Thus far only on the matter of chattel slavery did change come too late to avoid major surgery in the body politic. In the relationship of religion and politics, there have been important changes across the generations during which the old Protestant establishment structures were dismantled.

In 1838, in his great *Commentaries on the Constitution*, Justice Joseph Story—after Chief Justice John Marshall, the most important constitutional authority of the nineteenth century—still felt free to say that America was a Protestant nation and Christianity part of the common law of the land.[3] In 1892, in a case whose name is one of my favorites—Holy Trinity v. United States—the Supreme Court declared this to be a Christian nation.[4] In the Zorach case, Mr. Justice Douglas—certainly not the most traditional of court members—could still declare that, "we are a religious people whose institutions presuppose a Supreme Being."[5]

The identification of the U.S.A. with an established Protestant religion is evidently receding into the distance. For the time being, most Americans appear willing to leave it that in some sense we are a religious people, although there are occasional relapses—as when a lower official in the Reagan administration recently sent out instructions calling for religious activism on the part of officials on the ground that this is "a Christian nation."[6]

The Myths of the Beginning

The truth is that there are two myths about America's religious history that are destructive of a healthy affirmation of religious liberty and the interreligious dialogue that feeds it oxygen. One is the myth that the Founders of America were anticlericals and that they erected a "high wall of separation" between church and state. The French revolutionaries, and those who have esteemed their model, and the Russian revolutionaries, and those who follow that dream, were indeed hostile to organized religion. The American revolutionaries were *not*; they created a constitutional separation of the political covenant from the religious covenants, which is a different matter from hostile separation. From the Dartmouth College case (1819) through the Freedman's Bureau (1865-72) to the

---

[3]Joseph Story, *Commentaries on the Constitution* (Boston: Little, Brown & Co., 1891), 5th ed., par. 1873. First published in 1838.
[4]143 U.S. 457, 471 (1892).
[5]Zorach v. Clauson, 343 U.S. 306 (1952).
[6]At that he was only 193 years behind the times. During the 1980 campaign, Mr. Reagan referred to America as an association of "sovereign states," a matter settled when the Articles of Confederation were replaced by the Federal Constitution in 1791.

recènt contracts of the Office of Economic Opportunity, a friendly cooperation between religious agencies and government agencies has obtained.

The founders never contemplated America as a secular society: government was to be neutral and secular, while the churches were to work openly their full exercise and religious influence in the public forum. Massachusetts did not disestablish until 1834, and it was a century later that the Supreme Court ruled that under the "due process" clause of the Fourteenth Amendment the protection of First Amendment liberties also restrains government agencies below the Federal level.[7] In short the "separation" which obtains, and where it obtains, has been attained over generations of gradual disentanglement.

The second myth is that the founders of America established a Christian nation. This argument rests upon the fact that during the colonial period various Protestant institutions were supported and enforced by law, and that many of them continued by momentum long after the Constitution and the changed religious complexion of the population had rendered them redundant. But the argument itself can only be sustained by reversion to state-church theories and practices: it fits neither American constitutional development nor American political and religious realities.

An example of rather widespread misunderstanding is revealed by some of the most vivid and vocal court cases pressed against "establishment" (for example, the Walz case), usually accompanied by a great deal of sloganizing about the mythical "high wall of separation between church and state." These cases are obviously brought because of feelings and reactions generated under a repressive state-church system experienced in the old country. Black Baptist preachers, whose people have been here since long before the republic was founded, have no hesitation—for example in the Office of Economic Opportunity—to cooperate closely with government offices, even though at the same time the black preachers have been pillars in the fight against improper governmental intervention in religious affairs.

The exception to this generalization, and it may reveal—like the sanctuary cases—a fundamental theoretical conflict with serious future implications, is when "human rights" and First Amendment liberties come into conflict. In the Bob Jones University case most black leaders were opposed to continuing the school's tax-exempt status because of the record of discrimination on the basis of race, while many white church leaders believed that a successful intervention by an executive agency would set a precedent that jeopardized the future of religious liberty. They would preach on the matter—but not call on the government. It remains to be seen whether, in an age when there is much agitation for

---

[7]"We hold that the statute, as construed and applied to the appellants, deprives them of their liberty without due process of law in contravention of the Fourteenth Amendment. The fundamental concept of liberty embodied in that Amendment embraces the liberties guaranteed by the First Amendment" (Cantwell v. Connecticut, 310 U.S. 296 (1940).

abstract "human rights," traditional liberties and slow, orderly change can be maintained.

In the sanctuary cases, currently before the courts, another basic issue of religious liberty is at stake. The question is not whether a government has the right to restrict immigration; this may be debated as public policy, case by case, and if religious representatives disagree with public policy they may either change it or resist it and take the consequences. However, it has been revealed that spies attended religious meetings under false pretenses and taped over 100 hours of discussion. There could scarcely be a more blatantly un-American, unconstitutional, and immoral action than this—or one more likely to put at risk the free exercise of religion.

More recently a third myth has been brought forward, in an effort to present a synthesis of religious and political and social identities—and sometimes to re- duce the shifting boundaries between "human rights" and civil liberties. This is the idea that underneath the pluralities of existing religions there is in America an enduring "civil religion." "Civil religion" has an interesting history in America, from Andrew Jackson's affirmation that "the will of the people is the voice of God" to the recent writings of Sidney Mead, Robert Bellah, and Richard John Neuhaus.

But some of us have studied the course of civil religion in another setting and are not beguiled. *Positives Christentum* ("non-sectarian religion") was once, like "civil religion" in recent American writings, an appealing intellectual game played on the margins of major religious establishments—in Europe, legal estab- lishments; in America, social establishments. The German experience with "civil religion" is instructive. In 1920 it was incorporated as Article 24 of the NSDAP Platform, and it then moved outside the academic precincts. As an important component of the will to power it was bound to expressions of hostility to historical religious communities.

> We demand freedom for all religious sects in the state in so far as they do not endanger the state or work against the customs and morals of the German race. The Party as such represents the point of view of a positive Christianity without binding itself to any particu- lar confession. It fights the spirit of Jewish materialism inside and outside of our ranks.[8]

No believing Protestant or Roman Catholic, and no alert Jew, should have missed the true import of German "civil religion" when it became something more than a game of the mind in emancipated academic circles. And in America, too, our respect for the dignity, integrity, and liberty of other persons and faith communities must have more secure grounding than the illusion that when all

---

[8]Translated in Franklin H. Littell, *The German Phoenix* (New York: Doubleday & Co., 1960), p. 3.

the water has been boiled out of the pot we shall find left at the bottom the common ground of all religions.

A viable concept and reality of religious liberty cannot be based upon a baseline of popular myths or academic propositions. Since 1791 the American experiment, breaking from the model of European Christendom, has no stake in *either* persecution *or* toleration—which are, in fact, two sides of the same coin. The American model for the free exercise of religion creates a reserved area, from which all agencies of secular government are explicitly restrained and within which religious truths and practices may be freely debated, evangelized, witnessed, dialogued, pamphleteered, preached, criticized, and taught. In sum, under religious obligation I am bound to refute the errors of my neighbor's faith and affirm its values; at the same time under political obligation I am bound to join with him or her in resisting the intervention of legislatures, courts, and executive agencies—Federal, state, and local—into all matters of ultimate concern.

The Historical Beginnings of Religious Liberty

The Virginia Bill of Religious Freedom, which we celebrate this 200th anniversary year, like the provisions of the First Amendment which followed in its wake, contemplates a society in which high religion and good government progress naturally from two poles: *voluntary* religious commitments and *secular* government. As James Madison insisted, the enemies of high religion and good government have been, across many centuries, religious cabals that manipulate political power and arrogant political officers who manipulate religious loyalties and institutions.

Historically and logically, the quest for religious liberty begins with the "free exercise of religion" and not with the prohibition of establishment per se. Arcot Krishnaswami stated that "there is no doubt that historically the principle of separation of state and religion emerged as a reaction against the privileged position of the Established Church as the State religion, and that its purpose was to assure a large measure of equality to the members of various religions."[9] *Toleration* indeed began there, and it was a grant of government—which could, of course, be withdrawn in another season. But *religious liberty* had other beginnings.

Historically, the first witnesses and martyrs of religious liberty were protesters that the union of church and state in "Christendom," in the Holy Roman Empire, had from the time of Constantine and the Council of Nicaea (325 c.e.) so corrupted true religion that only a radical restitution of primitive Christianity

---

[9] Arcot Krishnaswami, *Study of Discrimination in the Matter of Religious Rights and Practices* (New York: United Nations, 1960), p. 47.

(represented in a restored *rechte Kirche*), sundered from political control, was worthy of the name "Christian."[10]

Logically, the foundation of religious liberty has been stated again and again across the centuries, but nowhere better than by Garrit Smith (1797-1874) during the abolitionists' appeal to the Higher Law.

> Our political and constitutional rights, so called, are but the natural and inherent rights of man, asserted, carried out, and secured by modes of human contrivance. To no human charter am I indebted for my rights. They pertain to my original constitution; and I read them in that Book of books, which is the great Charter of man's rights. No, the constitution of my nation and state create none of my rights. They do, at the most, but recognize what is not theirs to give.[11]

The prohibition of establishment has as its first purpose to facilitate the free exercise of religion by all citizens and groups. Derivative of this is the realization that secular government—government that does not deal at all with ultimates, government that is free of religious manipulation, government that has limited objectives and pedestrian programs—is preferable to any government religiously colored or ideologically tainted.

By Way of Contrast

More than a century ago the great ecumenical pioneer and church historian, Philip Schaff, put the American experiment in its world setting:

> The glory of America is a free Christianity, independent of the secular government, and supported by the voluntary contributions of a free people. This is one of the greatest facts in modern history.[12]

And just a decade later a great European theologian, confronting a thrust for power within his own Roman Catholic communion, put the matter on the high ground:

> It must be clearly understood how great the gulf is which divides the holders of this principle [*liberty of conscience*] from those who reject it, both in faith and morals. He who is convinced that right and duty require him to coerce other people into a life of falsehood . . . belongs to an essentially different religion from one who recog-

---

[10]Cf. Franklin H. Littell, *The Origins of Sectarian Protestantism* (New York: Macmillan Co., 1964), paperback of rev. ed., passim.

[11]Quoted in Dwight L. Dumond, *The Antislavery Origins of the Civil War in the United States* (Ann Arbor: University of Michigan Press, 1939), p. 231.

[12]Philip Schaff, *Germany: Its Universities, Theology, and Religion* . . . (Philadelphia and New York: Lindsay & Blakiston/Sheldon, Blakeman & Co., 1857), p. 105.

nizes in the inviolability of conscience a human right guaranteed by religion itself, and has different notions of God, of man's relation to God, and of man's obligation to his fellows.[13]

The difference between liberty and toleration, and the qualitative worth of the former over all systems of preferment—let alone persecution—are still not widely accepted, even though the Universal Declaration has staked out important ground. Some of the present difficulties in America arise from the fact that some communal spokespersons are still thinking within the context of "Christendom," of achieving and defending toleration on the European pattern rather than strengthening religious liberty as the American constitutional tradition contemplates it.

For example, even as advanced a statement as the Declaration on Religious Freedom of Vatican II, sometimes called "the American declaration" because of the influence of Father John Courtney Murray and Francis Cardinal Meyer, still fails to appreciate that voluntary religion and secular government are vital to religious liberty. It does indeed mark a considerable advance in strengthening the affirmation of "the free exercise of religion," but, because of the continuing exclusive claims at that time of Franco Spain and certain Latin American dictatorships to a proprietary religion, the authors of the Declaration were unable to declare the essential conditions of voluntary religious support and governmental restraint from meddling in ultimate concerns. The Declaration on Religious Freedom (*Dignitatis humanae personae*) was in the end a broad-gauged declaration of toleration.[14] Today, the American experiment still stands in contrast to most of the religiopolitical adjustments on the world map, including some that now tolerate dissenters and nonconformists.

In many parts of the world the traditional religious establishments, with their customs of privilege and/or persecution, have been replaced by modern ideological *Ersatzreligionen* under which the same repressive practices obtain.

A recent survey of governments represented in the United Nations revealed the following religious/ideological breakdown:

Marxist dictatorships	26
Muslim dictatorships	17
Christian dictatorships	29
old fashioned despotisms, traditional religions	14
republics, new and precariously situated	30
constitutional monarchies, tolerant	9
republics, stable and with tolerant establishments	12
republics, stable and with religious liberty	13

---

[13]Ignaz von Döllinger, quoted in A. D. Lindsay, *The Essentials of Democracy* (London: Oxford University Press, 1935), p. 69.

[14]Cf. Walter M. Abbott, ed., *The Documents of Vatican II* (New York: Guild Press/ America Press/Association Press, 1966), pp. 672-700.

The United States belongs, in principle, to the final bracket in the above list. But in America, for nearly 200 years a republic with religious liberty a basic constitutional provision, in the course of time social establishment and assimilation have produced many of the same problems which mark legal establishments. You will not be surprised to learn that in my opinion Arcot Krishnaswami's 1960 survey of discrimination in the matter of religious rights and practices was overly optimistic then, and that during the last quarter-century the situation has improved in few places—and worsened in many, including the U.S.A.

Contemporary America

Today, in America as well as in countries where a broad toleration has prevailed in recent generations (a toleration sometimes confused with religious liberty, which it is not), religious liberty is in more serious jeopardy than it has been for many years. Let a single fact serve as a sign of the deteriorating situation in the U.S.A.: there are today, according to watchdog offices, between 4,000 and 6,000 cases before the courts involving religious liberty—far more than during the entire history of the republic from 1791 to 1980. And principles are at risk and precedents are being set which we had thought—even as late as the 1976 Bicentennial Conference on Religious Liberty—to be secure.[15]

At the Fiftieth Anniversary Conference on the Barmen Synod, which was held at the University of Washington in the spring of 1984, some speakers stated that the situation had worsened to the point that the church was again compelled to adopt the final confrontational position toward the state—to stand *in statu confessionis*, as did the German Catholic hierarchy from 1930 to 1933, and the Barmen Synod of May, 1934, in condemning the idolatry of the *Führerstaat*. Whether things have gone that far or not, there are increasing evidences of a slide into pre-totalitarian *Gleichschaltung* (leveling). And, unhappily, just as during the final months of the Weimar Republic, some of the religious agencies and offices are here assisting—either actively, or by complacency—the government's burgeoning intervention in the affairs of congregations and denominations.

The precedents are being set, of course, in cases involving unpopular "sects and cults"—such as the Bhagwan and *sannyasin* now on the front pages of the newspapers. Out of thousands of recent cases threatening to religious liberty in recent months in America, a few may be picked out to illustrate the creeping arrogance of the modern American nation-state. In a famous case, the Rev. Sun Myung Moon was singled out, prosecuted, and sent to prison for a disputed tax sum slightly over $7,000—while in the same weeks the Internal Revenue Service let go corporate directors and politicians who had for their own selfishness robbed the taxpayers of hundreds of thousands and millions of dollars. The

---

[15]Cf. Franklin H. Littell, ed., *Religious Liberty in the Crossfire of Creeds* (Philadelphia: Ecumenical Press, 1976).

principle against which precedents are being set is more important than the $7,000: that a church official may, if the members so desire, hold in trust the finances of the church. Standing in the Free Church tradition, I find that principle questionable, but far more questionable is the proposition that any agent of government should be the determiner of ecclesiastical polity!

In Oklahoma, a court has intervened and preempted church authority in a church-discipline case. A civil court in southern California had levied a draconian fine of $23,000,000 against Hare Krishna, on the complaint of an apostate member that the religion had not made her a better person as promised. In Kansas, a law has been put forward which subjects to criminal prosecution groups that fundamentally alter personality traits in members—an effect which was (some time ago) a matter of pride to, *inter alia*, Quakers, Baptists, and Methodists, but is now evidently thought to be a monopoly of despised "cults and sects."

In Nebraska a law was enacted that required registration and submission of annual reports of churches to the Secretary of State—something for which we have freely criticized the Russian government's harassment of Baptists and Pentecostals, but which is evidently thought acceptable by those who hound "sects and cults" in the U.S.A. Moreover, to some of us who have studied the history of registering religious groups and deregistering, this technique is especially ominous. It was Reinhard Heydrich, who was also entrusted with the implementation of "the final solution to the Jewish problem," who issued the first list of "deregistered" "sects and cults" in the Third Reich (on July 20, 1937). Among others on that list were the Jehovah's Witnesses, who were more savagely persecuted than any other religious group in the German population, and who were also—until over a dozen Supreme Court cases built a wall of protection around them—the special targets of the American disciples of St. Torquemada during those same years.

In Portland, Oregon, a fine of $39,000,000 was levied a few months ago on a similar complaint against the Church of Scientology. In this case the judge had second thoughts, realized his court had been used to try a religion, and declared a mistrial. After the Portland mistrial, a great victory for religious liberty, the lawyer for the complainant immediately announced an appeal. And here we come to one of the most difficult but most critical issues in the whole contemporary scene.

These apostate cases have become a big business for a small stable of shyster lawyers, who are making fortunes scurrying across the country to take up a multimillion-dollar suit for damages wherever an accommodating client can be found —and not only from among a certain kind of lawyer have interest groups been gathered. In some ways, as the recent series of conferences sponsored by the so-called Christian Family Foundation has made clear, the assault on heartfelt religion led by a small clique of psychiatrists is even more ominous. Just a few weeks ago, for example, a closed conference at the Johnson Foundation center, "Wingspread," brought together an international gathering of chasers of "sects and cults," promoters of persecuting legislation—and psychiatrists. Psychiatrists played a most important part in the "final solution," of course.[16] In protest to the Wingspread Conference, the president of the Church of Scientology called it a " 'final solution' conference," pointing out that one of the psychiatric leaders of the conference was openly antireligious and had called in his writings for "a medical solution" to the problem of religious devotion.

In California, suit was brought against a pastor for counseling without professional psychiatric accreditation a young man who later committed suicide; the civil court took the case but decided for the church. In Australia, today, a psychiatrists' association is pressing a bill requiring that persons engaged in religious counselling must be licensed by them in order to function as professional counsellors.

Maintaining the Integrity of Free Religious Communities

On the active encouragement of measures dangerous to the "free exercise of religion," nothing has been more damaging than these interventions on the part of government. And nothing has been more disturbing than the way some communal agencies, especially in the Jewish community, have energetically participated in the hounding of so-called "sects and cults." In Western Europe, where the model of "Christendom"—with its alternating record of persecution and toleration—is still strong, a Cottrell Resolution which urges the fourteen governments of the Council of Europe to take political measures to suppress unpopular religion is not surprising. However, in America, where one would have supposed the blessings of liberty should be deeply engrained in the consciousness of all of us—and especially in the minds of those who themselves have suffered so grievously from persecution in the past—such retrogression is heart-stopping. We have yet to learn, it appears, a fundamental axiom in maintaining liberty in a pluralistic society: that liberty is indivisible, and that we cannot enjoy liberty for our own community without being ready to defend the liberty of those with whom we disagree. The risk is great that religious liberty can be lost because groups speak up only for their own rights and view with disinterest the assaults on the rights of others.

There is another risk built into the American experiment in religious liberty: removal of governmental discipline must under religious liberty be substituted by internal discipline. The religious communities must maintain the order that secular government cannot and should not supply. In the old state-church system, the government could be counted upon to provide structures of authority

---

[16]Cf. Benno Müller-Hill, *Tödliche Wissenschaft: Die Aussonderung von Juden, Zigeunern und Geisteskranken 1933-1945* (Hamburg: Rowohlt Taschenbuch Verlag, 1984); on their definition of the religious as "schizophrenics," Jews, and "estranged from society," see pp. 87-88.

in religion. Educational requirements for the clergy, minimal standards in maintaining parish groups, and keeping records—all are subject to order provided by government. On the other hand, in a free-church area all matters of standards, for the clergy and for the membership, are dependent upon the religious community's own sense of responsibility. Whereas in the state-church system the conflicts over discipline involve both political and spiritual centers of power, the basic problem is otherwise under religious liberty. Here the problem is, as the Jonesville tragedy demonstrated, that government is put under pressure from public opinion to move in when church discipline has broken down and religious supervisors have failed to do their jobs.

Under the free-church system, the individual members are called upon to maintain the delicate balance between freedom and discipline which is of the essence of personal responsibility—whether in a political democracy or in a church where "the whole people of God" has some say in matters. What is the relationship of personal liberty of conscience to church discipline? Certainly there is no more sensitive area than this, and it has direct effect upon the relation of church to government; more and more cases are being accepted in civil courts, where there was once practice of judicial restraint, which involve individual protests against church discipline. In a subtle way the recourse to civil discipline is related to the collapse of internal discipline and authority: quite clearly the early enactment of the Prohibition Amendment and pressures today for abortion legislation are related to the religious leaders' inability to maintain internal church discipline.

If the churches do not maintain high standards of discipline, the relationship between churches may also be tainted, for sometimes the person fleeing from his or her promise to uphold one denomination's standards will join another with standards more flexible at that point. This has been markedly true of whites fleeing churches that have taken a strong stand on racial justice, but there have been some on other issues—for example, clerical celibacy, the Tridentine Mass, the ordination of women. Here the issue is not transfer as such, but tensions that may arise because the church of refuge does not itself maintain high standards— that is, make careful inquiry in respect to *all* applications for membership, as to the spiritual condition of the petitioner for admission.

Finally, the contribution of the denomination to the society as a whole is involved, and this is the *quid pro quo* for governmental restraint. Even the tax-free status of religious communities has been justified over the centuries first of all because of the general social contribution made by the churches. Perhaps a preliminary hypothesis would be this: the extent to which a church contributes to a healthy tension between liberty and discipline in the society at large will be a function of the balance between discipline and respect for the liberty and dignity of the human person within the church. The way in which members within a church treat each other is predictive of the way in which they will treat fellow-citizens in the outside world.

Put bluntly, the "School of Christ"—as the great pioneer of religious liberty

Caspar Schwenckfeld called it—may turn out to be a "school for dictatorship" or a "school for anarchy" if the church fails to maintain both of the poles of reference: liberty of conscience *and* voluntary discipline.

In Conclusion

The American experiment requires both a quality of self-restraint that governmental units are now neglecting and a quality of internal religious discipline that the churches are now neglecting. The danger of a slide into *Gleichschaltung* on the one side and of anarchy on the other is very real. And there is a parallel development involving the campuses, which were the other chief centers of criticism of government policy and action in recent years. There are dozens of cases today in which political agencies are invading preserves and abridging rights traditionally reserved to campus self-governance, just as there are many hundreds of cases involving the churches. On campus, as in the congregations, "freedom" is a plus word and self-discipline is hard to come by. On campus, as in the congregation, a vacuum of responsibility invites aggression by the modern nation-state.

When there is a vacuum created by lack of internal discipline in the religious communities or the universities, the modern nation-state fills it rapidly. Unless checks and balances are carefully maintained, the end of the modern nation-state is the highly centralized dictatorship—under which no independent centers of opinion and action are tolerated.[17]

Finally: when we study and discuss human rights and basic liberties, we are not engaged in an academic exercise, such that spiritual or intellectual laziness can be compensated by energetic effort in another course. Liberty cannot be kept alive without lively attention to the dialogue. There may be an armed truce between extended families or religious communities, reaching even across generations of co-existence, but without dialogue sooner or later the explosion will come. There is another and final axiom to be learned from the history of this Age of Genocide, which began with the slaughter of the Armenians and reached its keenest sign in the Holocaust: a society that does not constantly seek to expand the liberty of all its constituents does not stay static; *it goes bad*, sliding down the slippery slope from bigotry to repression, from persecution to genocide.

---

[17]Cf. Otto Kirchheimer, "In Quest of Sovereignty," *The Journal of Politics*, vol. 6, no. 2 (1944), p. 141: "Mere multiplication of organizational affiliations is without any significance when the organizations in question have only the character of satellites working in the same social zone as the main organization."

Franklin H. Littell (United Methodist) is Professor of Religion at Temple University and Adjunct Professor in the Institute of Contemporary Jewry at Hebrew University, Jerusalem. He chairs the boards of the William O. Douglas Institute, Seattle (for study of contemporary social issues), and the Hamlin Institute, Philadelphia (for study of religious liberty and persecution). He holds degrees from Cornell College (Iowa), Union Theological Seminary (N.Y.), and Yale University (Ph.D.), and is an ordained clergy member of the United Methodist Church. He has lectured at over 300 campuses around the world and authored twenty-two books and nearly 300 major articles or book chapters. His weekly column, "Lest We Forget," has appeared in several newspapers since 1978. He is a member of the U.S. Holocaust Memorial Council and the International Council of Yad Vashem. A graduate seminar he offered at Emory University in 1959 on "The German Church Struggle and the Holocaust" was the first to be offered on this theme and—along with his *The Crucifixion of the Jews*— spawned Holocaust studies in the U.S. and a rethinking of Christian Antisemitism. He was the Consultant on Religion and Higher Education for the National Conference of Christians and Jews from 1958 to 1983; founded the Institute for American Democracy (to study extremism and terrorism) and the Anne Frank Institute of Philadelphia; and co-founded both the Annual Scholars Conference on the Church Struggle and the Holocaust, and the National Christian Leadership Conference for Israel. An officer in the U.S. occupation of post-war Germany for nearly a decade, he received the Grosse Verdienstkreuz in 1959 from the German Federal Republic for aiding educational and religious institutions and movements and furthering U.S./German reconciliation. He also received the Jabotinsky Medal from Israel in 1980 for his work on behalf of Israel and Christian-Jewish understanding.

RELIGIOUS LIBERTY IN YUGOSLAVIA: A STUDY IN AMBIGUITY

Paul Mojzes

I. The Heritage of Intolerance

Balkan fractionalism, separatism, and intolerance are proverbial. Balkanization is neither recent nor finished. Some of the rivalries are "home made"; others were unwelcome imports by invaders which found fertile ground to fester vigorously because of the proximity of diverse peoples clamoring for identity and recognition.

The southern Slavic tribes settled on what is now the territory of Yugoslavia in about the seventh century c.e. Francis Dvornik's remark, "The early history of the Slavic nations is full of tragic incidents, of brilliant hopes, and promising possibilities which seldom found realization owing to the various circumstances and events beyond the control of the Slavic rulers,"[1] certainly applies to the southern Slavic people even to the most recent times. Religion, which was to play a multifaceted role in the history of the area, became a tool of separation practically from the outset of the conversion from the old Slavic religion to Christianity. The eastern and southern regions of what is now Yugoslavia came under the influence of the Byzantine Empire, which impressed upon its sphere of influence the Eastern Orthodox form of Christianity. The western South Slavic lands came under the impact of neighboring Rome, from which it inherited the rival Roman Catholic brand of Christianity. Both Rome and Constantinople aspired to the extention of their variant to the entire area; thus, the two forms of Christianity came into sharp conflict with each other, fostering fierce loyalties in the local population, each developing the mentality of "final outpost of the true faith in face of schismatic threat," which persists until today. The development of the Bosnian form of Christianity in the central regions, believed to be the Bogumil heresy by both the Orthodox and the Catholics, further complicated this initial state of rivalry.[2]

The fourteenth-century conquest of most of the territory by Ottoman Turks introduced another deadly religious conflict, namely, between an expanding Islam and a defensive Christianity. Islam, the religion not only of the conquering new settlers but also of many converts primarily from the ranks of the by-then-defunct Bosnian Church, reinforced the frontier-outpost mentality. Religion was a precious form of identification at times when politics were determined by

---

[1]Francis Dvornik, *The Slavs in European History and Civilization* (New Brunswick, NJ: Rutgers University Press, 1962), p. 2.

[2]John V. A. Fine, Jr., *The Bosnian Church: A New Interpretation* (Boulder, CO: East European Quarterly, 1975).

more powerful neighbors and where increasingly the clergy, especially among the conquered people, played the leadership role in the absence of other native governing authorities. The Turkish *milet* system—which divided people not so much into territorial units but into religious communities, granting a certain autonomy and responsibility to their religious leaders—tended to rigidify the traditional European identification of an ethnic group with a single religion. The religious leaders exhibited patriotism even in cases where the center of a religion, as in the case of Catholicism, was outside the country or where the rulers, like the Austrians and Hungarians, were likewise Catholic. Thus, the churches became the staunch supporters of the survival of a threatened identity of their membership, and religious affiliation became permanently welded to national consciousness. To this day, this ethnoreligious unity presents a strength, a challenge, or a problem, depending on the perspective of the viewer.

Then Protestants came onto the scene, further complicating the rivalries. The Reformation was moderately successful in Slovenia and Croatia, only to be nearly wiped out by the Counter-Reformation. In the nineteenth and twentieth centuries some of the newer Protestant denominations made their appearance, but they, too, added to the combative mood of intolerance. The larger group of Protestants were the folk churches of such national minorities as the Hungarians, Slovaks, or Germans. The free churches generally pursued a policy of proselytizing the more inert members of the other churches, which, of necessity, led to sharp conflicts.

With the formation of Yugoslavia at the end of World War I, the conflicts and intolerance persisted, changing only the group in power. Now Islam was in retreat, with Orthodox and Catholics receiving legal privileges as the established religions of their respective areas, each aspiring to a final vindication of its revival, hoping to absorb within its fold more or less the entire population. The ethnic rivalries of the two most numerous populations, namely, the Orthodox Serbs and Catholic Croats, culminated during World War II in a fratricidal civil war in which many old scores were settled by massacres and in which forcible conversions were attempted. Total bedlam prevailed.

The last to arrive on the scene was the "religion," or pseudoreligion, of Communism, originally in a Leninistic-Stalinistic totalitarian garb. This drove the most recent wedge into an already hopelessly fragmented population. The Communists did not side with any of the existing religions but had quarrels with all of them. They, too, aspired to eliminate all rivals. Nurtured on an intolerant soil, driven by an intolerant secular faith, and guided by an example of the militantly atheistic Soviet Union, the Yugoslav Communists were going to heal the rifts of disunity by bringing the entire country to reconciliation through the process of building socialism. This, too, made demands upon the body and the soul, with the ultimate result of bringing one more divisive loyalty into the region. Pluralism is the name; intolerance, the game!

II. Communist Policies toward Religion

The Communist Party of Yugoslavia was originally a loyal follower of the Communist Party of the Soviet Union and shared all its ideals and approaches. Two well-known Leninistic principles dominated this approach. One was the legal separation of church and state, declaring religion the private affair of every citizen. This had the effect of relegating religion out of the public sphere into the private spiritual domain of individuals. Religious liberty was understood narrowly as the freedom to worship or not to worship. The second principle was that it is the task of the Marxist party as the vanguard of the working classes to assist in what it considered the inevitable fading away of religion, thus assisting the process of individual and social liberation from superstitious and exploitative religious practices which are surviving merely as vestiges of the past.

In theory these two principles can be separated by stating that the government applies the first principle, while the Communist Party advocates the second. That theoretical distinction is a vain one, however, for in practice the government consists of the leaders of the Communist Party, and the second principle becomes decisive in interpreting the first. This conflict of approaches still colors the present situation despite some efforts to modify it by emphasizing legal aspects of the principles of separation of church and state which would tend to diminish state intervention in religious matters, thereby providing for greater religious liberty.

Several discernible stages mark this period from the Communist takeover in 1944/45 to the present.[3] These are presented here very concisely,[4] because a knowledge of them is necessary to understand the evolution of the theory and practice to the present moment—while the focus of this presentation is on the current status of religious liberties.

The first period was from 1945 to 1953, when the government and the party mounted an all-out attack on the churches despite a claim of religious liberty. Marxist scholars and even the government leaders admitted in the 1960's and 1970's that harsh measures were undertaken against religious institutions and individuals, including imprisonment, murder, the nationalization and destruction of property, and so forth.

From 1953 to 1965, the second period, there was a gradual reduction of the pressure against churches and religious individuals, though excesses—such as torture, imprisonment on false charges, and even murder by the secret police were still practiced from time to time, more in some parts of the country than in

---

[3]For a detailed description of church-state relations from 1945 to 1972, see Stella Alexander, *Church and State in Yugoslavia since 1945* (London, New York, Melbourne: Cambridge University Press, 1979).

[4]A more elaborate discussion of this is found in Paul Mojzes, "Christian-Marxist Dialogue in the Context of a Socialist Society," *Journal of Ecumenical Studies* 9 (Winter, 1972): 4-25.

others. Regional differences in the treatment of religion became even more pronounced, a feature which to this day characterizes Yugoslav church-state relations and which have increasingly been handled by the republican and provincial
rather than the federal government. What this means at present in practice is that
in one region of the country, for example, in Slovenia and Croatia, the authorities may show a great deal more tolerance and permissiveness toward religious
activities, while in another part, for example, in Macedonia or Kosovo, clergy
and believers are openly harassed and intimidated by the police, and very few
public pronouncements of the greater liberties in the other parts of the country
reach the local public.

The third period, from 1965 to 1971, was the most liberal period in the
treatment of the churches. Some call it the "golden age" in church-state relations. The system had opened up to such a degree that many religious practices
were unobstructed. Government interference in internal church matters was min-
imalized and in some instances was almost completely removed. The churches
were permitted to publish journals and books again; theological schools were
allowed to expand; clergy could travel freely in and out of the country; religious
education on church premises was sanctioned again; etc. A growing concern,
however, was expressed by the government and the press at the simultaneous
increase of politicization of the few larger religions, particularly the Roman
Catholic, but also the Islamic and Serbian Orthodox. The chauvinistic nationalist
excesses (demonstrations, riots, and terrorist actions) frightened Tito and the
other leaders to the point that they feared that the country and/or the social
system might collapse. They then undertook measures not only to purge the
Communist Party from "anarcholiberals" and "nationalists" but to tighten the
reins on religion as well.

This led to the fourth period, from 1972 to 1983, which was characterized
by an attempt to install more controls over church life and the suspension or
privatization of the Christian-Marxist dialogue which had commenced during the
previous period. A complete reversal of the concessions made during the previous
period did not take place, however. Certain aspects of church life did not suffer
at all but, rather, continued steadily, thereby giving additional weight to certain
freedoms (for example, noninterference in the curricula and teaching staff of
theological schools and fairly easily obtained permissions for repairs of church
buildings). In a few areas no progress was made (for example, no access to radio
or television), while in others there was some regress (for example, longer periods
of prior notification of authorities required if a foreign visitor was to preach in
a church). The situation altered not qualitatively but quantitatively. A certain
increase of confrontational practices could be felt.

After 1983 there seems to have been an onset of a new period,[5] although

---

[5]Other attempts at periodization have been made by other scholars. See, e.g., Zdenko
Roter, "Razvoj odnosov med katoliško cerkvijo in državo v socijalistični Jugoslavijii,"

there is a lack of clarity both as to whether that is the case and as to what direction the trend has taken. This lack of clarity corresponds to the confusion after Tito's death, not only with respect to national leadership and the direction of the beleaguered economy but also in the general feeling that the country is in a crisis. National conflicts seem to have increased, leading to the brink of open conflict (in which the churches are implicated and which they do not consciously seek to diminish). However, a new openness has been experienced—at least with regard to the freedom to discuss in the press and other media and at conferences —certain formerly taboo subjects pertaining to earlier and present failures of the leadership. This new period seems to contain not only possible pitfalls (especially seeking to divert the national focus on economic problems by attacking the churches as scapegoats) but also new opportunities for the expansion of liberties in a country which is without a long democratic tradition.

By and large, the general trend during these successive stages was toward an increase in the autonomy and liberty of religion, though oscillations were evident both in place and within the time periods. The government of Yugoslavia consciously attempted to create a system, usually called workers' self-management, which would be more open and tolerant than the Soviet model. They accepted as a reality that religion would not vanish as rapidly as they had originally expected and that, therefore, some accommodations must be made since religion exerts a considerable influence over large segments of the population. The increased participation in religious practices was interpreted by them as either a larger number of people "coming out of the closet" when the repressions eased, or as a genuine religious revival, particularly among the young. This necessitated at least a reassessment of the role of religion in the particular circumstances of Yugoslav history and for many Marxists an advocacy of more tolerant attitudes toward religion, as long as religious people spearheaded no open revolt against the government. The basic concession asked from the churches was not to oppose the socialist system but rather to recognize it at least tacitly. The slogan changed from "if you are not with us you are against us" to "if you are not against us you are with us." This called for a less doctrinaire approach to religion, which is today's hallmark of the Yugoslav government's attitude toward religion.

III. Recent Legislation concerning Religion

This section should be prefaced with some preliminary remarks regarding the Communist understanding of government and law. Theoretically, their understanding of the role of the government and the law is that they protect the interest of the ruling class. Whenever the perception of that interest changes, as

---

Teorija in praksa 7 (September, 1970): 1280-1282; and Pedro Ramet, "Catholicism and Politics in Socialist Yugoslavia," *Religion in Communist Lands* 10 (Winter, 1982): 257.

reality changes, there may be swift changes in the government form and person-nel as well as in the law. There is no judicial or legislative independence from the executive branch, which consists entirely of Communist leaders. The text of the law, and even more so its application, can be bent in any direction if this is in their interest. Hence, it is highly deceptive to point to the text of the law and regard it as normative for actual practices. The letter of the law may proclaim a variety of freedoms, but it is the executive branch which interprets and guides its application. The judicial branch will carry out the decisions which the executive branch makes, no matter how much bending of the law that may require. Many observers of the Communist countries have noticed that one of the greatest objective weaknesses of the Marxist form of governance is the problem of "social-ist legality." Since it is solely the party leadership which determines what is in the interest of the "working people," there is really little protection of human rights unless that happens to be interpreted as being of benefit to those in power. The meaning of many human rights is bent out of shape by spurious "double-talk."

This is not to say that what the laws say is totally unimportant. If the laws clearly guarantee certain rights or prohibit certain actions, rather than being vague or secretive, there will then be some pressure which can be exerted, at least in principle, to get the government minimally to observe the very laws which it created. In Yugoslavia, then, laws are not unimportant, though they are not decisive in the exercise of religious liberties.

The several post-World War II constitutions (1946, 1956, 1963, and 1974) affirm the basic freedom of religion and conscience, separation of church and state (including separation of schools from the churches), equal status for all religious institutions and individuals before the law, and the prohibition of the use of religion to incite national hatred and intolerance or to abuse religion for political purposes.[6] Article 174 of the constitution of 1974 maintains that the practice of religion is an individual affair, so that no one may be forced to join or be prevented from joining a church, and it recognizes religious communities as legal persons which are free to conduct worship services, rites, and religious affairs (the latter was left undefined). The government may provide financial support for specific purposes. Religious communities may own properties within the limit of the law. While the constitution gives the appearance of guaranteeing freedom of religion without any consequences for the citizens' status, this is neither clearly spelled out in theory, nor carried out in practice, for it is quite impossible for an explicitly religious person to attain higher ranks in government, education, the army, or economic management.[7] The constitution guarantees

---

[6]Most of the information on legislation regarding religion is from Ivan Lazić, "Pravni i činjenični položaj konfesionalnih zajednica u Jugoslaviji," in Zlatko Frid, ed., *Vjerske zajednice u Jugoslaviji* (Zagreb: NIP "Binoza," 1970), pp. 45-77; and Stella Alexander, "Yugoslavia: New Legislation on the Legal Status of Religious Communities," *Religion in Communist Lands* 8 (Summer, 1980): 119-124.

[7]There was even some discussion as to whether the selector and coach of the national

equality of all citizens, but religious people have nearly always experienced "second class citizen" treatment. The right to participate in public life is denied to the religious communities, and *de facto* individual believers also are limited in their participation in public life, particularly in major decisions.

In 1953 the first special legislation on religion was promulgated, called "The Basic Law of the Legal Position of Religious Communities." In it the federal government expanded the constitutional regulations, specifying the rights and obligations of the confessional groups as well as rights and responsibilities of government organs dealing with religion. These laws became well known to the religious communities and gave a modicum of stability to church-state relations because they at least made clear what the norms were upon which the government insisted.

The second attempt to provide the legal framework for the developing church-state relations was different from the first in that the regulations were not on the federal but the state (republican and provincial) level. This not only reflected the decentralization of power in the government which had taken place, but it also made it possible for the different religious situations in particular states to be treated in a more diversified way. The laws were submitted to public discussion in 1975 and 1976 and have been enacted subsequently (mostly in 1978).

This newest comprehensive legislation guarantees that the religious communities may publish, and it sets the conditions for these publications—with minor variants among the states. Clergy are allowed to visit their members in hospitals and homes for the elderly, but not in prisons or in the army. Social and economic activities are forbidden to the religious communities, which tends to stop all charitable activities (which were occasionally permitted in the past), as well as any recreational and educational activities for children and youth which are not strictly tied to some religious observance. Religious education for the ministry and of children are permitted. Theoretically, a child under fourteen (in Macedonia under ten) may be compelled to participate in religious education if the parents insist, but generally the consent of both parents and the child are required. In actuality, serious pressures are brought to bear upon children and believers not to take part in such religious education. This is mostly accomplished in schools or at parents' place of employment, making it nearly impossible for members of the League of Communists of Yugoslavia (the Communist Party's altered name since the 1960's) to resist.

All places of worship and church real estate must be registered with the government, as must all religious communities. No special permission is needed for activities within church buildings, but for any out-of-door activities permits must be sought, and such permits have often been denied. There is a ban on topics of a political nature at religious gatherings. No pressures may be exerted

---

basketball team could be a former star who had become a Mormon during his stay in the U.S.A.

on people to participate in any religious activities. Fines and some imprisonment have been imposed for violating these laws. While there is a feeling that some of these laws are more restrictive than the ones of 1953, there is also a feeling that one may appeal for redress against violations of these laws, though in practice religious communities have rarely, if ever, sought to prosecute a government official who may have mistreated them. One of the most dramatic cases of a confrontation between a church and an official whom the church felt to be a threat was the 1985 statement by the Serbian Orthodox Church that a high official of the Commission for Religious Affairs of Serbia, Radovan Samardžić, was *persona non grata* because of comments he allegedly made, which the Serbian Orthodox Church considered inimical to its interests.

IV. Reports of Mistreatment and Abuse

Even good laws are of no avail if they are not conscientiously applied. Yugoslav laws on religious communities are still somewhat restrictive, but they may well be one of the best sets of laws of any Eastern European socialist country. The larger question is whether there are not abuses of authority in the implementation or nonapplication of laws, resulting in the mistreatment of individuals and intimidation of communities. There is considerable arbitrariness in the application of the laws by local officials, which is condoned by the higher authorities. There is little effective control exercised by the higher over the local officials. The rule of thumb is that the one with the less tolerant attitude toward religion will prevail in determining the actual government position toward the local churches. Those who are more tolerant are generally more timid in asserting their views. In regions where the conflicts between church and state are greater, the abuses tend to be greater. Abuses also tend to be greater where more authoritarian or doctrinaire officials are in power. For instance, with the fall of Alexander Ranković in 1965 from the vice-presidency of the country, his hold on the organs of internal security (U.D.B.A.—the secret police) was broken, and a period of relaxation ensued not only for the churches but also for life in general. Thus, the orientation of a key leader or local official can determine to what degree human rights are respected.

The evidence shows that the greatest conflict exists between the government and the Roman Catholic Church, which was reflected by the many more arrests and trials of Catholic clergy than of other church officials. The following is a list of arrests and other repressive acts reported by AKSA, the Catholic News Service from Zagreb,[8] from October, 1982, to September, 1985:

1. The three-and-a-half-year sentence of friar Jože Zovko of Medjugorje,

---

[8]As reported in *AKSA Bulletin*, an English translation made by Stella Alexander and Muriel Heppel, and distributed by Keston College in England, hereafter abbreviated as *AB*.

who was accused of inventing and orchestrating the apparitions of the Virgin to several teenagers, which brought about mass pilgrimages from home and abroad, was reduced to one-and-a-half years by an appeals court.[9]

2. Only a section of a mosaic in the church at Stražeman containing the likeness of the late Alojzije Cardinal Stepinac (rather than the entire mosaic) will be removed.[10]

3. Zeljko Slonjsak, a parish priest at Kutina, has been sentenced to three years of imprisonment for spreading false information in a collection of sermons, "Flora of Vinogorsko," that he edited—which was a crime according to Article 187 of the Croatian Criminal Code.[11]

4. Marija Car from Duga Resa was expelled from the League of Communists because her husband, a nonparty-member, had christened their child. Her expulsion was sustained despite her appeal.[12]

5. A representative on the Water and Sewage Board in Split was called upon by her youth organization to give an account of her interest in religion.[13]

6. The municipal council in Split prohibited the completion of work on, and usage of finished sections of, the Church of St. Peter in Split. Frane Cardinal Franić protested that the church did nothing illegal.[14]

7. The Veterans' Association of Gornje Černiljev disassociated itself from verbal offenses in an argument over building a local church. Apparently this was not the first time where the bigotry of state officials has been moderated by the Veterans' Association.[15]

8. The priest of the Holy Cross Church at Siget (Zagreb), Fr. Emmanuel Hosko, issued denials against the accusation that he organized disco dances and sporting events for the youth, apart from spontaneous singing and play after religious instruction.[16]

9. Ivan Lalić, head of the Commission for Religious Affairs of Croatia, cited examples where Catholics carried Croatian flags without the red star and sang old Croatian patriotic (nationalistic) songs at religious gatherings. Such events are not uniformly punished; in Split such infractions draw fines of fifteen to thirty days' imprisonment, while an Orthodox priest and a teacher in Bosnia-Herzegovina were sentenced to five years' imprisonment for singing *Chetnik* songs.[17]

10. Andjelka Jagnić was imprisoned fifteen days for claiming to have seen a vision of the Virgin in Gala. A journalist of *Slobodna Dalmacija* criticized authorities for the absence of legal grounds for such a sentence. He quipped, "Would Andjelka Jagnić have been sentenced to a month's imprisonment if she had seen her with the child Jesus in her arms?"[18]

---

[9]*AB*, October 21, 1982, p. 8.
[10]Ibid.
[11]*AB*, December 17, 1982, p. 9.
[12]*AB*, August 5, 1983, p. 9.
[13]Ibid.

[14]*AB*, September 12, 1983, p. 4.
[15]*AB*, November 22, 1983, p. 8.
[16]*AB*, December, 1983, p. 3.
[17]Ibid.
[18]*AB*, February 21, 1984, p. 10.

11. Great controversy was caused by a statement attributed to Bishop Zazinović of Krk at the Eucharistic Congress in which he allegedly said that godless materialism must be fought by all honorable means, including the shedding of blood. The secular press accused him of favoring inquisitional methods; he defended himself by saying that he criticized not materialists but materialism and that the shedding of blood was a reference to Christians' willingness to shed their own blood. He also complained that attempts had been made to discourage believers from attending the Eucharistic Congress.[19]

12. Ivica Mašturko, a Marxist scholar, criticized militant atheization. He pointed out that the Socialist Alliance of the Working People of Yugoslavia, which is supposed to gather people irrespective of their beliefs, is almost completely dominated by Communists and that such monopoly runs counter to self-management.[20]

13. Prof. Jože Krašovec of the Theological School in Ljubljana was sentenced to a month's imprisonment for the following passage in his book *Christians for the Future*:

> Militant atheists and the champions of man's functional role in a collective are particularly aware of how powerful and efficient is the religious faith of a community. Hence they deceive the people with slogans saying that religion is a purely private, individual affair. They know that a man must be isolated; then he will become their submissive subject, an element in their system.

The prosecutor maintained that such a passage incites bad feelings among citizens, while Krašovec defended himself by saying that the passage had been taken out of context.[21]

14. Bishop Kos of Djakovo complained about the Commissions for Relations with Religious Communities of Vojvodina and Sremska Mitrovica because, during the celebration of the elevation of the parish church in Sremska Mitrovica to a pro-cathedral, they banned a procession of clergy into the church and withdrew transportation facilities to pilgrims just before the onset of festivities. He complained that these acts were illegal.[22]

15. At a meeting of the secretaries of the Communist organizations of Slovenia several prominent members of the Central Committee admitted that there were still cases of discrimination against believers but that these were cases of arbitrariness which harm both believers and unbelievers. Militant atheism is being superseded by a more moderate revolutionary view.[23]

16. The Coordinating Council of the Regional Committees for Relations with Religious Communities of Serbia sharply attacked the Serbian Orthodox religious press for taking a pastoral attitude toward Serbs outside of Serbia, thereby incit-

---

[19]*AB*, March 29, 1984, pp. 8-9.   [22]*AB*, July 6, 1984, p. 5.
[20]Ibid., p. 14.   [23]Ibid., p. 7.
[21]*AB*, May 10, 1984, p. 6.

ing national and religious intolerance. The writings of Prof. Atanasije Jeftić were singled out, stating that "it was unacceptable that a theologian and trainer of students at the theological faculty should treat questions unconnected with the church."[24]

17. Reporting on the meeting of the Holy Synod of the Serbian Orthodox Church, *Pravoslavlje* stated that permission to build churches where they were destroyed in World War II had still not been obtained in many places, while church property, including court yards and grave yards, had been seized illegally, pupils harrassed by school authorities, they and their parents pressured not to go to church or celebrate holy days, and "attempts are even made to force them to eat forbidden foods on fast days."[25]

18. The inconsistencies of application of the law which was noted by *Pravoslavlje* were also contained in a letter to the editor of *Svijet* by the Orthodox priest Željko Gavrilović, who wrote, "One could write a book about the sectarian attitudes toward religion on the part of members of the LCY in different areas."[26]

19. The Archbishop of Ljubljana, Dr. Alojzije Šuštar, stated that there are still many historical distortions and attacks on the church, although there has been a marked improvement with respect to obtaining permission to build new churches, visit the old and the sick, print new brochures, and obtain social security and health insurance for clergy. However, he stated that church members often complain that the "good relations" between church and state, which the government declares, "are just empty words, because of unfortunate personal experiences."[27]

20. The Franciscan friar Vlado Buntić, assistant pastor at Drinovići, had been at that point imprisoned for two months on a summary conviction, without trial; no written copy of the sentence was sent to the parish office.[28]

21. The building of a cemetery chapel at Cerci was halted by a building inspector, although a permit to build had been received. The local Communists complained that the cross of the chapel would be too high and that a road and a House of Culture should be finished first.[29]

22. At a series of seminars for Communists in Dalmatia, it was reported that "hostile, malevolent or sectarian attitudes towards believers still exist and that divisions between people based on their world-views are still prevalent: intolerance towards believers has become a sort of religious attitude."[30]

23. Armin Prebeg, a priest from Split, was sentenced to fifty days in prison for allegedly forcing a woman in a hospital to go to confession.[31]

24. The secretary of the Central Committee of the League of Communists in Bosnia and Herzegovina, Dr. Ivan Cvitković, otherwise a sociologist of religion,

[24]Ibid., p. 8.
[25]*AB*, August 23, 1984, pp. 7-8.
[26]Ibid., p. 8.
[27]*AB*, October 11, 1984, p. 4.
[28]Ibid., p. 5.
[29]Ibid., p. 8.
[30]*AB*, November 16, 1984, p. 5.
[31]*AB*, June 20, 1985, p. 7.

stated in a lecture that there are conflicts of conscience for believers, such as a Catholic physician who must perform abortions in the hospital although his beliefs forbid him, or a Muslim serving in the army who is not able to eat everything since no provisions are made for religious dietary regulations.[32]

25. The Franciscan friar Emmanuel Jurić from Tuzla was imprisoned for forty days for "insulting the patriotic feelings of citizens" in a confession.[33]

26. The Macedonian Veterans' Association warned that the spread of religious education in Macedonia is harmful, particularly among Albanian Muslims who send their children to *medressas* rather than public schools.[34]

27. Several high government officials blamed the Catholic Church for violating the principles of the Protocol between the Vatican and Yugoslavia, saying that a section of the Catholic clergy is misusing their rights for "nationalist, antisocialist, and anti-Yugoslav ends."[35] (These oft-repeated charges of clericalism are leveled mostly at Catholic, but also at Serbian [not Macedonian, however] Orthodox and Muslim, religious leaders.)

28. Franjo Cardinal Kuharić of Zagreb criticized the attempts to suppress religion and deny religious liberties and rights.[36]

29. A member of the Seventh-day Adventist Church was sentenced to two-and-a-half years in prison for refusing to bear arms.[37]

30. Religious activities are increasingly described as nationalist or cleronationalist, according to both Serbian Orthodox and Roman Catholic Croatian sources.[38]

These ample illustrations are not exhaustive, nor are they a particularly investigated account of violations of religious rights, but primarily the ones that have been reported in the secular or religious press. Many violations are not reported by the victims (analogous to rape victims) for fear of making their situations worse. I personally know the case of a young man who, while serving in the army, confided after several months to a "friend" that he was a Seventh-day Adventist. He was immediately reprimanded by his commanding officers, sent for psychiatric observation, and later dismissed from the army without any indication of what further steps might be taken against him. He and his sister, a student, both shared their impression that it is best not to admit to anyone that one is a believer because there are unpleasant consequences for one's education or career or one's parents' careers.

The Yugoslav police, security organs, and prison guards are known for their

---

[32]Ibid., p. 8.

[33]*AB*, July 25, 1985, p. 4. A somewhat different account is given on p. 6, where a Franciscan priest, Branko Jurić, was reportedly sentenced to fourteen days for saying in the confessional that, if his penitents were swearing at God, why not swear at Tito and the state.

[34]Ibid., p. 5.

[35]Ibid., p. 6.

[36]Ibid., p. 7.

[37]*AB*, August 16, 1985, p. 7.

[38]Ibid., pp. 5 and 6.

brutal methods of investigation and treatment of those who are arrested. From conversation with a man who was imprisoned only several years ago, I learned that during preliminary hearings he was tied to a radiator, and two masked policemen beat him repeatedly with rubber truncheons until he was ready to "admit." After serving two years in prison, he wet his bed every night for a long time. Although a large, strong man, he admitted crying like a child and begging for mercy when he was beaten.

The case of a young worker who attended some Marxist "dissident" meetings, was interrogated in 1983 by the police, and was later found dead has become well known in the West. The police claimed he committed suicide, but it obviously was a case of police-murder.

It is not suggested that these two illustrations of police methods were specifically against believers. The last such case of police-murder known to me was of a Methodist minister from Macedonia, Asen Palankov, in 1958.[39] If they are willing to use harsh methods against some, they certainly are able to use it against others, including religious offenders. This is not merely a logical inference but is empirically confirmed. For instance, other Methodist clergy in Macedonia have been threatened by the police that their "guts will hang from the rafters just as Palankov's did." The clergy are often summoned by the police for "friendly discussion" sessions which are secretly tape-recorded. At such sessions they are requested to submit membership lists and asked about their own and their members' political views; requests for church repairs are denied for decades, and church members' legal appeals are consistently denied. This results in a general feeling of helplessness and resignation, since they know that their rights have much less chance of being defended than those of persons who are not religious. It also brings divisiveness into the ranks of church leaders and laity as to how one should respond to such pressures. Generally, those who are more intimidated or conciliatory tend to gain an upper hand and set a tone of timidity and compromise. This, in turn, often alienates younger people who have not been directly exposed to such harsh treatment.

V. On the Brighter Side

Nevertheless, enormous progress has been made in the degree of openness and freedom for religion in the past twenty years. There seem to be no current prisoners for purely religious cases, and the length of imprisonment for the mixed religiopolitical cases is shorter than in the past.

The sociological studies of religion have become scholarly in nature and have not only discovered inaccuracies in the traditional Marxist notions of religion but

---

[39]Paul Mojzes, "A History of the Congregational and Methodist Churches in Bulgaria and Yugoslavia" (unpublished doctoral dissertation at Boston University, 1965), p. 598.

have also admitted the very significant explicit or latent religiosity of the majority of Yugoslavs. Among these sociologists, the vast number (to mention the most prominent ones, Esad Ćimić, Zdenko Roter, Marko Kerševan, Srdjan Vrcan, Stefica Bahtijarević, Ivan Cvitković, Ivica Mašturko, Nikola Dugandžija, and the philosophers Branko Bošnjak and Andrija Krešić) have pressed for a genuine separation of church and state where the state would not be an advocate and promoter of anti-theism but a truly a-theist state which would favor neither nonbelievers nor believers. Their influence, while not determinative, is significant. The Yugoslav Communists are not at all like-minded on how to deal with religion, and a considerable struggle is taking place in which the moderates seem to be gaining in influence. Should they prevail, religious liberty would be guaranteed more effectively.

In the decade from 1970 to 1980, five times as many religious as Marxist publications (with a circulation of 15,580,000 against 3,478,000) were reported by the theoretical party journal *Komunist*.[40] While there is no complete freedom of publication, it is astonishing for someone who has known how restrictive that policy used to be in Yugoslavia, and still is in the rest of Eastern Europe, to see how wide the scope of research, writing, translating, and publishing is in Yugoslavia with respect to books, journals, and newspapers. Material critical of the government and even of the system have been published. The religious press is not among the more outspoken critics, but it has definitely benefited from the enlarged scope of the freedom of the press. There seem to be few if any restrictions in the number of copies, size, or nature of publications, though the religious press is not supposed to treat solely political or social issues. Yet, criticism of government social policies did appear in the religious press (for example, anti-abortion statements in the Catholic press). The Bible, Qur'an, Talmud, and other scriptures have been newly translated, published in Yugoslavia, or imported from abroad and have been disseminated not only through the churches—many book stores also carry them as standard items. In some parts of the country there is no shortage of scriptures, but in other parts the demand still outstrips the supply.

While the secular press frequently takes pot-shots at religion, such attacks are by no means universal. Often journalists or even government officials will treat religion positively and will advocate more moderate policies. Sometimes, but not always, letters to editors critical of the paper or of some government policy will be printed. Many feel that the cooperation of believers and nonbelievers is much more desirable than conflict. From time to time, in specific cases, the journalist will take the side of a religious group over against an official's or court's action.

Pilgrimages to Rome, Jerusalem, Mecca, Padua, as well as sites in Yugoslavia, such as Marija Bistrica, Medjugorje, and the medieval Serbian monasteries, take place in large numbers with the assistance of travel and transportation agencies.

---

[40]*AB*, November, 1984, p. 5.

Masses and services in native and foreign languages are provided for tourists and locals and announced in prominent places (the authorities even permitted the celebration of a Mass at an international nudist assembly, though it did provoke considerable discussion in the church as to whether the officiating priest should be nude—that is really on the bright side!).

Travel abroad by all, including clergy, and visits by foreign religious leaders have not been impeded since about the late 1960's. Such visitors as the Moscow Patriarch, the Vatican Secretary of State, or other prelates and dignitaries (for example, Billy Graham) are allowed to preach and to visit with their peers, and they are received by government officials. Even more encouraging are visits and public lectures by such notable theologians as Hans Küng and Jürgen Moltmann. Each year there is an international seminar on the future of religion which takes place at the Inter-university Center for Post-graduate Studies in Dubrovnik. International learned societies discussing the theme of religion have met in Yugo-slavia with no interference, and foreign missionaries or professors have been allowed to preach or teach in Yugoslavia.

The youth have shown considerable interest in religion and considerably less interest in state-supported atheism. The weekly *NIN* asked, "Who attracts young people? Two thousand people attended a talk on religion and mysticism in the Youth Centre and five hundred people stood and listened for hours to a discus-sion on religion in the Student Centre."[41] And this took place in Serbia, where the interest in religion is not as visible as in Croatia. At the 1984 Eucharistic Congress at Marija Bistrica,[42] the majority seem to have been young, and many walked fifty miles or more to the Congress singing Christian songs.

Christian-Marxist dialogues have taken place, both in public and in publica-tions, scholarly or otherwise.[43] The scholarly dialogue does not seem to have a direct impact on the relations between government leaders and higher clergy, however. The negotiations between officials of church and state occur in a less generous atmosphere, but the fruits of the dialogue do render the context of negotiations more constructive.

After years of being denied permission, the Serbian Orthodox Church re-ceived the authorization to continue the construction of the Cathedral of St. Sava in Belgrade, and the church at the site of the former concentration camp of Jasenovac has been finished, while the Archbishopric of Split has been granted the right to proceed with its cathedral church. After the earthquake of Skopje all faiths were allocated ground for building churches or mosques according to a carefully developed urbanization plan, and financial assistance from abroad for such buildings has been allowed. In fact, the government has become aware of the potential financial benefit of some religious activities, especially during the

---

[41]*AB*, May 10, 1983, p. 9.

[42]Christopher Cviic, "An Outburst of Faith," *The Tablet*, October 6, 1984, pp. 964-966.

[43]Paul Mojzes, *Christian-Marxist Dialogue in Eastern Europe* (Minneapolis: Augsburg Publishing House, 1981), pp. 128-158.

difficult economic crises, and it has tended to move pragmatically to share in the benefits. Funds have been granted by the government for the repair and restoration of historical religious monuments.

No quota has been imposed on theological schools, so they are able to admit as many students as there are applicants. On the whole, there seems to be a satisfactory number of clergy, though some churches, mainly for internal reasons, experience greater problems in recruitment than others. The curricula of these schools are entirely in the hands of the churches. Clergy are allowed to form professional associations, which have been resented by certain hierarchies but defended by the governments as consistent with the social system. Social security and health insurance have been made available to clergy. The churches are allowed to provide pastoral care for the immigrant communities of Yugoslavs working abroad.

Thus, one can see that the rights exercised by religious communities in Yugoslavia are not inconsiderable. As a rule, the list of permitted activities has expanded steadily.

VI. *The Ambivalence of the Present Situation*

If one were to notice only the bright side, then Yugoslavia's record in religious liberties would be exemplary and its future bright. However, if one were to look only at the previously itemized instances of government repression, one would conclude that the situation is bleak—certainly not as bleak as in Albania, the Soviet Union, or Bulgaria, but, nevertheless, bleak. Many believers in Yugoslavia as well as observers dwell at length on this aspect of the limitations of religious liberties. For instance, Jure Krišto stated,

> The relationship between the Roman Catholic Church and the Communist regime in Yugoslavia is almost as bad now as in the immediate postwar period (1945-1953). The Communist Party began its relentless, organized attack on the Catholic Church in 1971 through the media and other channels; this onslaught peaked in 1981. Unreasonable, escalated antireligious propaganda and imprisonment of a number of priests took place.[44]

Pedro Ramet observed the ambiguity as it applies to the Catholic Church in this perceptive manner:

> The Catholic Church certainly enjoys more freedom in Yugoslavia than it does in any other Communist country. But it has to fight to win and maintain that freedom, and there remain distinct limits to

---

[44]"Relations between the State and the Roman Catholic Church in Croatia, Yugoslavia in the 1970's and 1980's," *Occasional Papers on Religion in Eastern Europe* 2 (June, 1982): 22.

what the Communist authorities will tolerate. . . . Thus the Church remains a tolerated species, but one destined for extinction in the ripeness of time . . . the Church finds itself being nudged to the periphery of social and cultural life—to say nothing of its official banishment from politics—to a niche in which it cannot be content. . . . Its defense of human rights and of the national aspiration of the Croats is part and parcel of that aspiration. But that aspiration . . . is precisely the LCY's definition of the "mortal sin" of clericalism.[45]

A Roman Catholic theologian from Zagreb, Vjekoslav Bajsić, described the situation as being more or less the same since 1963 with some oscillations (for example, improvement after the signing of the Protocol between Yugoslavia and the Vatican). When the relations between the great power blocs deteriorate, it makes an impression on church-state relations, even in neutral Yugoslavia, because there is less room for walking on a tight-rope. The church more or less does what it wants, but some individuals experience pressure—for instance, if they send their children to religious education or if someone carelessly said something tactless. It is not clear who instigates actions against the believers; it is not always by instructions from above, but since the country is not monolithic many people take the initiative in creating difficulties for believers. In Yugoslavia it is difficult to say what the official line is and what is only a press attack. The inconsistencies are marked. In Split nuns were prevented from providing child day-care centers, while in Zagreb they continue to do so. In Slovenia there is an association of Catholic journalists who have frequently criticized and accused government officials for their attitude toward the church, while in Croatia that cannot be done. In Croatia there are local obstructions to the building of churches, while this is not the case in Slovenia. In early 1985 there were sharp attacks upon the Roman Catholic Church, but at the great festival of Sts. Cyril and Methodius in Djakovo in the summer of 1985 everything went well. Likewise, the great Marian pilgrimage and Eucharistic Congress in Marija Bistrica, the largest religious gathering ever in Yugoslavia (about 200,000 to 300,000 people), experienced no hitches.

In Bajsić's opinion the relationship between church and state will not significantly change. There are no particular trends, toward either reconciliation or sharper attacks. The government does not want to see an increased role for the churches and realizes that if religion does not organize itself it will not be dangerous. Thus, the great issue is the presence of religion in public life. Since nationalism is the most potent formula for gathering people, the government is most nervous about the linkage between nationalism and religion. In Yugoslavia, religion, indeed, tends to be national, which means that due to nationalism one cannot love one's enemy as one's own group. If there were Christian solidarity in Yugoslavia, then the party would face a serious rival, but this is not the case.

---

[45]"Catholicism and Politics," pp. 271-272.

Structurally, the Communist Party holds the nationalities of Yugoslavia together in a precarious balance.[46]

A similar assessment was made by Martin Hovan, a Methodist minister from Novi Sad. He stated that respect for religious rights has definitively improved since the middle 1960's. The government does not interfere in internal matters of the church, though it does sometimes request information about what is going on. The government completely accepts the internal regulations of churches and regards those church people who break such rules as having made an error. The officials are informed and may even give church leaders legal advice, but they do not step in to settle an issue (a specific problem in the Skopje Methodist Church was cited as an example). The laws disallow to churches anything that is not strictly religious (such as sports, recreation, dances, excursions, etc.), but the religious press is free. There is no prior censorship. One copy of each published issue must be submitted to the justice department, and the public prosecutor may seek the banning of distribution of a particular issue if the court agrees that the material is objectionable. Importation of literature from abroad is more problematic. Up to three copies can be received without problems, but a special permit must be issued by the government for bulk shipments. When a bulk shipment is sent without permission, the customs office notifies the respective church that it cannot be delivered for lack of permit.

According to Hovan, there is no excessive arbitrariness, but there are regional differences. For instance, in Macedonia there is less objection about an educator who goes to church than in Serbia. In Slovenia and Croatia the overall situation is better than in Serbia. If there are problems, the churches relate to the Commission for Relations with Religious Communities on the federal, state, provincial, or municipal levels.[47]

VII. Conclusion

The responsibility for the conflicts and ambiguities of the Yugoslav situation with regard to religious liberties rests not only on the government; the churches themselves have frequently initiated or contributed to the tension. To proclaim religious liberty and human rights when until very recently the same institution denied it to others and still shows disrespect for the rights even of some of its own members sounds hollow and hypocritical. The past behavior or misbehavior of many of the religious communities is one of the serious obstacles to a successful affirmation of such rights today. The very narrow scope of the present religious concern for human rights weakens the effectiveness of any church's witness. The Yugoslav churches have not shown any great creativeness in broadening the notion of religious liberty. The link with nationalism gives some of the

---

[46]Interview with Dr. Vjekoslav Bajsić in Zagreb, Yugoslavia, August 2, 1985.
[47]Interview with the Rev. Martin Hovan in Novi Sad, Yugoslavia, August 6, 1985.

churches the clout to defend their own minimal rights, and, regretfully, most have been satisfied to continue to travel this same route. They seem to feel that an ever greater claim of being the defender of a certain nationalism will increase their freedom and influence, possibly to the position of a favorite status. Very few churches have sought to find in their own religious treasure some creative responses or initiatives which would not at the same time threaten the liberties of other churches. As long as the government continues to be the sole guarantor of at least legal equality among the religious groups, the churches will be ineffective as authentic embodiments of the proclamation and practice of religious liberties and human rights.

The main source of the denial of religious liberties, however, lies directly in the attitude of the League of Communists, as implemented by the government. While the League of Communists has considerably softened its original extremely intolerant attitude, making the situation currently much more bearable, its prevailing view is still that religion does not belong to the socialist order. By one means or another, religion is to be limited, isolated, marginalized, attacked, and —in the long run—eliminated. As long as this persists, religious people will not feel at home in their own country, and Communists will continue to suspect them as an alien nuisance and threat. Only a minority of Marxist intellectuals have worked at discovering a more conciliatory formula which would recognize the right of religious people to full civil liberties; while their views have had some impact, it cannot be said that they have been accepted by the power-wielders.

The precariousness of the present situation, frought with ambiguities and pitfalls, reflects, at least for the time being, Yugoslavia's way of handling religious liberties.

Paul Mojzes (United Methodist) is Professor of Religious Studies at Rosemont (PA) College. Born in Yugoslavia, he became a naturalized U.S. citizen in 1965. He was educated at Belgrade (Yugoslavia) University Law School, Florida Southern College (B.A.), and Boston University (Ph.D. in Eastern European church history, 1965), and has traveled extensively in Eastern Europe. He is secretary of Christians Associated for Relationships with Eastern Europe, and a member of the Europe Committee of the Division for Overseas Ministries (both National Council of Churches of Christ in the U.S.A.). Co-editor of the *Journal of Ecumenical Studies*, he is author of *Christian-Marxist Dialogue in Eastern Europe* (Augsburg, 1982), and editor of two *J.E.S.* special issues: *Varieties of Christian-Marxist Dialogue* (1978) and *Christian-Marxist Encounter: Is Atheism Essential to Marxism?* (1985). He is co-editor of *Society and Original Sin* (with Durwood Foster; Paragon, 1985), and author of over fifty scholarly articles. Founder and editor of *Occasional Papers on Religion in Eastern Europe*, he has received numerous fellowships, including three post-doctoral fellowships.

RELIGIOUS FREEDOM IN EGYPT:
UNDER THE SHADOW OF THE ISLAMIC *DHIMMA* SYSTEM

Abdullahi Ahmed An-Na'im

The existence of religious conflict and strife in Egypt today cannot be denied. Feelings of animosity and distrust between Muslims and non-Muslims often erupt in riots and communal violence. Muslim-Coptic clashes in 1972 resulted in the death of forty-eight people. Similar clashes in 1981 led to the death of eight and the detention of more than 1,500 political and religious personalities, including Pope Shenouda III, the head of the Coptic Church.

The state of religious freedom and tolerance in Egypt reflects centuries of conflict, tension, and interaction among the main religious communities in the area, namely, Muslims, Christians, and Jews. The Islamic-Jewish dimension, however, has both been complicated and alleviated by the rise of Zionism and the establishment of the State of Israel. While the social isolation and economic and political difficulties of Egyptian Jews were intensified with charges of allegiance to an alien entity and doubts as to their loyalty to the Egyptian polity, post-World War II conditions and the establishment of the State of Israel encouraged Jewish migration to Israel as well as to other parts of the world. The current official peace between Egypt and Israel is too recent and too uncertain to have had a significant impact on Muslim-Jewish relations in Egypt.

Christians, mainly Copts, constitute the main religious minority in Egypt today. Exact figures are hard to come by in this field, but reliable estimates put the Copts at about 9,000,000, which is about twenty percent of the total population. There also are, of course, some non-Coptic Christians, Jews, Baha'is, and adherents of other religions, as well as atheists and agnostics. Current discussions of the problems of religious freedom and tolerance in Egypt, however, tend to concentrate on Muslim-Coptic relations in view of the size and relative importance of these two communities. From the point of view of religious freedom as a fundamental human right, however, the issues are the same with regard to any religious or nonreligious belief. The illustration and discussion of the problem in terms of Muslim-Coptic relations may be dictated by the availability of current information, but it does not indicate indifference to the problems faced by other groups.

To put the subsequent discussion in context, there is a brief outline of the present Egyptian legal and constitutional system, followed by a brief survey of relevant sources in order to outline a working definition of the concept of religious freedom as established by current international standards. Examples of violation of religious freedom and instances of intolerance are then cited as background for a discussion of some of the underlying causes. Finally, suggestions on remedial action that may be undertaken in Egypt, and possibly in other parts of the Muslim world, are offered.

Legal and Constitutional System

The present Egyptian legal and constitutional system is the outcome of intellectual and political developments going back to the beginning of the nineteenth century.[1] Following the invasion of Egypt by Napoleon in 1798, French civilization and political ideology acquired a strong hold on Egyptian elite classes. Although the General Council, a consultative body, and the Institute of Egypt, a scholarly/scientific body, established by the brief French administration were disbanded following the expulsion of the French by an Anglo-Turkish expedition, French intellectual and legal traditions endured. Mohamed Ali, the ruler of Egypt from 1805 to 1848, undertook an extensive modernization program, including the introduction of a state school system to supplement the preexisting religious education. He also started the practice of sending Egyptians abroad for education.

As a result of the policies of Mohamed Ali and his successors, Egypt gradually moved to adopt a Western-style legal system, along the lines of the French continental model. There was first the concession to demands by the consuls of Western powers to have jurisdiction over disputes affecting their own nationals living in Egypt. The system was then regularized within the framework of the general legal system by replacing consular jurisdiction with courts staffed by European and Egyptian judges who applied a code derived from European sources. The jurisdiction of these "Mixed Tribunals," as they came to be called, was extended to cover most civil and commercial law matters, leaving the Islamic *Shari'a* Courts with jurisdiction over only family law and inheritance for Muslims. The civil code applied by the Mixed Tribunals was formally promulgated when the British occupied Egypt in 1882. Mixed Tribunals were gradually abolished in the 1930's and 1940's, and a revised civil code was enacted in 1949, combining Islamic law principles with the French continental concepts of the previous code. Specialized Shari'a Courts were abolished in 1956 as ordinary judges who received training in Islamic Shari'a law as part of their regular legal training assumed jurisdiction over family law and inheritance for Muslims, together with their general territorial jurisdiction.

On the constitutional and political plane, there were first the developments leading to what may be called constitutional monarchy early in this twentieth century, specially since the adoption of the 1923 Constitution. Britain continued to occupy Egypt from 1882 to 1922, and it exercised considerable influence in Egypt's internal affairs until after the Army's Revolution of 1952 and the final evacuation of all British forces in 1956.

The Egyptian Army took over from King Farouq and his liberal parliamen-

---

[1]The following survey is based on John H. Barton et al., *Law in Radically Different Cultures* (St. Paul, MN: West Publishing Co., 1983), pp. 16-36, and various Arabic sources.

tary system on July 23, 1952. A brief power struggle within the "Free Officers Organization" which led the coup followed before Jamal Abdel Nasser emerged as the undisputed leader of the new regime. He continued in power, under several constitutional instruments, until his death in 1970. The single-party state established by Nasser was taken over by his successor, Anwar Sadat, who promulgated the current Egyptian Constitution in 1971 and undertook some political reform in the mid 1970's by introducing a limited measure of democratic liberties within the Arab Socialist Union, the only legal political organization in post-revolution Egypt until 1983.

Under the 1971 Constitution, the president, who is elected to office by popular vote after nomination by the Peoples Assembly, dominated the political process, with powers to appoint vice presidents, the prime minister, and the cabinet, in addition to having veto power and emergency powers to issue binding decrees when authorized to do so by the Peoples Assembly. President Sadat consolidated and utilized these powers in his economic and political reforms of the mid-1970's. From the point of view of the present essay, however, it is important to note that the extensive powers of the president, combined with some domestic political considerations, tempted President Sadat to try to manipulate the support of Muslim fundamentalist groups in Egypt against opposition forces. When he realized the dangers of the encouragement he gave to the Muslim fundamentalists and attempted to check them following the religious riots of June, 1981, it was too late for him personally. President Sadat was assassinated by a Muslim fundamentalist group on October 5, 1981.

The next president of Egypt, Husny Mubarak, went further in trying to accommodate all factions of political opposition by allowing multi-party politics for the first time since 1952. Several political parties, including the Muslim Brothers, a fundamentalist group advocating the immediate and total implementation of Islamic Shari'a law, contested the elections of 1984. Through an alliance with the Wafd moderate traditional political party, the Muslim Brothers have now gained an influential voice in the mainstream of legitimate Egyptian politics. They are currently employing peaceful political pressure in the advocacy of the implementation of Shari'a law. Other factions of the fundamentalist movement may even be prepared to use force in support of their demands for Islamization.

In relation to religious freedom, it is interesting to note that all Egyptian constitutions since 1923 have had explicit provisions on the matter.[2] Article 3 of the 1923 Constitution provided that all Egyptians are equal before the law,

---

[2]All modern Egyptian constitutions and organic documents since 1805 and up to 1971 are published in Arabic, with an analytical table of contents, in *Ad-Dasatir al-Masrya, 1805-1971* (Markaz At-tanzim wa Al-microfilm, 1977). In the following section, I have tried to present the contents of the relevant provisions in English without the benefit of an official translation.

and that they are equal in the enjoyment of civil and political rights and public obligation, without discrimination on grounds of origin or language or religion. Article 13 of the same Constitution added the specific obligation of the state to protect freedom of worship "in accordance with customs observed in Egyptian territory, provided that such observance does not violate public order and is not inconsistent with morals." This proviso seems to have been designed to preserve the traditional relative status of the major religions in the region at the time, namely, Islam, Christianity, and Judaism. There was supposed to be equality before the law, but religious observance had to conform with preexisting custom, even if that custom, as seems to have been the case, sanctioned inequality between Muslims and non-Muslims. The 1930 Egyptian Constitution reiterated the same provisions of the 1923 Constitution, presumably with the same implications noted above. Similar language was also used by the Constitutional Declaration of the Commander-General of the Armed Forces and Leader of the Army's Revolution on February 10, 1953, following the July 23, 1952, Revolution, and the Constitutions of 1956 and 1964.

President Sadat's Constitution of 1971, however, introduced two elements into this formula. Having dropped, for the first time, the limitation of observance with reference to custom, this Constitution complicated the issue of religious freedom in Egypt by making Islamic Shari'a law a main source of legislation. The provision that Islam was the state religion and that Arabic was its official language was first introduced by Article 3 of the 1956 Constitution. The 1971 Constitution added to this provision the clause that "the principles of Islamic Shari'a law shall be a main source of legislation." This clause was subsequently amended in 1980 to read, "the principles of Islamic Shari'a law shall be *the* main source of legislation."[3] The change from "a main" to "the main" was clearly intended to emphasize the role of Shari'a, thereby giving constitutional support to demands for immediate and total implementation of Shari'a. As we shall see below, this is detrimental to the cause of religious freedom and tolerance. Muslim fundamentalists are now seeking the actual revision of existing legislation in order to provide for the immediate and total implementation of Shari'a. They seemed to have suffered a temporary setback on May 4, 1985, when the Peoples Assembly voted to review the Egyptian legal system "gradually and scientifically" and revise aspects found to be inconsistent with Shari'a.[4] This formula may allow some time for the debate on reform of Shari'a in order to provide for, *inter alia*, a greater religious freedom, as suggested in this essay. To appreciate the need for reform, it is proposed first to establish some working definition of religious freedom before trying to assess the position in Egypt in light of that definition.

---

[3]*1985 Facts on File, Inc.*, August 2, 1985, p. 578E1.
[4]Ibid.

Scope and Necessary Implications of Religious Freedom

There is growing support now for the view that basic international documents such as the Universal Declaration of Human Rights are legally binding on all nations as customary international law, regardless of membership in the United Nations or expression of support for the Declaration. Membership in an international treaty such as the United Nations Charter and specialized human-rights instruments would, of course, create a positive obligation under international law as treaties, without need to invoke the principles of customary international law. In the present context, this means that Egypt is bound by the customary international-law principles of religious freedom as defined in the Universal Declaration, which Egypt supported at its inception in 1948.[5] However, since Egypt is not yet a party to the International Covenant on Civil and Political Rights, with its more specific provisions on religious freedom, treaty obligation can only be derived from the general treaty of which Egypt is a member, namely, the Charter of the United Nations. Respect for religious freedom as defined in international documents may, therefore, be a legal obligation.

These and other documents, moreover, may have a powerful moral and political impact on popular attitudes and official policies even when not legally binding. The practice of other nations, as reflected in their own constitutions and regional international documents to which leading states are parties, may also have some influence on attitudes and policies. It is in light of these considerations that we refer to the provisions of international documents in relation to religious freedom.[6]

The history of international concern with religious freedom is the history of the international human-rights movement itself. One of the earliest challenges to the notion that a state has exclusive sovereignty over its own citizens was based on the principles of humanitarian intervention on behalf of religious and religo-ethnic minorities. It is true that at the beginning these were efforts by members of one religion on behalf of their co-religionists elsewhere. But the movement gradually shifted into genuine international humanitarian concern regardless of narrow national or religious interest.[7] Thus, Britain was strongly critical of Turkey, its own ally, for the latter's treatment of Armenians in the late nineteenth

---

[5]Egypt was one of the few Muslim countries which was independent and a full member of the United Nations in 1948, when the Universal Declaration of Human Rights was adopted. It voted in support of the Declaration, which was adopted without dissenting vote by the General Assembly on December 10, 1948.

[6]Space here does not permit the detailed discussion of the historical background and the description of the nature of the legal system needed for meaningful comparative reference to religious freedom under other legal systems. For a comprehensive treatment of the issues under English law, e.g., see St. John A. Robilliard, *Religion and the Law: Religious Liberty in Modern English Law* (Dover, NH: Longwood Publishing Group, 1984).

[7]Evan Luard, "The Origins of International Concern over Human Rights," in Evan Luard, ed., *The International Protection of Human Rights* (1967), p. 9; and Arthur H. Robertson, *Human Rights in the World*, 2nd ed. (1982), pp. 19-21.

century. International protests against Russian pogroms against Jews in 1891 and 1905 were at least partially motivated by genuine concern for the principle of religious freedom. The need to provide for religious freedom ranked high in many international treaties until the concept was consolidated and developed by the peace treaties of 1919 and the efforts of the League of Nations. It is very significant to note here the close relationship between regional and international peace on the one hand, and religious freedom on the other, in recognition, no doubt, of the historical fact that religious tension and conflict has always been a major cause of war and armed conflict. Viewed from this angle, the need to protect religious freedom and promote tolerance would be part and parcel of the obligation of all states under the Charter of the United Nations. This is particularly so for Egypt, on whose suggestion the positive state obligation to respect human rights received specific mention in the Charter back in 1945.[8]

The Universal Declaration of Human Rights was designed to specify and elaborate upon the human-rights provisions of the United Nations' Charter. Besides the general provisions of Article 1 for freedom and equality in dignity and rights for all human beings, and the prohibition of discrimination on grounds of religion under Article 2, both of which are relevant to questions of religious freedom, Article 18 of the Universal Declaration reads as follows: "Everyone has the right to freedom of thought, conscience and religion; this right includes freedom to change his religion or belief, and freedom, either alone or in community of others and in public or private, to manifest his religion or belief in teaching, practice, worship and observance." The provisions of the Charter are directly binding on Egypt as treaty obligations. The provisions of the Universal Declaration, moreover, are binding both as the most authoritative interpretation of the Charter's human-rights provisions and as customary international law.[9]

The Charter and the Universal Declaration were part of the same process that produced the International Covenant on Civil and Political Rights of 1966.[10] Egypt is not a party to this treaty and may not, therefore, be legally bound by its provisions, but since the Covenant has been signed and ratified by more than seventy states, including many Muslim countries,[11] it can at least be said to have significant persuasive authority in relation to Egypt.

---

[8]Egypt was one of the countries which suggested the amendment to the Dumbarton Oaks Proposals in 1945 so as to state definitely the United Nations' obligation "to promote respect for human rights and fundamental freedoms" (U.N. Conference on International Organization, vol. 3, pp. 453 ff.). See John P. Humphrey, "The U.N. Charter and the Universal Declaration of Human Rights," in Luard, *International Protection*, p. 40.

[9]Robertson, *Human Rights*, pp. 27-28.

[10]In accordance with the resolution of the General Assembly of February 12, 1946, the Economic and Social Council directed the Human Rights Commission to prepare the International Bill of Rights, which was later divided into the Universal Declaration of 1948 and the Civil and Political Rights and the Economic, Social, and Cultural Rights Covenants of 1966. See, generally, Louis B. Sohn, "A Short History of the United Nations Documents on Human Rights," in *The United Nations and Human Rights*, 18th report of the Commission to Study the Organization of Peace, pp. 59-60.

[11]Iran, Iraq, Jordan, Lebanon, Libya, Mali, Morocco, Senegal, Syria, and Tunisia are

Article 18 of the International Covenant on Civil and Political Rights added three specific implications to the general provisions of Article 18 of the Universal Declaration: freedom from coercion which impairs freedom to have or adopt a religion or belief of one's choice; restriction of limitations on freedom to manifest one's religion or beliefs only to limitations which are prescribed by law and are necessary to protect public safety, order, health, or morals, or the fundamental rights and freedoms of others; and respect for the liberty of parents or legal guardians to ensure the religious and moral education of their children in conformity with their convictions.

Another source of internationally accepted standards of religious freedom is the recent Declaration on the Elimination of Intolerance and Discrimination Based on Religion or Belief, adopted by the General Assembly of the United Nations on November 25, 1981.[12] Article 2 (2) of this Declaration defined intolerance and discrimination based on religion or belief as being any "distinction, exclusion, restriction or preference based on religion or belief and having as its purpose or as its effect nullification or impairment of the recognition, enjoyment or exercise of human rights and fundamental freedoms on an equal basis." Article 3 condemns such discrimination, while Article 4 calls upon states to take effective measures, including enactment and rescindment of legislation, in order to prevent and eliminate such discrimination. Article 5 elaborates upon and regulates the principle of moral education of children in accordance with the wishes of parents or legal guardians. Activities that may be undertaken in exercise of the right to freedom of thought, conscience, or belief mentioned in Article 6 by way of *inter alia* are clearly intended as illustrations of the right, not as an exhaustive list.

Following Article 7 on state obligation to implement through national legislation the rights and freedoms set forth in the Declaration, Article 8 provided that nothing in the Declaration may be construed as restricting or derogating from the rights defined in the Universal Declaration on Human Rights and the International Covenants of Human Rights. This particular Article is important in the Egyptian context because the Declaration does not expressly mention the right to change one's religion, while Article 18 of the Universal Declaration and Article 18 of the International Covenant on Civil and Political Covenant do include this freedom in their formal definition of religious freedom. By endorsing the text of Article 8 of the Declaration on Religious Tolerance, Egypt has reaffirmed its commitment to religious freedom as defined at least in the Universal Declaration, if not also in the Covenant on Civil and Political Rights.

---

members of the Covenant. Other countries where Muslims constitute a significant proportion of the population, if not the majority, such as Guinea, Tanzania, and Kenya, are also members of the Covenant.

[12]Such a Declaration would not be, in itself, binding, because it is not a treaty, but it may be taken as further evidence in support of an international obligation to maintain standards of religious freedom.

Guarantees against discrimination on grounds of religion or belief and sub-stantive freedoms of religion and belief are also provided for in all three regional human rights instruments, namely, the European Convention for the Protection of Human Rights and Fundamental Freedoms of 1950, the American Convention on Human Rights of 1969, and the African (Banjul) Charter on Human and People's Rights of 1981. Besides the special significance of the African Charter to Egypt as a member of the Organization of African Unity and signatory to the Charter,[13] all three regional documents may be cited in support of the proposi-tion that the protection of religious freedom in these terms has become an estab-lished principle of customary international law binding on all states. These docu-ments also add to the moral and political authority in support of this freedom.

When we turn to the available empirical evidence in the case of Egypt, we find that religious freedom has historically been violated and continues to be so violated today. The scale and magnitude of such violation is likely to increase drastically in the near future unless very specific positive steps are taken to guard against this very real possibility.

Religious Freedom and Tolerance in Egypt

Prior to its initial Islamization in the seventh century, Egypt was a predom-inantly Christian province of the Byzantine Empire. Having adopted the Monoph-ysite doctrine (only one nature in Christ), the Egyptian Church of Alexandria was at odds with the Byzantine Orthodox Church, and Egypt was consequently the scene of bloody religious strife at the time of the Muslim-Arab conquest of 640 C.E.[14] It was not surprising, therefore, that the Egyptians welcomed the Mus-lim Arabs as liberators—especially since the new administration showed promis-ing signs of religious tolerance and political accommodation for the indigenous Coptic population. Although the system of *dhimma*—the compact between a "tolerated" religious community and the Muslim rulers—clearly violates religious freedom by modern standards, in the context of the seventh century that system was a tremendous relief and significant advancement on then-prevailing standards of religious oppression and intolerance. The majority of Egyptians gradually converted to Islam, but a significant minority of Christians and Jews remained subject to the system of *dhimma* as practiced, and often distorted, by genera-tions of Egyptian rulers, religious leaders, and the general population.

Without going into the controversy of the pros and cons of the *dhimma* system, or trying to apportion blame for excesses in its practice, we can still

---

[13]Egypt has fully ratified this Charter, which was adopted by the African Heads of States in Nairobi in June, 1981. The Charter has not yet come into force because, as of July, 1985, it had achieved only fifteen out of the twenty-six necessary ratifications.

[14]Y. Masriya, "A Christian Minority: The Coptics in Egypt," in Willem A. Veenhoven, ed., *Case Studies on Human Rights and Fundamental Freedoms: A World Survey*, vol. 4 (Hingham, MA: Kluwer Academics, 1976), p. 90.

make the following two remarks which are extremely significant from the point of view of the present realities of religious freedom and tolerance in Egypt. First, we should note that in the field of social attitudes and tolerance of other groups, what often counts is the predominant popular perception, or misconception, of historical experiences, regardless of the "true" or "scientifically" proved historical facts. In the specific Coptic-Muslim situation in Egypt, the Copts seem to perceive their history in Muslim Egypt as "a lengthy tale of persecution, massacres, forced conversions, of devastated and burned churches."[15] The Muslims, on the other hand, appear to resent what they see as favorable treatment accorded the Coptic minority by Western powers, which they perceive as a conspiracy between co-Christians against Islam and the Muslim majority in Egypt. Unable to retaliate against the alien powers, the general Muslim population tended to direct its hostility toward the Copt next door—hence, the periodic instances of religious riots and violence referred to at the beginning of this essay.

The second general remark concerns the nature of the *dhimma* system and principles of Shari'a with regard to non-Muslims in general, and Copts in particular. By citing specific examples of discriminatory and harsh principles of Islamic Shari'a law, especially when considered in the modern context of religious freedom and tolerance, non-Muslims in Egypt achieve the double objective of supporting their claims of historical persecution, while at the same time highlighting present and possible future violations of their religious freedom.

This analysis is supported by the available evidence of recent and contemporary distrust and hostility. When the Wafd political party encouraged Copts to participate in national politics in the 1920's and 1930's, it was accused of being dominated by the Copts. In 1937, for example, King Farouq utilized the influential Azhar Islamic University in his bid to discredit the Wafd party as being controlled by the Copts, and therefore unworthy of the confidence of the Muslim majority because the Qur'an provides that a Muslim should not befriend or seek the support of an infidel.[16] In the face of such politically damaging propaganda, the Wafd party, naturally enough, sought to disassociate itself from the Coptic minority.[17]

On the more concrete level, and despite the constitutional provisions noted above guaranteeing equality before the law and freedom of religion in every Egyptian constitution since 1923, Egyptian Copts seem to have faced discrimination at all levels.[18] Not well represented in Abdel Nasser's regime, they suffered serious difficulties as a result of the rise of Muslim fundamentalism, especially during President Sadat's later years.[19] In 1957 the Copts protested against per-

---

[15]Ibid., p. 84.

[16]Ibid., pp. 86-87.

[17]Leland Bowie, "The Copts, the Wafd, and Religious Issues in Egyptian Politics," *Muslim World*, vol. 67 (1977), pp. 106-126.

[18]Edward Watkin, *A Lonely Minority: The Modern History of Egypt's Copts* (1963).

[19]J. D. Pennington, "The Copts in Modern Egypt," *Middle Eastern Studies*, vol. 18 (1982); pp. 158-179.

secution and restrictions in building churches, new laws affecting the personal
status of Christians, and discrimination in public office, distribution of land,
housing, etc.[20] Again, in the summer of 1972, Coptic religious leaders formally
protested to President Sadat against "recent provocations and the planned persecutions publicly announced by the Ministry of WAKFS (supposedly, the Ministry of Religious Affairs).[21] According to a report published in 1983, moreover,
with the rise of Muslim fundamentalism and intensive governmental efforts at
Islamization, the Copts have suffered.[22] Finally, the exile of Pope Shenouda III
and placement of several bishops and priests under house arrest by President
Sadat following the 1981 disturbances are seen by Copts as further evidence of
persecution and discrimination, because their religious leaders were singled out
for harsh retaliation while they were merely defending their community against
violence incited by fanatic Muslim fundamentalists.[23]

This sense of continued official as well as popular persecution has led some
Coptic leaders to declare that it is necessary for Christians in the Arab world to
develop a Muslim identity because it is suicidal for a religious community to
isolate itself.[24] The very fact that such a solution is suggested is in itself evidence
of the ultimate violation of religious freedom: telling the minority that, in order
to live, it has to cease to exist as a community!

This suggestion in fact echoes a previous attempt by Christians in the region,
including the Copts in Egypt, to seek reconciliation with the Muslim majority
through the concept of Arab nationalism. Copts, like other Christians in the
Arab world, did in fact turn to Arab nationalism and sought to establish an Arab
identity in order to avoid religious classification with its consequent persecution
and discrimination. It has been argued, for example, that, by emphasizing the
Coptic contribution to Arab nationalism in Egypt and their patriotism and rejection of domination by any foreign church, it would be possible to support
greater liberty and tolerance in Egypt.[25] Coptic apprehensions regarding the
development of Arab nationalism and the tensions between Islamic and nationalist revivals are also discussed in the context of a call for reassessment of the basic
concepts of the historical background to the relations among Copts, Islam, and

---

[20]P. Rondot, *Man, State, and Society in the Contemporary Middle East* (1972), p. 276.
[21]For the text of the official telegram sent by Coptic religious leaders to President Sadat,
see Masriya, "A Christian Minority," pp. 91-92.
[22]Shawky F. Karas, "Egypt's Beleaguered Christians," *World Views*, vol. 26 (1983); pp.
53-54.
[23]*The Reflector* (Essen Coptic Church, Iowa), June, 1982, cited by *Human Rights Internet Reporter*, vol. 7 (1982), p. 970. *The Copts: Christians of Egypt*, vol. 12 (1985), pp. 1-2,
complains that Pope Shenouda III, since his release from detention, has been prevented by
the authorities from conducting services and delivering his weekly sermon in St. Mark's
Cathedral in Cairo, and that he has been barred from visiting Alexandria.
[24]Per Dr. George Bebawi, a deacon in the Coptic Church and former secretary to the
Patriarch, reported in an article by Sharon Lefever, "From a Coptic Leader: A Recipe for
Moslem Coptic Accord," in *Monday Morning*, vol. 10 (1981), pp. 50-55.
[25]See, e.g., Yusuf Abu-Sayf, "The Copts and the Arab National Movement" (in Arabic),
Al-Mustaqbal Al-'Arabi 4 (August, 1981): 83-91 and 114-122.

Arab nationalism.[26] The need for free and candid democratic dialogue is also seen by other writers who see the problem of sectarian strife in Egypt as a political and social problem.[27] The tendency to blame imperialism and Zionism for the problem reflected in some current Arab writings is certainly inconsistent with the spirit of objectivity and candor required for such debate. Foreign influences may have sometimes aggravated the tensions and conflict between Muslims and Copts in Egypt, but they could not have done so if the problem were not there in the first place.

As indicated earlier, it is important to note that other non-Muslims in Egypt also suffer violations of their religious freedom. Muslims who become Baha'is or atheists have been declared by Egyptian courts and authoritative legal pronouncements (*fatwa*) to be apostates, a status which entails a variety of serious legal consequences even under current Egyptian law.[28] According to a superior Egyptian court, a Baha'i marriage is invalid even if both parties are Baha'is, if either party was previously a Muslim, because, as an apostate from Islam, he or she lacks all capacity to make contracts, including a contract of marriage.[29] With reference to arguments based on religious freedom under the Constitution, the court is reported to have held that the Egyptian Constitution does not protect "fabricated sects which are trying to be elevated to the ranks of heavenly religions."[30] The court was not prepared, it seems, either to explain the source of the competence it granted itself to determine whether beliefs are "fabricated" or to state the criterion by which such determination could be made!

On Underlying Root Causes

The pursuit of causes of human behavior is a hazardous and uncertain endeavor, especially if one purports to identify the most fundamental cause or causes in an exhaustive or exclusive sense. Causes of human behavior are difficult to identify because of the complexity of individual psychic and group-dynamics factors that determine motivation for action and reaction within various levels of group interaction. Another source of difficulty is the multiplicity of factors that contribute to the shaping of social and political structures and opportunities for response and accommodation. In relation to the question of religious freedom in Egypt in particular, there is also the lack of independent reliable sources for verification of the various aspects of the historical experience of the various religious

---

[26]Yusuf Abu-Sayf et al., "On the Copts and Arab Nationalism" (in Arabic), *Al-Mustaqbal Al-'Arabi* 4 (March, 1982): 121-134.

[27]Foreign forces are accused of forcing issues and trying to exploit the situation by such writers as Jamal Isma'il in his article, "Could What Happened in Lebanon Occur in Egypt?" (in Arabic), *Ad-Dustor* 13 (September 12, 1983): 27-29.

[28]Rudolph Peters and Gert J. J. DeVries, "Apostasy in Islam," *Die Welt des Islam* 17 (1976-1977): 11.

[29]*The Human Rights Internet Reporter*, vol. 10 (1985), p. 406.

[30]Ibid.

groups and communities. This tends to enhance the importance of private perceptions based on unreliable oral traditions which are influenced by such factors
as early socialization of individual persons within their families and within other
significant groups. All this tends to create a vicious circle of self-fulfilling prophecies as the actions of one side are taken to justify the reaction of the other side
which, in turn, is taken into account by the first side in reenforcing initial attitudes and justifying further action.

Despite these difficulties, some hypothesis on underlying causes is necessary
for treatment or remedial action. It is useful, nonetheless, to note the difficulties
and limitations of causation theorization.

In the context of religious freedom and tolerance in Egypt, there are, on the
one hand, Coptic perceptions of historical experience interacting with elements
in individual socialization and group dynamics in relation to the Muslim majority. On the other hand, there are Muslim perceptions of historical experience
interacting with elements of individual socialization and group dynamics not
only in relation to the Copts but also in relation to other religious minorities.
Out of this complex process of interaction within and across religious boundaries, initial fears and apprehensions of one side are confirmed and used to justify
patterns of behavior that confirm the fears and apprehensions of the other side.
Coptic prophecies about Muslim attitudes and behavior toward Copts prompt
certain Coptic responses that, in turn, confirm Muslim prophecies about Coptic attitudes and behavior toward Muslims and prompt certain Muslim responses.
It is obvious that this vicious circle must be broken through candid, objective
dialogue.

To break the circle, one side must take the first step in bridging the centu-
ries-old credibility gap. It is herein suggested that the Muslims must not only
initiate such dialogue but must also do so with such a degree of candor and
objectivity as is necessary under all circumstances. There are at least two main
reasons why it is imperative that the Muslims initiate this interchange. There is
first the tactical factor, namely, that only the dominant majority can afford to
take the first step in bridging the credibility gap. The second reason is substantive in that the Muslims have to demonstrate that the repression and persecution
of the *dhimma* system are not going to be repeated.

The *dhimma* system and related aspects of Shari'a rules on the status of
non-Muslims are obviously fundamental to the whole process described above.
Besides its extremely significant historical role, with its impact on current attitudes and responses, the *dhimma* system and related rules will be reintroduced
in Egypt today if the Muslim fundamentalists succeed in achieving immediate
and total implementation of traditional Shari'a. Major features of this system
and other discriminatory rules are bound to apply even if Shari'a is introduced
"gradually and scientifically," as planned by the current Egyptian People's
Assembly, unless the highly original reform technique suggested at the end of
this essay is employed first to revise Shari'a rules before any legislation is undertaken. The following brief survey will show why the *dhimma* system and related

rules of Shari'a had that historical role and continue to pose such a grave threat to religious freedom not only in Egypt but also throughout the Muslim world.

Categorization and discrimination on grounds of religion or belief is fundamental to traditional Shari'a law. As stated by Majid Khadduri forty years ago, "Human Rights in Islam, as prescribed by the Divine law, are the privilege only of persons of full legal capacity. A person with full legal capacity is a living human of mature age, free, and of Moslem faith. It follows, accordingly, that non-Moslems and slaves who lived in the Islamic states were only partially protected by law or had no legal capacity at all."[31] According to Shari'a, a person's status, legal rights, and capacity are determined by one's religion, whether he or she is a Muslim, a *Kitabi* who is a believer in one of the heavenly revealed scriptures, mainly Christians and Jews, or a non-*Kitabi* non-Muslim. Only the first group, Muslims, are full citizens of an Islamic state enjoying all the rights and liberties of a citizen. *Kitabis* may be tolerated as a community enjoying a limited degree of independence under a compact of *dhimma* with the Muslim rulers. A non-*Kitabi* non-Muslim has no rights whatsoever under traditional Shari'a law, except under a license of *aman*, a license or safe-conduct allowed to foreign emissaries and merchants. Polytheists and other unbelievers are not supposed to be tolerated at all as permanent residents of an Islamic state governed by traditional Shari'a law. Their historical or contemporary existence in Muslim countries may be dictated by political expediency or other considerations in violation of strict rules of Shari'a.

This approach to personal status and legal rights is obviously highly objectionable from the point of view of human rights in general and religious freedom in particular. This is clearly illustrated by the briefest review of the relevant rules of Shari'a. A Muslim who abandons Islam, whether or not he or she subsequently embraces another faith, is guilty of the crime of apostasy, which is punishable by death under Shari'a law. Apostasy also involves several civil-law consequences. Besides losing the capacity to conclude any contract, whether in disposition of property or in relation to personal status such as a contract of marriage, an apostate loses all his or her property to the state. If married to a Muslim, his or her marriage is immediately dissolved.[32]

Personal status and legal rights of *Kitabis* are determined by the particular compact of *dhimma* the community concluded with the Muslim rulers, subject to the general rules of Shari'a. In other words, the degree of communal autonomy and range of individual legal rights granted to the particular community of believers in one of the heavenly revealed scriptures are determined by the terms

---

[31]"Human Rights in Islam," *Annals of the American Academy of Political and Social Science*, vol. 243 (1946), p. 79. Reference to slaves is not of historical interest only, because the legal principles governing the status of slaves remain valid within Islamic jurisprudence, although slavery has ceased to exist in practice.

[32]On the meaning and consequences of apostasy, see Peters and DeVries, "Apostasy in Islam."

of their compact with the Muslim rulers within the framework of Shari'a law.[33] Originally modeled on the example of the compacts concluded during the first decade after Hijra (622 to 632 C.E.) between the Prophet and the Jewish and Christian tribes of Arabia, the compacts of *dhimma* drawn up by generations of Muslim rulers varied with geopolitical conditions—and sometimes with the temperament and personal inclination of the particular ruler. At best, the compact granted the religious minority the "right to collect taxes for their own communal institutions, the right to administer justice in matters of personal law, freedom of religious education and worship, and recognized the official status of the head of each community."[34] Often, unfortunately, the *dhimma* lost its original character and became "the formal expression of a legalized persecution."[35] All compacts of *dhimma* are subject to general Shari'a rules that provide for the imposition of the humiliating personal tax (*jizia'*), exclusion from public office, inequality before the law, and other measures designed to segregate and humiliate the tolerated unbelievers in Islam.

Unbelievers in God, as identified by Shari'a, are not tolerated at all within a Muslim state except under temporary license. Hindus and Buddhists, as well as adherents of all "fabricated sects which are trying to be elevated to the ranks of heavenly religions," according to the formula used by the Egyptian court quoted above, are never to be tolerated except under temporary license. They have no rights whatsoever outside the terms of that license.

In the light of this brief survey, one can hardly fail to appreciate the deep resentment and grave apprehensions of Copts and other non-Muslims in Egypt. Historical controversy aside, the best *dhimma* system in conception and implementation would still discriminate against Christians and Jews and violate their religious freedom. Further, the violation of the fundamental rights of other non-Muslims is even much more objectionable in the context of a modern national state.

Toward Greater Religious Freedom

Given that Muslims are the dominant majority which oppresses—or is at least perceived as oppressing—Copts and other non-Muslims in Egypt, the credibility of any proposal to increase and enhance religious freedom depends on the willingness of the Muslims to discuss all aspects of the problem. In particular, Muslims must be prepared to see the full implications of *dhimma* and other Shari'a

---

[33]The following survey is based on the great wealth of detail and documentation provided by Bat Ye'or in her book, *The Dhimmi: Jews and Christians under Islam*, tr. David Maisel, Paul Fenton, and David Littman (Rutherford, Madison, Teaneck, NJ: Fairleigh Dickinson University Press; London and Toronto: Associated University Presses, 1985).

[34]Ibid., p. 49.

[35]Ibid., p. 48.

rules on non-Muslims from the point of view of Egyptian non-Muslims who are the victims of these rules.

However sympathetic a modern Muslim may be, little can be done within the framework of existing Shari'a law. The rules discriminating against non-Muslims and subjecting them to the various limitations outlined above are the necessary product of Shari'a rules of *'usol al-fiqh*, which are the techniques by which detailed Shari'a rules on any given question are determined. Given the sources of Shari'a and the techniques by which rules are derived from those sources, discrimination against some non-Muslims and the total intoleration of others are unavoidable. The only way out is to revise the rules of *'usol al-fiqh* themselves so that alternative Islamic Shari'a rules may be derived from the basic sources of Islam, albeit at variance with some Shari'a principles as known to Muslims today. In other words, to develop modern Islamic Shari'a law, Muslims need to revise the rules that govern the making of rules.

The basic sources of Islam are the Qur'an and Sunna, the first being the literal word of God as revealed to the Prophet, while the second is the example set by the Prophet through his utterances and other traditions. The traditions of his leading companions (*sahaba*) also enjoy varying degrees of authority according to the relative status of the particular companion because the Prophet himself said that his companions are capable of offering guidance to Muslims. With the growth of the Muslim domain and the development of Islamic civilization, learned scholars and jurists turned to the task of the articulation and tabulation of legally binding principles of Shari'a law out of the basic sources indicated above. This involved a highly technical process of authentication of traditions, determination of the relative weight of sources, reconciliation of apparently contradictory authorities and the general rationalization of the emerging body of jurisprudence as a whole.

Of particular significance to the proposed reform of Shari'a rules on *dhimma* and non-Muslims are the rules of abrogation (*naskh*) which determined those parts of the Qur'an and Sunna that were operative as sources of legally binding rules and others which were not so operative, although remaining part of the Qur'an and Sunna. According to these rules, the verses of the Qur'an advocating freedom of choice in religion, for example, do not mean what they appear to say; they should rather be read in the light of the legally operative verses of *jihad* and the status of non-Muslims. Thus, Chapter 18, verse 29 of the Qur'an, which instructs the Prophet to tell people that he is bringing forth the truth as he received it from the Lord and that they are free to believe or disbelieve does not mean that one can remain an unbeliever in Islam without suffering adverse consequences or that a Muslim is free to repudiate his or her faith in Islam. By citing other sources, the early Muslim jurists have determined that the verses of the Qur'an advocating freedom of choice in religion are subject to abrogation or repeal (*naskh*), thereby becoming not legally binding. This is the current position under Shari'a—hence, the rules on *dhimma* and non-Muslims referred to above.

The techniques by which general principles and rules were to be derived from the basic sources came to be known as the science of *'usol al-fiqh*, largely attributed to Imam Ash-shaf'y, the founder of one of the four major Sunni schools of Islamic jurisprudence. The substantive part of Shari'a dealt with rules governing every aspect of public and private, communal and individual, domestic and international life. Sunni and Shii'te schools of jurisprudence differ on many points of detail, but they all agree on the broad principles of *dhimma* and discrimination against non-Muslims outlined above. It is futile, therefore, to seek the abolition of these principles through research into differences between the various schools of jurisprudence or differences between the various jurists and scholars. As indicated above, given the sources and the established techniques for deriving detailed principles and rules from those sources, no Muslim jurist or scholar can possibly reach different conclusions.

It is not possible to change the source of the law and remain within Islam, because Islam, by definition, is the norms, ethical principles, worship practices, etc., to be derived from the Qur'an and Sunna. It may be possible, however, it is suggested, to revise the techniques for deriving detailed rules. In other words, it may be possible to develop a modern version of the science of *'usol al-fiqh*, because it was the work of ordinary men of piety and learning who applied themselves to the sources of Islam in order to meet the needs and expectations of their society in its particular historical and geographical context. What is to prevent pious and learned Muslims of today from applying themselves to the same sources, but with a fresh modern perspective?

One pious and learned Muslim who did precisely that was the late Sudanese scholar Ustadh Mahmoud Mohmed Taha.[36] Space does not permit a full exposition of the thought of Ustedh Mahmoud, but the main implications of his thinking in relation to religious freedom may be summarized as follows.[37] He conceded that the technique of abrogation (*naskh*) mentioned above was necessary and desirable to enact the body of law suited to that stage of human development. Such abrogation, however, was not designed to be a permanent and final abrogation of the verses of freedom of choice in religion, but rather a postponement until such time when the exercise of that freedom of choice and its full implications were the proper norm of the day. In this way, abrogation may now be reversed to enact the verses supporting religious freedom and repeal or abrogate the legal effect of verses restricting such freedom.

To avoid any misunderstanding of the position of Ustadh Mahmoud, it

---

[36]Ustadh Mahmoud was executed by former President Numeiri of Sudan on January 18, 1985, because he opposed the immediate total implementation of Islamic Shari'a law without undertaking the reform process he advocated. Numeiri had suddenly undertaken a policy of total Islamization in 1983, until his overthrow on April 6, 1985, three months after he executed Ustadh Mahmoud.

[37]Ustadh Mahmoud published about twenty books in Arabic and many essays and articles in daily newspapers and magazines in the Sudan. The present author has translated Ustadh Mahmoud's main book, *The Second Message of Islam*, into English, but it has not yet been published because he was imprisoned until recently by Numeiri.

should be emphasized that he did not propose to discard any part of the Qur'an or undermine its divine nature. What he did suggest, however, was that Muslims should undertake modern legislation to enact those verses of the Qur'an which were previously deemed to be abrogated in the sense that they were not made the source of legally binding rules (*ayat al-ahkam*). In relation to religious liberty, for example, he argued that the verses emphasizing freedom of choice and individual responsibility for such choice before God should be the bases of modern Islamic law. To do that, Muslims need to abrogate the verses of compulsion and discrimination against non-Muslims, in the sense of denying them legal efficacy in modern Islamic law. Such verses shall remain part of the holy Qur'an for all purposes except the purpose of legally binding rules. In other words, in the same way that early Muslim jurists employed the technique of abrogation (*naskh*) to rationalize and develop a body of law for their time, modern Muslims should undertake a similar process in order to develop a body of law for modern society. The only difference is that some of the verses of the Qur'an which were not deemed to be legally binding in the past are to be legally enacted into law today, with the necessary consequence that some of the hitherto-enacted verses are to be rendered unbinding in the legal sense. The resultant law would be modern Islamic law because it is derived from the Qur'an to satisfy the needs and aspirations of modern women and men.

This is one way—and in the view of the present author a very promising way—for reforming Shari'a rules to abolish *dhimma* and all discrimination against non-Muslims under Shari'a. Unless these are abolished, there is no prospect for religious freedom in Egypt or anywhere else in the Muslim world which purports to apply any part of Shari'a. The immediate and total implementation of Shari'a demanded by Muslim fundamentalists would make a difficult situation completely intolerable.

Abdullah Ahmad An-Na'im (Muslim) became a Visiting Professor of Law at the University of California at Los Angeles School of Law in 1985. After graduation from the University of Khartoum (Sudan), he attended the University of Cambridge (England), receiving an LL.B. and Diploma in criminology, and the University of Edinburgh (Scotland), receiving a Ph.D. in Law (1976). He taught law at the University of Khartoum, 1976-81; was a Rockefeller Fellow in Human Rights at Columbia University, 1981-82; and returned to the University of Khartoum till his detention in May, 1983, because of his opposition to the implementation of *Shari'a* in the Sudan. After the fall of President Numeiri (April, 1985), he received a Ford Foundation grant to do research on human rights in Islam. A leading member of the Sudanese Islamic reform movement, *jumhoryon*, started by the late Mahmoud M. Taha (executed in January, 1985, by President Numeiri), he has published in Arabic and English on Sudanese law and human rights, and has translated Taha's major work into English. He is presently doing a major study of religious tolerance in Muslim countries and communities.

RELIGIOUS LIBERTY AND HUMAN RIGHTS
IN THE SUDAN

Khalid Duran

The Sudanese case might be a particularly apt example to illustrate the inter-relatedness of the various categories determining the present conference project. Protest movements against the violation of human rights have assumed the form of civil war—patent in the South and simmering in the North. The focal point of this struggle for human rights is the question of religious liberties. The conflict is (a) one within a religion, namely, Islam, involving the cardinal issue of (alleged) apostasy, for which capital punishment was no longer held just as a threat but was actually meted out. It is (b) a conflict within a nation, inasmuch as religious intolerance is largely responsible for the civil war between the North and the South of the country—a civil war that once lasted for some seventeen years and, after an interval of a decade of comparative peace, has been ravaging the Sudan again for over a year now, with ever-increasing intensity. In a way, it is also (c) a conflict between nations, a conflict within the international community; at least it is perceived as such in many parts of Africa. Black Africans tend to view the war in the Sudan as one between an Arab nation in the North and an African nation in the South, with the North occupying the South by way of an age-old expansionism in the name of the Islamic religion. This opinion is held not only by Christians but also by many Muslims in such neighboring countries as Uganda and Kenya. The domination by the North of the South is a cultural-linguistic and an economic-political one. As such it has all the trappings of a national conflict, especially since there is a growing tendency among non-Arab Muslims to side with their non-Muslim compatriots against Arab Northerners. This may seem paradoxical, but it is not without parallels in other parts of the world; for example, black Muslims in Mauritania might occasionally be more sympathetic to Senegalese Christians than to white Mauritanian Muslims.

Much of what is to be said here about religious intolerance in the Sudan might, at the moment, be more potential than real. The fall of the Numeiri-Turabi dictatorship as the result of a popular uprising in March and April, 1985, led to a considerable improvement of the situation. Yet, the same forces of intolerance that backed the ousted regime's controversial "Islamization" program are still very much at work. Not only do they enjoy moral and material support from abroad, but their concepts of religiocultural domination over the rest of the population have also found acceptance with a vocal, though small, section of the educated class. In October, 1985, it was demonstrated on the streets of the capital that this type of highly motivated, well-funded, well-organized religious fanaticism, along with its paramilitary forces, is bent on blocking the process of democratization in order to enforce its ideological notions, regardless of the majority opinion among both Muslim and non-Muslim Sudanese. The rule of the "Muslim Brotherhood" ("National Islamic Front") in the name of *Shari'a* (Islamic law) from 1983 to 1985 is, therefore, not a matter of past history; rather, it is still an unresolved issue, boding ill for the future of the Sudan.

The antagonism between Northern and Southern Sudan, or between Arabic-speaking Muslims and Christian-led Animists, has its roots in the large-scale slave-trade that was common practice till near the end of the nineteenth century. Even after independence in 1956, Southerners used to be called *'abid* (slaves) in common Northern parlance. Accordingly, the government had to appeal to the public to desist from the use of such derogatory terms if national unity was not to be jeopardized.

The responsibility for the slave-trade continues to be a hotly debated issue. Northerners refer to the abolition of slavery by order of Ottoman viceroy Mehmet Ali, under whom Egypt was made into an independent power of its own and expanded its hold over the Sudan and even into parts of what is now Uganda. Actually, however, under Mehmet Ali's absolutist rule even sections of the Egyptian population were made to live in a state of semi-slavery. This was especially apparent in the way peasants were forcefully recruited into the army. Some of the Christian missions in Southern Sudan may not have given full priority to the abolition of slavery in the regions under their sway, but it hardly seems tenable to accuse them of having abetted slavery, as some Northern Sudanese and Egyptian authors are fond of alleging. This is not the place to apportion the blame for slavery. The major problem today is that even highly educated Sudanese from the South have valid reasons to complain about a condescending attitude toward them among sections of the Northern Sudanese population, the root cause being that they are regarded as people just emancipated from slavery. A Northern Sudanese professor of political science betrayed this state of mind—perhaps unwittingly—when he was asked about the acceptability of a Southerner as president of the country (instead of their being confined to the role of vice president, if anything at all). Despite this otherwise progressive stance, he felt that this would be out of the question—just as most people believe a Black could not possibly become president of the United States.

What makes things worse—and is relevant in the present context—is that the way out of this predicament might be conversion to Islam. Some Muslims tend to view this as Islam's emancipationist force. To non-Muslims, however, this is discrimination and religious coercion. Past attempts by Northern administrators to impose Arabic (Muslim) names on Southern school students were regarded by non-Muslims not as a readiness to integrate them but as a first step toward a more-or-less-forced conversion.

Language is another issue. The requirement of Arabic—or at least its official or semi-official promotion—is not just a nationalist concern of Northern Sudanese Muslims. It has a religious dimension insofar as Arabic is regarded as a holy language—a belief that is totally unacceptable to non-Muslims. It can safely be said that Southerners would have resisted Arabization less had there not been this religious dimension to the issue. As a secular language with a purely functional purpose, Arabic might be welcomed by many, because it is an admirable language and a useful instrument.

Muslim Sudanese certainly have a point in charging British colonialism with having deepened the antagonism by virtually cutting off the South from the North, in order to Christianize it. This is not based on historical conjecture, because there is too much evidence to prove that colonial policy aimed to create a "Christian belt" to halt the southward advance of Islam into black Africa. Pent-up resentments caused Southerners in the post-independence Sudan to rise in revolt against the central government, with the result that hundreds of Muslim army officers, administrators, and civilians from the North were killed. The Northern side blamed Christian missionaries from abroad—which was not entirely without foundation—and took strong action against them, at least over a number of years. Keeping in view the fact that the origin of the conflict goes back to the ruthless expeditions of Northern slave traders, it is surprising that the South did not embrace Christianity *en bloc* or *en masse*. The Southern Sudan is still predominantly Animist, and there is also a sizable number of Muslims among the tribespeople—people who embraced Islam freely, not through forced conversion or coercion. Despite the gigantic efforts by European missionaries, Christianity remains restricted to a fairly small minority of Southerners, though they are certainly influential because of the education provided by the mission schools.

The Addis Ababa Agreement of 1972 that ended the first Sudanese civil war provided the South some degree of autonomy. For a number of years it seemed that the Christian-Muslim conflict was amicably resolved. During that period the central government did not go out of its way to integrate Southerners, but instead it made a number of efforts to counter Southern suspicions. The system of government was fairly secularist (politically, not philosophically). There was open confrontation with those Northern forces that had always clamored for the introduction of an Islamic constitution and the conversion of the Sudan into an Islamic state. The one-party system, with the S.S.U. (Sudanese Socialist Union) as the all-embracing political institution, was certainly defective in many ways, but in the particular and peculiar circumstances of the Sudan it was meant to fulfill a specific role—to bridge the gap between North and South, between Muslims and non-Muslims. (Such categorization always implies a degree of generalization!) The Sudan was a member-state of the Arab League even then, but its official designation was the "Democratic Republic of the Sudan," not the "Arab Republic of the Sudan."

Much as the dictatorship of the ousted President Numeiri is now blamed for all the ills of the Sudan, and rightly so, it is also true that during the first seven or eight years it held the country together on what was, at least, a semi-secularist basis. The long duration of this dictatorship—altogether sixteen years—cannot be understood if this erstwhile positive aspect is not taken cognizance of. Things began to take a turn for the worse with the policy of "national reconciliation" ushered in by President Numeiri in 1977. This meant reconciliation of the regime with the forces of Muslim totalitarianism, who are usually subsumed under the term "Islamism," that is, believing in Islam as a primarily political ideology, one superior to all other -isms such as capitalism or communism, nationalism or socialism, liberalism or secularism, etc.

As soon as the leaders of political parties with a Muslim fundamentalist or Islamist outlook had returned to their country—with some in important government positions—they made every effort to erode the secularist system from within, seeking gradually to carry through their old design of introducing in the Sudan what they call the "Islamic system." This rekindled fears in the South, causing increasing unrest, and leading eventually to the outbreak of another civil war. The "national reconciliation"—that actually meant the reintegration of the Islamist forces into the political mainstream—was accompanied by economic deterioration, culminating in the disastrous starvation of 1985. In the late 1970's this had already caused fresh resentment in the South. Although the North suffered no less from abject poverty (in fact, the worst-affected regions are in the North), the South felt that its sufferings were due primarily to Northern neglect and economic discrimination.

Islamist ideas—the concept of Islam as a political ideology—are promoted chiefly by two parties in the Sudan. First and foremost is the traditional Umma Party as the political arm of the *ansar* sect, which is probably the strongest Sudanese sect in its number of adherents, although it is only one among many contending forces on the religiopolitical battlefield. The *ansar* sect is of special historical significance, since it enshrines the legacy of the Sudanese Mahdi (Messiah) who died almost exactly 100 years ago, in 1885. He enjoys a special prestige as a kind of national liberator, because he succeeded in driving out—at least temporarily—the Turko-Egyptian occupation forces. His aim, however, was not nationalistic in the sense that we would understand it today. He aimed to establish a theocratic rule not only over the Sudan but also over the entire Muslim world and, ultimately, beyond.

From the viewpoint of human rights, the Mahdi's record was negative with regard to both Muslims and non-Muslims. For the Mahdi, and even more so for his successor, the Khalifa 'Abdallahi, there was simply no question of tolerating Christianity—or any other religion, for that matter. Hundreds of Levantine Christians, who constituted the bulk of the business community in the Sudan in those days, could save their lives only by converting to Islam. Those who wished to return to their faith could do so only after the British had conquered the country and put an end to Mahdist rule. Muslims fared even worse than did Christians under Mahdist rule, because those who did not accept the Mahdi as the "Promised Messiah" were put to the sword, and their wives and children were enslaved. No reading material was allowed except for the Qur'an and the one treatise the Mahdi had written. In order to control the population of the capital, even mosques were pulled down so as to have everyone appear five times a day at the one remaining mosque. Especially the thirteen years of the Khalifa's reign were extremely bleak if examined from the viewpoint of human rights, particularly those concerning religious liberties.

Here one might argue that this is no longer fully relevant because the Mahdi's successors (his offspring) became increasingly moderate, and the Umma Party proved to be pro-British, with all that this entailed in terms of benign conservatism. The best known among the present leaders, a great-grandson of the Mahdi and a former prime minister, is a highly sophisticated graduate of British universities, who is very much at home in the international corridors of political life. Among the Islamists, Sadiq al-Mahdi is comparatively moderate, in some sense almost reformist. He is at loggerheads with his brother-in-law, Dr. Hasan A. al-Turabi, who heads the more radical party, the "Muslim Brotherhood." After a recent split of the "Muslim Brothers," he combined several radical Islamist factions into the "National Islamic Front" (N.I.F.). Sadiq al-Mahdi took a bold stand against Turabi, when the latter was the chief propagandist of the repressive "Islamization" policy under Numeiri. The rank and file of the *ansar* sect, however, still adhere to the fanatic notions of Muslim supremacy over the rest of the population and seek to establish an Islamic state. There is little to distinguish them from the "Muslim Brothers," whose members are often of *ansar* origin. Among the *ansar* elite, too, there has been no critical assessment of their own history, no "revision" of history or coming to terms with the past on the pattern of what the Germans would call *"Vergangenheitsbewältigung."* Instead of a self-critique or a genuinely religious introspection, even Sadiq al-Mahdi himself frequently indulges in untenable apologetics and Islamist slogan-mongering that put his intellectual stability in doubt.

For both non-Muslims and non-Mahdist Muslims the memories of those theocratic atrocities are still vivid. One century is not that long a time span, and there are still a few grandparents around who can relate stories from their childhood under the Mahdi's successor. This would be enough of a psychological burden even if the present *ansar* leadership were to dissociate itself clearly from that past and proffer a new interpretation of Islam. Since this has not been the case, or only so in a minimal way, the majority of Sudanese (who are not Mahdists) have every reason to fear the influence of this force in politics. In the Sudan it is less a question of "experimenting" with Islam as, for example, in Pakistan. In Khartoum, the "Islamic system" is not projected as an alternative to be implemented for the first time in history, as the Khomeini regime purports to do in Iran. The Sudan, or at least sections of the Sudanese population, celebrated in 1985 the centennary of "Islamization." Even without the tragic events of 1983-1985, we are faced here with the gigantic task of undoing a century-old legacy, with all that this entails in terms of fears and suspicions, of ingrained attitudes and prejudices.

The "Muslim Brotherhood" or N.I.F. as a more modern manifestation of those theocratic ambitions can best be analyzed as fascism in the world of Islam. It bears a close resemblance to the Falange ideology of *nacionalcatolicismo* in Franco Spain. Violent clashes in Khartoum in October, 1985, between "Muslim Brothers" and others, especially non-Muslims from the South, took on an almost racist character, as there were street battles between brown and black. There might be, though, a sad advantage to this aggravation of the situation, inasmuch as people are coming into the open with their real attitudes and true positions. There is no longer any camouflaging of religious intolerance by endless apologetics and untiring rhetorics—with people pointing accusing fingers at others. The N.I.F. now openly demands from the interim central government that the South be crushed with military might and that Shari'a be enforced throughout the country—according to its own narrow interpretation of Shari'a, not according to a consensus of Muslim majority opinion, of course.

Previously, separatist aspirations were largely confined to the Southerners. This trend continues in the full-fledged separatist movement calling for the establishment of a "Savannah Republic" in the southern Sudan. Another idea, however, seems to predominate as a result of the military strength of the insurgent "Sudanese People's Liberation Army" (S.P.L.A.). It advocates an alignment of Southerners with dissident Northerners, be they brown Christians or black Muslims. Together they should subdue Arab-Muslim suprematists and establish a truly secularist order in the Sudan. As a result, Islamists in the North have turned into separatists. Previously, they upheld national unity as the uppermost ideal and wished to exorcise separatism from the South. Now there are voices among the *ansar*, especially among the N.I.F.'s followers, saying that either the South should accept our "Islamic system" or it had better secede, so that we (the Islamists) are no longer blocked. The South, which was seen formerly as easy prey for Islamization, is now regarded as a deadweight encumbering Northern Sudan and preventing it from advancing toward its Islamist destiny.

Beginning with the "national reconciliation" of 1977, the Numeiri regime gradually veered away from its erstwhile secularist stance. Whatever might have been the reasons, personal or political, the dictator came closer and closer to the positions of the Islamists, till he finally made a bid to outpace them by proving to be even more fundamentalist than the "Muslim Brothers." September, 1983, saw the introduction of Shari'a. For most Muslims "Shari'a" has an ethical connotation. They view it less as legal injunctions than as moral precepts. Actually, Shari'a stands for a large variety of religious demands, ranging from rules of cleanliness and a sexual code of behavior to business regulations and questions of social welfare. Modern Islamists have greatly mystified this large mass of precepts as an inexhaustible source of answers to all the questions of life. They have created the myth of a panacea for all the ills of society, a kind of *deus ex machina* on whom Muslims could easily rely. They would then fare much better than by emulating the West.

It may not be without significance that such stalwarts of Muslim orthodoxy as Afghanistan and Morocco, to mention only two, never attached as much importance to the Shari'a as do present-day Islamists who wish for something of their own by which to compete with totalitarian ideologies. In Afghanistan and Morocco, as in most parts of the Muslim world, the mass of the population has mostly followed indigenous law dating from pre-Islamic times. Some sections of the populations integrated a number of elements from the Shari'a into their customary law; others did not do even that. It became something like a standard practice of Islamic religion to have Shari'a and *'urf* (customary law) side by side. The Sudan is no exception to this rule, except that there this organic development, which elsewhere was mostly harmonious, experienced two disturbing interferences—in the nineteenth and in the twentieth centuries. While this made the Sudanese experience differ from that of many other Muslim countries, it is not the only case of this kind. It has a model character for a few other countries. This applies also to the Sudan's having been turned into an experimental field by outsiders. For a new international religious establishment created in Saudi Arabia as a fundamentalist pseudo-church of Islam (in particular, the "Muslim World League" with its enormous network of sub-organizations), the Sudan is of utmost importance. It is regarded as a launching pad for Islamization (in the sense of Shari'a-enforcement) in the rest of Africa. In this poverty-stricken country numerous institutions have been created with impressive funds from oil-rich Gulf states, which are intended to combat popular religion (manifested in the mystic fraternities) and to substitute fundamentalism for it. The next step envisioned is to make this "purified" Islam or, rather, Islamism, spread out from the Sudan into the neighboring countries of black Africa.

Both of the Sudanese experiments with the Shari'a—under the Mahdi 100 years ago, as well as under Numeiri-Turabi till the Spring of 1985—emphasized the punitive aspects of it, such as the severing of hands and feet, public flogging, and harsh prison terms. The prohibition of alcohol received much publicity, but in essence the entire Shari'a-enforcement boiled down to increased political repression—similar to what had happened under the Mahdi's theocracy. For this reason most people in the post-Numeiri Sudan prefer to speak of the "September Laws." In part, this is expressive of the desire not to blemish the Shari'a with the excesses of a regime generally considered to have been perverse. The term "September Laws" stands symbolically for the worst type of repression witnessed by the country during the twilight of the Numeiri-Turabi government. Important segments of the Sudanese people wish for some kind or other of Shari'a-enactment, but there is a general consensus that it should not be the way the Islamists understand it—and certainly not in the manner in which it was done by the previous regime. The demand for a clear-cut abrogation of the "September Laws" has been voiced in the North even more persuasively than in the South. The South, however, has taken to armed rebellion against them—a desistance from the Shari'a is one of the primary conditions posed by the S.P.L.A. for peaceful negotiations with the central government. This created a dilemma for the interim government, insofar as it found itself unable to do so because of outside pressure, particularly from the oil-rich neighboring Arab states. Therefore, the "September Laws" have been suspended—but not repealed. A democratic government that is to result from the free and general elections announced for April, 1986, will thus be burdened with a pending issue which promises to turn into a major controversy of international proportions. Such Sudanese developments are bound to have far-reaching effects on large parts of the Muslim world and on other parts of Africa.

Islamists take particular pride in the Shari'a notion of quick justice. Western judicial procedures, with their sheer endless possibilities of appeal and long-lasting lawsuits, are considered decadent if not corrupt. This is a constant theme that is harped upon wherever Islamists are in force, especially in Iran. There might be a grain of truth in this, but the experience in all those countries has been discouraging: overzealous judges, keen on proving the swift effectiveness of Shari'a, committed blunders, and dozens of innocent people were maimed by severe physical punishments. The interim government following upon the Numeiri regime has every good intention of compensating people for the wrongs of the past. However, it could do little to repair the damage done to the victims of rushed justice in the name of the Shari'a. Severed hands and feet cannot be restored to those who proved, at last, to be innocent!

On August 29, 1984, the United Nations Sub-Commission on Prevention of Discrimination and Protection of Minorities adopted a resolution recommending that the United Nations' Commission on Human Rights urge governments which have legislation or practices providing for the penalty of amputation to provide for punishments other than amputation. The resolution cites Art. 5 of the Universal Declaration of Human Rights, which prohibits cruel, inhuman, or degrading punishment. The International Secretariat of Amnesty International reported on "Political Imprisonment in Sudan" (October 31, 1984) that, since September, 1983, at least forty-four amputations had been carried out, including twenty-eight of the right hand upon conviction of theft, and sixteen of the right hand and left foot upon conviction of armed robbery or persistent theft. Several hundred men and women have been flogged with between twenty-five and 100 lashes upon conviction of alcohol offenses, adultery or intended adultery, corruption, and other offenses under Shari'a. After the fall of the dictatorship in 1985, a number of amputated Sudanese, victims of the "September Laws," formed an association, but they were unable to get it registered, and their members continue to suffer much intimidation and a wide variety of discriminations.

Despite all this, one should guard against painting a picture that is nothing but bleak. As in other Third World countries, the experience with colonialism was bitter and left the Sudanese very irritable. They certainly have difficulties in accepting criticism from the "Christian West," which has contributed its own share to exacerbating the country's predicament. Hence, it is especially important to pinpoint exactly where the violations of religious rights takes place, rather than to present too global a case. In this context we stand to benefit from the typology outlined in the preliminary report by Elizabeth Odio-Benito. Examining her points one by one, we discover that the infringement of religious rights is not total. In other words, there is a density of violations at a few points, whereas with regard to other points Sudanese authorities are justified in declaring that there is nothing to complain about. The following comments deal with the Sudanese situation vis-à-vis the nine specific rights enumerated in her report (though not in the same order as she presented them):

1. "The freedom to worship or assemble in connection with a religion or belief, and to establish and maintain places for these purposes."

A number of Christian sections in Northern Sudan adduce considerable evidence concerning obstructions to the establishment of new churches. In the South, such obstructions are less direct, but indirect obstructions are manifold. The Sudanese Catholic Church has evidence to substantiate its complaint that:

> We were constantly refused the right to build churches or cultural centers; some of our churches were closed, our activities were reduced even though well organized for the profit of Christians as well as Muslims; and in national affairs we were unknown, as if we do not exist.[1]

2. "The freedom to establish and maintain appropriate charitable or humanitarian institutions."

This is a point of special grievance because the funds for such purposes usually come from abroad. The representatives of foreign missions wishing to aid Christian communities have to go through the central government. During the sixteen years of Numciri's rule, even most minor aid operations had to be sanctioned by the president's office. This caused enormous delays, and often nothing came of it at all. Thereby, the impoverished Sudan deprived many of its citizens of substantial foreign assistance because of religious bigotry.

3. "The freedom to solicit and receive voluntary financial and other contributions from individuals and institutions."

Here, much the same situation applies as in the previous point.

4. "The freedom to train, appoint, elect or designate by succession appropriate leaders called for by the requirements and standards of a religion or belief."

Here, obstructions due to individual attitudes have to be distinguished from government policy, which showed some degree of indifference, for the most part.

5. "The freedom to observe days of rest and to celebrate holidays and ceremonies in accordance with the precepts of one's religion or belief."

There has been no obvious obstructionist government policy, except that some authorities did occasionally create hurdles as a result of personal bias. In this case, the behavior of Christians has at times been almost provocative. Khartoum used to witness Christmas processions that assumed the character of paramilitary marches—something hardly seen elsewhere in the world. It is difficult, indeed, to see any connection between those marches and Christmas. The phe-

---

[1]Statement by the Archbishop of Khartoum, Gabriel Zuheir Wako, on behalf of the Sudanese Catholic Church, concerning the introduction of the Shari'a in the Sudan, Khartoum, September 23, 1983. Published in *Mashrek International*, February, 1985.

nomenon can be understood only as a militant reaction by a Christian minority embittered by all kinds of injuries, past and present.

6. "The freedom to establish and maintain communications with individuals and communities in matters of religion or belief at the national and international levels."

Here, obstructions have been of a more general nature, as a matter of an overall totalitarian government policy, but rarely is it specifically anti-Christian.

7. "The freedom to teach a religion or belief in places suitable for these purposes."

While there has usually been sufficient freedom to do this, it has, nonetheless, been an issue where Christians often felt aggrieved. They are free to teach their religion but find themselves confronted by an educational policy devised by Muslims with a clear bias in favor of the Arab North. Christians in Pakistan would have a very similar complaint (Hindus in Pakistan, even more so!). This observation raises doubts whether this useful nine-point typology is comprehensive enough. It might be necessary to reformulate some of the points or add other ones.

8. "The freedom to write, issue and disseminate relevant publications in these areas."

This point is somewhat similar to the last one. We should ask what good this freedom is if a poor minority community which is hardly able to produce its own publications is swamped by publications of an opposing majority—moreover, one with government support and sometimes even done through official channels. Islamists such as the "Muslim Brotherhood" and the newly formed N.I.F. receive unlimited funds from the oil-rich Gulf states. Some Islamist factions are heavily financed by Iran, others by Libya. Since this is a question of rivalry, some "Muslim Brothers" look out for who is bidding the most; others cash in from several sources. The net result is that this is by far the richest political party in all the Arab and Muslim states. No matter the sometimes insignificant number of their adherents—the Islamists have the means to produce abundant literature of all kinds and in all languages. They produce direct and indirect propaganda, maintaining dailies and weeklies and monthly and quarterly journals, for old and young, for male and female, for every taste. This literature is beautifully printed and is distributed free-of-charge or for a nominal price. It makes an impact even at American and European universities, not to speak of one of the poorest countries of the world, like the Sudan, where students are starving for reading matter.

When Russian and Chinese propaganda literature was first permitted on the Pakistani book market, it had an immediate effect and succeeded in stimulating leftism. For one generation, the basic issue was whether to decide for Moscow or for Beijing. Later, the Islamists flooded the market with their literature. Leaving aside the question of quality, the "battle of the books" was won by sheer

numbers. At present there is nothing that can match Islamist literature in the
Muslim world in quantity. Keeping in mind that we are speaking about propaganda, not truly educational or religious materials, we may even call its quality
superior. For a new generation of Muslims the question now is whether to decide
for Riyadh or for Teheran or perhaps for Tripoli. Non-Muslim minorities, especially in the Sudan, find themselves almost overwhelmed by an aggressive missionary activity, and they have little to counter this spate of publications. The
Animist majority in the Southern Sudan suffers most from this onslaught, because Christians at least have their own publications to fall back upon, however
disadvantaged those may be.

9. "The freedom to make, acquire and use to an adequate extent the necessary
articles and materials related to the rites or customs of a religion or belief."

This became a major problem under the Numeiri-Turabi dictatorship because
of the total prohibition on alcohol, which went so far as to punish Christian
clergy for the mere possession of mass wine. I should like to caution against
giving this single issue too much prominence, because it has often diverted attention from other problems that perhaps were more crucial. Nonetheless, it is an
issue that bedevils Christian/Muslim relations wherever Islamist rule enforces the
prohibition of alcohol. Under the Sudanese "September Laws" it came into the
limelight, but it exists elsewhere as well. Moreover, it has a special psychological
dimension because of the implied association of Christianity with moral corruption. The public flogging of the Catholic priest, Giuseppe Manara, in 1984,
because he was found in possession of sixteen bottles of mass wine, is to be seen
not only as an individual violation of human rights; it was also clearly designed
to intimidate the Christian community as a whole and to stimulate prejudice
against it.

Significantly, the typology used in the preliminary report does not seem to
touch upon the cardinal issue or issues of the Sudanese case. If this is to prove
anything, it merely proves the speciality of the Muslim dimension or, rather, its
complexity. The cardinal issue is that of non-Muslim citizens' being subjected to
a penal law which they have no right to challenge in any way, a law which their
elected representatives have no chance of altering, because a dominating class
of Muslims declares this evidently human-made law to be divine in origin, and,
therefore, unalterable. Manifestly, there is some similarity to the situation in
those countries where "democratic people's constitutions" assume a sacrosanct
nature comparable to the theocratic system of the Islamists. Both instances stand
out for their exceedingly harsh punishments, although the Islamist practice of
mutilating ordinary thieves hardly knows any parallel.

The objections of the Sudanese Catholic Church, summarized in the statement by the Archbishop of Khartoum on September 23, 1983, highlight the
ramifications of this issue:

> The Christians who do not have the Islamic Shari'a as their behav-
> ioral guidance would certainly lack the motivation to obey the law.

> The Islamic Shari'a encourages the Muslims who are in litigation with the Christians and other non-Muslims. The Christians feel that everybody has the same equitable rights.
>
> An accurate understanding of the law is essential in order to adopt just attitudes toward it. The Christians consider that the adoption of the Islamic Shari'a is a coercive measure imposed by the law to become Muslim.[2]

An application made in 1983 by the president of the Omdurman Bench of Magistrates, Eitidal Muhammad Fadul, and the president of the El Obied Bench of Magistrates, El Rayah Hassan Khalifa, challenged the constitutionality of the new Shari'a legislative provisions, reasoning that:

> Some of the positive duties under the Shari'a violate the rights and liberties of non-Muslims. . . . It therefore follows that this section provides for discrimination on the ground of religious belief in violation of article 38 of the Constitution which states as follows: "All persons in the Democratic Republic of the Sudan are equal before courts of law. The Sudanese have equal rights and duties, irrespective of origin, race, locality, sex, language or religion."

The full implementation of the Shari'a as understood by the Islamists also signifies separate taxation for Muslims and non-Muslims. This does not necessarily imply higher taxes for non-Muslims. In fact, many Muslims might well be more heavily taxed according to the rules of *zakat* (the religious tax), but it does constitute a discriminatory practice. The crucial point is that the viewpoint of the non-Muslims be taken into account at all. The Islamist attitude is to point out the advantages their system is supposed to have for non-Muslims. While this is, objectively speaking, sometimes true, it implies a disenfranchisement of the non-Muslims, because they have no choice but to accept what the majority community believes is best for them. An example from India illustrates this point. Under the rule of enlightened Moghul emperors such as Akbar, taxation was secular in nature; Hindus and Muslims were subjected to the same type of government taxes. Later, Emperor Aurangzeb introduced the traditional Shari'a taxation, according to which Muslims had to pay the *zakat* and non-Muslims, a tax called *jizya*. A delegation of Hindu peasants appealed to the authorities to return to the former system; though they had to pay less under Shari'a taxation, they preferred to pay more—as they had done till then—because they did not want to be classified as a kind of citizen different from their Muslim neighbors. In modern parlance we would say they were prepared to pay higher taxes in order not to be declared second-class citizens. The same is the opinion of non-Muslim Sudanese. It would be an important task of human-rights activists to bring this point home to the Islamists who display much insensitivity in this regard.

---

[2]Ibid.

Under the "September Laws," non-Muslims were not yet exempt from military service. However, should the Shari'a-application be taken to its logical conclusion, the defense of the country would become a preserve of Muslim citizens, with the army closed to Animists and Christians.

In Pakistan, Islamists have developed the concept of a "separate electorate." In this system, Muslims can vote only for Muslim candidates; non-Muslims, only for non-Muslims. Again, this is in tune with the ancient Shari'a. In the modern context, however, its primary purpose is to prevent Muslim politicians who are sympathetic to the minorities from gaining votes or being elected with non-Muslim support. A rule of the "Muslim Brotherhood" or N.I.F. in the Sudan would lead to a similar system.

There is yet another aspect of the application of the Shari'a that does not seem to implicate non-Muslims directly; indirectly, however, it affects them all the more. This is the position of women, which definitely differs from the concept of equal rights for all found in the United Nations' human-rights charter. Whatever arguments the advocates of the traditional Shari'a adduce in favor of its equity, this is certainly one of the most controversial issues. No doubt, in its time (seventh-century Arabia) the Shari'a brought about a revolution and greatly improved the lot of women. This dynamic process, however, came to a halt, and even became retrogressive in part. No wonder, then, that the question of women's rights figures prominently in the literature of contemporary Islam. There is the large apologetic strand endeavoring to prove that true female emancipation can only be found in Islam. On the other side are many Muslim reformers and modernists who are highly conscious that all is not well with the position of women according to the Shari'a as an ossified code of conduct. This issue, more than any other, prompted reformists to demand a further development of the Shari'a in tune with the social developments of the age.

There are numerous Muslim thinkers all over the world, both men and women, who criticize the inferior status of women in the Shari'a handed down to us. At first sight this looks like a headache for Muslim women alone, but the general and detailed restrictions imposed upon women by the Shari'a have their effect on public life as a whole, so that non-Muslim women stand to suffer almost as much as their Muslim sisters. It is not so much the chances for education that diminish as it is the possibilities to put acquired education to use. There is the danger of women's being confined to the "classical careers" in education and medicine. Stringent Shari'a interpretations impose restrictions even in those domains, and in some countries women no longer enjoy the professional scope previously achieved. There are some segments among Sudanese Islamists who hold that women teachers can teach only female pupils, that women physicians can treat only female patients, and that female nurses should serve only in women's wards.

According to the traditional Shari'a as it is understood by mainstream Sudanese Islamists, a woman's testimony is worth only half that of a man's. So, if two witnesses are needed, but only one male witness is available, there must be two female witnesses to replace the second male. The supposed emotional in-stability of women is said to render them unfit for most jobs in the legal profes-sion, and this is not the only career becoming taboo if the traditional Shari'a is applied. For non-Muslims this is an altogether unbearable hardship. It closes many careers to female academics. However, this issue also meets with particu-larly stiff resistance from the bulk of the Muslim community, from most of those believers who do not subscribe to the Islamist ideology. The above-mentioned stipulations became law in Pakistan in 1984. The redeeming feature is that this law was passed only under the aegis of a military dictatorship. There was tremen-dous opposition to it, and it can safely be said that a parliament emerging out of really free elections is, more likely than not, going to repeal this "law of testi-mony." Similarly, in the Sudan the overwhelming demand that the "Septem-ber Laws" be annulled is linked to such justified fears. Muslim women are the vanguard of this protest. The issue of women's rights in the religious context acquired added significance in the Sudan because of the bold stand taken by Mahmoud M. Taha, who was of the opinion that the legal career was a very suitable field to absorb the ever-increasing number of female academics. His writings on this subject throw this issue into bold relief. They constitute both a comprehensive and profound as well as very courageous and conscientious critique of the traditional Shari'a. Moreover, they come from an Islamic perspec-tive and are based on interiorized religious convictions. Significantly, his conclu-sions are diametrically opposed to those of the Islamists.

It cannot be emphasized enough that opposition to the Shari'a, at least in the shape it assumed as "September Laws," is opposed by Muslims just as much as by Christians and Animists. As a matter of fact, the most sustained effort to rebut the notion of a traditional Shari'a without any further development in light of the present was made by the Northern Sudanese Muslim reformer Mahmoud M. Taha and his movement of the *jumhuriyun* ("Republicans"). In a strictly Islamological perspective, this is certainly a heretical movement, but so were most reform movements in the world of Islam throughout history. Funda-mentalists such as the Wahhabis in Saudi Arabia or the Mahdists in Sudan were considered heretical by the majority of Muslims, at least during the initial period. The important fact is that a large segment of educated Sudanese public opinion sympathizes with much of M. Taha's message. In addition, his reform ideas are gaining ground in other parts of the Muslim world.

Sudan's history with the traditional Shari'a as understood by the Mahdist fundamentalists and modern Islamists might explain why such a reformer as M. Taha should rise from that country rather than from neighboring Egypt, with its leading role in Muslim modernism. He was brought to trial with four of his disciples on January 7, 1985. A court, consisting of a single judge with less than two years of judicial experience, took less than two hours to condemn all five to death. He was executed mainly because of his courageous opposition to the "September Laws" and his demand that the civil war be stopped immediately. He insisted, from a purely religious point of view, on the equality of all citizens, regardless of their religion. To this end, he rejected the Islamist concepts of an "Islamic system," an Islamic state, and an Islamic constitution.

The case of M. Taha leads to another issue of special relevance to the typology outlined in the preliminary report to the United Nations. A visitor to the Ministry of Religious Affairs in Khartoum through the years could not help receiving the impression that this seemed to be a Ministry of Islamic Affairs instead. Despite the fact that at least one-fourth of the Sudanese population is non-Muslim, there was little indication that this Ministry also catered to the needs of the other religious communities. For this reason, it was criticized by M. Taha, who demanded that it really serve as a Ministry of Religious Affairs, rather than as an Islamic propaganda office or missionary establishment. This greatly upset some Islamists who denounced him for his criticism. Their attacks leave no doubt regarding their inability even to conceive of a joint ministry for the religious affairs of all communities. To them religious liberties cannot assume the characteristics of a pluralist society, only those of a symbiosis of semi-autonomous communities.

M. Taha's self-sacrifice for his convictions brought another cardinal issue to the fore, namely, that of apostasy in Islam—or, to be more precise, the freedom of Muslims to hold different views or interpretations of Islam diverging from those adopted by a given government as the official doctrine. Taha never renounced his faith. On the contrary, all his life was devoted to the cause of Islam as he understood it. The capital punishment prescribed by the traditional Shari'a is, therefore, not merely a threat to those Muslims who choose to abandon their inherited faith, but also is a menace to all who can arbitrarily and all too easily be declared apostates by a religious establishment—while they might actually be fervent believers who do justice according to all the criteria of orthodoxy but differ from others on a few points of interpretation.

What is of special importance in the present context is the convergence between the *jumhuriyun* opposition to the "September Laws" and the objections raised by the Sudanese Catholic Church. M. Taha's teachings correspond to the conclusions of Gabriel Zuheir Wako, Archbishop of Khartoum, when the latter said:

> There are other means to avoid crimes, which are much more harmonious with the nature and dignity of mankind:
> — an effective prevention of crime;
> — an education showing the advantages and the disadvantages of both a criminal and an honest life;
> — a proper religious formation.[3]

The convergence between Christian and Muslim advocacy of human rights is most evident with regard to the public flagellation of women. Thus, Northern Sudanese such as the *jumhuriyun*—but many other Muslims no less—would fully subscribe to the Catholic Church's position as formulated by Wako: "We usually

[3]Ibid.

associate women with motherhood. No one could ever bear to see his mother beaten in public or even in private. To beat a woman can raise very strong negative feelings within the community."[4] Finally, the archbishop neatly evoked the tenets of Islam's Holy Scripture, the Qur'an, when he concluded:

> If we follow the retaliation law, "an eye for an eye, and a tooth for a tooth," we would soon be a blind nation. We rarely name God as Just, however; we prefer to call God the Merciful. Our laws should express this splended attribute of God which is mercy.[5]

This tallies with the majority opinion among Sudanese Muslims and has found a forceful restatement in Mahmoud M. Taha's major work, *The Second Message of Islam.*[6] A complaint frequently heard from Muslim Sudanese during the Numeiri-Turabi years was: Why do outsiders pick up their cudgels on behalf of Christian Sudanese alone? Are we Muslims suffering less? We feel the infringement upon religious liberties not only as dictatorship; for us it also means a perversion of the noble precepts of our religion. Every Muslim prayer is a call to God "the Compassionate, the Merciful."

---

[4]Ibid.

[5]Ibid.

[6]The English translation of this work, by Abdullahi Ahmed An-Na'im, is awaiting publication.

APPENDIX

The following excerpts are from *Al Montada*, no. 109-110 (September-October, 1984), pp. 16-18, which carries the full statement, "The Position of the Christian Churches with regard to the Enforcement of the Islamic Shari'a and to the Declaration of the Sudan Being an Islamic State."

We, Christian churches, reaffirm our respect for Islam and for Muslims. We highly regard the spiritual values found in Islam. We profess our loyalty to the Sudan and our commitment to its welfare. . . . We recognize our duty . . . to contribute to the well-being of our country. . . . It is our right to express this act of loyalty and sincere respect by speaking the truth as we see it, rather than to flatter or keep silent. . . . The road to unity and peace is through understanding, mutual respect, and dialogue. The role of the state is to work for and promote the common good of all citizens without excluding any. The state cannot bring about unity or carry out its role by being discriminatory to the exclusion of a number of citizens, in our case, well over a third. . . . We . . . once more voice our objection to the enforcement of Islamic Shari'a on all citizens, irrespective of their beliefs, religion, or culture. We also object to . . . declaring the Sudan an Islamic state when over a third of its citizens are non-Muslims. . . . The oath of loyalty on the Qur'an excludes Christian citizens from participation in the construction and the life of the country; it reduces them to second-class citizens without rights and without freedom. The enforcement fosters divisions in the country [and] . . . gives rise to religious conflicts. . . . The enforcement would tend to force non-Muslims to become Muslims. Non-Muslims would lose their rights as citizens. It violates the right of any human being to freedom of conscience. Legislation based entirely on Islam cannot in justice bind a nation of diverse religions and cultures. . . .

In spite of the declaration that Islamic Shari'a was not applicable to Christians, we now see that Christians and other non-Muslims have also become the target of these laws . . . The Christian religion is abused in the public media and in public speeches. . . . Its teaching, legislation, traditions, and practices are ridiculed. The local church leadership, which is 100 per cent Sudanese, has been ignored. They could have been consulted for the common good.

The conflicts within our country have been attributed to Christianity, thus arousing ill-feeling against Christians, and diverting the attention of the nation from the real causes of unrest which are injustice, falsehood, and disregard for other human beings. Christians are being treated as foreigners, when in fact they are real and full citizens of the country. Muslims must live by the dictates of their religion, but they have no right to impose their convictions on others who have different beliefs. In the name of peace, justice, and unity, in the name of the well-being of our country, we make an urgent appeal to the legislators to re-affirm the present and permanent constitution which takes into account the diversity of races, beliefs, religions, and cultures in our country.

Signed by the following church leaders:

Butrus T. Shukai, Bishop of Khartoum
Clement Janda, S.C.C. General Secretary
Daniel M. Zindo, Bishop of Yambio
Rev. Samwïil Jangul Angollo, the Sudanese Church of Christ, Omdurman
Rev. Matthew McChiening, Presbyterian Church in the Sudan, Khartoum
Ephraim A. Natena, Provost, All Saint's Cathedral, Khartoum
Gabriel Zuheir Wako, Archbishop of Khartoum
Joseph Pellerino, Bishop of the Catholic Church, Rumbek
Joseph Nyekindi, Bishop of the Catholic Church, Wau
Paride Taban, Bishop of the Catholic Church, Torit
Vincent Majwok, Bishop of the Catholic Church, Malakal
Joseph Gasi Abangite, Bishop of the Catholic Church, Tombura
Paolino Lukudu Loro, Archbishop of the Catholic Church, Juba

Khalid Duran (Muslim) was born in Germany to a Moroccan father and Spanish mother; was educated in Spain, Pakistan, and Germany (political science and sociology at the Universities of Bonn and Berlin); and became an associate professor in the Islamic Research Institute in Pakistan in 1968, where he also taught at Islamabad University (sociology) and the Pakistani National Institute of Modern Languages. He wrote book reviews and articles for the daily *Pakistan Times*, the weekly *Outlook*, and the quarterlies *Islamic Studies* and *Islam and the Modern Age* (New Delhi). Involvement with the Islamic "left" led to his expulsion from Pakistan in 1975. He has been a research scholar since 1978 at the Deutsches Orient-Institut in Hamburg, Germany, at its Egypt-Libya-Sudan desk. A frequent lecturer in European and American institutions and at interfaith conferences, he has become a disciple of the late Mahmoud Taha of the Sudanese Islamic reform group, Republican Brothers. A founding member of the Committee for Christian-Muslim Dialogue for the biannual Protestant *Kirchentag* in W. Germany, he also founded the "Islamic Academy Hamburg" as a forum for Muslim socialists and instituted a study circle on liberation theology in Latin America and the Muslim world along with exiled Argentinian priests and members of the German Protestant student community. A frequent contributor to scholarly journals in several languages, he has also lectured at the teacher-training institute in Hamburg to help German teachers cope with problems with students from Turkey and other Muslim countries. In 1985 the Deutsches Orient-Institut, Hamburg, published his *Islam und politischer Extremismus: Einführung und Dokumentation*.

Otto Luchterhandt (Protestant) is a lawyer who has been a scholar at the Institut für Ostrecht at the University of Cologne, West Germany, since 1975. He studied law, Slavic studies, and Eastern European history at the Universities of Freiburg, Bonn, and Cologne, receiving his Dr. jur. from Cologne. He has received a second doctorate from Cologne in public law, church-state law, and Eastern European law in 1986 (Habilitation). His first dissertation was published in 1976: *Der Sowjetstaat und die Russisch-Orthodoxe Kirche* (Cologne). Among his other books are: *UN–Menschenrechtskonventionen–Sowjetrecht–Sowjetwirklichkeit: Ein kritischer Vergleich* (Baden-Baden, 1980); *Die Gegenwartslage der Evangelischen Kirche in der DDR* (Tübingen, 1982); and *Der verstaatlichte Mensch: Die Grundpflichten des Bürgers in der DDR* (Cologne, 1985).

THE HUMAN RIGHT OF FREEDOM OF RELIGION
AND SOVIET LAW

Otto Luchterhandt

I. *The Presuppositions of International Law and Their Consequences for a Fundamental Assessment of the Human-Rights Problematic in the U.S.S.R.*

The freedom of religion has both an individual and a collective or institutional legal character. It is a comprehensive human right, which takes shape in many particular rights. These rights represent in part the concretizing of other human rights within a religious framework. These rights today are guaranteed— to a more or less broad extent—by those states which are bound to the European-North American constitutional tradition and which have made human rights and freedom the basis of their political systems. Therefore, the laws of individual freedom of religion show far-reaching similarities, while the differences with respect to the legal status of churches and religious communities could be considerable. Here, historical traditions, confessional peculiarities, and cultural idiosyncracies of the countries of course play a great role.

It would be a grave methodological error—unfortunately, very frequently committed in the literature—to pick out an ideal Western nation with the greatest measure of individual and collective freedom of religion and to criticize the legal and social situation of religious persons and communities in the socialist, ideological states against this standard. It is apparent that such a procedure is arbitrary and incorrect. The question of the standard is a difficult one. Happily, the difficulties are essentially eliminated for us by fundamental, international human-rights agreements which the Soviet Union has not only signed but has also ratified and which, moreover, today enjoy a far-reaching recognition in the international legal community. These are of significance:

1. the International Covenant of December 16, 1966, concerning civil and political rights;
2. the International Covenent of December 16, 1966, concerning economic, social, and cultural rights;
3. the UNESCO Convention against discrimination in education of December 15, 1960;
4. the I.L.O. Convention against discrimination in employment and profession of June 4, 1958; and
5. the Declaration of November 25, 1981, on religious intolerance and discrimination which, unfortunately, is not a legally binding international norm.

These international conventions guarantee the following special rights, which —taken together—constitute the human right of freedom of religion as it is legally binding, by international covenant, on the Soviet Union. From the critical perspective of a liberal, democratic, constitutional state, it is barely more than a minimum standard:

1. The freedom for each person—adult or child—to choose for her or himself a religion or worldview, to hold it, and to change it (Art. 18, para. 1, Civil Rights Covenant).

2. The right to be permitted to make use of these rights without external coercion (Art. 18, para. 2, Civil Rights Covenant).

3. The freedom to confess one's religion or worldview alone or in community with others *privately* through worship, in the form of religious customs, or through education or other practices (Art. 18, para. 1, Civil Rights Covenant).

4. The freedom to confess one's religion or worldview *publicly*, whether alone or in community with others (Art. 18, para. 1, Civil Rights Covenant).

5. The freedom for parents or other authorized teachers to educate children in accord with their religious convictions (Art. 18, para. 4, Civil Rights Covenant; Art. 5, UNESCO Convention).

6. The freedom for parents to delegate the religious and moral education of their children to a third person (for example, clergy) (Art. 18, para. 4, Civil Rights Covenant; Art. 13, para. 3, Social Rights Covenant; Art. 5, UNESCO Convention).

7. The right of parents to choose educational institutions independent of the state so as to secure the religious and moral education of their children or, if such institutions do not yet exist, to found them (Art. 13, para. 3, Social Rights Covenant).

8. The fundamental rights of equality for all religious persons, that is, the right to practice all the human rights guaranteed in the international conventions without discrimination on account of religious affiliation.

This means especially:

9. The right not to be discriminated against because of religious views when practicing freedom of opinion, freedom to spread opinions, and freedom of information (Art. 2, para. 1, and Art. 19, Civil Rights Covenant); in other words, religious freedom of opinion, propaganda, and information.

10. Correspondingly, the right to meet for religious purposes results from supra (Art. 2, para. 1, and Art. 21, Civil Rights Covenant).

11. In the same way, the right to found and join religious societies is derived (Art. 2, para. 1, and Art. 22, Civil Rights Covenant).

12. The right not to be hindered from the practice of general freedom of movement in one's homeland on account of religious affiliation (Art. 2, para. 1, and Art. 12, para. 1, Civil Rights Covenant).

13. The right not to be hindered from leaving (Art. 2, para. 1, and Art. 12, para. 2, Civil Rights Covenant) or entering the country on account of religion (Art. 2, para. 1, and Art. 12, para. 4, Civil Rights Covenant).

14. Equal access of religious citizens to all public educational institutions, both general and professional (Art. 2, para. 2, and Art. 13, para. 1, Social Rights Covenant; Art. 1, UNESCO Convention).

15. Equal access of religious citizens to professional and work places, including those of "public service" (Art. 2, pars. 2, and Art. 6 or Art. 7, Social Rights Covenant; Art. 25, Civil Rights Covenant).

16. Equal participation of religious citizens in the political affairs of the country and equal access to the positions of political leadership (Art. 2, para. 2, and Art. 25, Civil Rights Covenant).

17. The right of religious minorities "together with other members of their group to attend to their own cultural life, to confess and practice their own religion or to make use of their own language" (Art. 27, Civil Rights Covenant).

While the prohibitions against discrimination are valid without reservation, the freedom rights stand under the well-known condition of "public order"; that is, according to Art. 18, para. 3 of the Civil Rights Covenant, "The freedom to manifest one's religion or worldview is to be subjected to only those legal limitations which are necessary for the protection of public security, order, health, morals or the basic rights and freedom of others." This reservation means, doubtless, a strong relativization of the guarantee of freedom. It does not represent an "escape clause," however, which is open to just *any* interpretation. The authorization conceded to a state to limit freedom of religion as well as political freedom and freedom of movement through this provision is itself subject to specific limitations, namely:

1. The limitations must be made normative in a formal way through a *"law"*; a legislative act of a lesser rank or an administrative measure does not suffice.

2. The law is permitted to provide only for *"limitations"* (cf. Art. 18, para. 3). Explicitly forbidden is not only the formal but also the actual abrogation of rights through their legal undermining (Art. 5, para. 1, Civil Rights Covenant; also Social Rights Covenant).

3. Freedom of religion may not be set aside through emergency measures; it is not to be jeopardized by crises (Art. 4, Civil Rights Covenant).

4. The legal limitations may not affect the prohibition against religious discrimination.

5. Freedom of religion may be limited only for the protection of enumerated, general, elementary legal norms of the society as well as for the protection of fellow citizens' human rights. The restrictive character of this delimitation is such that, in contradistinction to specifically political human rights such as freedom of opinion, of the press, of assembly, and of association (cf. Art. 19, 21, 22, Civil Rights Covenant), the criterion of "national security" is inapplicable (cf. Art. 18, para. 3, Civil Rights Covenant).

Notwithstanding these distinctions, moreover, all the measures a state might enact for the limiting of human rights stand under the prohibition against abrogating them *de facto* or, indeed, *de jure*. Herein lies a grave problem by which the characteristic situation of the human right of freedom of religion in ideologically closed Communist states moves into sharp focus. The Soviet Constitution of October 7, 1977, linked the practice of personal religious and political freedom and of other democratic rights to the reservation that they be in *positive* "agreement with the goals of the building of Communism" (cf. Art. 47 and 51, Soviet Constitution), or likewise "in accordance with the interests of the people and in order to strengthen and to develop the socialist system" (cf. Art. 50, Soviet Constitution).

Moreover, each and every basic right of the Soviet citizen stands under the following duties, which are to be interpreted in accordance with the official Soviet ideology, to wit: "to respect the rules of socialist community life," "to prove oneself worthy of the high calling of a citizen of the U.S.S.R." (Art. 59, para. 2, Soviet Constitution) and, furthermore, "to protect the interests of the Soviet state and to contribute to the strengthening of its power and authority" (Art. 62, para. 1, Soviet Constitution).

The full juridical meaning of this attendant, obligatory qualification of Soviet basic rights first reveals itself when one looks at Art. 6 of the Soviet Constitution. There it is determined that the Communist Party of the Soviet Union alone possesses the exclusive power to determine authoritatively the interests of the people, the political goals of the Soviet state, and the measures for their realization. That means nothing other than that the practice of the fundamental rights of the Soviet citizen stands under the sovereign reservations of the party and state leadership or, to put it another way, that under Soviet constitutional law—I emphasize: *law*—the practice of fundamental rights consists essentially in the fulfillment of party directives. This is precisely, however, no longer a "limitation" in the sense of the human-rights conventions but rather the *abolition or abrogation of human rights per se.*

The meaning of human rights does not consist in the dutiful furtherance of the common good according to the directives of the party-state, but rather in the free development of individuals in moral self-responsibility with respect for the equal rights of their fellow human beings and for the elementary conditions of a peaceful common life in community in the free participation in the shaping of the political order by having at their disposal an indeterminate number of spiri- tual and political behavior alternatives among which they can freely choose.

Indeed, the individual also possesses *duties* with regard to the state—thus, Art. 29 of the General Declaration of Human Rights of December 10, 1948—but they represent something other than rights. Unfortunately, one must point out this self-evident fact with respect to the Communist states. Art. 19, para. 3 of the Civil Rights Covenant, which speaks of the "special duties and a special obli- gation" with regard to the practice of freedom of opinion, would be meaningless if the basic right of expression of opinion had already been conceived—as it un- fortunately is in the Soviet Constitution—as a duty.

With this abrogation of human rights and freedom placed in the very struc- ture of the Soviet Constitution, there arises a profound problem for freedom of religion. Religion does not have, so to speak, a sharply defined, clearly demar- cated area as its object; rather, it flows out of the entire spiritual and practical life of human beings and thus stands in an indissoluble, mutual relationship with all intellectual and, of course, political activities of human beings. Because the freedom of the spirit is indivisible, the (partial) muzzling of the spirit by the dominant, institutional, secular ideology, with its claim to absoluteness—which, in principle, is not different from the state religion of a confessionally exclusive state of the seventeenth or eighteenth centuries—necessarily endangers freedom of religion. This remains true even when religion is broadly tolerated and effective, as it is today in Poland and the German Democratic Republic. These two examples from the Communist-ruled world show that a limited coexistence and a relatively far-reaching tolerance of religious citizens—given the circumstances—are possible even in an ideologically Communist state with its attendant human-rights nihilism, given a pragmatic attitude on the part of the party and state leadership.

The Soviet Union is also capable of making such accommodations, as was initially demonstrated by the relatively liberal *modus vivendi* which existed between the Soviet state and the religious communities, namely, the Russian Orthodox Church, between 1943 and 1958. It is therefore in no way *prima facie* senseless to direct corresponding human-rights demands to the address of the U.S.S.R., even apart from the fact that the observance of human rights in principle must be insisted upon for all states, especially for those—such as the U.S.S.R.—which have admitted, for whatever motives, the international, binding, legal nature of such rights.

II. The Typical Violations, Restrictions, and Discriminations concerning Religious Freedom and Religious Citizens in the Soviet State

In the following expositions, aspects of individual rights as guaranteed by international law will be dealt with systematically from the perspective of the restrictions and discriminations hostile to human rights to which they are subject.

A. Freedom of Religious Profession—Freedom of Religious Opinion

Insofar as freedom of religious profession is a part of the freedom of religious opinion, it shares the chief problematic of this human right in the Soviet state, namely, its strangulation by the application of certain penalties:[1]

1. Art. 190, para. 1 of the Russian Federation (R.S.F.S.R.) Penal Code (hereafter abbreviated *R.F.P.C.*) considers as punishable "the spread of consciously false fabrications that defame the system of the Soviet state and society." The infamous Art. 70 of the *R.F.P.C.* ("anti-Soviet agitation and propaganda") formally elevates this action to a crime, if the person expressing the opinion

---

[1]A broad discussion of freedom of speech is found in Otto Luchterhandt, *UN-Menschenrechtskonventionen—Sowjetrecht—Sowjetwirklichkeit: Ein kritischer Vergleich* (Baden-Baden: Nomos Verlagsgesellschaft, 1980), p. 107.

simultaneously intended with his or her "falsifications" the "subversion or weakening of Soviet power." With the assistance of these totally capriciously interpreted definitions, Soviet criminal prosecution authorities and courts have long suppressed critical remarks about the actual and legal situation of religious communities in the Soviet state as well as about the religious politics of the party and state leadership—whereby it was completely irrelevant to them if the criticism dealt with provable or proved facts. This means that critical examination of their own status in the Soviet state is forbidden to religious Soviet citizens. In this regard they must comply with the official regulating of speech, which—as the foreign propaganda of the Moscow Patriarchate sufficiently proves—describes religious affairs in the U.S.S.R. in the most favorable light.

2. In practice, the direction of Art. 142 of the *R.F.P.C.* (March 16, 1966, version) operates with further limitations. It considers punishable the *production* of any kind of documents—including "letters"—which call for the nonfulfillment of religious legislation, in order to circulate them on a wide scale. This regulation is directed particularly against the exercise of the right of petition by religious citizens, because the mere production of a petition demanding the change or lifting of anti-religious regulations is enough for the courts to determine the culpability (this is interpreted as a call for disobedience). The *subjective* intention of mass circulation is indisputably concluded from the *objective* suitability of the documents for circulation.

3. Also threatened by these realities of political criminal law are religious citizens who through the confession of their faith separate themselves critically from atheism and thereby particularly from the atheistic premises of Communist ideology. An energetic apologetics, one not restricted to nebulous formulations, oversteps the limits of tolerance of religious freedom in the Soviet Union (judging from how the authorities act). This is also totally consistent, since, in a Communist worldview which takes itself seriously, criticism of atheistic materialism must be considered a direct attack on the bases of the Constitution. From this there result direct and serious consequences for the content of sermons. Through the special (investigatory) censorship of sermons by the authorities the meaningful addressing of listeners in everyday Soviet life is for the most part prevented.

4. Art. 227 of the *R.F.P.C.* standardizes a further express restriction of religious freedom which is directed against certain sects. According to the article, one becomes liable to punishment if one occasions "the renunciation of societal activity." That "participation in public life" is a criminally protected section of the law may appear odd to a citizen of a liberal, democratic, constitutional state, to whom retreat into private life is for the most part open. As noted, active support of the state is a constitutional obligation in the Soviet system. Renunciation of community life arouses mistrust and, if practiced for any length of time, leads to personal difficulties. For the rest, the evidence of criminality rests on the solid tenet of anti-religious education that the best "cure" for religion is participation in public affairs, the incorporation of religiously "infected" people into the "collective."

B. The Freedom to Spread Religious Opinions

The religious freedom to spread opinions is a further aspect of the freedom of confession. It concerns the *process* of confession, which can happen privately or publicly, orally or in writing. The freedom of religious propagation was expressly guaranteed in the Constitution until 1929.[2] It then disappeared from the Constitution; since then, only the right "to confess a desired religion and to practice religious rites" stands over against the freedom of atheistic propagation that is guaranteed in Art. 52 of the Soviet Constitution. Soviet authorities derive from it to this day a general prohibition of religious propagation.[3] One must conclude from practice that they tolerate the oral spreading of religious views through *private* conversations and intervene administratively only when they assume the character of a systematic canvassing. Profession in private correspondence is exempt from punishment.

The *public* spreading of religious views is forbidden, however. Insofar as it occurs orally, it is treated as an infringement of the community order; when it occurs in written form, the authorities consider it an evasion of the comprehensive censorship provisions whose formal observation is protected by the regulations of the political criminal law. Religious propagation not authorized by the state is considered per se a "defamation of Soviet reality" or "anti-Soviet propaganda." As it deals here with such materials as *samzidat*, one refers mostly to other crimes, especially to "involvement in forbidden business" (Art. 162, *R.F.P.C.*). What is meant here is, for example, the business of a religious printer, as in the case of the underground publisher "Christianin," through which the Reformed Baptists formerly published religious writings in large numbers, but whose collaborators without exception have been sentenced to a more or less severe punishment.

The forbidding of public religious propagation, however, is not without exception. Strictly speaking, one could include sermons here. However, they are of course an integral component of the worship service and therefore belong to the freedom of worship. It is different with religious literature, especially with magazines, which the spiritual leadership of the licensed religious communities of the Soviet state are permitted to publish, above all the journal from the Moscow Patriarchate, which even has its own publishing department at its disposal.

It is juridically decisive that these exceptions to the prohibition of religious propagation are completely at the political discretion of the state authorities. Consequently, religious citizens have no legal claim for the editing of religious literature, because that permission is granted them upon the fulfillment of cer-

---

[2]See Otto Luchterhandt, *Der Sowjetstaat und die Russisch-Orthodoxe Kirche* (Cologne: Verlag Wissenschaft und Politik, 1976), p. 89.

[3]Elaborated in Otto Luchterhandt, *Die religiöse Gewissensfreiheit im Sowjetstaat*. Teil II: *Die Rechtstellung der Gläubigen nach dem Grundrecht der Gewissensfreiheit*. Berichte des Bundesinstituts für ostwissenschaftliche und internationale Studien 40 (Cologne, 1976), pp. 20-24.

tain legally determined and realizable prescriptions. The prohibition in principle of religious propagation cannot be justified by the criteria of internationally recognized law, the *"ordre public,"* the public order and safety, the health and rights of fellow citizens. Its sole aim lies in the attempt to restrict artificially the developmental possibilities of religious citizens.

Apart from that, the juridical prohibition of religious propagation in the U.S.S.R. violates international law's prohibition of discrimination, for, in contrast to the religious Soviet citizen, the atheist citizen is expressly empowered, as noted, to practice "propagation" corresponding to his or her convictions. Art. 2, para. 1, and Art. 19, para. 1 of the Civil Rights Covenant are thereby violated.

C. Negative Freedom of Conscience[4]

The stipulation of Art. 18, para. 2 of the Civil Rights Covenant, that no one may be subject to "pressure" which encroaches on one's freedom to have or accept a religion or conviction of one's choice, encounters absolutely insolvable problems in an ideological state, and this is especially the case with the U.S.S.R. For, contrary to the liberal, anti-clerical phrase that was taken over by the Bolsheviks, "Religion is a private matter," and contrary to Lenin's express injunction against the statistical determination of religious membership, Soviet authorities have long striven to record religious citizens by name. This was done especially through observation of local congregations, through the obligatory state-controlled registration of all religious functions, and through methods of empirical social research. The determination of religious membership and the social composition of the congregations form the decisive condition for the so-called "individual work with believers." This is the technical Soviet term for the systematic ideological indoctrination of the religious citizen at the workplace, at school, and at home through primary and secondary agitators. From an organizational viewpoint, this is a system of psychically enforced atheisization in which authorities, services, educational institutions, unions, the Komsomol, and the Pioneer organizations—as well as further special organizations—work together as one, and according to plan, under the direction of the local party committees. The work of this machine constitutes a flagrant infringement, even a mocking, of the negative freedom of conscience of the religious Soviet citizen. It clearly runs counter to Art. 18, para. 2 of the Civil Rights Covenant.

D. The Freedom of Religious Association

Because the practice of religion regularly takes place within the community, and usually occurs within the context of organized religion, the freedom of religious association occupies a central significance. This is especially true for the Soviet Union because religious practice there is restricted to the legal religious communities, outside of a private area that is hardly worth mentioning (more

---

[4]On this, see ibid., pp. 55-68.

about this later). The freedom of religious association consists of the right to start a religious community, or a part of one, as well as the right to join an existing religious community.

Religious associations in the U.S.S.R. are either local "societies," that is, groups of at least twenty adult founders, or "groups of believers," which must consist of at least three founders with the same worship views.[5] The associations may assume their activity when they have been accepted by the state. This occurs through the act of registration, for the granting of which the Council for Religious Affairs of the Council of Ministers of the U.S.S.R. in Moscow is responsible. The Council decides on the application according to its political judgment. Thus, citizens have no legal right with regard to permission. There is also a religious association prohibition, from which exception can be made in unusual cases, but in reality this does not happen very often, for the Soviet state is not interested in the blossoming of religious associations but, in accordance with its own ideological declaration, in their "dying out."

There is an absolute prohibition of association for a list of "sects" whose doctrinal teachings and activities have an "anti-state or gruesome and fanatical character," a very indistinct description that is directed first and foremost against all religious associations that are not prepared to accept the repressive conditions of religious practice in the Soviet state.[6] Affected by name are the Jehovah's Witnesses, the Reformed Baptists, and other splinter groups from officially permitted religious communities or denominations. The members of those religious communities which are committed to resistance are persecuted in accordance with Art. 227 of the R.F.P.C. On the basis of these prohibitions, there is in the U.S.S.R. today practically a *numerus clausus* of religious societies.

Should the application for permission be allowed for a religious association, the founders receive at the same time consent to use a space for worship, be it in a church or other building. A special-use contract is concluded with the local state administration.

As far as the right to join is concerned, all members of a particular religious community have the right to become formal members of the local association in question. Nevertheless, in actuality the authorities have long demurred to admit more than twenty to thirty persons (so-called *dvadcatki*, or "Communities of Twenty").

E. The Extent of the Right of Organized Worship

The sanctioned religious communities in essence are restricted to the worship service itself as well as the remaining activities which are absolutely necessary for the preservation of the cult (such as the preparation of future members).

---

[5]Ibid., pp. 25-30.

[6]Art. 23, instruction on the application of the legislation on worship of March 16, 1961; German translation is in Otto Luchterhandt, *Die Religionsgesetzgebung der Sowjetunion* (Berlin: Berlin Verlag, 1978), pp. 54-65.

Congregations may employ clergy, utilize houses of prayer, and cover their costs through financial contributions of those participating in worship services. They may have worship gatherings and celebrate religious rites, insofar as they do not disturb the public order and do not interfere with the rights of fellow citizens. Any social and charitable activities and any special organizations for men, women, youth, or children are forbidden, as are any kind of special religious/cultural presentations, conversation groups, libraries, etc. Religious rites may not be performed outside of the worship space, though the authorities may grant exceptions, especially for funerals.

The spiritual leadership of the religious communities (of the Moscow Patriarchate, etc.) may maintain teaching institutions within narrow limits, hold workshops for making worship objects (such as candles), publish religious literature, and maintain relations with religious communities at home and abroad.

All the aforementioned activities, with the exception of the religious rites that take place within the worship building, require state permission—which can be granted or denied according to the authorities' personal religious/political discretion. Likewise, a permission already granted can be withdrawn at any time without explanation. Thus, religious communities are completely without rights and at the mercy of the Council for Religious Affairs of the U.S.S.R. Council of Ministers and its supervision of religious communities. The state not only uses its power to control and dominate the organizational structures of the religious communities, but it also does not shy from exercising a more or less strong influence on the spiritual-theological content of religious communities with the aid of the largely pliable spiritual leaders. Furthermore, the state manipulates the spiritual leadership to carry out additional restrictions of worship practice in the religious communities not foreseen in the law, which creates the outside impression of "voluntariness." In this manner a portion of the party policy of religious oppression is veiled.

F. The Extent of the Right of Private Worship

As a matter of principle, private performance of religious rites is permitted in the home—that is, simple home and family devotions. They need permission only if clergy are required, such as for dispensing sacraments for the seriously ill or dying. In closed institutions and establishments, namely, in hospitals, the sacraments may be received only with state permission. Even in these instances the authorities decide according to their personal judgment. The legal prohibition against pilgrimages to cloisters and other "holy places" constitutes a serious attack on the individual right of the freedom of worship and of religious usage. Apparently it aims to do away with religious traditions that have deep roots among the people. The instruction in question infringes upon the freedom of movement with regard to religion, which is protected by international law. The religious Soviet citizen is discriminated against compared to atheists, who are allowed to travel freely to the "glorious sites of the Revolution."

G. The Right to Religious Education

A key aspect of the private right of worship is the right to religious education. In the U.S.S.R. this right lies in a gray area between legality and illegality.[7] The right for parental education is regulated in Art. 18 of the principles of marital and family legislation as follows: "Parents should educate their children in the spirit of the moral code of the founder of Communism, look after their physical development, the education and preparation for a societally useful activity . . . Parental rights are not to be exercised in conflict with the interests of the children."

The definitions amount to an indirect prohibition of children's religious education, for the "moral code" in whose spirit education is to be conducted can be found in the program of the Soviet Union's Communist Party. However, Communist and religious morality are mutually exclusive according to the immutable view of the party. While officially no formal prohibition of children's religious education by parents has been derived from this, it is unmistakably pointed out in the pertinent literature that a conscientious exercise of parental rights excludes religious education. In short, while religious education is not expressly forbidden, it is not allowed in the "well-understood" (read: "Communist") interests of the child—a point of view whose contradiction is resolved only when it is understood as an expression of an anti-religious, atheistic, repressive strategy. Since the desired express prohibition of religious education would lead domestically to a civil war with little chance for success and internationally to a loss of face for the state because of its blatant contradictions to human-rights conventions, only the path of political tactics can lead to the state's unchanging goal. While tepid religious education is indeed disapproved of though tolerated without sanctions, intensive religious education is opposed through administrative and juridical measures that include even the withdrawal of the right to education.

Absolutely forbidden, according to official judgment, are the use of physical or psychic force in religious education, as is delegating other people—especially clergy—to conduct it. Therefore, children's religious education can occur only in the family and can be conducted only by the parents.

These restrictions of parental rights obviously infringe on the standards of religious freedom in international law that have been recognized by the Soviet Union. If the pertinent human-rights conventions guarantee parents even the right of nonstate educational facilities, then the mere delegation of religious education to catechists of religious societies is clearly quite allowable. Indeed, one must say that in a state structure like that of the U.S.S.R., in which the entire educational system is nationalized, the carrying out of religious instruction within the religious societies represents a necessary component and is therefore utterly indispensable.

---

[7]Luchterhandt, *Die religiöse Gewissensfreiheit*, pp. 36-48.

The reluctance to allow nonstate, religiously instituted educational establishments infringes on the human right of religious freedom. The Soviet Union has rejected the observance of this duty on the basis that the right of nonstate educational establishments is valid only for those states in which such establishments already exist. That is to be firmly rejected, for Art. 13 of the Social Rights Covenant and Art. 5 of the UNESCO Convention also guarantee, as stated, the right to *found* private educational facilities with state recognition. The Soviet argument cannot be accepted—namely, that the nationalization of the educational system excludes applying the right to nonstate educational facilities—for then one could refuse to guarantee human rights at home on the ground that one's own constitution did not foresee them. If this were valid, then one would have to ask for what purpose international-law human-rights documents are ratified.

H. The Right of Religious Equality

The right of religious equality means two things for religious citizens: from a *formal* perspective, they are to have the same rights as other citizens, without consideration of their religion; from a *material* perspective, the general law is to respect their religiosity and not subject them to restraint of conscience. It allows them a much more deviating behavior in keeping with their religious conscience, where the conscience is fundamentally concerned and the guarantee of the religiously alternative behavior is acceptable to the state and therefore tolerated by it.[8]

The last prohibitions dealt with—of organizing religious instruction outside the family and of founding private educational facilities—are already evidence of discrimination against religious citizens in the area of the educational system. The very conditions in this area show that the religious citizen is not yet even provided with the formal right of equality. On the contrary, it borders on cynicism when Soviet legislation on one side prohibits discrimination against citizens on account of their religion but on the other side guarantees to religious as well as atheistic parents the right to the atheistic education of their children and to "equal" access to decidedly anti-religious state educational facilities. Such legislation that is apparently sympathetic to human rights endangers precisely the human right of religious freedom.

Further discrimination may be seen in that access to religious literature in public libraries is denied the religious citizen, while atheistic citizens may check out atheistic literature without hindrance. Another aspect of anti-religiously-motivated discrimination in the cultural area is the reluctance to grant religious societies access to state communications media.

In the political area, religious citizens are already discriminated against by constitutional law, because leadership in state and society is reserved exclusively for members of the Communist Party of the Soviet Union (see Art. 6 of the

---

[8]Ibid.

Soviet Constitution)—and religious citizens may not join the party, since party membership and religious membership are unreconcilable (Art. 2 of the party statutes). This violates Art. 25 of the Civil Rights Covenant. Political discrimination carries over into economic and professional areas. It finds expression in closing off the religious citizen's access to higher positions and even entire branches of state service, as well as positions in business and social organizations. From the official side, this is openly admitted and justified on the grounds that a religiously oriented functionary could not fulfill the main objective of the Soviet state, namely, the building up of Communism and the educating of fellow citizens "in the spirit of high Communist consciousness." Consequently, "religious membership" in matters of public personhood functions as a criterion of a qualification deficiency. The religious citizen's human right of the freedom to choose an occupation is therefore exceedingly restricted; there is a long list of forbidden occupations. Definitively excluded is any involvement with the educational system, culture, or science. This discrimination has already worked against admission to higher levels of education, especially universities.

The artificially contrived restrictions by the Soviet state (*numerus clausus*) in regard to access to theological-training institutions is one aspect of discrimination in the area of freedom to choose an occupation. It is well known that especially the academics and seminaries of the Russian Orthodox Church have to turn away a large number of student applicants because of the capricious state directives. There are also evidences of discrimination in the area of state social services. For example, citizens who are employees of religious associations or institutions for the maintenance of buildings for worship (boilertenders, custodians, guards, etc.) worry about being excluded by law from the state old-age and invalid insurance if they also attend worship services.

Since pilgrimages are a specifically religious form of tourism, their prohibition, as already noted, infringes on the current right available to all citizens to move freely within the territory of the state. Also, the state refusal to permit religious prisoners the minimal exercise of their beliefs is a discrimination vis-à-vis their atheistic fellow citizens as well as a directly serious restriction of the human right of religious freedom. On the contrary, the religious prisoners are punished because of their possible religious activity. They are denied the possession of religious literature (including the Bible). Considering the spatial and human isolation of prisoners, one must see an especially serious violation of the human right of religious freedom in the sense of Art. 18, para. 1 of the Civil Rights Covenant.

I. International Aspects of Religious Freedom

Because of the international character of the great world religions that expresses itself partially in an international organization of religious communities (the Catholic Church, etc.), as well as in more or less well-developed confessional, ecumenical, and interreligious contacts, the international dimension of the human right of religious freedom is of great importance. Naturally, this concerns not so much religious freedom as an individual right as it does the activities of religious societies. Several examples can be given: participation in international conferences, congresses, or other kinds of religious gatherings; the reception and exchange of religious literature; the sending or receiving of financial support; studying at a foreign religious institution; pilgrimages to Mecca, Jerusalem, Rome, Mt. Athos, Lourdes, or other places; visits with another or one's own church leaders, as in the case of the Lithuanian bishops with the Vatican; national religious societies' joining international religious associations or international nongovernmental associations; etc.

The ease of international relations depends on the permeability of the borders and the state's readiness to permit and foster private foreign contacts. As is known, the Soviet Union unfortunately has distinguished itself in this through an inordinate amount of repression. For the most part, the U.S.S.R. fulfills the negative expectations that one tends to have of a totalitarian system.

I can express myself briefly as to what concerns the *legal* side of the problematic. All international actions by Soviet citizens are, in principle, subject to the prohibition of the state by the withholding of permission, which in every case is granted (or not) by the appropriate party and state authorities. Complete control dominates. As always, the state also decides here, according to its political discretion (that is, there is no means of legal redress). Since it concerns a political judgment, the primarily repressive tendency of the party's religious policy also naturally operates here.

The practice of granting permission differs greatly and understandably fluctuates over time. Repression operates at its strongest against "simple" religious citizens; practically speaking, they have no possibilities of cultivating international religious contacts. Unequally more favorable is the situation of the leadership of the religious societies, especially in the case of the Moscow Patriarchate. Here the state has, as formulated in a resolution of the Central Committee of the Communist Party of the U.S.S.R. at the beginning of 1961, its own direct interest "in bringing religious organizations and their leading personages into the struggle for peace, the unmasking of anti-Soviet propaganda that is generated in foreign countries, as well as the explanation of Soviet legislation concerning worship and of the condition of religion in the U.S.S.R."[9]

Accordingly, the central state authority for supervision of religion (the Council for Religious Affairs of the U.S.S.R. Council of Ministers) is obligated to support religious societies "in the development of international ties, in the participation in the struggle for peace and the strengthening of friendship between peoples" (Art. 2 of the Statute of 1966). The officially sanctioned religious communities of the U.S.S.R. can develop their international contacts only at the price of placing themselves simultaneously in the service of party-state foreign politics and by fulfilling concrete assignments of the authorities. In practice, it

---

[9]See Luchterhandt, *Die Religionsgesetzgebung*, pp. 26-27.

can be determined that the state has on a number of occasions in past years allowed, especially on behalf of Lutheran communities, the introduction of religious literature from abroad and has proffered other assistance including, in rare cases, study at theological institutions in foreign countries. The Russian Orthodox Church, as is well known, has congregations outside the U.S.S.R. and evidently can care for this part of its organization without special hindrance from the state. With respect to international contacts, religious Soviet citizens are no better or worse off than their religiously indifferent or atheistic fellow citizens, for repression of the Soviet regime affects all Soviet people to the same extent.

III. Concluding Remarks

The comparatively favorable impression one receives from the notable practical opportunities that religious communities have for becoming involved in international matters cannot mask the fact that the typical Soviet citizen's ability to exercise the human right of religious freedom is restricted to conducting religious rites in a building of worship or within one's own four walls. Art. 52 of the Soviet Constitution, which regulates freedom of conscience and which the Soviets always praise when speaking about international relations, offers only a minimum of religious freedom; it is a standard of law that is not much beyond avoiding a prohibition. This falls far short of the human right of religious freedom's content, which the U.S.S.R. has pledged itself to respect and guarantee, in numerous international human-rights conventions.

This minimum of religious freedom in the U.S.S.R. does not result from the alleged natural dying out of religion, which Marx and Engels assumed to be a concomitant of the development of Communism. Rather, it appears to be the result of a constant suppression (at times severely, at other times more moderately, pursued) of citizens' and people's opportunities to develop religiously. A quick look at the history of the Russian Orthodox Church bears this out. In 1939 the Church had only several hundred congregations in the U.S.S.R. By 1945 there were more than 20,000; this number did not change till the end of the 1950's. Suddenly, by 1966 there were only slightly over 7,500 congregations. The numbers have diminished somewhat since then (approximately 6,900).[10] In comparison to the dramatic decline under Khrushchev, it has remained relatively stable.

The fluctuation is not hard to explain in light of the state's previously described opportunities for administrative intervention with regard to religious freedom. This policy's guiding principle is repression, and one of its chief characteristics is the anti-religious orchestration of religious legislation. Both factors rest on the fact that the U.S.S.R. as a closed worldview state denies religion's

---

[10]Otto Luchterhandt, "Geknebelt und dennoch lebensfähig. Die Russisch-Orthodoxe Kirche in der Ära Breschnew," *Herder-Korrespondenz*, no. 5 (1982), pp. 232-237.

right to exist, as a result of which it also denies the legitimacy of religious communities.[11] Therefore, the U.S.S.R. has separated itself from the spiritual foundation of tolerance, which is nothing else than the realization built into the state
apparatus that for the state there can be no final truth, because the breakdown
of the medieval system of the comprehensive rule has made the question of truth
an object of dispute for people. With these suppositions the state can fulfill its
basic function of being the union of peace for everyone living in a certain region
only if it wisely declares itself "neutral" in the question of truth and resists the
temptation to identify itself with a definite "partial" (that is, representing only
one side) "Truth." There is also the irony that the U.S.S.R. recognizes Art. 52
of the Constitution and guarantees both an unpronounced freedom of conscience
as a formal right of citizens and also openness on the question of truth, for the
"parity" of the religious and nonreligious conscience expressly pronounced here
has no other meaning in essence.

Seen in itself, this juridical definition of freedom of conscience is rooted
in the free human-rights tradition—no wonder, since it comes from the pen of
Lenin, who took it from the anti-clerical program of left-wing European Liberalism. Seen as such, freedom of conscience in the Soviet Constitution as a juridical
concept represents a liberal remnant that nevertheless cannot develop its human-
rights effect because both party and state base themselves exclusively on a philosophical Marxist meaning of the freedom of conscience, namely, in the sense
of a "liberation of the conscience from religious superstition" (criticism of the
Gotha Program of 1875).[12]

Only when the Communist Party of the U.S.S.R. is prepared to admit that
it is dealing with philosophical—that is, "party-bound"—truth which the state
cannot make compulsory for everyone can the door be opened for true toleration in the Soviet Union. Unavoidably, that would mean that the Communist
Party would voluntarily surrender its specific basis of legitimacy for exercising
dominance. Since such a far-reaching revolution in the ideological and political
bases of the Soviet state is not to be expected in the foreseeable future, one can
only hope and work toward the Soviet party's and leadership's lessening—out of
sober wisdom—the artificial pressure on religious citizens and, as is true in other
socialist nations, their conducting themselves with more "tolerance" with respect
to religious practice.

Translated by Alan Mittleman (Part I) and Arthur Turfa (Parts II and III)

---

[11]For this, see Otto Luchterhandt, "Die Religionsfreiheit im Verständnis der sozialist-
ischen Staaten," in Eugen Voss, ed., *Die Religionsfreiheit in Osteuropa* (Zollikon-Zurich:
G2W-Verlag, 1984), pp. 50-51.

[12]A more elaborate discussion of these two meanings of freedom of conscience in Marxist
philosophy is found in Otto Luchterhandt, *Die religiöse Gewissensfreiheit im Sowjetstaat.*
Teil I: *Rechtstheoretische Untersuchung der Gewissensfreiheit.* Berichte des Bundesinstituts
für ostwissenschaftliche und internationale Studien 37 (Cologne, 1976), pp. 8-40.

RELIGIOUS FREEDOM AND HUMAN RIGHTS IN KOREA

Yong-Bock Kim

In this essay, we will treat the practice of religious freedom in Korea and its suppression by the political power. For this, we will have to look into the historical background, including cultural and political history, which has affected the present practice of religious freedom in Korea. Then we will have to analyze the present situation of religious freedom, including some legal aspects. Furthermore, we must deal with the area of violations of religious freedom, particularly the freedom of mission, which is the practice of religious freedom in a concrete socioeconomic and political context. One of the fundamental assumptions of this essay is that religious freedom is suppressed whenever it seriously threatens the political power; hence, the issue of religious freedom may have to be seen in the context of power relations or power conflicts. This means that we may not only have to look into international power conflicts, national power relations, and power factors within religions, but we also may have to examine the nature of the powers that are engaged in relating and confronting. Today the ultra-efficient exercise of power by technological means has far-reaching implications for religious freedom.

I. The History of Religious Freedom in Korea

The term "religious freedom" did not exist until foreign missionaries, particularly Protestant missionaries, came to Korea around 1884. In fact, the Korean-American Treaty of 1884 did not include a clause of toleration for Christian worship in Korea. Only when the Korean-French Treaty was signed in 1886 was permission granted for Christian worship. While this treaty permitted foreign residents in Korea to hold worship services, it did not mean general tolerance for all the Korean people. Nevertheless, this treaty became a watershed for the development of Korean Christianity, which was allowed to propagate its faith among the Korean people.

Up to this historical point the Roman Catholic faith had been severely persecuted for about 100 years under the state ideology of neo-Confucianism.[1] This was the second most severe religious persecution in Korean history. The harshest persecution had been the neo-Confucian suppression of Buddhists at the beginning of the Chosun Dynasty, under the theory of anti-Buddhism (Ch'okbullon). Of course, the history of religion in Korea involves many religious-political conflicts. When religion is aligned with the ruling power, it becomes an ideology to

---

[1] Yu Hong-yol, *A History of the Catholic Church in Korea* (Seoul, 1962).

95

suppress the contending religion; when religion is intertwined with the opposing power, then that religion is persecuted. There have even been intrareligious persecutions, for example, by established Buddhism against so-called heretical Buddhism, and by orthodox Confucianism against "heretical" Confucianism. In all these cases, the power—the political power—is the critical factor in the persecution of religion.

During the period of the establishment of the Three Kingdoms there were religious persecutions. The first historically recorded persecution was against the Buddhist religion, as illustrated in the story of the Buddhist martyr, I Ch'a-don,[2] who was executed due to political pressure by the king's court. However, the occasion became a turning point for the stronger influence of Buddhism in the Silla Dynasty. When Buddhism was established, it suppressed populist Buddhist sects such as Maitreiya Buddhism, which is often associated with political opposition.[3] Kung-ye, the founder of Hukokuryo, was associated with the Maitreiya sect of Buddhism and called himself the Messiah Buddha.

However, the real suppression of Buddhism had taken place with the foundation of the neo-Confucian Dynasty by Li Song-kye in 1392. It was systematically argued that the ruin of the kingdom was caused by the Buddhist teaching, which was false. The most famous critic was the ideologue of Chosun Dynasty, Chong To-jon, who fiercely argued against Buddhism, largely drawing upon the neo-Confucianist arguments.[4] During the Chosun Dynasty (1392-1910) Buddhism was suppressed and was at best a second-class religion. One important point is that Confucian teachings and Buddhist teachings generally co-existed before neo-Confucianism became the state ideology of the Chosun regime. In fact, neo-Confucianism became an orthodoxy unable to tolerate other religious or philosophical teachings; it prohibited any deviant or heterodoxical interpretation of Confucianism. When Buddhism was associated with political opposition or popular uprising, then it was ruthlessly suppressed together with the popular movement.

When Roman Catholic books were introduced from China in approximately 1603, their teachings were viewed in essentially the same way as Buddhism had been: Roman Catholic teachings are morally faulty, and they undermine the moral and social order of the Chosun Dynasty. When Roman Catholics began to

---

[2]I Ch'a-don: The first Buddhist martyr under the reign of Silla King Pophung in C.E. 527. Kim Pu-sik, *Records of Three Kingdoms*; Il-yon, *Inherited History of Three Kingdoms*, etc.

[3]Throughout Korean history, populistic Buddhism, such as Maitreiya Buddhism, was closely associated with political and social uprisings, although one time—at the peak of Silla power—the Maitreiya Buddha was utilized as the cohesive national symbol to unify the people.

[4]Chong To-jon, *Bulssi Chappyon* (Various Criticisms against Buddhism). The most important points of his criticism were that the Buddhist ethical teaching is faulty and that it undermines the Confucian social order.

practice their beliefs and do away with ancestral worship and sacrifice, not only was the religion officially banned, but also its believers were ruthlessly executed, suffering the cruelest deaths. The persecution of Catholic believers in the Chosun Dynasty was very severe, reaching its peak in 1839, when the anti-Catholic decree was issued. It reads, in part:

> Alas! Who can be born without a father, and who can grow up with-
> out a mother? They call the ones who gave birth to me the parents
> of the flesh; they call Ch'onju (Heavenly Lord) the parent of the
> soul, and they only worship and love Him, but cut themselves off
> from their parents. And this is unforgivable, because it breaks the
> filial relationship. The ancestral worship has been practiced from the
> beginning of time . . . and the filial son cannot bear the death of his
> parents without ancestral rites. And yet they destroy ancestral tab-
> lets and prohibit ancestral worship.[5]

This situation continued until the Western religions were tolerated *de facto* as a result of the opening of the country to the Western nations. The only trace of formal tolerance is found in the 1886 treaty of amity between Korea and France, allowing worship services by foreigners in Korea. By this time, 20,000 Roman Catholics had been executed.

Then, in 1894, there was a conflict between the Chosun regime and a reli-gious-political movement called the Tonghak Rebellion. Tonghak was treated like a heresy or heterodoxy, which could not be tolerated, and its founder, Ch'oi Che-u, was executed under charges of subversion. Tonghak was first of all an indigenous religion, not associated with any political movement; but, because its belief in equalitarian values began to materialize into religious practice in the Tonghak Rebellion, it was ruthlessly suppressed with the reluctantly solicited aid of China and Japan.

About this time the social conditions were ripe for the rapid growth of Christianity, which was also making impact upon the social and political reform movement of the Independence Club. One mission agency official in the United States observed:

> The leading spirit in the Independence Movement is a Christian. Most
> of the patriotic demonstrations were made . . . by Christians . . . One
> spoke, "Society must be turned upside down. There is no hope in the
> upper classes. Christianity begins at the bottom. After all, a man's a
> man, be he King, noble or coolie. . . . Christianity is essentially an
> emancipating religion, and leads inevitably to the desire for free gov-
> ernment, peace and popular institutions."[6]

---

[5]*Ch'oksa Yuneum* (Royal Edict against Evil Teachings), October 18, 1839.
[6]Robert Elliott Speer, *Missions and Politics in Asia* (New York and Chicago: Fleming H. Revell Co., 1898), p. 287.

When the Independence Movement and Christian leaders in it began to put their beliefs into practice, advocating free government, the Chosun regime immediately dismantled the organization and put its leaders into prison. At this time there was the fear that Protestantism might face a fate similar to that suffered earlier by Roman Catholicism.

However, the question of religious freedom became a serious issue under Japanese colonialism. When the Japanese colonial power took control of the Korean peninsula in 1905, right after the Russo-Japanese War, it began to curtail the influence of Christianity in Korea, for the Christian religion advocated freedom from all sins and evils. This meant that the Christian faith was a liberating religion for the oppressed people. As soon as Japan formally annexed Korea in 1907, the colonial regime created the fabricated Case of Conspiracy to Assassinate Terauchi, the Governor General. This was to suppress Korean Christians, who held religious beliefs that were conducive to their involvement in the independence struggle against Japanese colonialism. Missionaries documented the case and published a report titled "Korean Situation," which is nothing other than a report of the violation of human rights.[7]

The Japanese colonial government wanted to curtail the influence of Christian religion in schools, since mission schools and Christian private schools outnumbered the government schools at that time. The colonial government banned all religious instruction during regular class hours in the mission schools. The doctrine of separation of state and church was used by the state to eliminate religious instruction from educational institutions, public or private, and the colonial regime actively carried out inculcation of a national ideology based upon the Meiji Education Rescript, which demands loyalty to the Japanese Emperor and nation.[8] Here again the political power limited and suppressed religious practice.

One missionary described the situation as follows:

> These new regulations prohibit religious instruction in all private schools in Korea. The Educational Senate of the Federated Missions in Korea . . . offered to bring its schools into line with the government curriculum with one additional study, that of the Bible. This had no effect. . . . The Educational Senate asked to make the Bible study purely optional. This was refused. . . . Schools in Korea can have Bible instruction neither as a compulsory nor as an optional subject, neither in school hours nor out of school hours. The school must be completely separated from the church.[9]

The most dramatic suppression of the churches and Christians by Japanese

---

[7]See the 1912 report of the Federal Council of Boards of Foreign Mission, U.S.A., "Korean Situation: Conspiracy Case."

[8]See the 1913 Japanese Government General of Chosen *Manual of Education in Korea*, pp. 60 ff.

[9]A letter by E. K. Loomis (1916?).

colonialism was during the March First Independence Movement in 1919. Christians participated wholeheartedly in the movement, which was a nonviolent-resistance movement against the Japanese colonial regime. According to the Governor General in Korea, Christians gave leadership to 220 events between March 1, 1919, and March 1, 1920. The entire church was involved. The Japanese suppression was brutal, as manifested in the story of their burning down a whole church full of people at Cheamri. It is generally recognized that by ratio the Christians suffered most in this suppression, although we do not have exact figures. There is a detailed human-rights report on the suffering of the Korean people on this occasion.[10] Once again when religious beliefs were practiced in a political context, in opposition to the political power, it led to suppression of the religion by that power.

Religious persecution intensified during the 1930's, for the Japanese colonial power demanded "religious" loyalty to the Japanese emperor, forcing Shinto worship upon all Koreans, including Christians. This was especially difficult for the Christians, for they believed that the Shinto worship was idolatry. Christian books and literature were banned selectively, in addition to forced Shinto worship. In this situation Christians were forced to become either martyrs or betrayers of their religion. The persecution and political oppression reached apocalyptic proportions. Christians were forced to deny their faith against their will and to submit themselves to the emperor worship; many were imprisoned and became martyrs.[11] The Japanese ultra-nationalist ideology and military adventurism, proposing to conquer Asia and establish the so-called Greater East Asia Co-prosperity Sphere, harshly pressed the Korean people, including Christians, to submit themselves totally to the Japanese Empire.

Persecution on a massive scale again rose at the end of World War II. The U.S.S.R. military forces occupied the northern half of the Korean peninsula and established a Communist regime, while the U.S. military forces occupied the southern part and established a military government and then the Republic of Korea in 1948. The people in Korea were subjected to an ideological and military conflict imposed by the two superpowers' Cold War. The Korean War became the most tragic expression of this conflict. In this context the suppression of religion—especially Christianity—again took place in Korea. It was Christians who suffered most under the Communist regime. It is claimed that there were 2,000 churches and 300,000 Christians in North Korea right after World War II; all these churches disappeared completely. Vast numbers of Christians escaped and fled to the south, and many were martyred. During the Korean War,

---

[10]Besides the official report, "The Korean Situation: Authentic Accounts of Recent Events by Eye Witnesses" (issued by the Commission on Relations with the Orient of the Federal Council of the Churches of Christ in America), there is an unpublished report, "Korean Independence Outbreak," that was written anonymously in 1919. Reportedly, 360 Presbyterian leaders were imprisoned.

[11]In July, 1940, more than 2,000 Christians were imprisoned; of them, about fifty had died as martyrs by 1945.

churches and Christians in the south suffered war-time suppression in the North Korean Communist-occupied territory, which covered the whole of the Korean peninsula except for a small part of the Taegu-Pusan area. Christians, being classified as agents of imperialism, were regarded as the enemy by the Communists. The nature of the Communist regime in its totalitarian power did not allow any room for religious tolerance, especially of the Christian religion.[12] It is again clear that the dominant political power will suppress any religion or religious practice when it perceives this as a challenge to itself in both ideological and political terms. This is particularly true when the political power makes an absolute claim on ideological or religious truth.

II. The Present Situation of Religious Freedom in Korea

The situation of human rights in general and religious freedom in particular is complex. We need to analyze the factors in Korean society which create the situation of violations of human rights and religious freedom. From the above survey of Korea's story of religious freedom—or, rather, the violations of this freedom—we can discern a traditional factor: that is, the authoritarian power, which asserts its claim over what is right and wrong—religiously, ethically, and ideologically. The neo-Confucian orthodoxy of the Chosun Dynasty is the main traditional factor. This factor has a strong hold on the authoritarian powers in Korea, creating a political and cultural environment for violations of human rights. Korean regimes have used authoritarian Confucian values to consolidate and to justify hierarchical power relations and arbitrary exercise of power. For example, the traditional concept of loyalty (to the king) is used to boost the authority of the president. Another example is that the legal tradition of neo-Confucian orthodoxy emphasizes the punitive function of the law. That is, the law is used to punish people, rather than to protect innocent people.[13] This is manifested in a law process which constantly violates the rights of the people. In fact, the Confucian factor is so diffuse and pervasive in the Korean political culture that it undermines the democratic rights of the people.

Ideology, as utilized by the ruling power, is a newly emergent cause of violation of the rights of the people. The grave issue before the independence of Korea was the semi-ideological, semi-religious Japanese emperor system with its militarist and ultra-national chauvinist traits. Since the defeat of Japan, the ideology of Communism has become a critical issue—particularly under the Cold War situation. The ideological situation in South Korea has been governed to a large extent by anti-Communism, a negative stance against the political ideology of North Korea. The ambiguous linking-up of people's thoughts, writings, and

---

[12]Some say that more than 400 church leaders became martyrs or were abducted by the North Korean Communists during the Korean War.

[13]Hahm Pyung-choon, *Korean Political Tradition and Law* (Seoul: Hollym, 1967).

acts with the Communist ideology has been used to suppress voices and actions critical of the ruling regime, including religious thoughts and actions.

The situation is one of fierce hostility and tension due to the uneasy cease-fire at the demilitarized zone (DMZ). What is worse is the military confrontation over the past thirty years between the interlocking military alliances of South Korea and the United States on the one hand, and North Korea, the U.S.S.R., and China on the other. This confrontation has not only threatened peace on the peninsula but has also done immeasurable damage to the basic rights of the people living under the divided and hostile regimes. The modern concept or doctrine of total national security has opened the door to the militarization of society, so that all aspects of national life become security matters. As a result, the national-security concern—defined and dominated mainly by military considerations—is paramount, overshadowing even human-rights considerations. National survival becomes the supreme goal of the society, not merely a basic objective. And yet, ironically, the national security doctrine has been the pretext for the suppression of human rights in many parts of the world.

The Japanese military "heritage" and subsequent U.S. and U.S.S.R. occupation have thrust the Korean people into the forefront of the ideological and military battlefield and into a localized arms race, under the aegis of the Cold War between the superpowers. The two parts of divided Korea have been locked into the competing global military-strategic systems, which are engaged in a fierce confrontation that threatens the earth. Under this situation, where the military and security objectives take precedence, there can be no serious consideration given to human rights. On the contrary, in the name of war, human rights are violated and restricted.

Under these circumstances, the military takes direct or indirect command of national life, of politics, and of economics. Its political control covers not merely governmental affairs but also social relations, cultural life, and even religious and spiritual life. The ruling power commands elaborate systems of police and security to maintain tight and total surveillance of the entire population. It controls the cultural institutions such as the educational system and the information and communication media, which it actively manipulates. Modern technology is applied with efficiency and sophistication to achieve such control. The establishment of efficient and sophisticated systems of control by technological means is closely related to the role of transnational corporations, which seek to expand and control the world's resources for maximum profits. This process equals or surpasses the nation-states' pursuit of security. Penetration of the giant international corporations into countries such as Korea has been a real contributing factor to the limiting of human rights. For example, restrictive labor laws have been instituted to attract international investment and safeguard its profits.[14]

---

[14]The Foreign Capital Inducement Law of 1966 and the Provisional Exceptional Law restrict labor in foreign-invested companies. See Christian Institute for the Study of Justice and Development, *The Power of TNC's in Korea* (Seoul, 1981), p. 15.

The presence of the giant international business corporations is the vital link in the equation of the global capitalist system as it affects third-world countries. The multinational corporations exert pressures upon economic, social, political, and cultural institutions in such a way that human rights are more likely to be violated, especially when there are no effective measures to safeguard them, or when those measures are weakened under the efficient political control of the ruling powers in those countries. The logic of control in this case is expressed in terms of its absolute necessity for social and political stability for economic growth and development; thereby, the rights of workers, farmers, and the poor can be restricted or postponed.

III. Patterns of Human-Rights Violations in Korea

The most consistent and sustained patterns of human-rights violations in Korea have been related to movements opposing the political power. The ruling regimes of the Chosun Dynasty and the Japanese colonial period, the Northern Communist regime and the regimes in the South have consistently suppressed opposition without any tolerance. Under Park Chung-hee, any opposition to his regime was ruthlessly put down. When the Park government negotiated the normalization treaty with Japan in 1965, the Korean church opposed the terms of the treaty, asserting that it was too compromised to be meaningful. In retaliation against this Christian opposition, the Park regime sought the enactment of a series of laws to restrict religious activities and tax religious organizations. The most far-reaching proposal was the Law on Registration of Social Organizations, aimed at the control of religious organizations. That legislation was abandoned due to the strong opposition of the Korean churches.[15] However, the Park regime continued to view the Christian churches as a hostile force.

The Park regime attempted to perpetuate itself through a constitutional amendment permitting a third presidential term, which was barred by the Constitution of the Republic of Korea. This was strongly challenged by the leaders of Korean society, especially by Christians, who saw democracy as an ethical mandate rising out of their faith, and believed that the perpetuation of one-man rule was against democracy. The leading person was the Rev. Dr. Kim Chai Choon, who had a large following among ecumenical Christians in Korea. This was the beginning of the real confrontation between the Park regime and Christians on the issue of human rights and religious freedom.

When the Park regime introduced the Yushin (Revitalization) Constitution under martial law in October, 1972, there was all-out opposition, for this consti-

---

[15]Yong-Bock Kim, "Church and State since the Liberation of Korea," in CISJD, *The State Power and Christianity* (Seoul, 1982).

tution allowed the life-long presidency of Park and severely curtailed the rights of the people. The Christians' view was that the Park regime and the Yushin Constitution were effectively undermining any democratic development for the Korean people. Naturally, Christians became the forefront of the human-rights movement in Korea in the 1970's. They issued their theological position on the situation in 1973, as follows:

> We make this declaration in the name of the Korean Christian community. But under the present circumstances, in which one man controls all the powers of the three branches of government and uses military arms and the intelligence network to oppress the people, we hesitate to reveal those who signed this document. . . . We are under God's command that we should be faithful to his Word in concrete historical situations. It is not a sense of triumphant victory that moves us today; rather it is a sense of confession of our sins before God to speak the truth and act in the present situation of Korea. . . . We as a Christian community believe 1) that we are commanded by God to be representatives before God the Judge and Lord of history, to pray that the suffering and oppressed people may be set free; 2) that we are commanded by our Lord Jesus Christ to live among the oppressed, the poor, and the despised as he did in Judea; and that we are summoned to stand up and speak the truth to the powers that be, as he did before Pontius Pilate of the Roman Empire; 3) that we are compelled by the Spirit to participate in His transforming power and movement for the creation of new society and history, as well as for the transformation of our character; and that this Spirit is the Spirit of the Messianic Kingdom who commands us to struggle for socio-political transformation. Therefore, we express our theological convictions as follows: 1) The present dictatorship is destroying the rule by law and persuasion; it now rules by force and threat alone. . . . No one is above the law except God. . . . If any one poses himself above the law and betrays the divine mandate for justice, he is in rebellion against God. . . . 2) The regime in Korea is destroying freedom of conscience and freedom of religious belief. There is freedom neither of expression nor of silence. There is interference by the regime in Christian churches' worship, prayer gatherings, content of sermons and teaching of the Bible. . . . 3) The dictatorship . . . is using systematic deception, manipulation and indoctrination to control the people. The mass media has been turned into the regime's propaganda machine to tell the people half-truths and outright lies, and to control and manipulate information to deceive people. . . . 4) The dictatorship . . . uses sinister and inhuman and, at the same time, ruthlessly efficient means to destroy political opponents, intellectual critics, and innocent people . . . People are physically and mentally tortured, intimidated and threatened, and sometimes even disappear completely. These are indeed diabolical acts against humanity. . . . 5) The present dictatorship is responsible for the economic system in Korea, in which the powerful dominate

the poor. The people, poor workers and rural peasants, are victims of severe exploitation and social and economic injustice. . . ."[16]

On the basis of such religious convictions, Korean Christians acted to advocate the cause of human rights and to aid the victims of human-rights violations. In November, 1973, the National Council of Churches in Korea issued a declaration of human rights in five areas: religious freedom, rights of workers, women's rights, academic freedom, and freedom of speech.[17] In the Korean church there are mission groups which advocate the rights of the people through legal aid; there are educational programs, and statements are issued in support of the human-rights causes of particular groups. These include groups of workers, journalists' groups, students, and groups of intellectuals such as university teachers and writers—organized to fight the violation of their own human rights. A special Commission on Human Rights was set up in 1974, under the National Council of Churches, to document human-rights violations, to give legal aid to political prisoners, to communicate with international and national Christian communities, and to enlist support for the human-rights cause in Korea. The National Council of Churches and the Korean churches organized prayer meetings for the victims and conferences to discuss issues related to human rights.

Such activities by religious organizations, individuals, and churches are under constant pressure, harassment, surveillance, detention, house arrest, arrest without warrant, imprisonment, torture of the persons involved, and "trial by media" to discredit the particular organization or persons. The congregational life of pastors who are also human-rights activists is constantly harassed. Worship services, including prayers and sermons, are monitored for their contents. Special prayer meetings such as the KNCC-sponsored Thursday Evening Prayer Meeting for victims of human-rights violations are a primary target of suppression. Public lectures and consultations on issues of Christian mission are constantly harassed and monitored, and several pastors have been prosecuted for the contents of their sermons or speeches.

Mission organizations advocating the rights of the poor, industrial workers, farmers, the urban poor, and pollution victims also suffer constant pressure from the powers-that-be. Evangelistic work among the workers, for example, is tolerated, but education, conscientization, organization, and advocacy of labor rights are not. In fact, there is now a legal provision to prevent any influence by so-called third parties, for example, Christian mission organizations, in labor disputes. This restricts the mission of the churches among the workers. Mission organizations which act for the workers are branded by the public media as "impure elements" or "pro-Communist groups," in an attempt to isolate the churches' mission among the workers from public opinion. Christian mission among students and intellectuals is also persecuted. Christian student groups on

[16]Theological Declaration of Korean Christians, 1973.
[17]Human Rights Declaration, KNCC, 1973.

campuses are free to do evangelistic work, but as soon as they show concern for human rights or other sociopolitical issues, their activities are harassed and restricted. The Korean Student Christian Federation and its activities are *de facto* banned on campus. Activities by Christian intellectuals, including writing, publication, study and research, and the collection of materials are also under constant pressure from the authorities. Theological work comes under public attack for any content dealing with socioeconomic, political, or cultural issues.

Numerous cases can be cited. The persistent violation and restriction of religious freedom is related to the involvement of religion with social issues, based on religious convictions. The Korean church refers to this question as the problem of freedom of mission. Traditionally, the mission of the church was understood primarily as evangelistic activities. Religious freedom is upheld in the Constitution of the Republic of Korea; public worship, prayer, and other religious activities such as religious propagation are free. However, those religious convictions and practices that call for support of human rights—and the social and cultural rights of the people—are restricted and under constant pressure. This is the consistent pattern of violation and restriction of the freedom of religion in the recent Korean situation. The churches and the state are in constant conflict and tension over the interpretation of mission.[18] One time a government representative ventured the interpretation of the scriptures; another time, another government official tried to define the role of the churches in Korean history. This is certainly a violation of the doctrine of separation of church and state. The authorities seek to define this doctrine in order to limit and restrict religious freedom, rather than to guarantee it.

There are several ways for the ruling powers to limit and restrict religious freedom. Certain legal measures are routinely used; for example, security-related law contains some clauses allowing the suspension of human rights in extraordinary circumstances. These provisions are characterized by ambiguous definitions[19] of the extraordinary or emergency circumstances, and of the boundaries of violation of the law. This opens the door to the "liberal and convenient" use of this law to fabricate cases with the intention of suppressing certain persons or groups. Other legal measures, such as the criminal code and special measures, are also used to suppress and restrict human rights, including religious rights. Closely related to the above is the due process of law. Illegal arrests, detentions for periods of interrogation without lawyers and in isolation, and torture are often used to intimidate, to extract confessions, and to punish.

Due to the availability of highly sophisticated technological apparatus and to the lack of any control over the use and misuse of that apparatus in political and criminal proceedings, a wide range of violations of human rights and religious

---

[18]Statement on Freedom of Mission, KNCC, 1974.
[19]See reports on human rights from World Council of Churches-C.C.I.A. and Amnesty International for details.

freedom is practiced without much public notice. In addition to the modern intelligence and surveillance network, various information channels and the media are used to suppress and discredit religious organizations and religious leaders who are involved in the mission of the church.

There are several areas of violation of the freedom of mission, which may be summarized as follows: (1) Freedom of expression of religious thought is under attack. There are restrictions on the publication of theological formulations, and, even when published, these can be banned. They are subject to prosecution, to public attack in the media, and to other forms of restriction.[20] (2) Religious communication is also restricted. For example, the Christian Broadcasting System—formerly a fully functioning radio medium with news, commentary, and entertainment, as well as religious programs—is now limited to the communication of so-called purely religious matters, while matters pertaining to mission are banned due to their sociopolitical implications. This applies likewise to other forms of Christian journalism. (3) The development of religious relations and fellowship across national boundaries is restricted by blocking exchanges of experiences and information and by restricting travel. Passports are often denied or restricted for travel to religious conferences abroad. (4) Religious gatherings, both indoors and out, are under constant surveillance and monitoring; at times, gatherings for prayer are physically prevented. (5) The practice of one's religious convictions comes under pressure when these convictions are related to questions of justice and human rights. The consistent pattern of restriction and suppression of religious freedom in Korea is in the form of violation of the freedom of mission.

IV. Concluding Remarks

There is religious freedom in Korea today, to the extent that religion avoids touching critically on any questions about the policies or the power of the ruling regime. When the economic, social, political, and cultural implications of religious beliefs and convictions are expressed and acted out in the mission work of religion, and they touch upon the legitimacy, policy, and power of the ruling regime in a critical way, then the freedom of religion is not tolerated. However, it is an integral part of religious practice to advocate the socioeconomic, political, and cultural rights of the people as well as their basic human rights. At least this is an integral part of the mission of the Christian churches.

This phenomenon of the restriction and violation of the freedom of mission of the church is widespread in Latin America, Asia, and Africa, and it is sometimes manifested in the Christian West as well.

Today's political and economic powers are very difficult realities; they cannot be controlled or restricted by law, by popular democratic institutions, or by

---

[20]Minjung (people's) theology—a Korean theology—and liberation theologies are subject to such harassment.

public opinion. In this sense democracy—parliamentary democracy—is in crisis, as are the authoritarian and totalitarian powers. There is no secure legal guarantee of human rights and religious freedom under this political situation. The political powers are the primary culprits responsible for human-rights violations, and the powerful economic corporations—which defy all legal and democratic control—undergird the forces that violate human rights. The nature of the power of modern political and economic institutions, with their enormous size and their technological sophistication, can easily lead to the violation of the rights of people anywhere.

The question of religious freedom is, therefore, directly related to the question of how to limit the political and economic powers, which are institutionalized as the state and as the giant transnational corporations in the world today. The question of economic, social, and cultural rights is bound together with that of basic human rights; thus, religious freedom cannot be thought of in an isolated way. Religious faith, religious truth, religious thought—and the practice of all of these—are essential for the creation of a social order which maximizes popular rights and limits the unbridled powers of political regimes and giant economic corporations. Thus, religious freedom is not something to be granted by the state, but rather it must be viewed as the foundation of human freedom for the people's enjoyment of all their rights. This means that religious freedom in the broadest sense should properly be the freedom of mission.[21]

---

[21]This is a summary report of research done by the writer, who hopes to be able to present the full study at a future date.

Yong-Bock Kim (Presbyterian Church of Korea) is an ordained minister serving the Sandol Presbyterian Church in Seoul, Korea, and is the Associate Director of the Third-World Church Leadership Center at the Presbyterian Theological Seminary in Seoul. He has a B.A. from Yonsei University, and an M.Div. and Ph.D. (1969) from Princeton Theological Seminary, with concentration on theology and modern intellectual history of East Asia. He has lectured at several institutions including Princeton, San Francisco, and Presbyterian (Seoul) Theological Seminaries; Sophia University (Tokyo); the Ecumenical Institute at Bossey, Switzerland; and Ewha Women's University. He has directed a dozen research projects at the Christian Institute for the Study of Justice and Development since 1979, and has been involved with projects on economic justice, church and state in Korea, the church's response to the division of Korea, and non-Christians' attitudes toward Christianity. He has worked with a wide variety of ecumenical agencies and conferences throughout the world and has written numerous articles in Korean and English on social and theological issues. His books on Korean Minjung theology were published in Korean in Seoul and in English in Singapore, in 1981.

EXPLORING THE POSSIBILITY OF
HINDU-MUSLIM DIALOGUE

Kana Mitra

Islam and Hinduism have been present in the Indian sub-continent for over 1,000 years. During this time there has been a great deal of violence; even today it is not infrequent. There have also been periods of peace. However, whether in war or in peace, Muslims and Hindus have not reacted in a way that indicates mutual understanding and appreciation of each other. In their day-to-day encounter, there is at most a superficial civility during peace; during confrontation they look upon each other as sub-humans. During the 1945-46 riots, I was present in Dacca (Bangladesh). As a Hindu child I was frightened and angered by the war cry of the Muslim rioters, "Allah O Akbar." I did not know that it meant, "God is great!" Similarly, I imagine the war cry of Hindu rioters, "Bande Mataram" (hail to the mother), did not suggest maternal mercy to Muslim children. The brutal, inhuman behavior of both peoples during confrontation is all too well known.

Of course, there are a few rare cases of genuine friendship between individual Hindus and Muslims. There are even some cases of intermarriage. However, by and large, Muslims and Hindus have stereotyped understandings of each other. Muslims, in general, consider Hindus idolators and polytheists, and educated Muslims are contemptuous of the inequality of the Hindu caste system. Likewise, in general, the Hindu stereotype of Muslims is that they are meat-eating brutes who marry their sisters (cousins), and educated Hindus are contemptuous of Islamic intolerance and *jihad*.

This mutual contempt and isolation of Muslims and Hindus in India seems even more amazing in view of the fact that a large number of Muslims in the Indian sub-continent are of Hindu ancestry. Some recent anthropological studies even indicate the presence of remnants of Hindu attitudes among some Muslims of the sub-continent. For example, Adrian Mayer refers to the presence of caste among Muslims;[1] some Muslims indicate a preference for a vegetarian diet, as it is considered more pure, while Hindus venerate Muslim "pirs" as saints. However, overall, there is an attitude of competitiveness and mutual intolerance between Muslims and Hindus. Is dialogue between them even a possibility?

In order to explore what Muslims and Hindus think about each other's religion, I searched for writings of Muslims of the sub-continent on Hinduism and

---

[1]Adrian Mayer is an anthropologist of the London School of Oriental and African Studies. His research on Islam in India is referred to by Agehananda Bharati in *Hindu Views and Ways and the Hindu-Muslim Interface: An Anthropological Assessment* (New Delhi: Munshiram Manoharlal, 1981).

vice versa. So far, I have found no Muslim author writing exclusively on Hinduism. In Muslim writing, Hinduism is referred to in the context of showing its inferiority to Islam. Even a liberal Muslim such as Amir Ali in his *The Spirit of Islam*[2] has nothing but derogatory remarks about Hinduism and Buddhism. Aziz Ahmed, in *Studies in Islamic Culture in the Indian Environment*,[3] displays no insight into Hinduism when he admires Schimmel's description of the contrast between Hinduism and Islam: "Hindu genius flowers in the concrete and the iconographic; the Muslim mind is on the whole atomistic, abstract, geometrical, and iconoclastic."[4] Likewise, I found no book by a Hindu author which was written exclusively on Islam. Rammohan Roy, Rabindranath Tagore, Gandhi—all were appreciative of Islamic monotheism. However, they wrote no works on Islam. A contemporary Hindu scholar such as Anil Chandra Banerjee refers to the Islamic Shari'a to demonstrate the intolerance of Islam, in his *Two Nations: The Philosophy of Muslim Nationalism*.[5] It is quite evident that even the scholars among the Muslims and Hindus have not made any serious effort to understand each other's tradition.

Causes for Apathy and Indifference

There are complex historic, anthropological, psychological, sociological, economic, and political reasons for Muslim-Hindu conflict and apathy, some of which are very obvious. The first Muslims who came to India came as conquerors, and the vanquished were the Hindus. There is competitiveness between Hinduism and Christianity, but the first Christians who came to India were missionaries, not political conquerors. That is one of the reasons for lesser hatred and animosity between Hindus and Christians in the sub-continent. Buddhist missionary activity started under the patronage of King Asoka, but it did not lead to empire-building. That is one of the reasons for lesser hostility toward Buddhists by people of other faiths. The historical situation of the encounter between Islam and Hinduism is an important reason for the hostility between the two.

The Arabic culture in which Islam originated and the Indian environment in which Hinduism is nurtured are quite different. Patterns of behavior, standards of civility, attire, food, language—all are different. Meetings of alien cultures naturally produce distrust and misunderstanding. Human beings' ethnocentricity makes them distrust and ridicule the unfamiliar. Moreover, the Indian sub-continent, politically, was never one country. First, Muslim rulers, and later British, made it into one political unit. The nationalistic feeling of belonging to one

---

[2]1st ed. (Karachi: Pakistan Publishing House, 1961). The 1982 ed. was used for this essay.
[3](Oxford: Clarendon Press, 1969).
[4]Quoted in Bharati, *Hindu Views*, p. 74.
[5](New Delhi: Concept Publishing Co., 1981).

political unit was a later development among the people of the sub-continent. When nationalistic feelings started to emerge, they were often colored with religious feelings, and controversy over one or two nations for the sub-continent became almost inevitable. Religion has often been used for political purposes in the sub-continent. Sometimes it was used for Hindu-Muslim cooperation against the British, as in the case of the Sepoy Mutiny of 1875, or against each other during pre-partition, mostly by the British, and even after partition, by various political parties. Methodical research into these factors which are causes of the conflict between Muslims and Hindus is vital to the promotion of understanding between them.

Religious Causes

The characteristics of Islam and Hinduism as religions also contribute to the isolationism of these two traditions. Their worldviews seem to be quite different. In Islam, unity of one God and uniformity in ways of belief and patterns of worship are fundamental. Islam advocates one God, one scripture, one seal of prophecy. In other words, singularity or unity is characteristic of Islam as a religious tradition. Hinduism is, instead, characterized by plurality. A Hindu can be a Hindu worshipping many gods or one God or no God. The focal point of Hinduism is not one God but to be worshipful, which is usually referred to by such a Hindu philosopher as Radhakrishnan as respect for truth—*Sraddha*. So, it is said there are 330,000,000 gods in Hinduism, and there may be as many ways of worshipping God. Hinduism, therefore, does not refer to one God, one scripture, or one prophet. Just as unity is characteristic of Islam as a religious tradition, plurality is characteristic of Hinduism as a religious tradition.

Islam and Hinduism are distinctive in other respects also. Islam advocates a kind of theocracy—religious law needs to be political law. The universal ideal needs to be concretized in society and in history. Human beings are vicegerents of God.[6] The Hindu attitude is that the concrete is a stepping stone to the universal ideal but the universal can never be fully concretized in history. That is why, by and large, the Hindu ideal is a-historical or a-political. Islam believes in a final day of judgment; Hindus believe in the cycle of creation and dissolution, the cycle of birth and death. Islam is a missionary religion. F. S. C. Northrup wrote, "For an orthodox Mohammedan, missionary zeal, military power, and political control go together."[7] For Hinduism, the ideal is spiritual freedom, which may not be related to political freedom. This is expressed even in the

---

[6]Seyyed Hossein Nasr, *Islam and the Plight of Modern Man* (London and New York: Longman, 1975), p. 18.

[7]From F. S. C. Northrup, *The Meeting of East and West* (New York: Macmillan, 1946), p. 414. Quoted in Allen Hayes Merriam, *Gandhi vs. Jinnah: The Debate over the Partition of India* (Columbia, MO: South Asia Books [in association with Minerva Associates, Calcutta], 1980), p. 9.

leadership of the movement for independence in India. Gandhi worked for political freedom more as a spiritual leader; therefore, he never accepted any governmental post. Sri Aurobindo changed from a fight for political freedom to a fight
for spiritual freedom. The majority of Hindu monastic orders do not become
directly involved in political movements.

Allen H. Merriam, in *Gandhi vs. Jinnah: The Debate over the Partition of
India*, presented a descriptive and nonvaluational contrast between Islam and
Hinduism:

> It may be helpful to view Hinduism as an essentially feminine doc-
> trine and Islam as being far more masculine in character. The Hindu
> worships the cow as the symbol of motherhood and fertility; many
> Hindu deities are female, and Hindu art is full of voluptuous female
> figures. . . . Muslims, on the other hand, worship a very masculine
> Allah; only men are allowed inside a mosque, and in most Islamic
> societies women are veiled when in public. It would be quite unusual
> to have a woman prime minister in an Islamic nation.[8]

He also described very clearly the contrasting concepts of social organization of
Hindus and Muslims. The dominant force of Hindu society is the caste system,
which is based on the conviction that different humans have different potentiali-
ties, determined by one's action in the previous incarnation. Caste and sub-castes
produced a decentralized social structure which safeguarded against penetration
of any outside force; thus, Hindu society could continue relatively unchanged
during the years of Muslim rule. The rigid regulation of caste prohibited the
intermixture of castes and of Hindus and non-Hindus, but, paradoxically, it bred
an attitude whereby plurality is considered a social norm. Merriam noted that
this acceptance of diversity prompted Najime Nakamura to state, "Toleration is
the most conspicuous characteristic of Indian culture."[9] Islam, on the contrary,
considers all humans equal by birth. Merriam noted, "All people are called to
unite and conform to one community of believers."[10] Islam's emphasis on dogma
and a democratic social order has meant the development of a strong sense of
community—particularly in India, since it is a minority there.

It is evident that the theological and social assumptions of Muslims and Hindus are different. The differences of convictions generated contempt or, at best,
indifference toward each other. Muslims and Hindus feel no need to learn about
or from each other. Islam proclaims that it is the only true way—the straight
path. The Qur'an and the tradition make some concessions to the "People of
the Book," of course. For example, they can gain protection by paying *jizya*
(IX:29); and, after the battle of Badr, Muhammad formulated a treaty in which

---

[8]Merriam, *Gandhi vs. Jinnah*, p. 9.
[9]From Hajime Nakamura, *Ways of Thinking of Eastern Peoples: India-China-Tibet-
Japan*, ed. Philip P. Wiener (Honolulu: East-West Center Press, 1964), p. 172. Quoted in
Merriam, *Gandhi vs. Jinnah*, p. 10.
[10]Merriam, *Gandhi vs. Jinnah*, p. 10.

the Jews were included within the commonwealth of Medina.[11] In the eleventh
century, Mawardi prescribed that the *Imam* (caliph) had the duty "to wage holy
war (*jihad*) against those who, after having been invited to accept Islam, persist
in rejecting it, until they either become Muslims or enter the Pact (*zimma*) so
that God's truth may prevail over every religion."[12] The conditions of the pact
suggest that subordination of the *zimmis* was tolerated, but at least their lives
were spared. However, the Qur'an and tradition are vehemently opposed to idolatry. Muhammad's war was against the idolatry in the Arabia of his time. He
did not meet any Hindus or witness any image-worship of the Hindus, but the
Muslims who came to India considered Hindus idolators because of the image-
worship. Therefore, many of them did not want to grant the Hindus the status
of *zimmis*. Only some rulers following the Hanafi School of Shari'a assigned
zimmi status to the Hindus. Hindu image-worship is one of the most important
reasons for Muslim contempt of Hinduism. Image-worship, from the Islamic perspective, is a compromise with the transcendence of God—it is *shirk*. That is why
Amir Ali could see nothing noble or sublime in the forms of Hindu worship:

> The sacrifice could be performed only by the priest according to
> rigid and unalterable formulae; whilst he recited the *mantras* and
> went through rites in a mechanical spirit, without religious spirit or
> enthusiasm, the worshipper stood by, a passive spectator of the wor-
> ship which was performed on his behalf. The smallest mistake undid
> the efficacy of the observances.[13]

Hinduism proclaims in many ways. From the Hindu perspective, not only
can there not be just one way to truth, but also no way can be the perfect and
faultless way to truth. Agehananda Bharati has often ridiculed Hindu tolerance.
He has identified some modern Hindus as "essential unity" preachers who are no
less competitive and polemical than are Christians and Muslims. In his article
"Radhakrishnan and Other Vedanta,"[14] he pointed out that Vedantists of the
Vivekananda and Radhakrishnan type believe in the superiority of monism. In
his chapter "Sohi Allah Wahi Ram? The Anthropology of the Hindu-Muslim
Interface," he wrote:

> Urban "essential Unity" Hinduism which includes the sermon of the
> English speaking Swamis in India and abroad—states that all religions
> are equal, but implies that since Hinduism is 'scientific' and tolerant,
> it incorporates what all other religions teach, and is hence at least a
> primus inter pares.[15]

---

[11]Ali, *Spirit of Islam*, pp. 56-59.

[12]Banerjee, *Two Nations*, p. 3.

[13]Ali, *Spirit of Islam*, p. 160.

[14]In Paul Arthur Schilpp, *The Philosophy of Sarvepalli Radhakrishnan* (New York: Tudor
Publishing Co., 1952), pp. 459-479.

[15]In Bharati, *Hindu Views*, p. 72.

From the perspective of Hinduism, any claim by any tradition to be exclusively true is arrogant, although the contrary Hindu claim seems equally arrogant to others. Hindus consider ultimate truth to be beyond words and letters; hence, the Muslim claim that the Qur'an is the literal word of God is, from the Hindu perspective, a compromise with the transcendence of truth. Since all Hindus—not only the "essential unity" preachers—have been historically surrounded with plurality, they cannot comprehend or sympathize with any doctrine of "One Way." They are contemptuous of such arrogance, or at least indifferent to it. If all ways are ways to truth, even though none is perfect, one can stick to one's own, and there is no need to learn about or from each other.

Inclusivism often generates indifference, whereas exclusivism often generates intolerance and violence. Hindus are critical of the intolerance and violence of Islam. Hinduism as a tradition believes in the transformative quality of religion. Transformation, according to Hinduism, implies a change of personality from fear to courage, from anger to love, from violence to nonviolence. Although an individual or a group of Hindus may not be less violent than an individual or a group of Muslims—as the history of their encounter indicates—nevertheless, in Hinduism nonviolence is considered a cardinal virtue. Hence, Islamic *jihad* is looked upon with contempt by Hindus. Hindus, even the college-educated, look upon Islam as an essentially militaristic tradition. One educated Hindu, although not an official "scholar," described Muslim *salat*, in which the group prays by synchronic postures and movements, as military training in preparation for war.

It is evident that Muslims and Hindus neither understand one another nor make any serious attempt to do so. They do not try to go beyond the surface and penetrate that which may not be so apparent to the outside observer. Not only the average Muslim or Hindu but even theologians and philosophers indicate no interest or understanding of each other. Islamic *kalam* developed primarily outside the sub-continent. Any immanentist tendency in Islam can be explained in terms of interaction with Hellenism. Sufism might have been congenial to the Vedantic point of view, but it need not be explained in terms of its influence. It seems that Muslim theologians, being repelled by Hindu image-worship, made no attempt to find out what lay underneath. In the same way, the post-Islamic Bhakti movement in Hinduism was perhaps stimulated by Islamic monotheism and devotionalism, but it need not be explained in terms of that influence. The nineteenth- and twentieth-century Hindu elites who studied and appreciated the Qur'an found nothing in it which they considered to be genuinely new or not present in Hinduism. No Hindu thinker made any attempt to penetrate Islamic exclusivism or militarism to find out what lay underneath. Muslims and Hindus have confronted each other, but they have generally felt no real challenge from one another to appreciate or learn from or about each other.

Encounter with the West

Muslim and Hindu encounter with the West is a different matter. Both felt a challenge and threat from Western civilization. Both simultaneously admired and condemned Western civilization and values. Muslims and Hindus recognize the value of the advanced scientific knowledge in the West. Apologists of both traditions try to demonstrate that scientific knowledge is part of their heritage as well, and both refer to their respective contributions in mathematics, astronomy, and medicine. Muslims and Hindus recognize and appreciate the value of democracy, individual dignity, and humanism. They do not think that these are recognized values of the West alone. Rather, in polemics, they try to show how these values have been jeopardized in the West. There is ambivalence about technology, industrialization, and material prosperity among Muslims and Hindus, but in general there is appreciation of the bountifulness, health, and hygiene of the West. Modernity, which is equivalent to "Westernity" to many people, has stimulated both Muslims and Hindus to question and reflect on their own traditions —although not about each other's.

The Western attitude toward the sub-continent can be classified as either contemptuous and patronizing or romantic. Modernists of the West tend to highlight the superstition, backwardness, poverty, and dehumanization present in the sub-continent. Romanticists who are concerned about the negative effects of modernism—secularization, manipulation, dehumanization—display an attitude of appreciation for the spiritual and philosophical contributions of the sub-continent. Max Müller in the nineteenth century and Aldous Huxley in the twentieth may be cited as examples of the latter. Both Muslim and Hindu thinkers reacted to the negative criticism of the West with polemics and apologetics, although some self-criticism and social-reform movements were also generated. Muslim and Hindu thinkers reacted to the romantic attitude of the West with a feeling of self-congratulation and complacence. Both Muslim and Hindu writers like to quote the Western scholars who praise their traditions! Muslims and Hindus did not react jointly in their depreciation of some of the Western attitudes, nor did they appreciate each other as a result of their appreciation by the West.

What Can Be Done?

Hindus and Muslims have lived in physical closeness for years, and yet they do not dialogue with each other and show no inclination toward it. I have attempted to analyze some of the causes of this situation. The nature of the respective traditions as such is not conducive to any dialogue, yet the dehumanizing and inhuman relationship between Hindus and Muslims makes it quite evident that dialogue between us is a practical necessity. How can we dialogue? I can see a clue for it in our relationship and reaction toward the West.

In the last half of the twentieth century it is becoming increasingly fashionable to criticize Western values. Awareness of the dangers inherent in modernity is a necessity. There are many good works on this subject.[16] However, when the anti-establishment becomes the establishment, there is the opposite danger.[17] Uncritical condemnation of modernity may lead to uncritical acceptance of all types of superstition. It may lead to complacence, self-congratulation, and passivity. With our awareness of the dangers of modernity, let us not be blind to its stimulating and liberating effects. The history of any religious tradition would indicate how modernity revitalized it by eliminating some of the stagnation. In his lectures to the Western people, Vivekananda—who is considered instrumental in making Hinduism a missionary religion—seemed to be one of its greatest apologists, yet in his lectures to Hindus he seemed to be a vehement critic of their religion.[18] After his tour of America and Europe, he indicated his appreciation and admiration of these people for their recognition of the dignity of the individual, hygiene, health, vitality, etc. Modernity generates self-reflection and can be an antidote to the dogmatic adherence to the beliefs of the forebears and mechanical repetition of what they did. Uncritical adherence to traditions can stagnate any religion, as is evident in our two religions of the sub-continent.

The question of human rights is asked and pursued in the Western context. What the rights of human beings as human are is often described in terms of Western categories. This runs the danger of ideological neo-colonialism. Raimundo Panikkar is concerned about this *de facto* neo-colonialism. He points out that at the present time there are three sociologically dominant cultures: technological civilization, the pan-economic systems, and what is popularly called the "Western way of life." He notes that most of the African, Asian, and Latin American cultures, for economic survival, are taking the categories of these dominant cultures for granted, but the indiscriminate adoption of methods that are alien to the local cultures is not producing the desired effects.[19] There is a need to investigate the meaning of human rights, of growth and progress, not simply from the perspective of the dominant cultures—but from the perspective of others as well.

Not only contemplation but also action is needed. Living cannot stop while we are finding out the meaning of life. Indeed, the meaning of living may emerge from living itself, as such existentialists as Camus indicate. Herein lies the contribution of such activists in the field of interreligious and interideological dialogue as Leonard Swidler. Very much aware of the strong points of Western civilization, Swidler indicates "one of the strengths of modern Western civilization has been its stress on effective human action, both individual and corporate." So, he

---

[16]E.g., Ernst F. Schumacher, *Small Is Beautiful* (New York: Harper & Row, 1973).

[17]Paul Tillich, *The Courage to Be* (New Haven: Yale University Press, 1952), ch. 4-5.

[18]Vivekananda, *Complete Works of Swami Vivekananda*, vol. 3, Mayavati memorial ed. (Calcutta: Advaita Ashrama, 1973), pp. 166-167.

[19]Raimundo Panikkar, "Alternatives to Modern Culture," *Inter-Culture* 15 (October-December, 1982): 2-4.

thinks: "The world cannot be 'saved' simply by trying to 'save' the individual persons; the social structure within which the individual persons live must also be 'saved.' "[20] The content of "saving" is not self-evident and would need on-going contemplation, but the situation of the relationship between Muslims and Hindus definitely calls for action. One such activity is dialogue, but we are not so inclined. The enterprise of dialogue by Western activists such as Swidler is helpful in this respect, because through such enterprise Hindus and Muslims are getting involved in dialogue.

However, Muslims and Hindus are often suspicious of the Christian initiative in dialogue, which is feared as a covert way of converting. Whatever it is, Muslims and Hindus can appreciate the greater, if not total, understanding about their traditions, understanding by more people from the West. Hans Küng may be cited as an example. His attitude toward Hinduism in *On Being a Christian*[21] – and more recently as expressed in his response to Heinrich von Stietencron in his attempts to dialogue with different world religions[22]–is a clear indication of better understanding. In the first case he finds more superstition and degradation in the Hindu tradition; in the second, more appreciation of its mystical bent. This example itself illustrates the potential of dialogue for the development of mutual understanding. Thus, if we Hindus and Muslims begin to engage in dia-logue, there is the possibility of better mutual understanding even if we start to do so reluctantly or half-heartedly by means of Western initiative.

The modern method of the critical approach to history and the different social and psychological sciences can also be helpful in generating an atmosphere of dialogue between Muslims and Hindus. A conventional way of writing Indian history by both Western and Indian historians is in terms of the religious tradi-tions of its rulers. Romila Thapar, in *Communalism and the Writing of Indian History*,[23] traces this tendency back to James Mill's *History of British India* (early nineteenth century). She indicates that Mill developed the thesis of dividing Indian history into the three periods which he called Hindu Civilization, Muslim Civilization, and British Civilization—but not Christian. Such characterization of history can and did generate misunderstanding and even hostility among the different religions. For example, Turkish, Persian, and Arab conquerors of India were Muslim, and they themselves often identified their conquest as Islamic. However, the plunder and destruction of Hindu temples by Ghazni (eleventh century C.E.) need not necessarily be interpreted as the intolerance of Islam. Thapar points out that the Hindu King Harsha even appointed an officer, *devot-*

---

[20]Leonard Swidler, "Interreligious Dialogue: The Matrix for All Systematic Reflection Today," paper for the conference, "Toward a Universal Theology of Religion" (held at Temple University, Philadelphia, October 17-19, 1984), p. 22.

[21](New York: Doubleday & Co., 1976), ch. 3.

[22]Hans Küng et al., *Christentum und Weltreligionen* (Munich: Piper Verlag, 1984); from typescript of English translation by Leonard Swidler of Küng's response to Heinrich von Steitencron on Hinduism.

[23](New Delhi: Peoples Publishing House, 1969), p. 4.

patananayaka (uprooter of gods), to plunder the wealth of Hindu temples, but this is not seen as the intolerance of Hinduism.[24]

The fourteenth-century Muslim historian, Zia-ud-din-Barani, in his *Fatawa-i-Jahandari*, condemned the Delhi Sultans for not being zealots in their fight with the infidels and idolators:

> If the desire for the overthrow of infidels and abasing of idolators and polytheists does not fill the hearts of the Muslim Kings; if, on the other hand, out of the thought that infidels and polytheists are payers of tribute and protected persons, they make the infidels eminent, distinguished, honoured, and favoured . . . how then may the banners of Islam be raised?[25]

Barani showed his admiration of eleventh-century Ghazni by saying that if he could come back again he "would have brought under his sword all Brahmans of Hind . . . cut off the heads of two hundred or three hundred thousand Hindu chiefs (and) . . . would not have returned his 'Hindu-slaughtering sword' to its scabbard until the whole of Hind had accepted Islam."[26] Barani definitely seems to have been an intolerant person, but his writings may well not prove intolerance in Islam. Indeed, his indignation about the Delhi Sultans also indicates that not all Muslim rulers were Hindu inquisitors. An analytical, critical approach to the presentation and interpretation of the events of history in India is very important to generate an atmosphere of dialogue. All-India Radio sponsored a 1968 seminar on "The Role of the Broadcaster in the Present Communal Situation," in which Romila Thapar, Harbans Mukhia, and Bipin Chandra presented their critical analyses to suggest the dangers of stereotyped communal understandings of history. Thapar noted that antagonistic projection of a popular group, sect, or religion in history is very harmful, but even "more harmful is the kind of historical writing which is based on communal or near communal assumptions, but such assumptions in a generally uncritical framework are no longer questioned or challenged."[27] This type of self-critical scholarship and its sharing via the mass media need to be encouraged.

In this context, I would like to refer to a misrepresenting stereotype, even in this conference which intends to generate mutual understanding and harmony between nations and between peoples. The constant conflict between Pakistan and India is referred to as between "Muslim Pakistan" and "Hindu India." This is a historical, political, and ideological misunderstanding of India. India never was and even now is not only Hindu. India does not recognize nationality on the basis of religion.

It is evident that critical historical research where the insights of psychology, sociology, and anthropology are taken into consideration is helpful for dialogue

---

[24]Ibid., pp. 15-16.
[25]Banerjee, *Two Nations*, p. 10.
[26]Ibid.
[27]Thapar, *Communalism*, p. 10.

between Muslims and Hindus. Good history cannot be a one-sided narration and analysis of selected events. For example, A. C. Banerjee (in *Two Nations*) gave extensive documentation to suggest that Islamic Shari'a is at the root of Islamic nationalism, but in this work he referred extensively only to the Shari'as which indicate an intolerance in Islam, but not one which shows its tolerance. Thus, one-sidedness may characterize even apparently good, well-documented scholarship. The tendency toward one-sidedness is present among many scholars. Moreover, in the understanding of another's tradition it is necessary to understand it as much as possible as the other does. Adolph L. Wismar disputed T. W. Arnold's[28] view that missionary work is not an afterthought in Islam. Arnold thought that Muhammad himself, and the subsequent missionaries following his example, showed patience and forebearance in their attempt to convert the unbelievers. Arnold quoted from the Qur'an to prove his case. Wismar's refutation is based on the assumption that the Qur'an is Muhammad's word, not God's, as the Muslims believe. He assigned many questionable motives to Muhammad and indicated that Islam is intolerant. Whatever evidence was to the contrary he considered nothing but trickery.

The sociological and psychological study of the phenomenon of religion can help Muslim-Hindu dialogue. James Fowler's study, *Stages of Faith*,[29] describes how faith is dynamic and relational. In *Life Maps*[30] he points out the correlation between stages of faith-development and the capacity of the individual to take on the perspective of another and to widen the circle of those with whom one identifies oneself. Intensity of faith also leads to broadening of faith. This is clearly evident among both Muslim and Hindu mystics. Even in the field of clinical psychology, Muslim and Hindu psychiatrists have tried to apply their respective religious teachings to therapy. Elzibair Beshir Taha of the University of Khartoum, Sudan, in a paper prepared for discussion at the Parliament of Religion held at McAfee, New Jersey, November 15-21, 1985, noted that qur'anic teachings could be utilized as a technique of cognitive behavior therapy for Muslim patients. At that conference, a Philadelphia psychiatrist mentioned his use of the Bhagavad Gita to help his patients. It is evident that Western ideology and training have stimulated many Muslim and Hindu scholars and thinkers. These people may start dialogues with each other, following the Western example, as many of them do feel the need for mutual understanding between Muslims and Hindus.

However, Muslims and Hindus need to be aware of the dangers of Western civilization as well, and a large number of Western-educated and -trained Muslims

---

[28]Adolph L. Wismar, *A Study in Tolerance as Practiced by Muhammad and His Immediate Successors* (New York: Columbia University Press, 1927), ch. 1. He refers to T. W. Arnold, *The Preaching of Islam*, 2nd ed. (London: Constable & Co., 1913).

[29]James W. Fowler, *Stages of Faith* (New York: Harper & Row, 1981).

[30]Jim Fowler and Sam Keen, *Life Maps: Conversations on the Journey of Faith* (Waco, TX: Word, Inc., 1978).

and Hindus are critics of Western civilization. They are acutely aware of secularization and its consequences which result from the so-called "scientific," "critical" perspective of the West. Seyyed Hossein Nasr discussed this point in *Islam
and the Plight of Modern Man*, pointing out succinctly how the Western scientific point of view reduces reality to only one layer, and the symbolic concept
of nature is debased by calling it "totemistic" or "animistic," terms loaded with
pejorative connotations. Nasr wrote that Muslims trained in modernity are "made
to believe that the transformation from seeing the phenomena of nature as the
portents or signs (ayat) of God to viewing these phenomena as brute facts is a
major act of progress which, however, only prepares nature for that ferocious
rape and plunder for which modern man is now beginning to pay so dearly."[31]

Swami Yatiswarananda, a monk of the Rama-Krishna order, met Carl Jung
in Switzerland. While he appreciated Jung's understanding of human spiritual
need, he was critical of Jung's secular perspective. Jung suggested that the super-
conscious of the Hindu was included in the unconscious. The Swami felt that we
need to reverse our secular perspective of thinking that the body is the outermost
layer, and mind and spirit are within it.[32]

Western scientism often leads to secularization, and scholarship of religion
ends in reductionistic tendencies. Many Western scholars of religion are also critical of this tendency, such as W. C. Smith. We Muslims and Hindus who are
engaging in dialogue by means of Western stimulation need to be aware of this
danger; however, critical scholarship can be very helpful in eliminating some of
the barriers which now prevent Muslim-Hindu understanding.

Dialogue on the Theological Level

A secular approach to fostering unity between Muslims and Hindus is neither
practical nor desirable. Jawaharlal Nehru, the first prime minister of India, had
a secular view of progress and advocated unity between Muslims and Hindus on
the basis of modern Western civilization. Syed Abdul Latif, who belonged to
the liberal Aligarh School of pre-independence India, clearly pointed out Nehru's
mistake. He noted that the peculiar philosophy of life is what provides vitality
to the people and cannot and should not be overcome by the unity fostered by
the steamroller of industrialization.[33] M. N. Roy found the resolution of Hindu-
Muslim conflict in Communism; only that mighty economic force would have
the capacity of cementing the diverse sects and religious creeds of India: "This
is the only agency of Hindu-Muslim unity."[34] This position forgets that Muslim

---

[31]P. 19.
[32]Swami Yatiswarananda, *Meditation and Spiritual Life* (Bangalore: Sri Ramakrishna
Ashrama, 1979), pp. 20-21.
[33]Syed Abdul Latif, *Islamic Cultural Studies* (Lahore: Shaikh Muhammad Ashraf; 1st
ed., 1947; 3rd ed., 1960), pp. 27-36.
[34]M. N. Roy, *Documents of History of the C.P.I.* (Delhi: Ed. G. Adhikari, 1970), p. 354.

and Hindu believers are rooted in the transforming and life-sustaining characteristics of their traditions and that not many would want to trade spirituality for
modern amenities. Herein lies the true basis of Muslim-Hindu dialogue: Both
have faith in more than a secular understanding of human nature, which is expressed in qur'anic *al-ftrah* and Hindu *sraddha*. Both trust that it is the sacred—
the spiritual—which enables the human to be truly human.

The recognized distinctiveness of the two traditions need not necessarily discourage dialogue. Raimundo Panikkar and W. C. Smith[35] distinguish between *faith*
and *belief*. They are of the opinion that contradictory beliefs may be rooted in
common faith. Panikkar notes that even such contradictory statements of two
persons as "I believe God exists" and "I believe God does not exist" can be
rooted in faith in truth. In one instance the faith in truth expresses itself in the
belief that "God exists," whereas in the other it is expressed in the contrary
belief that "God does not exist."[36] Muslims and Hindus believe in the eternity
or perenniality of truth. This is one reason for the Islamic insistence that the
Qur'an is the literal word of God and for Hindus' description of their religion as
Sanatana Dharma. This common trust in truth can enable Muslims and Hindus to
undertake what John Dunne describes as "passing over" and "coming back."[37]
We Muslims and Hindus need not define and understand our identity over against
one another; that produces psychological and sociological barriers and often even
spiritual atrophy.

Dialogue between Muslims and Hindus, which is a necessity, is not impossible. To begin, we Muslim and Hindu scholars may explore and investigate the
parallels that exist between our two traditions, despite their differences and
distinctiveness. The well-known Islamic scholar, S. H. Nasr, has written that
". . . the rich intellectual structures of Hinduism and Buddhism naturally present
many resemblances to Islamic intellectuality, since all of them possess a traditional character."[38] This suggests that the parallels can be brought out effectively
by a proper method of comparing common, historically initiated, congenial systems. Nasr suggests that Hindu *darsanas* can be compared with appropriate and
corresponding Islamic schools with profitable results. Finding parallels and similarities, however, is not enough. The Middle Eastern situation indicates that two
people belonging to two traditions which are doctrinally so close does not alone
necessarily promote congeniality between them. All the reasons for conflict need
to be explored. From the perspective of theology, the distinctiveness of traditions which causes confrontation needs to be recognized, together with the find-

---

[35]Wilfred Cantwell Smith, *Faith and Belief* (Princeton: Princeton University Press, 1979).
[36]Raimundo Panikkar, *The Intra-Religious Dialogue* (New York: Paulist Press, 1978),
p. 8.
[37]John S. Dunne, *The Way of All the Earth: Experiments in Truth and Religion* (New
York: Macmillan, 1972).
[38]Nasr, *Islam and the Plight*, p. 42.

ing of parallels, and the possibility of accepting and appreciating the confronting ideal from within one's own tradition needs to be explored.

One important theological reason for Islam's antagonism toward Hinduism is its image-worship. Muslims may explore whether it would be possible to penetrate beneath Hindu image-worship so as not to consider it idolatry—without compromising the Islamic conviction of the transcendence of God. This is only a suggestion. How and in what way Muslims can recognize and appreciate Hinduism is a matter to be explored by them. My task is to suggest ways by which Hindus can accept and appreciate Islam.

Interreligious dialogue is also intrareligious dialogue. My suggestion that Hindus need to recognize and appreciate Islam leads to the usual Hindu response, "We do that; we recognize and appreciate all religions." Anthropological studies, such as those done by Bharati, indicate different levels of tolerance toward Muslims and Islam among Hindus. He points out that there is some tolerance among grassroots village Hindus and primarily among "pamphlet" urban Hindus, while there is hardly any tolerance among the Sanskritists.[39] Even when there is tolerance toward Muslims, it is expressed neither socially in recognizing the Muslim as equal to the Hindu nor ideologically in accepting the exclusivism of Islam as equal to Hindu inclusivism. Socially or ideologically, Muslims and Islam are not considered to be on a par with Hindus and Hinduism. Hindus consider Muslims unclean. The fourteenth-century Arab traveler, Ibn Battuta, recalled the Hindu practice of breaking or giving away their utensils if they were used by a Muslim.[40] This was not done only in Battuta's time; even today many Hindus act similarly. An Afghan Muslim told about his childhood experience of interaction with Hindus. If he were to visit the store of a Brahmin—whom his own father had helped to establish the store—he knew that everything in the store would be washed after he left. This behavior is inhuman and dehumanizing—not tolerant. The Muslim animosity toward Hindus is not without provocation.

In the same way, the Hindu doctrinal tolerance of all religions is not enough, as it is often expressed as an intolerance of exclusivism. Hindu theologians need to explore how they can accept and tolerate exclusivism without compromising their conviction of the transcendence of truth. A clue can be found in the Hindu attitude toward *Ista Debata*. A Hindu who is totally dedicated and loyal to the *Ista* would not even recognize other manifestations of the same deity. This is *Ista Nistha*. The gopis of Vrndavan are examples. They were dedicated to cowhand Krsna of Vrndavan, so they would not even look at King Krsna of Dwaraka. Thus, it should be possible for a Hindu to appreciate the qur'anic *nistha* of the Muslim.

A major stumbling block to the appreciation of Islam for non-Muslims is *jihad*. In our dialogue, a Hindu could ask the Muslim partner precisely what it

[39]Bharati, *Hindu Views*, pp. 71-94.
[40]Merriam, *Gandhi vs. Jinnah*, p. 6.

means. Does it indicate that all non-Muslims should be killed, as Beruni suggested? Is there any room for the recognition of plurality in Islam? What is the ideal Islamic way to deal with the *de facto* plurality that exists in the world? Christianity, like Islam, has an exclusivistic tradition, yet it is very active theologically about the issue of plurality. Is anything similar possible in Islam?

In Conclusion

Muslim-Hindu dialogue *is* a possibility. The Western initiative for dialogue—its scientific, critical spirit—influences Muslims and Hindus to reflect critically about their own traditions. Through that route we Muslims and Hindus can start a dialogue with each other; it is a practical necessity for the Indian sub-continent. We can utilize the modern findings of the social sciences to generate that insight which would break the barriers that exist between us. We can cooperate in sharing our spiritual insights with the West in order to counteract the dangers of secularization, which leads to dehumanization. We can communicate in the depth of our spirituality—which has happened among the mystics of our two traditions. On the scholarly level we can seek parallels. On the theological level we can explore the ways by which we can accept and appreciate each other without compromising our own convictions. We can honestly ask questions about those factors about the other which we find difficult to understand or accept. Inter-religious dialogue cannot solve all the problems, but it is a worthwhile effort.

Kana Mitra (Hindu) teaches at both LaSalle University, Philadelphia, and Villanova (PA) University in their Religious Studies Depts., especially in the areas of Eastern and world religions, religious experience, mysticism, and Catholicism. She holds a B.A. and an M.A. from Calcutta University, and a Ph.D. (1980) in religion from Temple University. She has also taught at Temple and Calcutta Universities and at Swarthmore (PA) College. Her dissertation was on "Catholicism and Hinduism: A Vedantic Investigation of R. Panikkar's Attempt at Bridge-Building." An Associate Editor of the *Journal of Ecumenical Studies*, she has contributed abstracts and book reviews and three articles (on human rights in Hinduism, on women in Hinduism, and a Hindu reflection on consensus in theology) to that journal. Four of her articles appear in the *Encyclopedic Dictionary of Religions* (Corpus Publications, 1979), and an article on "Cultic Acts in Hinduism" in *Revelation as Redemptive Experience in Christianity, Hinduism, and Buddhism* (Herder, 1982). She participates frequently in interreligious dialogues and seminars on women in religion.

THE BASIS FOR A HINDU-MUSLIM DIALOGUE
AND STEPS IN THAT DIRECTION
FROM A MUSLIM PERSPECTIVE

Riffat Hassan

Hindus and Muslims have lived together in the subcontinent of India, Pakistan, and Bangladesh for over 1,000 years. During this time many kinds of conflict—for example, historical/political, socioeconomic, cultural, theological, philosophical, psychological, and personal—have existed between these two religious communities. There have also been periods of violence when members of one community (generally the majority community) have perpetrated acts of aggression upon members of the other (generally the minority community). Sometimes these acts of aggression have been brutal to the extent of being barbarous, and sometimes their magnitude is shocking, as was the case when—in the bitter aftermath of the partition of the subcontinent into India and Pakistan in August, 1947—a bloodbath took place in which tens of thousands of human beings (Hindus, Muslims, Sikhs, Christians, and others) were massacred. The nature and number of communal (particularly Hindu-Muslim) riots[1] which have taken place in post-partition India are undoubtedly causes of serious concern to those who would like to see the peoples of this ancient land live together in peace. The troubled history of Hindu-Muslim relations in this area is, thus, clearly recognized at the outset of this essay. I do not attempt to negate or mitigate the fact that, in a number of ways, Hindus and Muslims are, and have always been, antagonistic to each other's realities as well as aspirations—and that this leads at times to all kinds of negative consequences, including physical violence.

The perspective from which this essay is written, however, while acknowledging the problems of Hindu-Muslim relations in Pakistan, Bangladesh, and (chiefly) India, focuses on the possibilities of Hindu-Muslim dialogue in this region. This perspective is grounded in my belief that, despite all the problems that Hindus and Muslims have had vis-à-vis one another through the centuries, they have been able in their millennium of coexistence in one geographical area to develop and maintain a pluralistic society which is as genuine as may be found anywhere in the world.

Since human beings are imperfect, any human society they create is imperfect. No pluralistic society in the world is free from a sense of dis-ease or tension, but this state of dis-ease or tension is not necessarily an evil. In fact, very often it is a blessing since it militates against a society's becoming stagnant and apathetic.

---

[1]An interesting sociological analysis of communal rioting in India is contained in R. A. Schermerhon's monograph, *Communal Violence in India—A Case Study*, ed. Syed Z. Abedin (Kalamazoo, MI: Consultative Committee of Indian Muslims, 1976).

Pluralism is good precisely because it embodies points of view which are not identical or even harmonious and thus cannot lead to a totalitarianism in which human differences are not tolerated and all human beings are subjected to the supreme oppression of having to conform to uniformity imposed from without. It is the effort to evolve a pattern of "the good life" within the framework of differing perspectives and values which makes pluralistic societies creative and dynamic.

As most Americans have heard, "There is no such thing as a free lunch." There is a price to be paid for pluralism, just as there is a price to be paid for democracy. Hindus and Muslims in the subcontinent have paid, and are paying (especially Muslims in India[2]), the price for pluralism, but—given the state of the world in which we all live—I believe that their experience of coexistence represents a significant achievement. The spirit of this experience is reflected in what may be called "a dialogue of life," which has been going on for centuries between Hindus and Muslims of the subcontinent. Such a dialogue was, and is, unavoidable and inevitable, given the fact that Hindus and Muslims have inhabited the same physical and cultural world since the tenth century.

The dialogue of life which emerges out of the processes of life is not a contrived matter. It arises "naturally" as it were from the interaction, positive and negative, obvious and subtle, verbal and nonverbal, between various peoples or persons. This dialogue is not the sort of dialogue we talk about in academic meetings because this dialogue proceeds not in accordance with rationally debated, mutually-agreed-upon criteria or guidelines for dialogue but in accordance with the existential needs of those who generate this dialogue. However, to ignore either the reality or the importance of this dialogue of life in any discussion of Hindu-Muslim dialogue in the subcontinent is to cheat oneself of what is perhaps the most valuable resource available to those of us who are committed to bringing about better understanding and relations between the two major religious communities of this ancient and vast civilization. In today's world many theologians realize the need for making "theology from above" coalesce with

---

[2]The situation of Muslims in India is eloquently described by K. L Gauba, who converted to Islam from Hinduism but rejected the two-nation theory (according to which Hindus and Muslims were two separate nations and chose to live in "secular" India rather than in "Islamic" Pakistan), in *Passive Voices: A Penetrating Study of Muslims in India* (Lahore: Pakistan Foundation, 1975). The following passage summarizes the author's feelings and the intent of the book: "It is with some sorrow and regret that the work was undertaken as the writer was no believer of the two-nation theory, and strongly opposed the partition of the country into two dominions of India and Pakistan. But after over twenty years in India as an Indian citizen, it must with sorrow be declared that its much proclaimed secularism is hollow, and much as the American Negro, though American, cannot rid himself of his color the Indian Muslim, though Indian, is nevertheless by and large unable to survive the inferiority of being a Muslim. It is said he keeps aloof from the 'mainstream.' After reading the book the reader will be able to decide for himself whether the Indian Muslim does not join the mainstream or is successfully kept away from it" (p. x). Also of interest to those who want to understand the psychology of Muslims in India is chap. 6 of W. C. Smith, *Islam in Modern History* (Princeton: Princeton University Press, 1977).

"theology from below." Likewise, there is great need today to make "dialogue from above" coalesce with "dialogue from below." While it is true that the reflections and discussions of scholars produce ideas and schemata which play an important, perhaps even a crucial, role in molding the ideas and attitudes of the common people, it is even more true that grassroot dialogue is what has the greatest impact on pragmatic reality.

While we must never permit ourselves to forget the violations of human rights which occur in and between India, Pakistan, and Bangladesh and seek constantly to strive for justice on behalf of all those who are discriminated against by the political and cultural systems prevailing in these countries, we must also seek to remember that for a millennium Hindus and Muslims have not only been neighbors in one physical region but have also had to face the same kinds of problems: the curse of massive illiteracy, poverty, and superstition; the burden of an ever-increasing population pressure in an area where tremendous inequities exist in terms of distribution of power and wealth; the difficulties of survival in societies run by incredibly corrupt persons—to mention just a few of the many problems which confront the common Hindu and Muslim living in the subcontinent. Facing common problems creates a strong bond between human beings regardless of caste, creed, or color. Anyone who has lived in the subcontinent understands what is meant by the first whole truth of Buddhism—that life is *dukkha* (suffering)—and this truth which is learned experientially by the teeming masses of Indians, Pakistanis, and Bangladeshis militates against self-centered isolationism or selfish indifference toward the plight of others. Suffering may not always lead to wisdom or compassion, but wisdom and compassion are seldom found in those who have not suffered. It is my belief that the people of my subcontinent—Hindus, Muslims, and others—possess much wisdom and compassion and that this is born of their suffering.

It is perhaps an irony or a paradox that those who are able to suffer deeply are also able to rejoice deeply. In few places in the world have I experienced the deep sense of joy I have felt in the homes of the people of my subcontinent. It is hard to describe to those who do not belong to this world what human relations mean to people of this world—Hindus, Muslims, and others. In this world, human relations are cherished far above material things, and the joy which a person feels in having or in being a mother, father, brother, sister, spouse, child, relative, or friend to another radiates through all the vicissitudes of fortune. In their attitude to family and friends, Hindus, Muslims, Sikhs, Christians, and other peoples living in the subcontinent are amazingly similar. They are also very similar in believing that people should meet and greet each other with courtesy and respect, especially when they address someone older in age, and in considering hospitality to others a very important value and virtue.

Aside from these similarities which provide the basis for a dialogue of life between Hindus and Muslims (and others) in the subcontinent, there are also other cultural bonds. One of the most important of these is the bond of common language. Hindus, Muslims, and Sikhs who speak Punjabi, for instance, gravitate toward each other. I have met Hindus and Sikhs living in the Western world who become tearful when they hear that I come from Lahore, a city loved by all the Punjabis, even as Delhi is loved by all those who speak Urdu. How important language is to a people is illustrated dramatically in the case of the alienation of the people of what was formerly East Pakistan from the state of Pakistan. This process of alienation began in the early 1950's. Bengali was not given the status of Urdu, which was declared to be the one national language even though the Bengalis constituted the majority of the people of Pakistan. The insensitivity shown by the federal government of Pakistan to the East Pakistanis' sentiment regarding Bengali did not diminish with time and continued to exacerbate the problems existing between the two wings of the country.

Here it would not be inappropriate to refer to the supreme irony embodied in the secession of East Pakistan from Pakistan, a country which had been created so that Muslims could live together according to the Islamic Shari'a. Critics of the creation of Pakistan had always upheld that religion could not be made the basis of statehood. For instance, Maulana Abu'l Kalam Azad, an outstanding Muslim who became a disciple of Mahatma Gandhi, said in his autobiography:

> It is one of the greatest frauds on the people to suggest that religious affinity can unite areas which are geographically, economically, linguistically, and culturally different. It is true that Islam sought to establish a society which transcends racial, linguistic, economic, and political frontiers. History has, however, proved that after the first few decades, or at most after the first century, Islam was not able to unite all Muslim countries into one state on the basis of Islam alone.[3]

Having watched the course of events preceding the 1971 civil war from which East Pakistan emerged as Bangladesh from very close quarters as a senior officer in the Federal Ministry of Information in Pakistan, I am convinced both that East Pakistan would not have seceded from Pakistan if a political instead of a military solution had been attempted, and that the loss of East Pakistan represents not so much an inability on the part of Islam to hold together two physically noncontiguous and culturally diverse regions as it does the failure of the Pakistan government to uphold Islamic principles of justice in the country as a whole.

The creation of Bangladesh did not represent a rejection of Islam as a way of life, as the majority of the people of Bangladesh continue to be devoutly Muslim, nor did it represent a well-considered rejection of Pakistan as a state as is shown by the tragic fact that today there are tens of thousands of Bengalis from Bangladesh who are working in Pakistan, having acquired forged papers making them citizens of Pakistan. At the same time, it must be pointed out that cultural bonds can and do at times transcend religious convictions. During the

[3]*India Wins Freedom: An Autobiographical Narrative* (Bombay: Asia Publishing House, 1959), p. 227.

pre-1971 period, for instance, the East Pakistanis revolted violently when the government of Pakistan forbade Radio Pakistan, Dacca, from broadcasting the writings of Rabindranath Tagore since he was a Hindu. It is sad but not surprising that the culturally illiterate government of Pakistan should have failed to appreciate the universalism of Tagore since it is unable, to this day, to appreciate the universalism of Iqbal and insists jingoistically on making him exclusively the poet-philosopher of Pakistan.

Moving beyond the Hindu-Muslim dialogue of life, which is rooted in a common culture, I would like to refer to another extremely important realm of life in which Hindu-Muslim dialogue has existed since the advent of the first Sufis into India: this is the realm of spirituality. All students of this area know how deep the spiritual quest of the children of this soil has been since the worldliness of the Vedic Aryans was superseded by the otherworldliness of the Upanishadic way of life and vision as well as the teachings of Buddhism, Jainism, and other ascetic sects. The Muslim mystics who came to India found the ground prepared for their work. Their passionate proclaiming of the existence of a loving, forgiving, saving God with whom a personal relationship could be established through singleminded devotion touched many hearts. It was Muslim Sufis, not Muslim soldiers, who converted masses of Hindus to Islam. Such conversions ought to have pleased the custodians of the Islamic Shari'a and Muslim rulers in India, but they did not. To holders of both secular and religious power in Islam, the Sufis have, since the early centuries of Islam, appeared as a great threat since they acknowledge the authority and sovereignty of no one but God and also because their devotion to God does not always exhibit itself in prescribed ways. For instance, knowing how important music was to the worshipful people of India, many Sufis adopted music in their worship—a practice frowned upon by the so-called "Shari'a-minded" Muslims. Regardless, however, of the attitudes of the Islamic establishment toward them, the mystics of Islam developed a spiritual bond with masses of Hindus, both those who converted to Islam and those who did not. The influence of Islamic mysticism on the Hindu bhakti movement and of Hindu mysticism on Muslim spirituality is well known, and it is noteworthy to mention here that Iqbal was very proud of being "a Brahmin's son" who represented a synthesis of Hindu and Muslim spiritual insight.[4]

Many messianic ideas are also common to Hindus, Muslims, and the other peoples of the subcontinent, and veneration is shown generally to all "saints" irrespective of their religious origin. Muslim scholars such as Fazlur Rahman

---

[4]In this context, reference may be made, for instance, to the following verses:

Mir and Mirza have staked their heart and faith on politics,
it is just this son of a Brahman who knows the secrets (of reality)
(S. A. Vahid, ed., Baqiyat-e-Iqbal [Lahore, 1966], p. 225)

Look at me for in Hindustan you will not see
another son of a Brahman familiar with the secrets of Rum and Tabriz
(Zabur-e-'Ajam [Lahore, 1948], p. 17)

deplore the appearance of messianism in Islam and attribute it to foreign influences, but I believe that there were also substantial reasons and forces within the Islamic tradition which contributed to it and that, although the Qur'an does not provide explicit support for it, it nevertheless has important spiritual, psychological, and emotional value for the masses of Muslims and constitutes a bond with other people who share their messianic hopes and ideas across the barriers of differing religious ideologies.[5] I have heard of Hindus visiting Muslim shrines, and I used to know Bengali Muslims who kept icons of the goddess Kali in their homes as protection against the evil eye. These Muslims were not idolatrous, since they did not deify Kali but regarded her as a savior- or intercessor-figure to whom they could address their fears and aspirations in much the same way that they would to Sufi saints.

Besides the dialogue of life and dialogue at the level of spirituality and the interchange of ideas and practices related to messianic beliefs, Hindus and Muslims in the subcontinent have also had a continuing dialogue on the basis of their common intellectual-aesthetic heritage. Literature, music, and philosophy are but a few ares in which Hindus and Muslims have much in common. There are many Hindus who love Iqbal, just as there are many Muslims who love Tagore. I remember how deeply touched I was several years ago when as a doctoral student working on Iqbal's philosophy I asked Mulk Raj Anand, a noted Indian novelist and scholar, about his feelings toward Iqbal, and he told me that one of his life's deepest desires was to visit Lahore and pay homage at the tomb of Iqbal, who had been his mentor at one time and whom he loved deeply despite the alienation brought about between Hindus and Muslims by the Muslim separatist movement in India. A year later, Mulk Raj Anand wrote to me telling me that he was happy in that he had indeed been able to fulfill his desire and pay his respects at Iqbal's mausoleum.

Having mentioned the areas in which I believe a dialogue already exists between Hindus and Muslims in the subcontinent, let me refer now to two areas in which there is either no, or minimal, dialogue between Hindus and Muslims living in India, Pakistan, and Bangladesh. The first is that of dialogue relating to historical/political issues; the second, dialogue relating to theological issues.

The first area is exceedingly difficult for a number of reasons, including the basic one that dialogue presupposes that a peer relationship or a relationship of equality exists between the dialogue partners. Dialogue of certain kinds cannot take place between obviously unequal people. That is why dialogue seldom takes place between masters and slaves and between men and women. In India, Muslims are not equal to Hindus; in Pakistan and Bangladesh, Hindus are not equal to Muslims in many ways. In the matter of writing history, particularly of the last 1,000 years, the historians of the subcontinent encounter serious difficulties. There is great pressure on Hindu historians to write history from the Hindu and

---

[5]See my "Messianism and Islam," *Journal of Ecumenical Studies* 22 (Spring, 1985): 261-291.

the Indian nationalist point of view and on Muslim historians to write history
from the Muslim and the Pakistani and Bangladeshi nationalist points of view.[6]
Both viewpoints are obviously limited and biased. There is imperative need for
writing a history which is comprehensive and just, which shows the mirror to
Hindus and Muslims alike. Confronting our mutual history can sometimes be as
painful as confronting our personal history if this history is a checkered one, but
it is necessary to do so in order to be free of the shadows of the past. Knowing
what we did or did not do does not alter the history of the past, but this knowledge—if accepted with courage and honesty—can lead to a different kind of
future. It is one of the prime tasks of those interested in promoting Hindu-
Muslim dialogue in the area of historical-political discussion to emphasize the
need for an accurate chronicling of all the facts which led to the alienation of
Hindus and Muslims in the pre- and post-partition periods and leads, every now
and then, to violence and the violation of the rights of weaker people.

Included in this "objective" history must be the role played in Hindu-
Muslim relations by the British imperialists who left India in great haste once
they accepted the fact that the golden days of the British Raj were over. So
many problems—political, geographical, economic, cultural, and psychological—
were the legacy of this Raj to the people of India: Hindus, Muslims, Sikhs, and
others. Although almost four decades have gone by since the departure of the
British from their most prized imperial possession, people of the subcontinent
are still discovering how variegated, widespread, and vicious the results of the
British colonial policy of "Divide and Rule" have been. One very important part
of any endeavor to establish better relations among the peoples of the subcontinent must be a thorough review of the British role in India, so that the responsibility for the atrocities which were committed against the various victims under
the different phases of this rule—particularly the momentous upheaval of the
pre- and post-partition period—can be correctly allocated.

As a Muslim and a person committed to dialogue, I do not believe in carrying the baggage of recrimination and bitterness from one life-period to another,
but I do believe very strongly that peace is predicated upon justice, and a just
evaluation of the past is necessary for establishing peace in the present and the
future. Criticism of the British conduct in India does not, of course, mean that
the British should be made scapegoats for all the problems which arose among
the major religious communities in India. There are undoubtedly a number of
problems which preexisted the coming of the British and are related to fundamental differences among these communities.

---

[6]It is to be noted that the nationalist point of view also changes with every new government, particularly in Pakistan and Bangladesh. Each successive (mostly military) regime
orders the rewriting of history to "expose" the evils of the previous regime. In any case,
Muslim children living in Pakistan are taught that their history began with the first advent of
the Muslims into India; they have no sense of identification with the earlier history (including that of the Indus Valley Civilization whose major excavated remains are in Pakistan) of
the subcontinent.

Without honest and deep self-probing and self-criticism, authentic dialogue with oneself or another is impossible. Hence it is necessary for all the peoples of the subcontinent to look into their own traditions and into their own hearts and minds and souls to discover the sources of these negative feelings and thoughts toward the "other" that periodically erupt in destructive modes of conduct. As stated by a philosopher, those who do not know their history are condemned to repeat it. We who come from a civilization which is not only one of the oldest in the world but also one of the most complex and reflective must understand our history if our future is to be better than our past, but this understanding of history must be comprehensive, not selective. We have to look not only at those periods or events in history which prove our particular bias but also at all the good and the bad together, and to take responsibility, both as individuals and as communities, for our own contribution to the difficulties which exist in our part of the world. However, we must not acknowledge guilt for that for which we are not responsible. The world, it is said, consists of the givers and the takers. It also appears to consist of persons who acknowledge guilt for everything and those who acknowledge guilt for nothing. Neither attitude is correct from the perspective of Islam, for neither conforms to the idea of justice. A just evaluation of our past requires that the specifics of history be examined closely and that responsibility be allocated for significant events, negative or positive, after proper consideration of all available evidence. And even that is not enough. It is not enough to hold any group—Hindus, Muslims, British, or any other—responsible for any particular event without specifying also which person or persons within the group were involved and what other circumstances (such as the time period) surrounded the event. We distort history by simplifying it. An extremely good example of this is provided by the way in which American television gives world news, particularly in situations (for example, the U.S. hostage crisis in post-revolutionary Iran) in which Americans are involved, directly or indirectly.

Authentic dialogue is not based on abbreviations, even as it is not based on hairsplitting elaborations of known facts. It is based on a clear and careful understanding of what we call "facts" seen in their total historical context. Once we are able to identify the sources of a conflict correctly, it becomes possible to transcend the conflict—to forget and forgive, as it were—but as long as we continue to evade a just evaluation, we are trapped in a process of scapegoating either ourselves or others. This, in qur'anic terminology, is "Zulm," and God tells us not to be "zalimin."

While speaking of history, perhaps a few words are in order about the way in which Muslims and Hindus view it philosophically. According to Kana Mitra, for Muslims, "the universal ideal needs to be concretized in society, in history," whereas, for Hindus, "the concrete is a stepping stone to the universal ideal but the universal can never be fully concretized in history."[7] While her first state-

---

[7]See p. 111, above.

ment is correct, Muslims would have no difficulty in also affirming her second statement. Like Hindus, Muslims also do not believe that the universal or the transcendent can ever be fully embodied in a material entity. If they believed otherwise, they would be guilty of deifying history as the Marxists are. Here, the following quotation from W. C. Smith's *Islam in Modern History* is relevant:

> Not that Islam . . . even in its most legalist form, ever became fully idolatrous. Attention was never *confined* to the this-worldly manifestation of value. For the Muslims, involvement in history, though absorbing, is at the most only the obverse of their coin, the reverse of which, polished, brilliant, and pure gold, is in the other world. Islam begins with God, and to Him it well knows we shall return. Its endeavor to redeem history, though total, is derived; it is an endeavor to integrate temporal righteousness in this world with a timeless salvation in the next.[8]

Finally, we come to the area of theological dialogue between Hindus and Muslims in the subcontinent. This is, in a way, the most difficult or problematic of all the areas discussed so far. In view of the fact that I have virtually no personal experience of participating in a Hindu-Muslim theological dialogue, I am hesitant to theorize regarding the methodology to be employed in such dialogue. What I can offer are some reflections and suggestions which might be useful to those who believe, as I do, that theological dialogue between Hindus and Muslims is urgently required in order to eliminate the gross ignorance regarding the "other" which leads to unjust behavior in times of peace and to gross brutality in times of stress.

Any Hindu-Muslim dialogue on theological issues must be carried out against the backdrop of the fact that Muslims entered the subcontinent as conquerors and that it was natural for Hindus to identify the religion of the conquering people as an embodiment of imperialism and militaristic power. The scope of this essay excludes the possibility of exploring the conduct of various Muslim rulers in India in general to determine if and to what degree Hindu allegations regarding Muslim aggression toward non-Muslims in this area are warranted by history. Such questions, of course, need to be asked and must be answered in the context of the political/historical dialogue mentioned earlier. However, in the context of theological dialogue it is more pertinent to look at questions or issues which affect the way in which Hindus and Muslims perceive each other's religious traditions and the impact which such perceptions have on their daily lives.

There is no question at all that the overwhelming majority of the Muslims in the world, if they have heard of Hinduism at all, think of Hindus as idol-worshippers. In a religious tradition as strictly monotheistic as Islam, where even in the realm of art no human representation is permitted, the making and revering of icons is bound to be regarded as "*shirk*" or association of anything with the

---

[8]P. 4.

One and Only God of humanity and all creation. Not only do most Muslims see Hindus as "*mushrikin*," but they also see them as "*kuffar*" or disbelievers in the one creator God of Jews, Christians, and Muslims. In view of this belief, most Muslims consider interreligious dialogue with Hindus to be an exercise not only in futility but also in sinfulness, since believers ought not to take unbelievers for friends, and dialogue is a friendly encounter which should take place only between or among believers.

At this point it is pertinent to mention that, historically, Muslims have had little or no interest in interreligious dialogue even with other believers in God, including the "*Ahl-al kitab*" ("People of the Book"—Jews and Christians) with whom they have strong theological and historical links. A partial explanation of this attitude may also be found in A. Toynbee's statement[9] that all three religions of revelation which sprang from a common historical root—Judaism, Christianity, and Islam—have a tendency not only toward exclusivism and intolerance but also tend to ascribe to themselves an ultimate validity. Muslims, who consider themselves the recipients of the final revelation, have, in general, taken the truth of Islam to be self-evident and have not expressed any great interest in having an open-ended philosophical and theological dialogue with people of other faiths, except perhaps in places where they have formed a minority component in a pluralistic environment. Also, the fact that until colonial times it was relatively easy for Muslims to assume the superiority of Islam to all other religions is, at least in part, responsible for their unwillingness to probe deeply into the question of the nature and implications of their Islamic identity.

One means of persuading at least some Muslims to participate in a theological dialogue with Hindus is to point out to them that such dialogue is called for by the spirit of many statements in the Qur'an.[10] For instance, the Qur'an refers to the fact that God not only created and honored the humanity of all human beings (Surah 17: *Bani Isra'il*: 70) but also intended Muslims to communicate the message of Islam to all. That the Qur'an is addressed to all is stated many times in the Qur'an; for example:

> Blessed is He Who
> Sent down the Criterion (Qur'an)
> To His Servant, that it
> May be an admonition
> *To all creatures.*   (Surah 25: *Al-Furqan*: 1)

> This is no less than
> A Message and a Qur'an
> Making things clear:
> That it may give admonition

---

[9]*An Historian's Approach to Religion* (Oxford: Oxford University Press, 1956), p. 296.
[10]All translations from the Qur'an cited in this essay are taken from *The Holy Qur'an*, tr. A. Yusuf Ali. (All texts of this translation are identical.)

To any (who are) alive,
And that the charge
May be proved against those
Who reject (Truth).   (Surah 36: *Ya-Sin*: 69-70)

This is no less than
A Message *to (all)*
The Worlds.   (Surah 38: *Sad*: 87)

Verily this is no less
Than a Message
To (all) the Worlds:
(With profit) *to whoever*
Among you wills
To go straight.   (Surah 81: *At-Takwir*: 27-28)

The universal mission of the Prophet of Islam is also affirmed by the Qur'an; for example:

We have not sent thee
But as a universal (Messenger)
To men, giving them
Glad tidings, and warning them
(Against sin), but most men
Understand not.   (Surah 34: *Saba'*: 28)

There are a number of verses in the Qur'an which refer to God's mercy and justice toward all creatures; for example:

And God careth for *all*
And He knoweth all things.   (Surah 2: *Al-Baqarah*: 268)

Unto *all* (in Faith)
Hath God promised good.   (Surah 4: *An-Nisa'*: 95)

That plurality of religions is sanctioned by God and is, in fact, a part of God's design for humanity is attested by the Qur'an; for example:

To each is a goal
To which God turns him;
Then strive together (as in a race)
Towards all that is good.
Wheresoever ye are,
God will bring you
Together. For God
Hath power over all things.   (Surah 2: *Al-Baqarah*: 148)

If it had been God's Plan
They would not have taken
False gods: but We
Made thee not one
To watch over their doings,
Nor art thou set
Over them to dispose
Of their affairs.   (Surah 6: *Al-An'am*: 107)

If it had been thy Lord's will
They would have all believed,
All who are on earth!
Will thou then compel mankind,
Against their will, to believe!   (Surah 10: *Yunus*: 99)

That there is to be no coercion in religion and that the Prophet's mission is simply to communicate the message of Islam is stressed by the Qur'an in many ways; for example:

Let there be no compulsion
In religion.   (Surah 2: *Al-Baqarah*: 256)

But if they turn away,
Thy duty is only to preach
The clear message.   (Surah 16: *An-Nahl*: 82)

The Truth is
From your Lord:
Let him who will
Believe, and let him
Who will, reject (it).   (Surah 18: *Al-Kahf*: 29)

If then they turn away,
We have not sent thee
As a guard over them.
Their duty is but to convey
(The Message).   (Surah 42: *Ash-Shura*: 48)

That the Qur'an advocates gracious conduct and religious tolerance as a life-attitude is clearly seen from the following verses:

When a (courteous) greeting
Is offered you, meet it
With greeting still more
Courteous, or (at least)
Of equal courtesy,
God takes careful account
Of all things.   (Surah 5: *Al-Ma'idah*: 86)

Revile not ye
Those whom they call upon
Besides God, lest
They out of spite
Revile God
In their ignorance.
Thus have We made
Alluring to each people
Its own doings.
In the end will they
Return to their Lord,
And We shall then
Tell them the truth
Of all that they did.   (Surah 6: *Al-An'am*: 108)

. . . If the enemy
Incline towards peace,
Do thou (also) incline
Towards peace, and trust
In God: for He is the One
That heareth and knoweth
(All things).   (Surah 8: *Al-Anfal*: 61)

If one amongst the Pagans
Ask thee for asylum,
Grant it to him,
So that he may hear the word
Of God; and then exort him
To where he can be secure.   (Surah 9: *At-Taubah*: 6)

That God's message has been intended, from the beginning, for the guidance of all humanity is shown by the verse:

The first House (of worship)
Appointed for men
Was that at Bakka:
Full of blessing
And of guidance
For all kinds of being. (alamin) (Surah 3: *Al-'Imran*: 96)

And, further, the Qur'an holds the promise:

One day we shall rise
From all peoples a witness . . .   (Surah 16: *An-Nahl*: 89)

The first problem to be confronted by anyone interested in bringing about a Hindu-Muslim theological dialogue would be to motivate both sides to enter into such dialogue with openness and seriousness. To have such a dialogue in a Western setting where dialogues are in fashion nowadays is one thing; to have it in India, Pakistan, or Bangladesh is quite another, and to bring it about would require much talent and commitment. If Hindus and Muslims could be persuaded in the interest of truth-seeking or peace-making to engage in a theological dialogue, the major task would be to determine what should be the beginning point of this dialogue.

My experience of Muslim-Christian-Jewish dialogue has convinced me that it is disastrous to begin any dialogue with a discussion on the concept of God, which many theologians assume to be the natural starting point of any theological dialogue in the framework of monotheistic religious tradition. I have never seen any dialogue which begins with a discussion of the Jewish, Christian, or Muslim concepts of God get past the point of hair-splitting definitions and disagreements, leaving the dialogue partners flabbergasted and wondering whether they are indeed talking about the believers in the same God. Any theological dialogue between Hindus and Muslims which begins with a discussion of the concept of God is even more likely to be doomed to disaster. I do not see any way in which the great majority of Muslims can be persuaded to appreciate the 330,000,000 gods of Hinduism, even if they are told that these gods are not ends-in-themselves but merely symbols of ultimate reality. Iqbal is certainly an an exceptional Muslim in that he has the courage to say:

> The "kafir" with a wakeful heart praying to an idol is better than a "believer" asleep in a sanctuary.[11]

Such is the absoluteness and starkness of Islamic monotheism that any reference to images of God or incarnations of God turns Muslims off so deeply that most of them feel compelled, theologically as well as personally, to abandon the dialogue. Most of the theological problems which Muslims have had with Christians have also revolved around the issue of Jesus' being the incarnation of God. However, the case of Christianity is different from that of Hinduism in that it preserves the Creator-God of Genesis and thus, from the Islamic point of view, does not lapse into total idolatry.

In my view, in order to eliminate the Muslims' stereotype of Hindus as idol-worshippers, it is better to begin by looking not at Hindu concepts of God but at Hindu experiences of God, particularly at those experiences which Muslims can empathize with. It would, for instance, be very difficult for a God-loving Muslim not to be deeply touched by Tagore's *Gitanjali: Gift Offering of Songs of God*. Some Muslims may feel a little uneasy at the human imagery used by the Hindu poet to depict the divine, but, then, Islamic mystic literature also abounds with such imagery, and the Qur'an itself uses anthropomorphic images for God ("I made a human being with both my hands" [Surah 36: *Sad*: 72]).

---

[11]*Javid Namah* (Lahore, 1947), p. 40.

Some people—theologians and others—think that theological dialogue does, or should, lead to theological agreement. This, in my judgment, is an erroneous point of view. For instance, no amount of theological dialogue between Hindus and Muslims can lead to the reduction of the monistic principle upheld by many Hindus to the monotheistic belief held by all Muslims, and vice versa. But why should the achieving of theological agreement be so necessary? Why should it not be sufficient for Hindus and Muslims to understand correctly what the religious experience of each is without trying to merge them together? Like many other Muslims, I also believe that there are some Hindus who, in fact, do identify idols with Brahman and, thus, are idolators. But I also believe that there are some Muslims who identify the Word or Law of God with God and, thus, are idolatrous. Whatever be the religious experience of some Hindus or some Muslims, and whether we approve of it or not, I think that it is important to remember in the context of Hindu-Muslim theological dialogue that the two religious worldviews have some extremely important things in common.

To begin with: both Hinduism and Islam conceive of ultimate reality as spiritual, thus making the believer aware of that which is beyond the here-and-now, the eternal and transcendent, which gives human life a purposefulness it would not have if reality were confined to the material. Both Hinduism and Islam insist that all aspects of life are related and must be integrated in order to achieve wholeness, which is the goal of Hindu *yoga* and Muslim *salat*. Neither Hinduism nor Islam permits the bifurcation of life into mutually exclusive domains: the secular and the sacred, the public and the private, the inner and the outer. Again, both Hinduism and Islam hold that knowledge of external and internal reality is to be obtained not only through reason but through all other human faculties as well, with particular emphasis on "the heart," which the mystics regard as the seat of "intuition." People of the Western world—founded as it is upon the Graeco-Roman civilization which upheld reason as the highest human faculty through which alone one could obtain knowledge of ultimate reality—rarely understand what "the heart" or "intuitive faculty" is, but it is due primarily to this faculty that Hindus and Muslims have evolved what are perhaps the two greatest mystic traditions in the history of civilization.

Finally, both Hinduism and Islam have put unequivocal emphasis on the idea that human beings are accountable for their actions and that ethical action is the goal of religious striving. In both there is great emphasis on duty-fulfillment and on the idea that duty to God is inseparable from duty to fellow human beings.

Having pointed out some of the common perspectives on which a Hindu-Muslim theological dialogue can be based, I consider it necessary to point out also that, as a matter of fact, much assimilation of religious/cultural ideas and attitudes has occurred in the Hindu-Muslim world. Both Hindus and Muslims might wish to stress their distinct identities and insist that Hinduism and Islam are utterly different ways of life, but the plain historical reality is that Indian Islam bears the clear imprint of Hinduism, and Hinduism has absorbed much that is clearly Islamic in origin. For instance, while many Hindus have been deeply

affected by Islamic monotheism,[12] many Muslims follow a caste system as strictly as the Hindus and take great pride in being "high-caste" (which generally
means being descended from the Prophet Muhammad or his blood relatives),
even if they are so only by virtue of their descent from high-caste Hindus!

Before I conclude my comments on the various kinds of Hindu-Muslim dialogue which exist, or ought to exist, in the subcontinent, I would like to mention
something very close to my heart: the need for a dialogue between Hindu and
Muslim women. As a Muslim feminist, I have been deeply concerned for a long
time about some negative ideas/attitudes/customs relating to women which are
found widely among Muslims of the subcontinent. Some of these practices (for
example, demanding the dowry or bride-price for girls at marriage) and concepts
(for example, the husband is the wife's "*majazi khuda*" or god in earthly form)
are clearly unIslamic. In fact, the "deification" of the husband is tantamount to
shirk (association with God) and, thus, an unforgiveable sin. However, they have
become so deeply rooted in Muslim culture that their association with, or deriva-
tion from, Hindu culture has long been forgotten, and they are regarded by many
Muslims to be part of the Islamic "Shari'a." While there are woman-affirming
resources within both Islam and Hinduism, these have not been used for the
liberation of women from the misogynistic/androcentric and rigid patriarchalism
of these two religious traditions. In this era of women's freedom from age-old
shackles, Hindu and Muslim women continue to be among the most oppressed
"minorities" in the world. They need to dialogue with each other not only to
understand their common bondage and servitude and to give each other emotional and psychological support, but also to strive together to evolve academic
and sociopolitical ways and means or methods and strategies to change the religiocultural world in which they live and die unsung. In this context, my plea to
Hindu and Muslim (as well as all other "disinherited" women of the world) is
(with due apologies to Marx): "Women of the world unite; you have nothing to
lose but your chains!"

In conclusion, I want simply to say that, as a person belonging to what the
Qur'an describes as "a nation in the middle,"[13] I feel that I stand midway between my religious world which is Judaeo-Christian-Islamic (West) and my cultural world which is Hindu-Islamic (East). I have spent more than half my life in
the West, which has molded my mind but where my body and soul are still ill-at-
ease. All to often I feel a deep longing to return to the soil of the ancient mystic
land where I was born and to the people who speak my language and share my
grassroots values. To be divided—as I am—is to be in a state of perpetual exile.
To be in exile is not a happy state, but it enables one to experience more than

----

[12]Reference may be made here to Kana Mitra's statement on p. 110, above: "Rammohan
Roy, Rabindranath Tagore, Gandhi—all were appreciative of Islamic monotheism."
[13]Surah 2: *Al-Baqarah*: 143.

one kind of reality.[14] It is tragic that the world in which we live today is full of exiles. However, these exiles have a glorious opportunity for dialogue and can do much to create, out of the deep sense of their own fragmented and lonely lives, the vision of a world which is integrated and whole, in which all human beings can find peace.

---

[14]The Qur'an regards *"Hijrah"* (going into exile) to be a part of *"Jihad fo Sabil Allah"* (striving in the cause of God) and considers it to be a state blessed by God.

Riffat Hassan (Muslim) is Associate Professor of Religious Studies at the University of Louisville (KY), where she has taught since 1976. She has also taught at the Louisville Presbyterian Theological Seminary; the University of Punjab in Lahore, Pakistan (her birthplace); Villanova (PA) University; the University of Pennsylvania; and Oklahoma State University, Stillwater, OK. She holds a B.A. in English literature and philosophy and a Ph.D. in philosophy (1968) from St. Mary's College, University of Durham (England). She has been involved in the Kennedy Institute (Georgetown University) Jewish-Christian-Muslim Trialogue since 1979, and with several local, national, and international groups dealing with women of faith, peace concerns, and interreligious dialogue on both scholarly and popular levels. She has published widely in Pakistan and the U.S., especially on the life and work of Iqbal, including *The Sword and the Sceptre* (Iqbal Academy, 1978) and *An Iqbal Primer* (Aziz Publishers, 1979). Her articles in the *Journal of Ecumenical Studies* have concerned Islam and human rights, and Islam and Messianism. She is presently writing a major book on women in Islam and in the Qur'an.

RELIGIOUS FREEDOM AND HUMAN RIGHTS IN THE WORLD AND THE CHURCH: A CHRISTIAN PERSPECTIVE

Charles E. Curran

Human rights and religious liberty have been receiving worldwide attention in the last few years. In the past and even in the present there have been many violations of human rights in the name of religious belief. The source of the problem is evident. Most religions involve a belief in a divine power and gift which brings life, salvation, and liberation to human beings. This belief is certainly true of Christianity which professes Jesus as the Savior of the world. A conviction that belief in Jesus and in a particular Christian denomination is so important has been used for centuries to override the religious freedom and human rights of other people. There are many situations in the modern world in which religions do not grant religious liberty or toleration to others and in the process deny basic human rights. Think of the religious struggles in Iran, in the Near East, in Northern Ireland, in Bangladesh, in India, and in so many other parts of the world.

There is always a tension between passionate religious belief in salvation through one particular way and toleration of others or an acceptance of their religious liberty. For the nonbeliever or even for one who maintains that all religions are basically the same, there is very little tension between saving religious truth and the freedom of those who do not so believe. Even today problems emerge more often among religious fanatics and fundamentalists. It has taken mainstream Western Christianity a long time to work out a way of respecting human rights and liberty while holding on to the truth claims of Christianity.

Despite widespread practical violations of human rights and religious liberty in our modern world because of religion, great progress has been made in the world community on a theoretical recognition of the importance and meaning of religious liberty and human rights. The most significant embodiment of this important worldwide development is found in the declarations, conventions, and work of the United Nations. The Universal Declaration of Human Rights was adopted in December, 1948. This basic document has been developed over the years by subsequent statements, declarations, and conventions. In 1983 the United Nations published a 146-page compendium of international instruments of human rights.[1] The occasion was the celebration of the thirty-fifth anniversary of the adoption of the Universal Declaration of Human Rights. After a long and tortuous development, the Declaration on the Elimination of All Forms of Intolerance and of Discrimination Based on Religion or Belief was adopted without

---

[1]*Human Rights: A Compilation of International Instruments* (New York: United Nations Publications, 1983; Sales No. E. 83. XIV. 1).

a vote by the General Assembly of the United Nations on November 25, 1981. There are many aspects of these documents which can and should be criticized, but they nevertheless represent a great achievement and advancement for human-kind. Despite cultural, religious, linguistic, economic, political, and ideological differences, these documents point to a general consensus in the world commu-nity, at least in theory, on the matter of human rights in general and religious liberty in particular.

Mainline Protestant and Roman Catholic Christianity have also come to general agreement on the matter of human rights and religious liberty or toler-ance, which is not exactly the same as religious liberty.[2] Protestant Christianity was first to accept religious liberty, which only became a part of official Catholic teaching at the Second Vatican Council in 1965.[3] Mainstream Western Christi-anity is in basic agreement about the meaning of religious liberty. The right to religious liberty is not only the freedom to have a certain belief, but it also in-volves the freedom of religious expression, the freedom of religious association, and corporate and institutional religious freedom.[4]

Western Christianity has recently embraced the concept of human rights as exemplified in official statements by the Roman Catholic Church, the World Council of Churches, the Lutheran World Federation, and the World Alliance of Reformed Churches.[5] Human rights is a very complex issue, but official state-ments and theological writings have rightly recognized and even endorsed this complexity. At the first level, human rights are seen primarily as political and civil rights defending the freedom of individuals against the power of the state. In distinction to this approach of Western democracies, socialist nations have

---

[2]In the best sense of the term, tolerance seems to refer primarily to the moral sphere, whereas religious liberty refers rather to the social and juridical areas. In addition, tolerance has been used in the Roman Catholic tradition as something much less than religious liberty. While recognizing these significant differences, it is not impossible for practical purposes to use the words interchangeably.

[3]For the documentation from the early meetings of the World Council of Churches beginning in Amsterdam in 1948 and for a discussion of religious liberty in light of W.C.C. deliberations, see A. F. Carrillo de Albornoz, *The Basis of Religious Liberty* (New York: Association Press, 1963). Also see "Declaration on Religious Freedom" in Walter Abbott, ed., *The Documents of Vatican II* (New York: Guild Press, 1966), pp. 675-700.

[4]A. F. Carrillo de Albornoz, *Religious Liberty* (New York: Sheed and Ward, 1967), pp. 3-24. Carrillo, who was head of the World Council of Churches' Secretariat on Religious Liberty, wrote this volume as a commentary and analysis of the Declaration of Vatican II.

[5]For these statements and commentaries on them, consult the following works: Pontifi-cal Commission, *Justitia et Pax: The Church and Human Rights* (Vatican City: Vatican Polyglot Press, 1975); Allen O. Miller, ed., *A Christian Declaration on Human Rights* (Grand Rapids, MI: Eerdmans, 1977); Jørgen Lissner and Arne Sovik, eds., *A Lutheran Reader on Human Rights* (Geneva: Lutheran World Federation, 1977); Alan D. Falconer, ed., *Under-standing Human Rights: An Interdisciplinary and Interfaith Study* (Dublin: Irish School of Ecumenics, 1980); Arlene Swidler, ed., *Human Rights in Religious Traditions* (New York: Pilgrim Press, 1982 [this symposium originally appeared in the *Journal of Ecumenical Studies* 19 (Summer, 1982): 1-113, special pagination]). For a small pamphlet containing the significant bibliography, see Alan D. Falconer, *What to Read on Human Rights* (Lon-don: British Council of Churches, 1980).

insisted on social and economic rights. Third World considerations have developed the concept of rights even further, and recent rights discussions have recognized rights to development, to a good environment, and to peace. In general Catholic and Protestant statements and theologians insist on the broad approach to human rights. There are different understandings of the grounding of human rights and religious liberty, but there exists remarkable agreement among mainline Protestants and Catholics on the meaning, nature, and extension of these rights.

Western Christianity, however, has taken a long time and a tortuous path to arrive at its acceptance of religious liberty and fundamental rights. Christians can only rejoice at what has occurred, but there are aspects of the question which continue to be of importance for both society at large and the church. The first aspect concerns how the mainline Protestant and Catholic churches came to the acceptance of these rights. This question has not only historical and theoretical significance but also practical bearing. Perhaps history can help to show how other religions and the world itself can come to the same acceptance of human rights. The second aspect of the question concerns the recognition of freedom and human rights within the churches themselves. How in theory and in practice do the churches themselves recognize and safeguard the religious freedom and rights of their own members? These two aspects will be developed in the two major sections of this essay.

I. An Analysis of the Past

In general, Roman Catholic and mainline Protestant Christianity contributed little or nothing to the original acceptance of religious liberty in the West. The Christian churches and Christian theology arrived on the scene both late and breathless. Church and theological support for religious liberty in the West came only after religious liberty had already been well accepted in the world at large. Protestantism in general embraced religious liberty much earlier than Roman Catholicism. American Protestantism accepted religious liberty before European mainline Protestantism, but recall that religious establishment continued to exist in Massachusetts until 1833.[6] However, even in the 1960's prominent Protestant scholars such as Thomas Sanders and Philip Wogaman pointed out that, while American Protestantism had for a long time supported religious freedom, there was no commonly accepted theological understanding and grounding of the principle of religious liberty.[7]

It seems that two factors played a very important role in the acceptance of

---

[6]Thomas G. Sanders, *Protestant Concepts of Church and State* (Garden City, NY: Doubleday Anchor Books, 1965), p. 15.
[7]Ibid., pp. 330 ff.; Philip Wogaman, *Protestant Faith and Religious Liberty* (Nashville: Abingdon Press, 1967), pp. 42, 43.

religious liberty in Western civilization from the seventeenth century on. These two factors are the secularization of the state and the recognition of the existence of religious pluralism. The secularization of the state and the breakdown of the old Christendom model put into historical actuality the dualism between church and state. There can be no doubt that in many countries the secularization of the state was based on some antichurch and antireligious motives which made it all the harder for some religionists to accept the religious liberty proposed by such advocates. The existence of religious pluralism was also a very pragmatic reason for accepting religious freedom. Religious freedom was the only practical solution in the midst of religious pluralism which was above all exemplified in the United States.

The historical circumstances affected the approach of the Christian churches to religious liberty. There was no doctrine of religious liberty in the Reformation, and the seventeenth-century solution *cuius regio eius religio*—the religion of the people follows the religion of the prince—was the recognized approach of mainstream Protestantism. Later, however, not only the Protestant sects but also the mainline Protestant churches often found themselves as a minority religion striving for their own existence and survival. Religious liberty was intimately connected with their continued existence and development. Even when some churches gained religious liberty for themselves, as in England for example, they saw no need to extend it to others, such as Jews and Catholics.

The Roman Catholic Church only accepted religious liberty fully in the 1960's. Before that time the famous distinction between thesis and hypothesis appeared to many as sheer opportunism. That Catholic position exhibited a willingness to accept religious liberty in those situations in which religious pluralism existed, but it maintained that the ideal is the denial of religious liberty and the union of all in the one true Catholic faith. In practice where Catholics were the overwhelming majority, religious liberty was denied; but where Catholics were a minority, religious liberty was accepted. Thus, historical factors brought about the acceptance of religious liberty in the West, and its later acceptance by the churches was heavily motivated by self-interest and institutional concerns.

Although the emergence of religious liberty in the West was not originally due to the churches or theology and although practical reasons of institutional self-interest were of great importance in the churches' acceptance of religious liberty, there are theological resources within the two major Christian traditions in the West which could be used to justify and support religious freedom. In the course of time both Protestants and finally Roman Catholics have found this support in their own traditions.

The fact that Protestantism embraced religious freedom before Catholicism is not due only to more pragmatic reasons, for in general Protestantism has always given more importance to freedom than has Catholicism. Specifically from the perspectives of theology, epistemology, ethics, political ethics, and ecclesiology, Protestantism has given a more central role to freedom than has Roman Catholicism. From a theological perspective, Protestantism has emphasized salvation by faith which frees Christians from the law. Freedom is the description often given to the redeemed status of the believer through the gracious gift of God in Christ Jesus. Roman Catholicism has always insisted on both faith and works and has not been accustomed to speaking about the redeemed state of the believer primarily in terms of freedom. The very ethos of Protestant thought has accentuated freedom. The basic thrust of Protestantism was a reaction against the authoritarianism of the Church of Rome. The Protestant Reform appealed to freedom and gave it an important role in its self-understanding.

Epistemologically, Roman Catholicism has insisted that the word and work of God are mediated in and through reason and human nature. Reason and reason's ability to know the truth have been stressed in Catholicism. Orthodoxy has always been a very central consideration, as well as the church's ability to know with certitude and to communicate the truths of faith. Such an approach leaves little room for tolerance and freedom with regard to religious truth. This emphasis on the ability of human beings to reason and to know the truth with certitude has not been as central in Protestantism. In more recent times Paul Tillich developed what he called the Protestant principle—which is basically the protest against any absolute claims made for finite and relative reality.[8] Our knowledge of God is never perfect but always inadequate and always under the judgment of the absolute. The Protestant principle is much broader than the question of truth, but it is applicable here. In the light of such a principle the Protestant approach could never be as totally self-confident of the truth as the Catholic position. Philip Wogaman has invoked this Protestant principle to criticize all absolute claims on the basis of which religious liberty could be denied.[9] Contemporary Catholic thought, however, with its more eschatological emphasis, often finds itself quite sympathetic to Tillich's Protestant principle.

Protestant ethics, although not as developed as Catholic ethics, has given great centrality to freedom.[10] Perhaps it is this very emphasis on freedom which has contributed to the fact that Protestant ethics has not been developed as systematically as Catholic ethics. God in Protestant ethics is often understood in terms of freedom. God freely chooses to make a covenant with human beings and to redeem the human race. God is ever and always free to intervene in history, for God is the sovereign of history. Catholic ethics puts less stress on freedom both in God and in human beings. God acts in accord with the divine plan. The natural law is nothing more than the participation of the eternal law in the rational creature. Human reason reflecting on human nature can arrive at the divine plan for the world. James Gustafson has recently pointed out an interesting convergence which has occurred in the last few years in Christian ethics.

---

[8]Paul Tillich, *The Protestant Era* (Chicago: University of Chicago Press, 1948), especially pp. xii-xxix.

[9]Wogaman, *Protestant Faith*, pp. 109-115.

[10]For a contemporary systematic Protestant approach to freedom, see Peter C. Hodgson, *New Birth of Freedom: A Theology of Bondage and Liberation* (Philadelphia: Fortress Press, 1976).

Protestant ethics is searching for some structure to overcome the occasionalism and existentialism that came from too great an insistence on freedom, whereas Catholic ethics is striving to overcome the traditional emphasis on order and to find room for responsible openness.[11] Historically and traditionally, however, Protestant ethics has stressed freedom, whereas Roman Catholic moral theology has insisted on order.

In social ethics there has been much discussion about the relationship of the different faiths to democratic government. Historically, Roman Catholicism opposed the early democratic revolutions and was not favorable to democracy. Until very recently, Catholic thought was indifferent about the form of government and saw no great advantage in democracy.[12] There seems to have been some affinity between later Calvinism and democracy, but again this depended somewhat on circumstances.[13] In Europe Calvinism was often associated with efforts to revolt from the absolute power of the ruler and therefore supported democratic forms of government, but a form of Calvinism continues to support the government of South Africa with its apartheid principles. Protestantism in the United States was a strong supporter of democracy. The traditional Protestant emphasis on sin has also played a role in Protestant acceptance of democracy by recognizing possible abuse of power and the need to protect people against such abuses. The division of powers among the executive, legislative, and judicial branches has often been defended in Protestantism on the basis of the need to protect against the abuses arising from sin. No one individual or group should be trusted with all the power. Reinhold Niebuhr has maintained that it is human beings' capacity for justice that makes democracy possible, but human beings' inclination to injustice makes democracy necessary.[14] Even in social ethics, Catholic thought until recently has not seen freedom as an important value. This aspect of Catholic social ethics will be developed later in greater detail.

The Protestant emphasis on freedom has also strongly affected Protestant ecclesiology and its difference from Catholic ecclesiology. From the very beginning, Protestantism has insisted on the freedom of the believer. Catholic theology with its emphasis on the human has always taken mediation seriously. The word and work of God are mediated in and through the human. Thus the church as a human reality mediates the divine gift of salvation. The church community is a sign or sacrament that makes visible and present the mercy and presence of God in our world. In all of theology mediation has characterized the Catholic approach with its traditional insistence on the "and"—faith and reason, grace

---

[11]James M. Gustafson, *Protestant and Roman Catholic Ethics: Prospects for Rapprochement* (Chicago: University of Chicago Press, 1978), pp. 30-94.

[12]John F. Cronin, *Social Principles and Economic Life*, rev. ed. (Milwaukee: Bruce, 1965), pp. 281 ff.

[13]Sanders, *Protestant Concepts*, pp. 262-274.

[14]Reinhold Niebuhr, *The Children of Light and the Children of Darkness* (New York: Scribners, 1944), p. xi.

and nature, scripture and tradition, Jesus and the church, divine law and natural law. The abuse in the Catholic understanding is to absolutize what is only the mediation, and this has often happened in different areas, especially in ecclesiology. Thus, the role of the church has been absolutized, and for many people the church was supreme even over the scriptures themselves. Protestantism has stressed the immediate relationship of the believer with God and downplayed the role of the visible church. The church is not seen as mediating the word and work of Jesus to the believer through the visible community itself. The believer is in immediate contact with the word of God in the scripture. Catholic ecclesiology has tended to be more communitarian, whereas Protestantism has tended to be more individualistic. Not only has Catholicism insisted on the role of the church as visible community, but the community is also hierarchically structured with special powers of teaching, ruling, and sanctifying given to the offices of pope and bishop. In reaction to Protestantism, post-Tridentine Catholicism tended to define itself not primarily as the people of God but as a hierarchically structured society. Most theologians agree that since the Reformation the Catholic Church became overly authoritarian, and Vatican Council II tried to overcome some of the theoretical and practical abuses of authoritarianism.

There can be no doubt that Protestantism historically has been more open to and supportive of freedom in general than has Roman Catholicism. This emphasis is not without problems of its own, as hinted at in some of the above analysis, but it does explain why Protestantism could historically be more open to religious freedom than Catholicism. However, there is a central tenet of Christianity that both Protestants and Catholics have appealed to in their later acceptance of religious liberty. The act of faith must be a free, personal assent. God's whole way of acting with human beings is to call for a free response to God's gracious gift. Many defenses of religious liberty have appealed to this fundamental tenet of Christian faith, but obviously what is called the social aspect of religious liberty includes much more than just protecting the private conscience of the individual.

The Roman Catholic rejection of religious liberty before Vatican II must be seen in the light of its opposition to what was called modern liberalism with an emphasis on liberty in all its forms. An overview of the historical development within Roman Catholicism will be helpful for this present study.[15] The heavy emphasis in Catholic thinking was on objective truth and the natural law. At best, one had to freely accept the truth in the speculative order and natural law

[15]Helpful studies of this historical development include the following: Roger Aubert, "Liberalism and the Church in the Nineteenth Century," in Joseph Masson et al., *Tolerance and the Catholic* (New York: Sheed and Ward, 1955), pp. 47-76; Fr. Refoulé, "L'Église et les libertés de Léon XIII à Jean XXIII," *Le Supplément*, no. 125 (May, 1978), pp. 243-259; Bernard Plongeron, "L'Église et les Déclarations des droits de l'homme au XVIIIᵉ siècle," *Nouvelle Revue Théologique*, vol. 101 (1979), pp. 358-377; Jean-Marie Aubert, "Les droits de l'homme interpellent les églises," *Le Supplément*, no. 141 (May, 1982), pp. 149-179; Ch. Wachenheim, "Comprendre l'attitude de l'Église," ibid., pp. 237-248.

in the moral order, but freedom was never an ultimate value. The most important realities were the objective realities themselves, and truth in both the speculative and the practical orders could be known without too much difficulty. This emphasis was the basis for the famous statement that error has no rights.

From such a philosophical perspective, this modern liberalism with its stress on freedom and human reason apart from God denied the natural law and the all-important human relationship to God. Human beings and not God became the center of the universe, and God's law was shunted aside. The political aspects of this liberalism, especially as seen in the French revolution, were clearly opposed to the Catholic notion of Christendom. In addition much of this liberalism was perceived to be anti-Catholic. Such liberalism with its emphasis on freedom also favored an individualism which was opposed to the Catholic understanding of society as an organic community of people working together for the common good.

In light of these perspectives it is somewhat easier to understand, but not completely justify, the opposition by the Catholic Church even in the nineteenth century to the modern freedoms. Pope Gregory XVI and Pope Pius IX condemned freedom of conscience and worship as a madness. Freedom of speech and freedom of the press were likewise condemned.[16] Their successor Pope Leo XIII continued this attack on the modern freedoms. There were some problems with the understanding of freedom proposed by liberalism, but Catholic thought refused even to dialogue with it and rejected the modern freedoms often by tenaciously holding on to a past that could no longer be a viable option.

The Catholic Church, which was the great enemy of freedom in the nineteenth century, gradually came to champion freedom in the twentieth century. Many factors explain this change, but a very important aspect was the emergence of a new opponent. In the nineteenth century, individualistic liberalism with its emphasis on freedom was seen as the primary problem of the age. However, as the twentieth century progressed a new problem appeared on the scene—totalitarianism. Catholic social ethics has always tried to find a middle path between individualism and collectivism. Against the collectivism of Fascism, Nazism, and Communism (but with much greater fear of the Left) Catholic teaching defended the dignity and rights of the human person. Human freedom became very significant. The development came to its climax in the 1960's. One can see a very significant change even within the writings of Pope John XXIII. In 1961 in the encyclical *Mater et magistra* Pope John insisted that the ideal social order should be based on truth, justice, and love.[17] In *Pacem in terris*, issued two years later, John added a significant element to this trilogy—truth, justice, love, and free-

[16]Aubert, "Liberalism and the Church," p. 59.
[17]Pope John XXIII, *Mater et magistra*, par. 212, in David J. O'Brien and Thomas A. Shannon, eds., *Renewing the Earth: Catholic Documents on Peace, Justice, and Liberation* (Garden City, NY: Doubleday Image Books, 1977), p. 102.

dom.[18] With this official Catholic acceptance of the importance of human freedom in society, the one remaining obstacle was the Catholic teaching on religious freedom which was changed by the Decree on Religious Freedom of the Second Vatican Council in 1965.

The acceptance of religious liberty in the council was based on the dignity of the human person. However, there was and still is some dispute about the exact grounding or basis of the right to religious liberty. John Courtney Murray, the American Jesuit whose influence on the Vatican II document was greater than that of any other person, based religious liberty on an understanding of limited constitutional government. For Murray religious liberty was primarily a juridical and constitutional question with theological and ethical overtones. For a number of French bishops and theologians religious liberty was primarily a theological issue which should be addressed from a specific theological perspective.[19] This discussion has important ramifications for our understanding of freedom and human rights in the church. By basing religious freedom on the nature of constitutional government, Murray's approach could be interpreted to separate and distinguish too much between freedom within society and freedom within the church. A more theological basis for religious freedom in civil society would also furnish more direct reason for affirming a greater role for freedom within the church.[20]

The analysis thus far has been related only to freedom and religious freedom, emphasizing how these realities came about in the Western world without a major contribution from the Christian churches or theologies. Subsequently, with no small help from self-interest, the churches have given a theological basis and justification for religious liberty.

What has been the general attitude of Western Christian churches to the other part of our consideration—human rights? Today the Protestant and Catholic churches are strong supporters of human rights understood in a rather complex way and including more than the traditional rights of Western liberties.[21] Very often today human-rights language becomes one way of talking about the whole of social ethics. It is impossible to discuss the whole history of Christian social ethics, but a brief comment will indicate how Catholic and Protestant churches and theologies have come to accept human-rights terminology and understanding. In both traditions there are strong strains of justice and social

---

[18]Pope John XXIII, *Pacem in terris*, par. 35, in ibid., p. 132.

[19]For Murray's discussion of this issue, see John Courtney Murray, *The Problem of Religious Freedom* (Westminster, MD: Newman Press, 1965), especially pp. 19-22.

[20]Murray himself—even in 1966—strongly urged a greater freedom in the church; see John Courtney Murray, "Freedom, Authority, Community," *America* 115 (December 3, 1966): 734-741.

[21]See, e.g., Sixth Assembly of the World Council of Churches at Vancouver, "Statement on Human Rights," *Ecumenical Review* 36 (January, 1984): 87-91; Otfried Höffe et al., *Jean Paul II et les droits de l'homme* (Fribourg: Éditions Universitaires, 1980).

concern, but it is only recently that both have come to accept and even endorse the terminology of human rights.

Human-rights language is not congenial to the Protestant tradition with its emphasis on the primacy of God and God's gracious gift of salvation.[22] To speak of human rights seems to start in the wrong place and makes the human being the center of all things. However, contemporary Protestant theologians have been able to accept the language of human rights and integrate it into a broader theological perspective. Thus the covenant and divine claims have been the grounding for human rights in some contemporary Protestant theologians.[23]

The language and the universality of human rights follows quite easily from a natural-law approach, but Protestantism has generally rejected such an approach and insisted on something distinctively Christian. However, on the basis of creation and covenant Protestant ethics has been able to support the universality of human rights for all. In practice contemporary Protestantism, especially through the work of the World Council of Churches, has encouraged interest in and participation by the younger churches of the Third World. As a result, the human-rights concerns of the Third World have been incorporated into the contemporary understanding of human rights in mainstream Protestantism.

The natural-law tradition associated with Roman Catholicism would seem in theory to be quite congenial with universal rights ontologically grounded in the human person. However, the Catholic tradition was slow to embrace the terminology of human rights. The first full systematic development of human rights in official Catholic teaching appeared in Pope John XXIII's encyclical *Pacem in terris* in 1963. Catholic teaching and theology were not at home with the language of human rights because the secular tradition supporting the "rights of man" was associated with individualistic liberalism which was strongly opposed by Catholicism in the eighteenth and nineteenth centuries. Even the language of rights indicated a human autonomy cut off from God and God's law. The Catholic teaching insisted on following the natural law and not on the rights of individuals. However, as the twentieth century progressed the Catholic Church began to defend and stress the dignity of the human person and the rights of the individual. One advantage of its earlier opposition to individualistic rights was the recognition of social and economic rights when it finally adopted the human-rights approach in *Pacem in terris*.

---

[22]In addition to the bibliography mentioned, the following articles are helpful in describing the approach to human rights in Protestantism: Roger Mehl, "La tradition protestante et les droits de l'homme," *Revue d'histoire et de philosophie religieuses*, vol. 58, No. 3 (1978), pp. 367-377; Th. Tschny, "Le protestantisme et les problèmes théologiques de droits de l'homme," *Le Supplément*, no. 141 (May, 1982), pp. 221-237.

[23]Jürgen Moltmann, *On Human Dignity: Political Theology and Ethics* (Philadelphia: Fortress Press, 1984), especially pp. 3-58; Max L. Stackhouse, "A Protestant Perspective on the Woodstock Human Rights Project," in Alfred Hennelly and John Langan, eds., *Human Rights in the Americas: The Struggle for Consensus* (Washington, DC: Georgetown University Press, 1982), pp. 142-158.

Contemporary Catholic social teaching continues its emphasis on human dignity and rights by calling attention to two significant human aspirations in the contemporary world—the aspiration to equality and the aspiration to participation, two forms of human dignity and freedom.[24] An older Catholic ethics was fearful of equality as destroying the organic nature of society in which the differentiated parts are organized in a hierarchical manner to achieve the common good. Now, however, equality is no longer seen as detrimental to communal human existence. An older approach understood society as being structured from the top down with the people even described as the ignorant masses who had to be directed by those in authority. Participation now stresses the right and need of all to share in creatively bringing about a more just social order for themselves and others. Thus the acceptance of and the importance of freedom, human rights, equality, and participation all point to a shift in Catholic thinking to a greater emphasis on the person and the dignity of the person.

What conclusions can be drawn from the first part of this study? First, today mainline Protestant and Roman Catholic teaching and theology support both religious liberty and human rights. Such support should help the practical struggle for human rights in our world and the effort to prevent religious intolerance from taking away human rights. Second, historically religious liberty explicitly came to the fore of consciousness without great support from the Western Christian churches or theology. Institutional self-interest played an important role in the acceptance of religious liberty by the Christian churches. However, in time the Christian churches found resources in their own traditions to accept religious freedom and tolerance. If history is any lesson for the present, there is bad news here. One cannot expect religions themselves on the basis of their own teaching to be in the forefront of defending religious freedom and tolerance. Some religions will probably continue to violate human rights in the name of religious truth. Other factors including the secularization of the state and plurality of religions will be much more important in bringing about the acceptance of religious freedom and tolerance in our world. One can, however, hope that the lessons of history will not repeat themselves.

II. Freedom and Human Rights within the Church

The subject of this second section on freedom and human rights within the Christian church must be reduced dramatically. The first limit will be to focus only on the Roman Catholic Church. This choice and limitation are not merely arbitrary. From the practical viewpoint it would be impossible to consider all the different Protestant traditions and denominations. The Roman Catholic Church is

---

[24]Pope Paul VI, *Octogesima adveniens*, par. 22, in O'Brien and Shannon, *Renewing the Earth*, p. 364.

clearly the largest single church. From a theoretical perspective, Roman Catholicism has had much more difficulty dealing with the reality of freedom in general and with freedom in the church than have mainline Protestant churches. In addition, Roman Catholic ecclesiology by its very nature has more tensions in dealing with freedom because of its insistence on the church as a visible society with God-given authority and structure. While the questions of freedom and basic human rights are significant for all churches, this section will be limited to the Roman Catholic Church.[25]

It is also necessary to recognize the complexity involved in concepts such as freedom and human rights. There have been volumes written and even libraries filled on these subjects. Freedom, especially in the sense of freedom from, can never be an absolute in any society or community. By its very nature any society —political, cultural, or social—requires the members to work together for the good of the society. Human society in general and the state or political society in particular certainly cannot absolutize freedom to the exclusion of all other moral concerns and values. This is especially true of the social aspects of freedom which are bound to tread on the freedom of others. Libertarians do tend to absolutize the reality of freedom, but they recognize that limitations on individual freedom are necessary precisely because of the freedom of others. The United States has traditionally taken great pride in its support of human freedoms, but even religious freedom in the United States is limited. The United States does not allow Mormons to practice their belief in polygamy. The children of Jehovah's Witnesses who need blood transfusions are legally taken away from their parents who oppose such transfusions so that they can obtain blood. Recently the Supreme Court declared that one had no absolute right to be free from work on one's religious days of observance. If freedom and even religious freedom are limited in secular society, freedom and religious freedom will be more limited in religious societies or more specifically in Christian churches. Here there are also "limits" on the content of belief. The Christian church is the community of disciples of Jesus who believe in the gospel message. There are certain limits to what it means to belong to the Christian church. One is not free to deny certain beliefs and be Christian. At the same time, however, Christians as members of churches have many freedoms that should be protected. The Christian tradition itself has frequently appealed to the important Pauline notion of Christian freedom, but again no one holds that Christian freedom can be a justification to believe or to do whatever one might want.

The concept of basic human rights is likewise complex and has received great attention in recent years. Human rights is not a univocal term. Mention has

---

[25]For some discussion of the question of rights within Protestant churches, see U. Scheuner, "Les droits de l'homme à l'intérieur des Églises protestantes," *Revue d'histoire et de philosophie religieuses*, vol. 58, no. 3 (1978), pp. 379-397; Norbert Greinacher, " 'For Freedom Christ Has Set Us Free,' " *Cross Currents* 31 (Summer, 1981): 185-193; Patrick J. Cogan, "The Protection of Ecclesial Rights in Other Churches: An Ecumenical Survey," forthcoming the *The Jurist*.

already been made of the different understandings of human rights in liberal, socialist, and Third World countries. David Hollenbach distinguishes three different aspects of rights—personal, social, and instrumental, which would apply to all the different content matter of rights—religious, economic, political, etc.[26] Again, I do not think, especially in the area of social rights in practice, that one can speak of absolute or exceptionless rights. Here, too, in the social area my rights might conflict with the rights of others.[27] Thus in any discussion of freedom and human rights it is necessary to underline the complexity of the concepts involved and to recognize that one cannot absolutize freedom, nor can one absolutize rights in the social area.

In a true sense one can use the categories of freedom and human rights as tools to deal with very many of the tensions being experienced in the Roman Catholic Church today. Most of the internal problems experienced in the church stem from the tension between authority and freedom. What is the proper use of authority, and what are proper roles of freedom? There will always be some tension between authority, understood in the sense of a God-given authority entrusted to the church and in a specific way to certain office holders in the church, and the freedom of the believers. However, it is possible to reduce these tensions.

From a theoretical viewpoint many contemporary Catholic theologians have attempted to rethink authority in the church in order to avoid the dangers of an over-authoritarianism which characterized pre-Vatican II Catholicism. The Constitution on Divine Revelation of the Second Vatican Council (par. 10) recognizes that teaching authority in the church serves the word of God and is governed by it: "This teaching office is not above the word of God but serves it, teaching only what has been handed on. . . ." Often in the past the question of authoritative church teaching was understood in two terms—authoritative church teaching and the conscience of the individual. Now the proper understanding requires a third term—the word of God, which both the authoritative church teaching office and the conscience of the believer, in different ways, try to discern.

A traditional Thomistic notion of authority also supports the above understanding. The Thomistic tradition has maintained an intrinsic and realistic approach which proposes that something is commanded because it is good. An extrinsic approach is voluntaristic and maintains something is good because it is commanded. For Aquinas, to command is to move another through intellect and will. Blind obedience has no place in a Thomistic understanding. Authority must conform itself to truth and not the other way around.[28]

---

[26]David Hollenbach, *Claims in Conflict: Retrieving and Renewing the Catholic Human Rights Tradition* (New York: Paulist Press, 1979), pp. 95-100.

[27]John Langan, "Defining Human Rights: A Revision of the Liberal Tradition," in Hennelly and Langan, *Human Rights in the Americas*, pp. 69-101.

[28]Jean-Marie Aubert, *Loi de Dieu, lois des hommes* (Tournai: Desclée, 1964).

A renewed ecclesiology shows that the church is primarily the community of believers. All the baptized share in the threefold office of Jesus as priest, teacher, and sovereign. In addition to the role of all believers there is also the hierarchical role and function in the service of the community. Thus, for example, in terms of the teaching office in the church, the hierarchical teaching office is not totally identical with the whole teaching function in the church. The older distinction between the *Ecclesia docens* and the *Ecclesia discens* cannot be maintained today. The relationship of the hierarchical teaching office to the total church is much more complex than it was often thought to be in the past.

Contemporary Catholic eschatology stresses the imperfection of all existing reality in light of the fullness of the reign of God. These eschatological considerations have affected the understanding of the church itself. The church is not the reign or kingdom of God as was taught in Catholic theology before Vatican II. The reign of God is much broader than the church, and the church always stands in judgment under the fullness of the reign of God. Future eschatological fullness reminds those existing in the present of the imperfection of all reality including the church. The church is no longer thought of as a perfect society but as a pilgrim community.

Epistemological considerations indicate that the search for truth is much more complicated and arduous than was assumed to be the case in the past. Historical consciousness, with its emphasis on the particular, the individual, and the contingent, has replaced an older classicism which stressed the eternal, the immutable, and the unchanging. Historical consciousness, properly understood, charts a middle course between classicism and sheer existentialism. Historical consciousness involves a more tentative epistemology and recognizes the role and importance of more inductive methodologies. One of the most startling statements accepting historical consciousness is found in *Octogesima adveniens*, the letter of Paul VI issued in 1971 on the eightieth anniversary of Leo XIII's groundbreaking encyclical *Rerum novarum*:

> In the face of such widely varying situations it is difficult for us to utter a unified message and to put forward a solution which has universal validity. Such is not our ambition, nor is it our mission. It is up to the Christian communities to analyze with objectivity the situation which is proper to their own country, to shed on it the light of the Gospel's unalterable words and to draw principles of reflection, norms of judgment and directions for action from the social teaching of the church.[29]

Historical consciousness recognizes the existence of and need for theological pluralism. No longer can there be the perennial theology and philosophy as the only way of trying to understand God's saving truth. Naturally there are limits

---

[29]*Octogesima adveniens*, par. 4, in O'Brien and Shannon, *Renewing the Earth*, pp. 353, 354.

to pluralism, but there is also the need to recognize and even promote theological pluralism in the church.

All these factors have influenced the theoretical understanding of authority in the Catholic Church and of teaching authority in particular. The concept of infallibility has been challenged by a few and reinterpreted by many, but infallibility as such does not have much practical significance in the daily life of the members of the church. In the more practically significant area of authoritative or authentic noninfallible teaching, there does exist the possibility of dissent within the church. Many people in reality are acting on the basis of such dissent so that it is having a practical effect on the life of the church. However, at the present time the hierarchical office holders in the church have been very reluctant in any way to accept and countenance the reality of dissent.

In accord with Catholic ecclesiology there are two levels to every question concerning the church—the theoretical understanding and the institutional and practical structures corresponding to the theoretical understanding. Official church teaching itself and contemporary theologians have proposed many newer understandings of the role of the church and of church authority, but there has been little or no change in ecclesial structures to correspond with this theoretical change.

Catholic social teaching in its attempt to favor both personalism and communitarianism, while avoiding the dangers of individualism and collectivism, has insisted on the importance of the principle of subsidiarity. According to this principle the higher and more centralized structures are a *subsidium* or help to do those things that cannot be done adequately on lower and less centralized bureaucratic levels.[30] The theoretical understanding of the church as the people of God involving a community of equals in the discipleship of Jesus with special teaching, ruling, and sanctifying offices which exist on local, regional, national, and worldwide levels provides the basis for the application of the principle of subsidiarity throughout the life of the church. Unfortunately, there are few structural modifications involving the principle of subsidiarity even in the new Code of Canon Law which has just been promulgated for the Latin Church. Authority remains highly centralized and without mechanisms geared to institutionalize the newer theological understandings.[31]

One important theoretical aspect of subsidiarity as applied to the church is

---

[30]For a contemporary understanding and use of this principle, see U.S. Bishops' Pastoral (First Draft), "Catholic Social Teaching and the U.S. Economy," *Origins* 14 (November 15, 1984): 355 ff.

[31]Before the publication of the new Code of Canon Law, severe criticisms were made of the proposed *Lex Fundamentalis*, which was never promulgated, as such. However, many of those criticisms are still applicable to the new Code itself. See Canon Law Society of America Task Force Subcommittee on the *Lex Fundamentalis*, "A General Analysis of the Proposed Schema on the *Lex Fundamentalis*," *Canon Law Society of America Proceedings* 32 (1970): 29-46; "A Critique of the Revised Schema of the *Lex Fundamentalis*," *Canon Law Society of America Proceedings* 33 (1971): 65-77; Giuseppe Alberigo et al., *Legge e Vangelo: Discussione su una Legge fondamentale per la Chiesa* (Brescia: Paideia, 1972).

the principle of collegiality involving the college of bishops functioning together. National and regional conferences of bishops are one institutional illustration of collegiality, but they have been very limited in what they can do. The Synod of Bishops is another instrumentality created after Vatican II, but the Synods that have taken place have been heavily controlled by Rome and have not really been a free exercise of collegial participation by the college of bishops throughout the world. Collegiality is badly in need of structures which can make it a reality. It is probably safe to say that true collegiality will not exist until a group of bishops can publicly express their differences with the Bishop of Rome, who holds the Petrine office in the church. The gross inadequacies of the structures set up to mirror subsidiarity and collegiality well illustrate the fact that church structures are badly needed to carry out the theoretical understandings agreed upon at Vatican II, to say nothing of further theological developments. In this connection it is important to recall that structures will never resolve the tensions totally, for there will always be a tension between saving truth and freedom, between church community and individual liberty. In addition, perfect structures can never exist. However, at the present time all must acknowledge that the existing structures are woefully inadequate in mediating even the theological understandings already recognized in official Catholic teaching.

Just as freedom in the church can be a way of dealing with most of the major problems facing the internal life of the church today, so the language of rights can be used as an instrument to deal with the major tensions facing the contemporary church. Rights language is the strongest ethical language that exists precisely because it makes a claim on other people to do something. Value language, for example, is not nearly as strong. It is not surprising that in the contemporary church people are using the language of rights to make their claims. Thus, for example, the Charter of the Rights of Catholics in the Church speaks about the right to dissent, the right for all to embrace marriage or celibacy, the right to decide in conscience the size of families and the appropriate method of family planning, the rights of the divorced and remarried to the sacraments, the right of Catholic women to the exercise of all the powers of the church, etc. Basically this document uses the format of the charter of rights to propose a blueprint for how the church should be renewed.[32] It is impossible to deal adequately with such a charter in one scholarly article, for one would have to examine individually each of the rights proposed. Thus it is possible to use the concepts of freedom and of human rights to deal with most of the internal questions facing the church today. This study can only point out some of the theological changes that have occurred and the lack of existing structures to mediate

---

[32]Association for the Rights of Catholics in the Church, *Charter of the Rights of Catholics in the Church*. This pamphlet is available from the Association c/o Dr. Leonard Swidler, Religion Dept. (022-28), Temple University, Philadelphia, PA 19122. For some similar statements, see Greinacher, "For Freedom," and Norbert Greinacher and Inge Jens, eds., *Freiheitsrechte für Christen? Warum die Kirche ein Grundgesetz braucht* (Munich: R. Piper, 1980), pp. 39-79.

these newer understandings. There is naturally a difference of opinion on how much should be done, but I have just made the minimum point that even the officially accepted changes in theological understanding have not been fleshed out in appropriate institutional structures.

The remainder of this study will concentrate on the question of the fundamental rights of members of the Catholic Church.[33] The new Code of Canon Law has a section on the fundamental rights and obligations of Catholics.[34] By its definition a list of fundamental rights or a bill of rights does not intend to be a detailed spelling out of all rights or a blueprint for governing the entire society. The first part of this study has mentioned the Universal Declaration of Human Rights of the United Nations, which contains only thirty articles. Many countries have adopted similar rights in their own constitutions.

As pointed out in the first part, Roman Catholicism has become a staunch supporter of human dignity, human freedom, and fundamental human rights in the political and social orders. "Justice in the World," the document of the 1971 Synod of Bishops, stressed the mission of the church in defending and promoting the dignity, freedom, and fundamental rights of human beings. The church itself must first strive to be just in its own community if it is to preach justice to others. This document then examines the modes of acting and lifestyle of the church and proposes what could be called a bill of rights for members of the church. Within the church, rights must be preserved—the right to a decent wage, rights of women to a share of responsibility and participation, right to suitable freedom of expression, rights of the accused, right to some share in determining and deciding what is done.[35]

The 1974 Synod of Bishops reiterated the same basic message. The church recognizes that its mission on behalf of promoting human rights in the world obliges it to a constant examination and an increasing purification of its own life, legislation, structures, and plan of action. Within the church itself violations

---

[33]There is also a large bibliography dealing with this subject, including the following: James A. Coriden, ed., *We, The People of God . . . : A Study of Constitutional Government for the Church* (Huntington, IN: Our Sunday Visitor, 1968); James A. Coriden, ed., *The Case for Freedom: Human Rights in the Church* (Washington, DC: Corpus, 1969); Johannes Neumann, *Menschenrechte—Auch in der Kirche?* (Zurich: Benziger, 1976); Greinacher and Jens, *Freiheitsrechte*; Eugenio Corecco et al., eds., *Les droits fondamentaux du chrétien dans l'Église et dans la société* (Fribourg: Éditions Universitaires, 1981). This last volume of 1328 pages is the proceedings of the Fourth International Congress of Canon Law, held in Fribourg in 1980. Helpful articles include the following: James A. Coriden, "Human Rights in the Church: A Matter of Credibility and Authenticity," in Alois Müller and Norbert Greinacher, eds., *The Church and the Rights of Man*. Concilium 124 (New York: Seabury Press, 1979); Frederick R. McManus, "Human Rights in the Church," in Falconer, *Understanding Human Rights*, pp. 114-132; James H. Provost, "Ecclesial Rights," *Canon Law Society of America Proceedings* 44 (1982): 41-62.
[34]*Codex Iuris Canonici* (Vatican City: Editrice Vaticana, 1983); *The Code of Canon Law: In English Translation* (Grand Rapids, MI: Eerdmans, 1983), canons 208-223.
[35]O'Brien and Shannon, *Renewing the Earth*, p. 400.

of human rights must be denounced.[36] There are other official church documents which make the same basic point.[37]

In light of this background one can only be astounded at what is found under the rubric "The Obligations and Rights of All Christian Faithful" embracing canons 208-223 in Book II of the new Code of Canon Law. The fundamental rights presented there are totally inadequate. The rights and obligations are mixed together in the space of sixteen canons. There are eighteen different rights which are mentioned in this section, but the inadequacies of the section on rights are glaring and manifold.

First of all there is a tendency to avoid as much as possible any mention of freedom. The first canon (208) asserts an equality with regard to dignity and action in the church, but no mention is made of the freedom of the Christian. Freedom appears only twice in these canons (215 and 278), dealing with freely founding associations and the freedom of inquiry for scholars. Freedom must play a much more central role in the theoretical understanding of the rights of Christians, to say nothing about the practical implementation of these rights. From a uniquely Christian perspective, Christian freedom is an important part of the faith tradition. Granted, as has been frequently stressed in these pages, freedom cannot be absolutized and can surely be abused, but it cannot be forgotten or left out. One of the primary functions of the church and its laws is to protect, defend, empower, and encourage true Christian freedom.

From the viewpoint of human rights, recent Catholic social teaching has emphasized basic human rights, grounding them in the dignity of the human person and stressing the fundamental importance of the freedom of the human person. However, in the section on fundamental rights in the Code of Canon Law, the freedom of the believer in the church is hardly mentioned. There seems to be a great fear of even using the word "freedom." Compare the approach to freedom found in the fundamental rights of Christians in the new Code with the role of freedom in a report on due process received by the American bishops in 1969 from a committee of the Canon Law Society of America. The Bishops' Conference recommended that the procedures found in this document be used by individual bishops in their dioceses. In their resolution the bishops maintained that, "The promotion of adequate protection of human rights and freedoms within the church is central to the bishops' role of service to the people of God."[38] This report begins with a preamble proposing the "conviction that all persons in the church are fundamentally equal in regard to their common rights

---

[36]1974 Synod of Bishops, "Statement on Human Rights and Reconciliation," *Origins* 4 (November 7, 1974): 318, 319.

[37]Jean Bernhard, "Les droits fondamentaux dans la perspective de la *Lex fundamentalis* et de la revision du Code de Droit Canonique," in Corecco, *Droits fondamentaux*, pp. 374-376.

[38]*On Due Process* (Washington, DC: National Conference of Catholic Bishops, 1969), p. 2.

and freedoms," and then spells out what could be called a bill of rights, specifically indicating the fundamental rights and freedoms of people in the church.[39]

Second, the enunciation of the fundamental rights in this section of the new Code is severely weakened by mixing together rights and duties and by qualifying the rights to such an extent that they fail to serve their real purpose. For example, the first canon (208) speaks about the genuine equality of all in the church, but it quickly adds a reference to inequality based on condition and office in the church. The second canon in the series (209) states the obligation to preserve communion with the church at all times. The fifth canon (212) calls for obedience to the sacred pastors.

Compare this approach with the enumeration of the rights of the members of the church given by the 1971 Synod of Bishops and with the enumeration of human rights in general given by Pope John XXIII in *Pacem in terris*. In both cases the rights are not mixed together with obligations, and the rights are not qualified and limited. Unfortunately, the framers of the new Code are out of tune with other church documents. In addition, the framers of the new Code did not take to heart the criticism made by a committee of the Canon Law Society of America concerning the first draft of rights proposed for a fundamental law of the church in 1969. This committee pointed out the excessive limitations and qualifications of the rights proposed in the original schema.[40]

Third, this section of the Code basically relies upon a pre-Vatican II ecclesiology which sees the church primarily as a hierarchical structure and not as the people of God. The basic dignity, freedom, equality, and participative rights of all must first be stressed. In the Code there are later sections on laity, clerics, bishops, religious, etc. These distinctions should not be brought into an explanation of what is common to all in the church. It is more than ironic that the very last canon in the section (223) maintains that ecclesiastical authority is entitled to regulate, in view of the common good, the exercise of rights which are proper to Christ's faithful. The ecclesiology at work in this section prevents it from being a declaration of the fundamental rights and freedoms of all believers in the church. By bringing into this section the hierarchical differences within the church, the framers have also logically called for many limitations on the rights mentioned.

Fourth, the final version of fundamental rights proclaimed in the new code is even more disappointing because it is actually a regression from what was found in the schema proposed in 1977.[41] For example, canon 17 in the proposed schema ruled out discrimination on the basis of descent, nationality, social condition, or sex; but there is no explicit mention of this in the new Code. Canon

---

[39]Ibid., pp. 4, 5.

[40]*Canon Law Society of America Proceedings* 32 (1970): 39.

[41]*Schema Canonum Libri II: De Populo Dei* (Vatican City: Vatican Polyglot Press, 1977). A translation was made in English and widely circulated by the National Conference of Catholic Bishops.

34 in the 1977 schema recognized the possible abuse of authority and power in the church and assured the faithful a proper redress. There is no mention of the abuse of authority in this section of the new Code. Also the earlier schema in canon 36 spelled out some of the due-process procedures which should be found in the church—the right to know the names of one's accusers, the right to hear the reasons for judgments given. These are not mentioned in the section of the new Code. It should be noted that even the 1977 schema does not mention the right not to incriminate oneself. Note, too, that the 1977 schema does not contain a final canon affirming that ecclesiastical authority is to regulate the exercise of all these rights.

Fifth, from a practical viewpoint, the most serious flaw in this section on rights is the failure to mention enlarged possibilities of administrative courts in the case of the violation of rights. The reason for this lack in this section is the fact that in the section on processes in the seventh book of the new Code there is no mention of the existence of administrative tribunals. All the preliminary schemata had provided for the possibility of such administrative tribunals on the diocesan, regional, and national levels, but the new Code left them out.[42]

The administrative tribunals were originally proposed as an easily available remedy for the violation of rights by administrative action. The 1969 report of a committee of the Canon Law Society of America dealing with due process pointed out that it is the administrative area of church governance which has lately experienced the greatest growth. Think, for example, of the creation of many new governing boards, departments, and agencies to supplement the bishop's personal administrative activities. Examples of these recent developments include personnel boards, liturgical commissions, parish councils, etc. Here the rights of many people need to be protected. In the old Code the only recourse against administrative decisions of bishops was to the Sacred Congregations in Rome, but such a process rendered such recourse practically unavailable to most people. To protect the rights of the faithful the American bishops, on the recommendation of the committee of the Canon Law Society, urged that individual bishops adopt the procedures proposed for conciliation (mediated dialogue), for arbitration (voluntary referral to an impartial referee), and for better ways of structuring administrative decisions in order to avoid unjust actions before they occur. The report also looked forward to the coming into existence of administrative tribunals in the forthcoming Code of Canon Law.[43]

The American canonists at that time and canonists in general until the final appearance of the new Code had every reason to believe that such administrative

---

[42]For a complete discussion of administrative tribunals, see Kevin Matthews, *The Development and Future of the Administrative Tribunal*, which is published in its entirety in *Studia Canonica*, vol. 18 (1984), pp. 1-233. Also see Thomas E. Molloy, "Administrative Recourse in the Proposed Code of Canon Law," *Canon Law Society of America Proceedings* 44 (1982): 263-273.

[43]*On Due Process*, pp. 11-15.

tribunals would be sanctioned by the new Code. The commission for the revision of the Code and the Synod of Bishops in 1967 called for the new Code to set up a series of administrative tribunals in the church and to evolve proper canonical procedures at each level for the protection of rights.[44] Pope Paul VI mentioned in 1977 that the new Code would have administrative tribunals. All the proposed schemata before the final version of the Code included provisions for these administrative tribunals. Their absence in the final document greatly weakens the practical defense of rights in the church.

One of the advantages of these administrative tribunals would be to recognize in practice the existence of the separation of powers so that an independent judiciary would function. The separation of powers has been looked upon as essential to real due process. Too often in the past on the local level the bishop has been both legislator or administrator and judge. Due process requires that the authority in question be subject to independent judicial review. One of the many criticisms of the present inadequate procedures of the Congregation for the Doctrine of the Faith in dealing with theologians whose writings are suspect is that the Congregation is both the accuser and the judge.[45]

This analysis shows the very inadequate nature of the fundamental rights of members of the church found in the new Code of Canon Law. Our analysis also bears out the suspicion raised in the first part of the study about the hesitancy to recognize freedom and its protection as an important value in the church. Recall that in the discussion on religious liberty there was a tendency on the part of some to base the argument for the existence of religious liberty on the nature of civil constitutional government, and not on theological and ethical values of freedom as such. Such an approach in itself can imply, and can be used by others to maintain, that such freedoms and rights should not be found in the church. In light of this reluctance, it is necessary to indicate why freedom and basic human rights must be found in the church too.[46]

The argument is heard that the church is a different type of society from the state. Freedom and fundamental rights exist in the state to protect the individual from the power of the state, but the church is a community which cannot be adversarial to the good of the individual members. Others maintain that the church by its very nature is an authoritative society understood as the authority of God shared by human beings. Such an understanding of the church is incompatible with the recognition of the freedoms of its members. However, these reasons in my judgment do not deny the need for legitimate freedom and its protection in the church.

Freedom is not just a secular value but is a truly Christian and human value. The freedom of the Christian is a very important Christian concept developed

---

[44]*Communicationes*, vol. 2 (1969), pp. 82, 83.
[45]Paulus VI, "Ad Praelatos Auditores et Officiales Tribunalis Sacrae Romanae Rotae," *Acta Apostolicae Sedis* 69 (1977): 152.
[46]Neumann, *Menschenrechte*, pp. 126-153.

especially by St. Paul. Freedom and liberation are important Christian realities which should have ramifications in all areas of the Christian's existence. The concept of freedom in civil societies is not based primarily on the nature of the state but rather on the dignity of the human person. Baptism and membership in the church do not take away one's basic human dignity and all that flows from it. The Catholic theological tradition has rightly given great importance to the human and in fact sees the Christian not as destroying the human but rather as the fulfillment of the human. Whatever is rooted in the dignity of the human person must be respected in the church.

It is true that civil political society and the church are not exactly the same. What is true and proper for the state will not necessarily be true and proper for the church. However, there is an analogy between the two and not total opposition. Since freedom and fundamental rights are based on human dignity, they must be found in both the church and the state—but in somewhat different ways. A contemporary Catholic ecclesiology no longer sees the church primarily as a hierarchical pyramid but as the people of God. The hierarchical office is at the service of the community of equal disciples. Within the church there can readily be abuses of power, and the members of the church need to be protected against such possible abuses. As discussed above, freedom is never an absolute, but the church must acknowledge and protect the freedom and the fundamental human rights that flow from the dignity of the human person. Official church statements in the area of social justice have recognized the need for freedom and basic human rights in the church, but for some reason these realities are not present in the new Code of Canon Law to the extent that they should be.

In conclusion, four basic steps are necessary to insure that the church and its law recognize and protect fundamental human rights and freedom in the church. More work needs to be done on all these levels, but this study has tried to make some contribution to this ongoing task.

The first step is to insist on the need for and importance of such freedom and rights in the church. The second step is to elucidate the proper grounding and basis for ecclesial rights. In my judgment, such rights should be based on the dignity of the human person as known through reason, experience, and revelation and on the fact of baptism.[47] The third step is to develop a theoretical model of what the fundamental rights of church members should be. Since other authors and groups have proposed such models, the present study did not go into this important task. Fourth, practical procedures must be put in place to institutionalize and protect these fundamental ecclesial rights.

In summary, this study has addressed the problem of religious freedom and human rights from some Christian perspectives. The first part indicated how the mainline Protestant and Catholic traditions gradually came to accept religious

---

[47]There has been much discussion about the grounding or basis of human rights for the Christian. For a summary and analysis of the literature in this area, see Gustave Thils, *Droits de l'homme et perspectives chrétiennes* (Louvain-la-Neuve: E. Peeters, 1981), pp. 49-96.

liberty, but only after the concept came to the fore through other agencies. This historical analysis might indicate some ways in which the struggles for religious freedom in our contemporary world can be helped. The second part moved from the area of the world to the area of the church and concentrated on how the Roman Catholic Church in its internal life tries to deal with the freedom and basic human rights of its members.

Charles E. Curran (Roman Catholic) is Professor of Moral Theology at the Catholic University of America, where he has taught since 1965 (following four years' teaching at St. Bernard's Seminary, Rochester, NY). He is a priest of the Diocese of Rochester. He holds a B.A. from St. Bernard's; an S.T.L. and S.T.D. (1961) from the Pontifical Gregorian University, Rome; and an S.T.D. with specialization in moral theology (1961) from the Academia Alfonsiana, Rome. He has served as president of the Catholic Theological Society of America and of the Society of Christian Ethics, and was the first recipient of the John Courtney Murray Award of the C.T.S.A. in 1972, for distinguished achievement in theology. Among his fourteen books are *Christian Morality Today* (Fides, 1966), *Catholic Moral Theology in Dialogue* (Fides, 1972; Univ. of Notre Dame Press, 1976, paper), *American Catholic Social Ethics: Twentieth-Century Approaches* (Univ. of Notre Dame Press, 1982), and *Critical Concerns in Moral Theology* (Univ. of Notre Dame Press, 1984). He and Richard A. McCormick have edited four volumes of *Readings in Moral Theology* for Paulist Press, 1979-84. He has lectured throughout the U.S. and abroad and has published numerous scholarly articles in English and the major European languages.

RELIGIOUS LIBERTY IN JUDAISM

Jacob B. Agus

I

Some two centuries ago, Moses Mendelssohn, the renowned Jewish philosopher, asked his friend, Christian Dohm, to present the case for the emancipation of Jewish people in the lands of Western Europe. Dohm complied with this request and wrote an excellent report, which expressed the liberal philosophy of the Enlightenment.[1] Mendelssohn appreciated the work of his friend, but he took exception to Dohm's suggestion that the Jewish community should have the right to excommunicate and expel those who disagree with or dissent from the practices of the community. A faith community must be allowed the latitude to legislate for itself and to impose its sanctions and disciplinary measures upon its own members. Mendelssohn disputed Dohm's contention on the ground that religion can only persuade, educate, and inspire, but it must not resort to force. In his work, *Jerusalem*, Mendelssohn expounded his thesis in detail, setting forth the liberal thesis that religion is an expression of humanity's inner life; hence, it cannot be subject to external manipulations.[2]

Mendelssohn's position was reinforced by a series of Jewish thinkers who identified themselves with the position of the European liberals. In fact, an alliance was forged between Jewish intellectuals and the international liberals, which at times went beyond the boundaries of philosophy and overflowed into the realm of politics and social relations. Not all Jewish thinkers agreed with Mendelssohn's vision of the future of the Jewish community. From time to time, the Zionist position was articulated as a possible alternative to the liberal view that the rights of the individual Jew were paramount.

Spinoza (1632-1677) was the first modernist thinker to suggest that the national aspect of Jewish life might be reasserted. He maintained that the establishment of a Jewish state in Palestine was a viable proposition.[3] In fact, there were two different versions of the Messianic era, ever since Maimonides in the twelfth century presented in his code a nonsupernaturalist interpretation of the coming of the Messiah: There will be no change in the laws of nature, but a scion of the House of David will arise to found a Jewish state in Palestine, gather the exiles, compel the people to follow the laws of Moses, rebuild the Holy Temple,

---

[1]Christian Dohm, *Über die bürgerliche Verbesserung der Juden* (Berlin, 1781).

[2]Moses Mendelssohn, *Jerusalem, or On Religious Power and Jerusalem*, tr. Allan Arkush. Intro. and commentary by Alexander Altmann (Hanover and London: University Press of New England [for Brandeis University], 1983).

[3]Baruch Spinoza, *Theologico-Political Treatise*, tr. R. W. Elwes (Dover Publications), ch. 4, p. 56.

reinstitute the schedule of public and private burnt offerings, reestablish the priestly gifts, establish a Sanhedrin, etc.

Nahmanides, a thirteenth-century Kabbalist, subscribed to the opposite view —the resurrection of the dead will take place at the time of the Messiah. The righteous will acquire an exalted body, which will not be subject to the ills of "flesh and blood." Even in this familiar physical world, there operates a "miraculous providence," side by side with the natural order. In the World to Come (*olam haba*) the miraculous order will come to predominate, culminating in the fulfillment of all human and Jewish hopes. Nahmanides promoted the mystical version of Judaism. So, every religious revival within Judaism would lead to a resurgence of interest in migrating to and settling in the Holy Land.[4]

The forerunners of modern Zionism were generally humanists, dedicated to the redemption of humanity as well as the salvation of the Jewish people. Some came from the socialist camp, for example, Moses Hess.[5] Some came from the ranks of nationalistic rebirth—such as Joseph Salvador.[6] George Elliot's novel *Daniel Deronda* was quite influential in the nineteenth century. The most enduring impetus was given to the Zionist movement by its founder, Dr. Theodore Herzl, at the turn of the nineteenth century. He was a liberal, not only in politics, but in all spheres of life: Reason and justice are capable of solving every problem. In him, liberalism as a cultural-social posture was united with Zionism. So, too, Labor Zionism blended the socialist-liberal ideal with the Zionist goal.[7]

Coming down to our times, the dialogue movement within Israel must proceed along two levels—*within* the Jewish and Arab camps and *between* the Jewish and Arab camps. Essential to both kinds of dialogue is a modicum of trust in the good will of the leaders in the opposite camp.

Insofar as the Jewish camp is concerned, there is ample justification for trust in the liberal movement. For two centuries the alliance between leading Jews and liberalism proved its strength and endurance.[8]

The term "liberalism" is here employed to designate a basic approach to reality, not a political, philosophical, or theological attitude. It refers to a belief in rationality and morality and openness to the revelation of saving ideals in the course of history. It is not devoid of mysticism, since it assumes that new and creative wonders of human nature are due to emerge in the course of evolution. A balanced liberalism is not contemptuous of the positive role played by religious movements in the maintenance of a stable emotional and psychological equilibrium in human affairs. The issue centers around the location of the in-

---

[4]H. D. Shevel and Mosad Horav Kook, eds., *Kitvai Rubenu Moshe ben Naḥman* (Jerusalem, 1963). Torat hashem Temima, p. 153.
[5]Moses Hess, *Rome and Jerusalem: A Study in Jewish Nationalism*, tr. Meyer Waxman (New York: Bloch Publishing Co., 1945).
[6]Joseph Salvador, *La loi de Moise*, etc. (1822).
[7]Dov Boruchow, theoretician of Poalai Zion Party, later known as Mapai.
[8]I. Friedlander, *Dubnow's Theory of Jewish Nationalism* (New York, 1905).

effable dimension. Is it in the emergence of human freedom and rationality? Or is it in the mystical tradition of myths and symbols?

II

Moses Mendelssohn joined the European liberals in defending the thesis that the emergence of freedom in history reflects the operation of the Divine Being. The philosophy of Henri Bergson in the first three decades of the twentieth century was a massive achievement of synthesis, comparable to the work of Aristotle in the ancient world and that of Maimonides in the twelfth century and Aquinas in the thirteenth century. Bergson completed his vision of "creative evolution" in the mid-1930's.[9] His philosophy contrasted the "open society" of democracy with the "closed societies" of the Communist and Fascist varieties. Pierre Teilhard de Chardin presented a Catholic revision of Bergsonism, reconciling the impetus of the biblical Hebrew prophets with the labors of Catholic mystics. Jacques Maritain contributed an intellectual emphasis to the Bergson-Chardin view of the triumphant advance of freedom in evolution and in history. Thus, pluralism was vindicated, and the concept of a free society was reinstated.

III

Now that the state of Israel is emerging from the shadows of mysticism into the light of freedom, which principles are likely to prevail in Israel—those of freedom or those of obedience to *Halackha*? Both principles are deeply rooted in the history of the Jewish people. Freedom is exemplified in the description of the Covenant at Sinai. All the people, whatever their rank, stood together, inspired by the same ideals. In the Midrash, we read that the Ten Commandments were spoken in the second person singular to indicate that the revelation was understood by each person "in accordance with his/her capacity."[10] Still, they voluntarily accepted a law which touched many aspects of their lives. The polarity of law and freedom determined the quality of Jewish life, preserving the Jewish community even in the lands of exile and allowing room for devotion and piety to make themselves felt in the life of the individual.

In Maccabees III we read of the Jews of Alexandria, Egypt. They were assembled in a vast hippodrome on the charge of separatism. They were threatened with an attack by drunken elephants—a fate which was averted when the elephants turned against their riders. Thereupon the loyal Jews, who abided by the dietary laws, implored their Ptolemaic soverign to give them the right to

---

[9]Henri Bergson, *The Two Sources of Morality and Religion*, tr. R. Ashley Audra and Cloudesley Brereton (New York: H. Holt and Co., 1935).
[10]Midrash Rabba, Exodus 28:6; 29:1.

punish their compatriots who violated the dietary laws.[11] This incident was characteristic of the practice of Jewish people in the Diaspora. The right to punish transgressors of Mosaic law was essential to the safeguarding of autonomy. The Mishna tells of the execution of a person who rode on a horse on the Sabbath, "in the days of the Greeks." It then cites the general principle "not that the law called for capital punishment in this case, but that the times demanded stringency in the application of the Law."[12]

During the long centuries of the medieval period, the Diaspora communities in the Christian and Muslim worlds frequently applied severe physical torture, even the mutilation of limbs, in order to enforce moral principles. For example, in Toledo, the year 1281 C.E. was marked by a wave of religious repentence and social reform. The rabbis and secular leaders called for the appointment of "supervisors in every street and square . . . to keep an eye on their neighbors, reprove them for their trespasses and eliminate wrongdoing."[13] A special effort was launched to expel from the community those who kept Muslim "slave-girls" in their homes. Those who resisted these communal ordinances were punished "by the lash, by cutting off an arm or a leg, and even by death."[14]

IV

Mutual distrust between Jews and Muslims in Israel and in Arab lands is a melancholy fact of life. The Arab and Jewish communities confront each other with their past and their future as well as with their contemporary conflicts. No one can foresee the future, but certain basic mental postures generate certain specific consequences.

For the Arabs, the long association of Jewish policy with liberalism can serve as a persuasive reassurance. While the fundamentalist attitude of the likes of Meir Kahane evokes images of biblical zealotry and hostility to the "peoples of the land," there is a history of two centuries when the Jewish communities built their institutions in keeping with the principles of liberalism—the rights of the individual, the dignity of the citizen, regardless of creed or color.

The Zionist ideal was conceived within the normal framework of free societies. Strong bonds of sentiment and idealism bind the State of Israel to the Jewish communities of the West, especially the United States. Since the Jews of the Diaspora are liberal in large part, the Arabs of Palestine can rest assured that the Reform, Conservative, and modern Orthodox communities will support them whenever the principles of liberalism so dictate.

---

[11]R. H. Charles, III Maccabees 7:10.
[12]B. T. Sanhedrin 46a.
[13]Yitzak Baer, *A History of the Jews in Christian Spain*, vol. 1: *From the Age of Reconquest to the Fourteenth Century*, tr. Louis Schoffman (Philadelphia: Jewish Publication Society of America, 1961), p. 258; Baer quotes from *Gates of Repentance*.
[14]Ibid., p. 261; Baer quotes from a responsum by Rabbi Solomon ibn Adret.

V

Issues of religious liberty arise in two areas—in reference to persons of the same faith and to those of other faiths.

Even fundamentalists may accord liberties to persons of other faiths that they would not grant to members of their own faith communities—on the ground that they are co-responsible for their brothers and sisters in faith but are not responsible for those outside their own faiths. However, generally speaking, liberals with respect to issues *within* the community are likely to act in keeping with their philosophy in regard to issues *between* communities.

The situation of Jewry in the Christian world was exceptional, from the very beginning. The Christian church had to wrestle with the uniqueness of Israel in order to cast light on its own identity and dignity. In Rom. 9-11, Paul dealt with this paradox—Judaism and Christianity belong to the same faith community, yet not entirely so. He takes care to walk on the razor's edge, inclining neither to the negation of Judaism nor to its complete affirmation. At the beginning of the German Enlightenment, Moses Mendelssohn likened this relationship to a two-story building—you cannot demolish the first story without causing the second story to come crashing down.[15]

In brief, paradox is at the heart of religion in society; freedom and self-restraint must go hand in hand.

What can we say of the shape of freedom of religion in Israel? Naturally, we cannot predict the future, but we can take note of the contending ideals, the clashing interests, and the areas in need of accommodation.

Within the Jewish community, there is an Orthodox rabbinate entrenched and determined not to afford recognition to the modern versions of Judaism. The rivalry between Orthodoxy in all of its variations and the Mesorati-Conservative-Reform fellowships is likely to be drawn into the political maelstrom of Israel. As a rule, the Orthodox are less concerned with the democratic cluster of ideals than the Conservative-Reform rabbis and laity. The Orthodox joined the secularists in condemning the "underground Jewish terrorists," but somewhat half-heartedly. They reject the views and policies of Kahane, but they provide recruits for groups of "settlers" in Judea and Samaria. The preaching of intolerance within the Jewish community generates waves of hostility that spread outward, overflowing into relations with the Arab world.[16] Can one gauge the consequence of attempts to demolish the two mosques on the Temple Mount?

Every effort must be made to nourish and cultivate the cultural roots of a democratic society. To this end, the non-Orthodox forces must be mobilized. At the same time, the frustrations and fears of the Orthodox must be addressed.

---

[15]See Charles S. Liebman, *The Religious Component in Israeli Ultra-Nationalism* (Cincinnati: University of Cincinnati Press, 1985).

[16]Yitzak Rabin, *The Rabin Memoirs* (Boston and Toronto: Little, Brown and Co., 1979), p. 333.

What if the Arab population within the present boundaries of Israel threatens to become the majority in the near future? Israel would then lose its special character as the Jewish state. However, if the West Bank and the Gaza strip are not annexed to Israel, then it is hard to see how the security of Israel's boundaries can be maintained. It is harder still to see how the rights of the Palestinian Arabs can be safeguarded.[17]

The problem is not insoluble, but a reasonable solution can be worked out only if the general atmosphere in Israel and in its neighboring land is not inflamed by jingoistic parties. A perspective of the near future is needed that is congenial to both communities and that encourages the upbuilding of mutual trust and tolerance. Such a vision should contain the following elements: a reduction of messianic fervor; a readiness to admit that a unique situation may require an unconventional, unprecedented arrangement, as an alternative to the structure of a nation-state; the vision of a trans-national state, serving not only its own citizens, but also a diaspora of noncitizens that enjoy the rights and endure the burdens of state-building.[18]

VI

The aura of messianism hovers over the State of Israel. Three great religions express their redemptive hopes in their own unique ways. The Jewish vision focuses on the return of the Divine Presence to Zion or Jerusalem. The Messiah is a scion of David. He is the instrument of redemption. Maimonides admits the lack of a consistent exposition of the Messiah's qualifications in our sacred scriptures.

"The king Messiah will arise and return the Kingdom of David to its original stature. He will build the Holy Temple and gather the scattered people of Israel. All the laws of Torah will come to prevail as in the first Kingdom. Sacrifices will be offered, *Shemittah* and the Jubilee years will be observed; as described in the Torah." All those who do not believe in this event and do not wait daily for the coming of the Messiah, do not simply disbelieve the words of some of the prophets—But, they deny the promise of the Torah itself (*Hilkdot Shoftim*-Melokhim, Chapter 11,1,2).

---

[17]Ibid. Rabin discusses the Arab Palestinian problem and the possibility of working out a feasible compromise.

[18]Amon Elon, in *The Israelis: Founders and Sons* (New York, Chicago, San Francisco: Holt, Rinehart and Winston, 1971), sums up his argument as follows: "Steeped in the liberal tradition of nineteenth-century nationalism, most of the early Zionist thinkers clearly envisaged a thoroughly secularized state. . . . In *Altneuland*, [Theodor] Herzl's blueprint for his proposed polity, the leading character, David Litwak, proclaims, 'The New Society is based upon the ideas that are a common product of all civilized people.' In Herzl's text, Litwak's words were immediately applauded warmly by the 'aged Rabbi Samuel.' We now know that on this score, too, Herzl's optimism was unfounded" (p. 328). The Holocaust could hardly have been foreseen in Herzl's day!

"Do not imagine that the King Messiah has to perform miracles, creating new things or revive the dead. It is not so. For R. Akiva was a great sage; yet he and the sages of his day acclaimed the son of Kosiba as the Messiah, until he was killed for sins. . . . The important thing to remember is that the Torah is eternal. Nothing can be added to it or detracted from it" (ibid., 11,4). The messianic hope is a popular creation. It is a more solemn and more solidly based expectation than the explicit articles of the Jewish faith because it is affirmed as an axiom by "all the prophets" and the common people.

A similar situation prevailed in the apostolic Christian community. Various descriptions of the Second Advent may be found in Paul's letters, in the parables relating to the *eschaton* in the book of Revelation and in the apocalyptic literature. But the messianic hope is charged with electric dynamism. To millions of Christians it is the heart of the Christian vision of life, literally a vision of unfolding events that will mark the end of history.

Muslim messianism is also poorly supported by verses from the Qur'an and authentic *hadiths*, but it is deeply grounded in the psyche of the Muslim masses. It is interpreted literally and assumed to be imminent. It looks ahead to a restoration of an ideal society, a mythical reunion of the dream world and reality. The *Mahdi* is always a contemporary personality as well as a second edition, as it were, of Muhammed.[19]

What is the relevance of the messianic aura in its three versions to the attainment of peace and freedom in Israel and its neighboring states? The conflicting images of the Messiah in the three faiths elevates each issue to the stature of a cosmic dispute. If the Messiah walks on a razor's edge between redemption and perdition, any help given to his cause may be of decisive significance for eternity. The stakes are enlarged; passions are inflamed; rationality and equality are abandoned. The galloping "horses of the Apocalypse" move to the foreground of history.

The reinterpretation of the messianic mythology in the three faiths for whom Palestine is the Holy Land will not by itself solve the Palestinian problem, but any attempt to attain a peaceful solution will have to be based upon such a demythologization, for we may assume that any revival of the messianic myth in one religion will awaken similar and opposite slumbering ghosts in the other faiths.

As we have suggested, a nonmessianic vision of the redemptive process must work out a model, a pattern of coexistence, that will allow room for the Diaspora as well as for the central political unit. The ideal of nationalism that emerged out of the French Revolution is in itself insufficient for societies like the Jewish global community. It is also incompatible with the ideal of Christendom and the concepts of the Muslim faith. In each of these cases, there is a "heartland" associated with myths from the past and a Diaspora that relates itself voluntar-

---

[19]Riffat Hassan, "Messianism and Islam," *Journal of Ecumenical Studies* 22 (Spring, 1985): 261-291.

ily to the heartland. The "fulfillment" of the Diaspora individuals consists in sharing the labors of upbuilding the central state and enhancing its quality of life. While the men and women of the Diaspora are attached to one ethnic community in the central state, their dedication should be directed to all the citizens of the central state, and vice versa.

In this perspective, Zionism is an attempt to endow ethnic feeling with the impetus of dedication to spiritual ideals. A special radiance is lent to the ideal of love of neighbor. Because particular citizens of the state do not belong to my ethnic group, I must undertake special efforts to guard their rights and to protect their interests. Because we share in the love of the overall community— citizens of the state and residents of the Diaspora—we are part of one spiritual community.

With this goal in mind, it becomes our duty to begin the process of molding patterns of personal life and a series of institutions that will express the spiritual dimension of religiocultural societies. Can we transform the hostile passions of nation-states to redeeming societies, bound by a chain of loyalties to the ideal of loving our neighbors?

Hard, indeed, is the task. However, our Sages have taught that "the greater the agony, the greater the *reward*." Consider what Arab-Jewish relations might have been had Arab lands welcomed the return of Jews fleeing from the Nazis, and had Zionist organizations launched a sustained effort to assist the Arabs to find their way into the modern world. Even now we must aim far beyond the vision of peace as an interval between wars. A true peace implies an active program for cooperation, not merely coexistence. Such is the call of the hour. Can we heed this call, each according to his or her capacity?

Jacob B. Agus (Jewish) was born in Poland, came to the U.S. as a child, graduated from Yeshiva College and was ordained a rabbi (1935) at the Theological Seminary of Yeshiva University. He has an M.A. and Ph.D. (1939, history and philosophy of religion) from Harvard University. He served as a rabbi in Cambridge, MA; Chicago; Dayton; and, since 1950, at Beth El Congregation, Baltimore, MD. He has been a visiting professor at Temple University, Reconstructionist Rabbinical College, Dropsie University (all Philadelphia), and St. Mary's Ecumenical Graduate Institute (Baltimore). He has served as editorial advisor to Arno Press, as consultant to A. Toynbee's "Reconsiderations" (vol. 12 of *A Study of History*), as a consulting editor of the *Encyclopedia Britannica* from 1956-68 for articles on Judaism and Jewish history, and as an Associate Editor of the *Journal of Ecumenical Studies* since 1978. He has written a number of books in Jewish thought, including French and Spanish translations of several, his most recent being *The Jewish Quest: Essays on Basic Concepts of Jewish Theology* (KTAV, 1983).

RELIGIOUS LIBERTY: A MUSLIM PERSPECTIVE

Mohamed Talbi

I. From Old Relations to a New Context

At the outset we have to remember that the problem of religious liberty as a common human concern and international preoccupation is relatively new. In former times the problem was totally irrelevant. During antiquity all felt that it was natural to worship the deities of their city. It was the task of these deities to protect the house, look after the family, and ensure the welfare of the state. Along with their worshippers they took the rough with the smooth. The deities of Carthage, for example, were by nature the enemies of the deities of Rome. In that context the refusal to worship the deities of the city was felt essentially as an act of disloyalty toward the state.

In the beginning the situation was almost the same in the biblical tradition. In the Bible Yahweh acts as the Hebrews' God. God constantly warns the people not to worship any other deity and to follow the Torah. This people with its one God is also an association of an ethnic entity—the twelve tribes descended from Abraham via Isaac and Jacob—with a land, Israel. The Hebrew community is an ideal prototype of unity: it obeys at one and the same time the *ius sanguinis, loci, et religionis*, the law of blood, place, and religion. It is the perfect proto-type of an ethnically homogeneous community rooted in religion and a land, shaped into a state. In a way, to speak of religious liberty in such a case is liter-ally absurd. There was no choice other than adhering to the state-community, or leaving it. Concretely, Jews who converted to another religion *ipso facto* ceased to belong to their state-community. Thus their conversions were felt as betrayals, and as such they warranted the penalty of death.[1] If we dwell on the case of the Jewish community as a prototype, it is because that case is not without some similarities to the classical Islamic *Ummah* as it has been shaped by traditional theology.

For historical reasons the situation changed completely with the appearance of Christian preaching and the destruction of the Jewish state in 70 c.e. From the beginning Christian preaching was not linked with a state: Jesus ordered his disciples "to render unto Caesar the things which are Caesar's, and unto God the things which are God's" (Mt. 22:21). This revolutionary attempt to dissociate the state and the religion and to ensure the freedom of the individual conscience failed. The time was not yet ripe. Consequently the early Christians and the Jews after 70 c.e. were often considered disloyal subjects by the Roman Empire be-cause of their refusal to pay homage to the deities of their city and of their social

---

[1]See Dt. 13:2-19; and Lev. 24:10-23.

176   Religious Liberty

group. Accordingly they were often treated as rebels, were even called atheists—because they were monotheists! The right to self-determination and religious liberty was denied to them as individuals acting freely in accordance with their consciences.

To make a long story short, let us say that political power and religion preserved more or less, or resumed, their old relations. They needed each other too much. The intolerance of the dominant social group asserted itself everywhere in the world with internal and external wars and many forms of more or less severe discrimination. Of course the Islamic world, though relatively tolerant, was no exception. As everywhere else in the world, human rights have been violated in this area, and it still happens that they are, here and there, more or less overridden. That does not mean, however, as we shall see, that Islam as such authorizes the violation of these fundamental rights.

Now, to avoid looking only on the dark side of things, we should note that our common past was not entirely so sombre and so ugly. We can also cite some brilliant periods of tolerance, respect, comprehension, and dialogue.[2] Nevertheless, we had to wait until the nineteenth century to see freedom of conscience clearly claimed. Political and philosophical liberalism were then in vogue, but in fact what was claimed was not so much the right of freedom of conscience as the right not to believe. Thus the concept of religious liberty unfortunately became synonymous with secularism, agnosticism, and atheism. As a result, a stubborn fight was launched against it as such. For us to deal with the subject honestly and with equanimity, we need to free ourselves of this false identification.

It must be granted that today religious liberty is, as a matter of fact, definitively rooted in our social life. Since the Declaration of Human Rights in 1948, this concept is henceforth an essential part of international law. Moreover, we already live in a pluralistic world, and our world is going to be more and more pluralistic in the near future. I have written elsewhere[3] that each person has the right to be different and that at the same time our planet is already too small for all our ambitions and dreams. In this new world which is expanding rapidly before our eyes there is no longer room for exclusiveness. We have to accept each other as we are. Diversity is the law of our time. Today, by virtue of an increasingly comprehensive and sophisticated mass media, every person is truly the neighbor of every other person.

In our Islamic countries we have since the beginning been in the habit of living side by side with communities of different faiths. It has not been always easy, as some recent events again make painfully clear. However, it is only recently that we have begun to be confronted with secularism. It is now our turn to

[2]See, e.g., R. Caspar, "Les versions arabes du dialogue entre le Catholicos Timothée I et le Calife al-Mahdi (IIe/VIIIe siècle)," *Islamochristiana*, vol. 3 (1977), pp. 107-175.
[3]M. Talbi, "Une Communauté de Communautés: Le droit à la différence et les voies de l'harmonie," *Islamochristiana*, vol. 4 (1978), p. 11.

experience from inside the growth of agnosticism and atheism.[4] We have to be conscious of this overwhelming change in our societies, and accordingly we have to exercise our theological thinking in this new and unprecedented context.

Before going further we must first ask more precisely what religious liberty is. Is it only the right to be an unbeliever? One may indeed say that religious liberty has very often been exclusively identified with atheism. However, this is only one aspect of the question, and from my point of view, a negative one. In fact, religious liberty is basically the right to decide for oneself, without any kind of pressure, fear, or anxiety, whether to believe or not to believe, the right to assume with full consciousness one's destiny—the right, of course, to jettison every kind of faith as superstitions inherited from the Dark Ages, but also the right to espouse the faith of one's choice, to worship, and to bear witness freely. Is this definition in harmony with the Qur'an's basic teachings?

II. The Qur'an's Basic Principles

In my opinion religious liberty is basically grounded, from a qur'anic perspective, first and foremost on the divinely ordered nature of humanity. A human is not just another being among many others. Among the whole range of creatures only humans have duties and obligations. They are exceptional beings. They cannot be reduced to their bodies because, above everything else, humans are spirits, spirits which have been given the power to conceive the Absolute and to ascend to God. If humans have this exceptional power, this privileged position, in creation, it is because God "breathed into him something of His spirit" (Qur'an, XXXII, 9). Of course humans, like all living animals, are material. They have bodies created "from sounding clay, from mud moulded into shape" (Qur'an, XV, 28). But they received the Spirit. They have two sides: a lower side—their clay—and a higher side—the Spirit of God. This higher side, comments A. Yusuf Ali, "if rightly used, would give man superiority over other creatures."[5] Humanity's privileged position in the order of creation is strikingly illustrated in the Qur'an in the scene where the angels are ordered to prostrate themselves before Adam (Qur'an, XV, 29; XXXVIII, 72), the heavenly prototype of humanity. In a way, and provided we keep humanity in its proper place as creature, we may as Muslims, along with the other members of Abraham's spiritual descendants, Jews and Christians, say that humanity was created in God's image. A *hadith* (a saying of the Prophet), although questioned, authorizes this

---

[4]See M. Talbi, "Islam et Occident: Au-delà des affrontements, des ambiguités et des complexes," *Islamochristiana*, vol. 7 (1981), pp. 57-77. A sociological inquiry held recently in Tunisia shows that 5% of the population declare openly that they are atheists, and 15% are indifferent. See A. Hermassi, "*al-Mutaccaf wa-l-faqih*," *Tunisian Review 15-21*, no. 8 (1984), p. 46.

[5]A. Yusuf Ali, *The Holy Qur'an: Text, Translation, and Commentary* (Leicester, U.K.: The Islamic Foundation, 1975), p. 643, n. 1968.

statement. So we can say that on the level of the Spirit all persons, whatever their physical or intellectual abilities and aptitudes may be, are truly equal. They have the same "Breath" of God in them, and by virtue of this "Breath" they have the the ability to ascend to God and to respond freely to God's call. Consequently, they have the same dignity and sacredness, and because of this dignity and sacredness they are fully and equally entitled to enjoy the same right to self-determination on earth and for the hereafter. Thus, from a qur'anic perspective we may say that human rights are rooted in what every human is by nature, and this is by virtue of God's plan and creation. Now it goes without saying that the cornerstone of all human rights is religious liberty, for religion, which is the "explanation of the meaning of life and how to live accordingly," is the most fundamental and comprehensive of human institutions.

It is evident from a Muslim perspective that humanity is not the fruit of mere "chance and necessity."[6] Its creation follows a plan and purpose. Through the "Breath" humanity has received the faculty to be at one with God, and its response, to have a meaning, must be free. The teachings of the Qur'an are clear: humans are privileged beings with "spiritual favours" (Qur'an, XVII, 70); they have not been "created in jest" (Qur'an, XXIII, 115); they have a mission and they are God's "vicegerents on earth" (Qur'an, II, 30). Proceeding from God, with a mission to fulfill, human destiny is ultimately to return to God. "Whoso does right, does it for his own soul; and whoso does wrong, does so to its detriment. Then to your Lord will you all be brought back" (Qur'an, XLV, 15).

For that to happen it is absolutely necessary that each person be able to choose freely and without any kind of coercion. Every person ought in full consciousness to build his or her own destiny. The Qur'an states clearly that compulsion is incompatible with religion: "There should be no compulsion in religion. Truth stands out clear from Error. Whosoever rejects Evil and believes in God hath grasped the most trustworthy hand-hold, that never breaks. God is All-Hearing, All-Knowing" (Qur'an, II, 256).

To the best of my knowledge, among all the revealed texts, only the Qur'an stresses religious liberty in such a precise and unambiguous way: faith, to be true and reliable faith, absolutely needs to be a free and voluntary act. In this connection it is worth stressing that the quoted verse was aimed at reproving and condemning the attitude of some Jews and Christians who, being newly converted to Islam in Madina, were willing to convert their children with them to their new faith.[7] Thus, it is clearly emphasized that faith is an individual concern and commitment and that even parents must refrain from interfering with it. The very nature of faith, as is stressed in the basic text of Islam in clear and indisputable words, is to be a voluntary act born out of conviction and freedom.

---

[6]See Jacques Monod, *Le hasard et la nécessité* (Paris: éd. du Seuil, 1970), wherein the famous biologist develops a materialist point of view.
[7]See Cheikh Si Boubakeur Hamza, *Le Coran: traduction nouvelle et commentaire* (Paris: éd. Fayard-Denoël, 1972), vol. 1, p. 97, who quotes Tabari, Razi, and Ibn Kathir.

In fact, even God refrains from overpowering humans to the point of sub-duing them against their will. This too is clearly expressed in the Qur'an.[8] Faith is then a free gift, God's gift. Humanity can accept or refuse it. It has the capacity to open its heart and its reason to God's gift. A guidance (*hudan*[9]) has been sent it. It is warmly invited to listen to God's call. God warns it in clear and unam-biguous terms. As it is underlined in the cited verse stressing human freedom, "Truth stands out clear from Error." It is up to humanity to make its choice. The human condition—and that is the ransom of humanity's dignity and sacred-ness—is not without something tragic about it. Humans can be misled. They are able to make the wrong choice and to stray from the right path. In a word, they have the capacity to resist God's call, and this capacity is the criterion of their true freedom.

Even the Messenger, whose mission properly is to convey God's call and message, is helpless in such a situation. He is clearly and firmly warned to respect human freedom and God's mystery. "If it had been thy Lord's will, all who are on the earth would have believed, all of them. Wilt thou then compel mankind, against their will, to believe!" (Qur'an, X, 99). A. Yusuf Ali, in his translation of the Qur'an, comments on that verse in this way:

> . . . men of faith must not be impatient or angry if they have to contend against Unfaith, and most important of all, they must guard against the temptation of forcing Faith, i.e., imposing it on others by physical compulsion, or any other forms of compulsion such as social pressure, or inducements held out by wealth or position, or other adventitious advantages. Forced Faith is no faith.[10]

The Apostle's mission—and all the more ours—is stringently restricted to advise, warn, convey a message, and admonish without compelling. He is ordered: "Ad-monish, for thou art but an admonisher. Thou hast no authority to compell them" (Qur'an, LXXXVIII, 21-22). In other words, God has set humanity truly and tragically free. What God wants is, in full consciousness and freedom, a will-ing and obedient response to the divine call, and that is the very meaning of the Arabic word "*Islam*."

Now we must emphasize that this does not mean that we have to adopt an attitude of abandon and indifference. We must in fact avoid both Scylla and Charybdis. First, we must, of course, refrain from interfering in the inner life of others, and we have already stressed this aspect of the problem enough. It is time to add that, secondly, we must also avoid being indifferent to every thing, being careless about others. We need to remember that the other is our neighbor. We must bear witness to and convey God's message. This too needs stressing.

---

[8]See Qur'an, XXVI, 4, and the commentary of Mahmud Shaltut, *al-Islam 'aqidatan wa shari'atan*, 2nd ed. (Cairo, n.d.), p. 33. See also Ali, *The Holy Qur'an*, p. 946 and n. 3140.

[9]See, e.g., Qur'an, II, 38; III, 4; V, 44, 46; VI, 157; IV, 33; XVI, 89, 102; XX, 123; XXVII, 2; XXXI, 3; XLVIII, 28; LXI, 9.

[10]Ali, *The Holy Qur'an*, p. 510, n. 1480.

We are too tempted today to shut ourselves up and to live comfortably wrapped in our own thoughts. But this is not God's purpose. Respectfulness is not indifference. God sets the example, for God is nearer to humanity "than the man's own jugular vein" (Qur'an, L, 16), and God knows better than we do our inmost desires, and what these desires "whisper (*tuwaswisu*)" to us (Qur'an, L, 16). Thus, God stands by us and speaks unceasingly to each one of us, warning and promising with a divine pedagogy that fits all persons of different social and intellectual classes, at all times, using images, symbols, and words that only God may use with a total sovereignty.

And God urges us to follow the divine example and to turn our steps toward all our sisters and brothers in humanity, beyond all kinds of frontiers, religious ones included. "O mankind! We created you from a male and a female; and we have made you into nations and tribes that you may know each other. Verily, the most honourable among you, in the sight of God, is he who is the most righteous of you. And God is All-Knowing, All-Aware" (Qur'an, XLIX, 13). A. Yusuf Ali comments on that verse in this way:

> This is addressed to all mankind, and not only to the Muslim broth-
> erhood, though it is understood that in a perfect world the two
> would be synonymous. As it is, mankind is descended from one pair
> of parents. Their tribes, races, and nations are convenient labels by
> which we may know certain differing characteristics. Before God
> they are all one, and he gets most honour who is most righteous.[11]

In other words, humans are not created for solitariness and impervious individuality. They are created for community, relationship, and dialogue. Their fulfillment is in their reconciliation at once to God and to persons. We have to find the way, in each case, to realize this double reconciliation, without betraying God and without damaging the inner life of the other. To do so we have to listen to God's advice: "Do not argue with the People of the Book unless it is in the most courteous manner, except for those of them who do wrong. And say: We believe in the Revelation which has come down to us and in that which came down to you. Our God and your God is one, and to Him we submit" (Qur'an, XXIX, 46). Let us note that the Arabic word used in the verse and rendered in the translation by the verb "to submit" is "*muslimun*" (= Muslims). So, to be a true Muslim is to live in a courteous dialogue with all peoples of other faiths and ideologies, and ultimately to submit to God. We must show concern to our neighbors. We have duties toward them; we are not isles of loneliness. The attitude of respectful courtesy recommended by the Qur'an must of course be enlarged to the whole of humankind, believers and unbelievers, except for those who "do wrong," that is to say, those who are unjust and violent and resort deliberately to the argument of the fist, physically or in words. In such a case it is much better to avoid a so-called dialogue in order to avoid the worse.

---

[11]Ibid., p. 1407, n. 4933. We generally follow his translation of the Qur'an.

In short, from the Muslim perspective that is mine, our duty is simply to bear witness in the most courteous way that is most respectful of the inner liberty of our neighbors and their sacredness. We must also be ready at the same time to listen to them in truthfulness. We have to remember, as Muslims, that a hadith of our Prophet states: "The believer is unceasingly in search of wisdom, wherever he finds it he grasps it." Another saying adds: "Look for knowledge everywhere, even as far as in China." And finally, it is up to God to judge, for we, as limited human beings, know only in part. Let me quote: "To each among you have We prescribed a Law and an Open Way. And if God had enforced His Will, He would have made of you all one people. But His plan is to test you in what He hath given you. So strive as in a race in all virtues. The goal of you all is to God. Then will He inform you of that wherein you differed" (Qur'an, V, 51). "Say: "O God! Creator of the heavens and the earth! Knower of all that is hidden and open! It is thou that wilt judge between Thy Servants in those matters about which they have differed" (Qur'an, XXXIX, 46).

III. Beyond the Limits Imposed by Traditional Theology

Though all Muslims are bound by the Qur'an's basic teachings, Muslim traditional theology developed in a way that, for historical reasons, does not, in my opinion, always fit in with the spirit of the Qur'an. Let us briefly recall two important cases: on the one hand, the *dhimmis* case—that is to say, the situation of the religious minorities inside the Islamic empire during medieval times—and, on the other hand, the apostate case.

Let us start with the *dhimmis*.[12] First, we must emphasize that, although the doors of many countries (not all of them, however) were opened (*fath*) by force or *jihad*[13]—as it was the general custom then—to pave the way for Islam, in practice Islam itself has almost never been imposed by compulsion. On this point the qur'anic teachings have been followed. They provided the *dhimmis* with a sound

---

[12]There is a large bibliography about that question. Cl. Cahen's article in the *Encyclopaedia of Islam* on "*dhimma*" gives the most important references. The basic book is still A. Fattal's, *Le statut légal des non-musulmans en pays d'Islam* (Beirut, 1958). See also B. Lewis' article, "L'Islam et les non-musulmans," *Annales* (Paris), no. 3-4 (1980), pp. 784-800. Bat Yé Or's book, *Le dhimmi, profil de l'opprimé en Orient et en Afrique du Nord* (Paris, 1980), is partial.

[13]It is not unimportant to recall that, from a Muslim perspective, *jihad* is neither war nor holy war. This is an orientalist's conception. The Arabic word "*jihad*" literally means "effort." The *jihad* consists in striving to fulfill God's purpose. Its highest form consists in fighting against our inner evil inclinations. It is for historical and contingent reasons that the wars fought by Muslims have more often than not been improperly called *jihad*. It is impossible to give a bibliography; the more recent book on this question is A. Morabia's doctoral thesis, *La notion de jihad dans l'Islam médiéval, des origines à al-Gazali* (Université de Lille III, 1975). See also M. Arkoun, M. Borrmans, and M. Arosio, *L'Islam religion et société* (Paris, 1982), pp. 60-62.

protection against the most unbearable forms of religious intolerance. In particular, with two or three historical exceptions, the *dhimmis* have never been prevented from following the religion of their choice, from worshipping, or from
organizing their communities in accordance with their own law. We can even
say that in the beginning their situation was often greatly improved by Islamic
conquest. They enjoyed long periods of tolerance and real prosperity,[14] very
often holding high positions in the administrative, court, and economic activities.

But it is a fact that at certain times and places they suffered from discrimination. Roughly speaking, things began seriously to worsen for them from the
reign of al-Mutawakkii (847-861 c.e.). The discrimination, especially in matters
of dress, took an openly humiliating shape. The oppression culminated in Egypt
during the reign of al-Hakim (996-1021 c.e.), who perhaps was not mentally
sane.

In the medieval context of wars, hostilities, and treacheries, this policy of
discrimination or open oppression was always prompted, or strongly backed,
by the theologians. To understand that, we have to remember that it was not
then a virtue—according to the medieval mentality everywhere in the world, and
within all communities—to consider all human beings as equal. How could one
consider as equal Truth and Error, true believers and heretics!

Thus, in our appraisal of the past we must always take the circumstances
into account, but above all we must strive to avoid the recurrence of the same
situations and errors. In any case, the Qur'an's basic teachings, whose inner
meaning we tried to put into relief, lay down for us a clear line of conduct. They
teach us to respect the dignity of the other and his/her total freedom. In a world
where giant holocausts have been perpetrated, where human rights are still at
stake, manipulated or totally ignored, our modern Muslim theologians must
denounce loudly all kinds of discriminations as crimes strictly and explicitly
condemned by the Qur'an's basic teachings.

However, we must consider the apostate case. In this field, too, traditional
theology did not follow the spirit of the Qur'an. This theology abridged seriously the liberty of choice of one's religion. According to this theology, though the
conversion to Islam must be, and is in fact, without coercion,[15] it is practically
impossible, once inside Islam, to get out of it. The conversion from Islam to
another religion is considered treason, and the apostate is liable to the penalty of
death.[16] The traditional theologians in their elaboration rely on the one hand on

---

[14]See S. D. Goitein, *A Mediterranean Society*, vol. 1, *Economic Foundations* (Berkeley
and Los Angeles: University of California Press, 1968); vol. 2, *The Community* (1971); vol.
3, *The Family* (1978). See also idem, *Letters of Medieval Jewish Traders* (Princeton, 1974).

[15]In the formulae of conversion to Islam it is explicitly mentioned that the convert has
"freely chosen Islam, without fear, in complete security against danger, and without any
kind of coercion." See Muhammad b. Ahmad al-Umawi al-ma'ruf bi-Ibn al-'Attar, *Kitab al-
watha'iq wa-l-sigillat* (Madrid: ed. P. Chalmeta and F. Corriente, 1983), p. 405; see also pp.
409-410, 414, 415-416.

[16]See 'Abd al-Rahman al-Gazari, *Kitab al-Fiqh 'ala al-madhahib al-arba'a* (Beirut, 1972),

the precedent of the first calif of Islam, Abu Bakr (632-634 c.e.), who energetically fought the tribes who rejected his authority after the Prophet's death and refused to pay him the alms taxes, likening their rebellion to apostasy. On the other hand they mainly put forward the authority of this hadith: "Anyone who changes his religion must be put to death."[17]

I know of no implementation throughout the history of Islam of the law condemning the apostate to death—until the hanging of Mahmoud Taha in the Sudan in 1985.[18] This law has remained mostly theoretical, but it is not irrelevant to draw attention to the fact that during the 1970's, in Egypt, the Islamic conservatives narrowly missed enforcing this law against Copts[19] who, without due consideration, converted to Islam, generally to marry Muslim women, and who, in case of the failure of the marriage, returned to their former religion. Recently, too, some Tunisian atheists expressed their concern.[20] So, the case of the apostate in Islam, though mostly theoretical, needs to be cleared up.

Let us first point out that the hadith upon which the penalty of death essentially rests is always more or less mixed with rebellion and highway robbery in the Tradition books. The cited cases of "apostates" killed during the Prophet's life or shortly after his death are all without exception of persons who as consequence of their "apostasy" turned their weapons against the Muslims, whose community at that time was still small and vulnerable. The penalty of death appears in these circumstances as an act of self-defense in a war situation. It is undoubtedly for that reason that the Hanafit school of *fich* does not condemn a woman apostate to death, "because women, contrary to men, are not fit for war."[21]

---

vol. 5, pp. 422-426. It has not been possible for us to have access to Dr. Nu'man 'Abd al-Razzaq al-Samarra'i's book, *Ahkam al-murtadd fi al-sari'a al-islamiya, dirasa muqarana* (The Apostate Status in Islam: A Comparative Study) (Ryad, Saudi Arabia, 1983). According to the Hanbalits, the apostate must immediately be put to death; according to the three other schools of fiqh, s/he is given three days to think it over, and it is only if s/he refuses to retract that s/he must be put to death. See also the formulae of conversion of Ibn al-'Attar, *Kitab al-watha'iq*, p. 407.

[17]For this hadith see, e.g., Buhari, *Sahih* (Cairo: ed. al-Sa'b, n.d.), IX, 19; Abu Dawud, *Sunan* (Cairo, 1952), II, p. 440. See also Buhari, *Sahih*, VIII, 201-202, and IX, 18-20; Abu Dawud, *Sunan*, II, pp. 440-442.

[18]Mahmud Taha was hanged by General Numeiri in Khartoum, Sudan, on January 18, 1985, at 10 a.m. as an apostate. Dr. 'Abd al-Hanrid 'Uways supported this enforcement of the law (see *al-Muslimun*, a Saudi weekly paper specializing in Islamic studies, March 23-29, 1985, p. 15).

[19]See Mohamed Charfi, "Islam et droits de l'homme," *Islamochristiana*, vol. 9 (1983), p. 15. See also Claire Brière and Olivier Carré, *Islam, Guerre à l'Occident?* (Paris: éd. Autrement, 1983), where we read: "Ainsi en 1977, une proposition de loi de peine de mort contre l'"apostat manifeste" est présentée au Parlement. Grosse affaire! Une telle loi, en effet, toucherait notamment les communistes militants. En effet, nous l'avons vu, ces derniers sont déclarés athées et apostats. Elle toucherait également les nombreux coptes qui, pour se marier avec une musulmane ou pour divorcer, se déclarent musulmans, puis representent publiquement leur pratique religieuse copte plus tard" (p. 185).

[20]See Talbi, "Islam et Occident," pp. 68-69.

[21]A. al-Gazari, *Kitab al-Fiqh*, V, 426.

Further, the hadith authorizing the death penalty is not, technically *muta-watir*,[22] and consequently it is not, according to the traditional system of hadith, binding. Above all, from a modern point of view, this hadith can and must be questioned. In my opinion, there are many persuasive reasons to consider it undoubtedly forged. It may have been forged under the influence of Leviticus (24:16) and Deuteronomy (13:2-19)—where the stoning of the apostate to death is ordered—if not directly, then perhaps indirectly through the Jews and Christians converted to Islam.

In any case, the hadith in question is as a matter of fact at variance with the teachings of the Qur'an, where there is no mention of a required death penalty against the apostate. Even during the life of the Prophet, the case presented itself at various times, and several verses of the Qur'an deal with it.[23] In all these verses, without a single exception, the punishment of the apostate who persists in rejection of Islam after having embraced it is left to God's judgment and to the after-life. In all the cases mentioned in the Qur'an, and by the commentators, it is a question on the one hand of time-servers—individuals or tribes, who, according to the circumstances, became turncoats[24]—and on the other hand of hesitating persons attracted to the faith of the "People of the Book" (Qur'an, II, 109; III, 99-100), Jews and Christians. Always taking into account the special situation, the Qur'an argues, warns, or recommends the proper attitude to be adopted, without ever threatening death.

1. The Qur'an Argues

From a Muslim perspective the Qur'an recognizes all the previous revelations and authenticates and perfects them: "Say: We believe in God, and in what has been revealed to us, and what was revealed to Abraham, Ishmael, Isaac, Jacob and the Tribes, and in that which was given to Moses, Jesus, and the Prophets, from their Lord. We make no distinction between any one of them, and to God we submit (*muslimun*)" (Qur'an, III, 84).

It does not follow that all are permitted, at the convenience of the moment, to change their religion as they change their coats. Such a behavior denotes in fact a lack of true faith. It is for this reason that the following verse insists on the universal significance of Islam, as a call directed to the whole of human-kind:[25] "If anyone desires a religion other than Islam, never will it be accepted of him; and in the Hereafter he will be among the losers" (Qur'an, III, 85).

Accordingly the apostates are warned: those who choose apostasy, after being convinced in their inmost thoughts that Islam is the truth, are unjust, and

---

[22]A hadith is called *mutawatir* when it is transmitted by several driving chains of reliable warrantors.

[23]Qur'an, II, 109, 217; III, 85-89, 91, 99-100, 106, 149; V, 57-59; XLVII, 25, 32, 34, 38.

[24]See Hamza, *Le Coran*, commentary on verses III, 85, 88, 91, 101, 106; IV, 31, 91, 106; V, 54; XLIX, 14.

[25]See M. Talbi, *Islam et Dialogue* (Tunis: ed. MTE, 1972), pp. 28-33; Arabic tr. in *Islamochristiana*, vol. 4 (1978), pp. 12-16.

as such they are bereft of God's guidance, with all the consequences that follow for their salvation. "How shall God guide those who reject faith after they accepted it, and bore witness that the Apostle was true, and that clear signs had come to them? But God guides not a people unjust" (Qur'an, III, 86; see also the following verses: 87-91).

Nevertheless, the Qur'an denounces the attitude of "the People of the Book," who exerted pressure on the newly converted to Islam to induce them to retract. There is no doubt that the polemics between the dawning Islam and the old religions were sharp. In this atmosphere the Qur'an urges the persons who espoused Islam to adhere firmly to their new faith, till their death, to close their ranks, to refuse to listen to those who strive to lure them to apostasy, and to avoid their snares. They are also reminded of their former state of disunion when they were "on the brink of the Pit of Fire," and they are exhorted to be a people "inviting to all that is good" in order to ensure their final salvation. Let us quote:

> Say: O People of the Book: Why obstruct ye those who believe from the Path of God, seeking to make it crooked, while ye were yourselves witness thereof? But God is not unmindful of all that ye do.
>
> O ye who believe! If you obey a faction of those who have been given the Book, they will turn you back into disbelievers after you have believed.
>
> And how would you disbelieve, while to you are rehearsed the signs of God, and His Messenger is among you? And he who holds fast to God is indeed guided to the Right Path.
>
> O ye who believe! Fear God as He should be feared, and die not except in a state of Islam.
>
> And hold fast, all together, by the Rope of God, and be not divided, and remember God's favour on you: for ye were enemies, and He joined your Hearts in love, so that by His Grace, ye became brethren; and ye were on the brink of the Pit of Fire, and He saved you from it. Thus doth God make His Signs clear to you, that ye may be guided.
>
> Let there arise out of you a Community inviting to all that is good, enjoining what is right, and forbiding what is wrong. They are the ones to attain felicity. (Qur'an, III, 99-104)

Thus, unceasingly and by all means, the Qur'an strives to raise the new Muslims' spirit, in order to prevent them from falling into apostasy. The argumentation is only moral, however. The Qur'an goes on: It is "from selfish envy" (Qur'an, II, 109) that "quite a number of the People of the Book wish they could turn you back to infidelity" (Qur'an, II, 109; see also III, 149); you have not to fear them, "God is your Protector, and He is the best of helpers, soon shall He cast terror into the hearts of the unbelievers" (Qur'an, III, 150-151); "your real friends are God, His Messenger, and the believers. . . . it is the party of God that must certainly triumph. . . . therefore take not for friends those who take your religion for a mockery or sport . . ." (Qur'an, V, 58-60). And finally, those who, in spite of all that, allow themselves to be tempted by apostasy, are forewarned: if they desert the cause, the cause nevertheless will not fail. Others will carry it forward:

> O ye who believe! If any from among you turn back from his faith, soon will God produce a people whom He will love as they will love Him,—lowly with the Believers, mighty against the Rejecters, striving in the way of God, and never afraid of the reproaches of a fault finder. That is the grace of God, which He will bestow on whom He pleaseth. And God is bountiful, All-Knowing. (Qur'an, V, 57; see also XLVII, 38)

Finally the apostates are given this notice: they "will not injure God in the least, but He will make their deeds of no effect" (Qur'an, XLVII, 32).

2. The Qur'an Warns

The young Muslim community is thus given many reasons to adhere to its new religion. The members of this community are also warned that for their salvation they should not depart from their faith. They are urged to follow the true spirit of Islam, and this spirit is defined in two ways: first they will love God and God will love them; secondly they will be humble among their brothers and sisters, but they will not fear the wrongdoers, and they will not join with them. If by fear, weakness, or time-serving, they depart from this line of conduct and fall into apostasy, the loss will be their own, and the punishment will be hard in the hereafter. "And if any of them turn back from their faith, and die in unbelief, their works will bear no fruit in this life. And in the Hereafter they will be companions of the Fire, and will abide therein" (Qur'an, II, 217). The apostates lay themselves open to "the curse of God, of His angels, and of all mankind" (Qur'an, III, 87), "except for those who repent thereafter, and amend, for God is Oft-Forgiving, Most Merciful" (Qur'an, III, 89). But there is no hope for those who persist in their apostasy (Qur'an, III, 90-91). These obstinate apostates will "taste the penalty for rejecting faith" (Qur'an, III, 106; see also III, 140). Such persons are entirely in the hands of evil (Qur'an, XLVII, 25). They secretly plot with the enemies (Qur'an, XLVII, 26-27), and "they obstruct the way to God" (Qur'an, XLVII, 32, 34). As a result "God will not forgive them" (Qur'an, XLVII, 34).

3. The Qur'an Advises

How should such obstinate and ill-disposed apostates be dealt with? How should those be treated who try to draw others into their camp or to manipulate others? Let us underline once more that there is no mention in the Qur'an of any kind of penalty, neither death nor any other one. To use the technical Arab word, we would say that there is no specified *hadd*[26] in this matter. On the contrary, the Muslims are advised to "forgive and overlook till God accomplishes His purpose, for God hath power over all things" (Qur'an, II, 109). In other words, there is no punishment on earth. The case is not answerable to the Law. The debate is between God and the apostate's conscience, and it is not our role to interfere in it.

Muslims are authorized to take up arms only in one case, the case of self-defense, when they are attacked, and their faith is seriously jeopardized. In such a case "fighting" (*al-qital*) is "prescribed" (*kutiba*) for them, even if they "dislike it" (*kurhun lakum*) (Qur'an, II, 216), and it is so even during the sacred month of Pilgrimage (Qur'an, II, 217; II, 194).[27] To summarize, Muslims are urged not to yield, when their conscience is at stake, and to rise up in arms against "those who will not cease fighting you until they turn you back from your faith, if they can" (Qur'an, II, 217).

It is thus evident that the problem of religious liberty, with all its ramifications, is not new within Islam. The Qur'an deals at length with it. At the heart of this problem we meet the ticklish subject of apostasy, and we have seen that with regard to this subject the Qur'an argues, warns, and advises, but it never resorts to the argument of the sword. This is because that argument is meaningless in the matter of faith. In our pluralistic world our modern theologians must take that into account.

We can never stress too much that religious liberty is not an act of charity or a tolerant concession toward misled persons. It is, rather, a fundamental right of everyone. To claim it for myself implies *ipso facto* that I am disposed to claim it for my neighbor, too. But religious liberty is not reduced to the equivalent of atheism. My right, and my duty also, is to bear witness, by fair means, to my own faith and to convey God's call. Ultimately, however, it is up to each person to respond to this call or not, freely and in full consciousness.

From a Muslim perspective, and on the basis of the Qur'an's basic teachings, whose letter and spirit we have tried to adduce, religious liberty is fundamentally and ultimately an act of respect for God's sovereignty and for the mystery of God's plan for humanity, which has been given the terrible privilege of shaping entirely on its own responsibility its destiny on earth and hereafter. Ultimately, to respect humanity's freedom is to respect God's plan. To be a true Muslim is to submit to this plan. It is to put one's self, voluntarily and freely, with confidence and love, into the hands of God.

---

[26]*Hadd* = legal penalty explicitly specified in the Qur'an.
[27]See Ali, *The Holy Qur'an*, p. 77, n. 209, commentary on II, 194.

Mohamed Talbi (Muslim) is Professor of the Faculty of Arts and Sciences of the University of Tunis, Tunisia; president of the National Cultural Committee of Tunisia; and editor of *Cahiers de Tunisie (Revue de Sciences Humaines)*. He holds a doctorate (1968) in medieval Muslim history from the Sorbonne, and has received many honors including Officier de l'Ordre de la République (Tunisia, 1965), Officier de l'Ordre de l'indépendance (Tunisia, 1975), Officier du Mérité Civil (Spain, 1972), Officier du Mérité Cultural (Tunisia, 1982), Premio Letterario Internazionale Mediterraneo (Palermo, 1979), and the Lukas Prize for Outstanding Contribution to Interreligious Amity (Protestant Theological Faculty of the University of Tübingen, 1985). He has published numerous articles and books, including *Histoire de la Tunisie, le Moyen Age* (Tunis, 1975), *Islam et Dialogue* (Tunis, 1972), and *Etudes d'Histoire Ifriiqiyenne et de Civilisation Musulmane Médiévale* (Tunis, 1982). He has been a participant in numerous conferences and congresses throughout Europe, Africa, Asia, and North America.

A BUDDHIST RESPONSE TO MOHAMED TALBI

Masao Abe

My first impression of Mohamed Talbi's essay, "Religious Liberty: A Muslim Perspective," is that Islam has two sharply contrasting aspects within itself: an aspect of respecting the liberty of choosing one's faith, and an aspect of discrimination and punishment of the apostate that includes the death penalty. As for the first aspect, by quoting the Qur'an, "There should be no compulsion in religion" (II, 256), Talbi states that, "The very nature of faith, as is stressed in the basic text of Islam in clear and indisputable words, is to be a voluntary act born out of conviction and freedom."[1] He also emphasizes, "In fact, even God refrains from overpowering humans to the point of subduing them against their will. This too is clearly expressed in the Qur'an."[2] At the same time, however, we are told "In the medieval context of wars, hostilities, and treacheries, the policy of discrimination or open oppression was always prompted . . . by the theologians."[3] And, according to traditional theology "The conversion from Islam to another religion is considered treason, and the apostate is liable to the penalty of death."[4] Further, "The punishment of the apostate who persists in rejection of Islam after having embraced it is left to God's judgment and to the afterlife."[5] However, "The apostates lay themselves open to 'the curse of God, of His angels, and of all mankind' (Qur'an III, 87) . . . [and] 'God will not forgive them' (Qur'an XLVII, 34)."[6]

I thus see in Islam two sharply contrasting aspects: the aspect of *the freedom to choose one's faith* and the aspect of *oppression* with regard to faith. Of course, we should not overlook that Talbi emphasizes the first aspect, the freedom to choose one's faith as the basic teaching of the Qur'an, whereas he discusses the second aspect, the open oppression of faith and the death penalty, as a deviation from the basic teaching of the Qur'an in such a case as the *dhimmis* (the situation of the religious minorities inside the Islamic empire during medieval times) and the apostate (the conversion from Islam to another faith). While I understand that such deviations have taken place for certain historical reasons in special social or international situations, nevertheless, these two aspects are so diametrically opposed that I can hardly reconcile them in a single living religion, Islam.

If a basic teaching of the Qur'an is that faith should not be forced but is a voluntary act based on conviction and freedom, how are such contrary devia-

---

[1] See p. 178, above.
[2] See p. 179, above.
[3] See p. 182, above.
[4] Ibid.
[5] See p. 184, above.
[6] See p. 186, above.

tions as open oppression and the death penalty of the apostate possible—even under special historical and social situations? If such a serious deviation from the basic teachings of the Qur'an is possible due to particular historical reasons and social situations, I am afraid there is no absolute authority for the Qur'an's basic teachings of the freedom of faith. If, as Talbi emphasizes, God refrains from overpowering humans to the point of subduing them against their will, why does God curse and not forgive apostates?

After a careful rereading of Talbi's essay, I came to understand that the Qur'an emphasizes the free choice of faith without compulsion in religion with regard to the conversion to Islam, but it does not emphasize the free choice of faith to leave and/or reject Islam. In fact, such rejection is seriously judged as treason, and the apostate is liable to the penalty of death. If I am not mistaken in this regard, then I understand the nature of God in Islam as follows: God created all human beings equally by inspiring into them God's "breath," and by virtue of this "breath" they have the ability to be at one with God and to respond freely to God's call. God is full of mercy and charity. At the same time, as the Qur'an clearly states, "God guides not a people unjust" (III, 86), because "How shall God guide those who reject faith after they accepted it, and bore witness that the Apostle was true, and that clear signs had come to them?" (ibid.). Why is God in Islam so ambivalent? I understand that God has two hands: a hand of mercy and a hand of justice. As the one absolute God, God can use these two hands freely. My question, however, remains: When it is stated, "God guides not a people unjust," why does a merciful God *not* guide a people unjust? Why does an all-loving God *not* forgive an apostate? And what does "unjust" mean? To what is one "unjust"?

God is merciful and quite tolerant with regard to conversion to Islam, whereas God is severe and intolerant with regard to conversion from Islam to another religion. The term "unjust," it seems to me, indicates "unjust" against God's authority as the one absolute God—or at least "unjust" against God's own righteousness as the sole standard of judgment. If this is the case, at least two problems may emerge: First, although God has two hands, namely, a hand of mercy and a hand of justice, the hand of justice often overwhelms the hand of mercy. As a result, discrimination, oppression, and the condemnation of the apostate to death take place. Second, such discrimination, oppression, and condemnation will provoke resentment, hatred, and revenge; such a negative and inimical reaction will create still further negative and inimical reactions, and this reciprocal relation will develop endlessly. With Talbi, I sincerely hope "modern Muslim theologians must denounce loudly all kinds of discriminations as crimes strictly and explicitly condemned by the Qur'an's basic teachings."[7] I also wholeheartedly pray that God's hand of mercy will overwhelm the hand of justice, rather than vice versa.

---

[7]See p. 182, above.

The Buddhist attitude toward the problem of heresy and apostasy is significantly different from that of Islam. Gautama Buddha, the founder of Buddhism, says:

> To an enemy intent on ill you are a good friend intent on good. To one who constantly seeks for faults you respond by seeking your virtues. Revilers you conquered by patience, plotters by blessings, slanderers by the truth, the malicious by friendliness.[8]

Buddhism does not advocate the notion of one absolute God but, rather, the "law of dependent co-origination," which indicates that everything in and beyond the universe is interdependent and mutually related. Not only human beings (in the universe) are interdependent, but also the divine (which is beyond the universe) and the human are interdependent. To the Buddhist, God who is transcendent, self-existing, and commanding is an unreal entity. Just as without the divine there is no human, so without the human there is no divine. Accordingly, in Buddhism there is no idea of an apostate. A stock Buddhist phrase in this regard is:

> "Not rejecting those who come;
> not running after those who leave."

Buddhism emphasizes wisdom and compassion rather than justice and charity. Just as in Islam charity without justice is not true charity, so in Buddhism compassion without wisdom is not true compassion. Like justice, wisdom makes distinctions clear, but, unlike justice, wisdom neither judges between the just and the unjust nor accepts the just alone while punishing the unjust. Rather, wisdom admits different things in their distinctiveness and acknowledges the different values of the things which are distinguished. While "justice" provokes resentment, hatred, and revenge, and thus creates an endless process of vengeful reactions, "wisdom" inspires understanding, acknowledgement, and mutual appreciation, and thus entails peace and harmony.

Islam is not lacking in the notion of wisdom; as Talbi emphasized, "A hadith of our Prophet states: 'The believer is unceasingly in search of wisdom; wherever he finds it he grasps it.' Another saying adds: 'Look for knowledge everywhere, even as far as in China.' "[9] In this connection, I would like to say to my Islamic friends: As your *hadith* states, please look for wisdom! However, it is not necessary to look as far away as China; rather, Islam can look to India, the birthplace of Buddhism.

---

[8]Satapañcaśatkastotra of Matriceta, 118-120, 122.
[9]See p. 181, above.

Masao Abe (Buddhist) is Margaret Gest Visiting Professor at Haverford (PA) College, 1985-87. He is Professor Emeritus of Nara (Japan) University of Education, where he taught philosophy from 1952 to 1980. A graduate of Kyoto (Japan) University, he studied and practiced Buddhism, especially Zen, with Sin'ichi Hisamatsu, as well as Western philosophy. As a Rockefeller Foundation Research Fellow, he studied Christian theology at Union Theological Seminary and Columbia University, 1955-57. He has been a visiting professor at several U.S. schools, including Columbia and Princeton Universities, the Universities of Chicago and Hawaii, and Claremont Graduate School. Since the death of D. T. Suzuki, he has been the leading exponent of Zen and Japanese Buddhism in the West. As a member of the Kyoto School of Philosophy, he is deeply involved in the comparative study of Buddhism and Western thought and in Buddhist-Christian dialogue. His recent book, *Zen and Western Thought* (University of Hawaii Press, 1985), collects his important essays on Zen in relation to Western thought. He has published in a wide variety of Japanese and Western journals, as well as serving on the advisory boards of five journals.

RELIGIOUS TOLERANCE AND HUMAN RIGHTS:
A BUDDHIST PERSPECTIVE

Masao Abe

In February, 1985, I was asked by Professor Leonard Swidler to submit, from a Buddhist standpoint, a paper on the subject, "Religious Tolerance and Human Rights," and to present it at this conference. Upon carefully reading the attached documents explaining the issues to be discussed at this conference and their implications, I felt I must attempt to make a response for two reasons. First, the issue of the relationship between human rights and religious freedom is one of the most urgent issues in contemporary human society; it is an issue that religious thinkers in particular can no longer ignore. Second, this issue derives fundamentally from the problematic innate in human existence and in the nature of "religion" itself. Consequently, the problem of the relationship between religious tolerance and human rights cannot be easily resolved, however urgent the issue may be.

From a standpoint different from that of Semitic religions predominantly discussed in the United Nations documents sent to me, perhaps Buddhism may contribute something new to consideration of this dilemma. The Buddhist view of "human rights" is significantly different from the views of its Western counterparts, as is the Buddhist attitude toward "religious tolerance." Since in most cases up to now both the notions of "human rights" and "religious tolerance" have been understood in terms of Western categories and have been discussed mainly from the Judeo-Christian-Islamic point of view, the Buddhist approach to these issues may help open up a new vista and may help provide an entirely new foundation to remedy serious conflicts in the contemporary world.

I

Before elucidating the Buddhist understanding of "human rights" and "religious tolerance," let me try to clarify the differences between the two main types of world religions. Western scholars often discuss religion in terms of a contrast between ethical religion and natural religion (C. P. Tile), prophetic religion and mystical religion (F. Heiler), and monotheistic religion and pantheistic religion (W. F. Albright, A. Lang), the first in each pair referring to Judeo-Christian-Islamic religions and the second to most of the Oriental religions.

This kind of bifurcation has been set forth by Western scholars with such "Western" religions as Judaism, Christianity, and Islam as the standard of judgment. Consequently, non-Semitic Oriental religions are often not only lumped together under a certain single category despite their rich variety but also grasped from the outside without any penetration into their inner religious core. Unlike

193

the Semitic religions, which most Western scholars recognize as having a clear common character, such Oriental religions as Hinduism, Buddhism, Confucianism, Taoism, and Shintoism exhibit significant differences in their religious essences and, hence, cannot legitimately be classified into a single category. To bring this point into sharper focus, I will take up Buddhism alone from among the Oriental religions and contrast it with Judaism, Christianity, and Islam.

Most Western scholars correctly characterize Judaism, Christianity, and Islam not as natural, mystical, and pantheistic religions, but as ethical, prophetic, and monotheistic religions. All three religions are based on the One Absolute God: Yahweh in Judaism, God the Father in Christianity, and Allah in Islam. In each of these religions the One God is believed to be a personal God who is essentially transcendent to human beings but whose will is revealed to human beings through prophets and who commands people to observe certain ethico-religious principles. Although we should not overlook some conspicuous differences in emphasis among these three religions, we can say with justification that they are ethical, prophetic, and monotheistic religions.

In contrast, Buddhism does not talk about the One absolute God who is essentially transcendent to human beings. Instead, it teaches the *Dharma*, which is *pratitya-samutpada*, the law of "dependent co-origination" or conditional co-production. This teaching emphasizes that everything *in* and *beyond* the universe is inter-dependent, co-arising, and co-ceasing (not only temporarily but also logically): nothing exists independently or can be said to be self-existing. Accordingly, in Buddhism everything without exception is relative, relational, nonsubstantial, and changeable. This is why Gautama Buddha, the founder of Buddhism, did not accept the age-old Vedantic notion of *Brahman*, which is believed to be the eternal, unchangeable reality underlying the universe. For a similar reason, Buddhism cannot accept the monotheistic notion of One Absolute God as the ultimate reality, but advocates *sunyata* (emptiness) and *tathata* (suchness or as-it-is-ness) as the ultimate reality.

In Buddhism, even the divine or the holy does not exist by itself, independent of and transcendent to the human or the secular. Just as the human does not exist apart from the divine, the divine does not exist apart from the human. The divine and the human co-arise and co-cease and are entirely interrelated and interdependent. The divine which exists by itself, or the God who exists alone, is considered in Buddhism to be an unreal entity. Again, "one" does not exist apart from "many," just as "many" is inconceivable apart from "one." "One" and "many" always co-arise and co-cease. Accordingly, an absolute "One" which is aloof from "many" is just as much a conceptual construction as a "many" which is unrelated to the "One." In Buddhism the ultimate reality is neither the divine God who is absolutely one nor human beings who are multitudinous but the relationality or "dependent co-origination" of everything, including the relationality between one and many, God and humans.

From a Buddhist perspective, human conflicts and human-induced suffering derive from ignorance of this law of "dependent co-origination" and the resultant self-centeredness. Accordingly, as the way of salvation from human suffering, Buddhism emphasizes the necessity of awakening to the law of "dependent co-origination" by breaking through the ignorance innate in human existence, that is, self-centeredness and attachment to anything, divine or human. Above all, those forms of attachment which absolutize the divine or the holy as something substantial, self-existing, eternal, and unchangeable must be overcome. Further, awakening to the law of "dependent co-origination" indicates awakening to the original nature of everything in the universe—and that awakening is simultaneously the awakening to one's own original nature or one's own true Self, for, without the awakening to one's own original nature, awakening to the original nature of everything in the universe is not possible.

In short, Buddhism fundamentally does not discuss a personal God, divine revelation, prophets, or salvation through faith; rather, it affirms the law of "dependent co-origination," self-awakening, the practice of meditation, and emancipation through nonattachment. Accordingly, I would like to characterize Judaism, Christianity, and Islam as "religions of divine revelation" and Buddhism as a "religion of Self-awakening." Expressed differently, the former are "religions of God," whereas the latter is a "religion of the true Self."

II

To provide a basis for the discussion of the Buddhist view of "human rights" and "religious tolerance" we must clarify three points derived directly from the law of "dependent co-origination."

1. *Anatman* or no-self: Although the law of "dependent co-origination" denies the self-existence and unchangeable substantiality of everything, including the divine or the holy, such interdependency and relationality are inconceivable without recognizing the particularity or individuality of the elements, human or nonhuman, which constitute that interdependency. Apart from the particularity or individuality of both sides of the relation, the very notion of relationality and "dependent co-origination" are not possible. An emphasis on relationality without a recognition of the individuality of the constituent elements will entail relativism which finally culminates in a nihilistic anarchism. This kind of relationality is static and merely formal, and it thus loses the dynamism between individuality and interdependency. However, if the particularity or individuality of either of the sides of the relation is substantialized or absolutized, the relationality or "dependent co-origination" will be destroyed. The law of "dependent co-origination" is possible only when each element involved in the relationship has a distinguishable particularity which is, however, nonsubstantial. This means that, due to the absence of unchangeable substantiality or enduring selfhood, each entity is entirely interdependent without losing its own particularity. Accordingly, the key point of the law of "dependent co-origination" lies in the

realization of the absence of unchangeable substantiality or enduring selfhood, that is, the realization of no-self which is traditionally called *Anatman*.

2. *Tathata* or suchness (as-it-is-ness): When everything is grasped in terms of "dependent co-origination" and thus is understood to be without enduring self-hood, the situation is very different from that in monotheistic religion. In mono-theistic religion, everything is understood, for instance, to be a creation of the One Absolute God, the creator. In this case, everything or everyone in the universe is equal before God, and, at least in Christianity, the resurrection after death is a resurrection in the form of a spiritual body (*soma pneumatikon*) which is the transformation of the physical body without the loss of identity: "Do you not know that your body is a temple of the Holy Spirit within you which you have from God?" (1 Cor. 6:19).

The individual is not absorbed in the divine at death but continues to be the same individual preserving his or her identity in a different mode.[1] This is because Spirit is the principle of individualization. Unlike Judaism and Islam, Christi-anity has a unique doctrine of resurrection in which distinction and identity of an individual person go together. In Christianity, however, this togetherness of distinction and identity is supported by the Holy Spirit of the One God. Accord-ingly, however dialectical the relationship between distinction and identity may be, it is understood or believed in within the framework of the One God, who calls people into fellowship with God. This implies at least the following two points: First, since the relationship between distinction and identity is realized in terms of the One Absolute God, both distinction and identity, strictly speaking, are not fully or thoroughgoingly grasped as such. Both distinction and identity— and their dialectical relationship—can be thoroughgoingly realized only by break-ing through the absolute Oneness of God. Second, in Christianity, the dialectical relationship between distinction and identity is applied only to a human being, not to individual things in the universe. This second point relates to the first point.

In this regard, Buddhism diverges from Christianity. In Buddhism, in which the One Absolute God is absent, not only all persons but also all things in the universe are thoroughly realized in such a way as to maintain their particularity or individuality without any transcendent, one absolute principle; yet, they are realized to be completely equal in the sense that regardless of their distinction all are equally and respectively grasped in their particularity or in their as-it-is-ness (suchness). For instance, an oak tree is thoroughly an oak tree and a pine tree thoroughly a pine tree in their distinctiveness; yet, an oak tree and a pine tree are equal in each one's being grasped in its own particularity or in its own such-ness. A fish is thoroughly a fish and a bird thoroughly a bird in their distinctive-ness; yet, a fish and a bird are equal in terms of each one's being grasped in its

---

[1]Lynn A. deSilva, *The Problem of the Self in Buddhism and Christianity* (New York: Barnes and Noble Imports, 1979; repr. of 1975 original), p. 111.

as-it-is-ness. Again, I am really I, and you are really you, with regard to our particular individuality; yet, you and I are equal in that each of us is realized in our own individuality and in our own personality. Exactly the same is true with the divine and the human. The divine is thoroughly the divine and the human absolutely the human; yet, the divine and the human are equal in the sense that both of them are equally apprehended in their essential characteristic or in their "suchness."

Accordingly, *tathata* or suchness (as-it-is-ness) includes complete distinction and complete equality, full distinctiveness and full sameness, dynamically and without contradiction. This is the reason Mahayana Buddhism often states that *Shabetsu-soku-byodo: byodo-soku-shabetsu*; that is, distinction as it is is sameness; sameness as it is is distinction (distinction *sive* equality; equality *sive* distinction). This dynamic relationship between distinction and equality extends not only to human persons but also more universally to nature and God as well. Such a dynamic relationship is possible because the One Absolute God is absent, and everything—including nature, humankind, and God—is realized without independent enduring selfhood or fixed unchanging substance.

3. *Madhyama pratipad* or the Middle Way: Gautama Buddha rejected both extremes of sensual indulgence and asceticism and espoused the Middle Way as the true method of religious practice. To him, this meant the Noble Eightfold Path of right view, right thinking, right speech, right action, right livelihood, right effort, right mindfulness, and right concentration.

The "middleness" of the Middle Way does not mean a mere compromise or a middle point between two extremes, as the Aristotelian notion of *to meson* might suggest. Instead, the Middle Way breaks through the two extremes by overcoming the dualistic standpoint as such, and it points to the nondual ultimate reality which is realized by the Buddha and every other awakened self.

This point will become clearer when we consider the Eightfold Negation set forth by Nagarjuna, the founder of Mahayana Buddhism. Interpreting Buddha's notion of Middle Way more radically than Gautama, Nagarjuna advocated the Eightfold Negation: neither birth nor extinction; neither permanence nor impermanence; neither unity nor diversity; neither coming nor going. In this connection, as I have stated elsewhere:

> There is no primacy of one concept over the other in these four pairs. In Nāgārjuna, the real nature of existence (tathatā) manifests itself when fixed concepts such as birth and extinction are removed. Hence the Eightfold Negation is synonymous with the Middle Path.[2]

In the same book I stated further:

> Nāgārjuna not only repudiated the eternalist view, which takes phenomena to be real just as they are and essentially unchangeable: he

---

[2]Masao Abe, *Zen and Western Thought*, ed. William R. LaFleur (Honolulu: University of Hawaii Press, 1985), p. 284.

also rejected as illusory the opposite nihilistic view which emphasizes emptiness and non-being as true Reality. This double negation in terms of 'neither—nor' is the pivotal point for the realization of Mahayana Emptiness which is never a sheer emptiness but rather Fullness.[3]

III

Next, I would like to discuss the Buddhist view of religious liberty and human rights. Some Western scholars say that Buddhism is a tolerant religion. Strictly speaking, however, this statement does not hit the mark of Buddhism. The term "tolerance" is a counterconcept of "intolerance," which implies active (often violent) refusal to allow others to have or put into practice beliefs different from one's own. Since Buddhism is not a monotheistic religion—for it is based on the realization of the suchness or as-it-is-ness of everything in the universe—in Buddhism the active refusal of allowing others to have beliefs different from one's own is absent, while the positive recognition and approval of others' beliefs in their different modes is clearly present. Buddhism cannot be defined by the term "tolerant" in the Western sense because it originally stands on a dimension transcending the duality of "tolerant" and "intolerant." The "tolerant" attitude of Buddhism is nothing other than an outcome of Buddhism's more fundamental attitude of "suchness" or "as-it-is-ness." In this connection one may distinguish negative from positive tolerance, the former referring to tolerance in the Western sense, the latter to tolerance in the Buddhist sense. Since the realization of everything's suchness or as-it-is-ness is itself the Buddhist faith, the deeper the Buddhist faith becomes the more tolerant the attitude toward other faiths. In Buddhism, deep faith and true tolerance do not exclude one another but go together. This fundamental attitude is applied not only to different beliefs within Buddhism but also to different views and beliefs of non-Buddhist religions and ideologies.

The basic Buddhist attitude toward different beliefs within Buddhism is not to reject, denounce, or punish them as heresy, but rather to evaluate them critically as different views and to subsume them into its own doctrinal system.

In his essay "Heresy," T. O. Ling wrote:

> Heresy is primarily a Western religious concept: there is no exact Buddhist equivalent. The nearest approximation is *ditthi* (Pali), *drsti* (Skt), literally a view, usually a "wrong" view, that is due not to reason but to craving or desire (tanhā). The most serious form of *ditthi* is to assert the reality and permanence of the individual human ego, i.e., the assertion of ātman. Since the Western concept of heresy implies an orthodoxy capable of denouncing heresy and willing to

---

[3]Ibid., p. 159.

do so, the approximation of Buddhist *ditthi* to Western heresy here comes to an end, since Buddhism has no authoritative hierarchy, and no sacramental sanctions. Even the most serious form of *ditthi*, assertion of reality of a permanent individual human "self," was maintained by certain Buddhists known as Pudgala-Vādins. They were regarded by all other Buddhist schools of thought as weaker brethren, and in error: but they maintained their existence and monastic institutions; as late as 7th cent. CE, Pudgala-Vādin monks amounted to about a quarter of the total number of Buddhist monks in India. On the whole, the attitude of other schools seem to have been that more prolonged meditation would eventually cause them to see error involved in this view, and its abandonment.[4]

In China and Japan, along with the establishment of various doctrinal systems and sectarian organizations, serious debates often took place among different Buddhist schools. Nichiren, a Japanese Buddhist leader of the thirteenth century, attacked Esoteric Buddhism, the Vinaya School, Zen, and particularly Pure Land Buddhism. His contemporary followers, who constitute the sect Nichiren-sho̊shu, are known for their aggressive attitude toward other Buddhist schools. On the whole, however, throughout the long history of Buddhism there has been no burning to death or any form of civil punishment due to different beliefs within Buddhism. Different views of the Dharma have been often regarded as *upaya*, skillful means to lead immature Buddhists to the ultimate truth of Buddhadharma.

In regard to the Buddhist attitude toward others of different faiths, the early Buddhist scriptures often emphasize, "Do not contend (*vivada*)." They also advocate non-controversy (*rana*). Gautama Buddha is called "One who cast aside contention" (*ranamjaha*). It is well known that Buddha answered with silence such a metaphysical question as to whether the world is eternal or not eternal, whether the world is finite or infinite, and whether the sage exists or does not exist after death. Buddha's silence on these metaphysical questions is often regarded as a form of agnosticism. For Gautama, however, concern with such metaphysical theories was unprofitable and did not tend toward religious salvation. His radically practical reason for an avoidance of commitment to any of the alternative doctrines mentioned above was brought out by Buddha himself,[5] as can be seen, for instance, in his response to the monk Malunkyaputta in the Majjhima-Nikaya, one of the earliest Buddhist writings. After emphasizing that the religious life did not depend on the dogma that the world is eternal or not eternal, Buddha said:

Whether the dogma obtain, Malunkyaputta, that the world is eternal,

[4]T. O. Ling, "Heresy," in Samuel George Frederick Brandon, ed., *A Dictionary of Comparative Religion* (New York: Scribner, 1970), pp. 324-325.
[5]Edwin Arthur Burtt, ed., *The Teachings of the Compassionate Buddha* (New York: New American Library, 1955), p. 32.

or that the world is not eternal, there still remain birth, old age, death, sorrow, lamentation, misery, grief, and despair, for the extinction of which in the present life I am prescribing. . . . This [dogma] profits not, nor has to go with the fundamentals of religion, nor tends to aversion, absence of passion, cessation, quiescence, the supernatural faculties, supreme wisdom, and Nirvana: therefore have I not explained it.[6]

Further, as E. A. Burtt has rightly pointed out, in the Buddha's view:

The assertion of any such theory naturally provokes the assertion of counter theories by others; this process generates heated and contentious argument, with its accompanying unresolved hostilities and mutual recriminations. It does not promote the humble self-searching and unity of understanding that are essential if the true spiritual goal is to be reached.[7]

Buddha's attitude toward sectarian dogmatism can be seen in the following exchanges with a monk extracted from the Sutta-Nipata, another early Buddhist scripture:

The Enquirer:	Fixed in their pet beliefs, these diverse wranglers bawl—"Hold this, and truth is yours"; "Reject it, and you're lost."
	Thus they contend, and dub opponents "dolts" and "fools." Which of the lot is right, when all as experts pose?
The Lord [Buddha]:	Well, if dissent denotes a "fool" and stupid "dolt," then all are fools and dolts—since each has his own view.
	Or, if each rival creed proves love and brains and wit, no "dolts" exist—since all alike are on a par.
	I count not that as true which those affirm, who call each other "fools"—They call each other so, because each deems his own view "Truth."[8]

The Buddhist attitude toward other religions may best be clarified in terms of the Middle Way. The doctrine of the Middle Way advocates the avoidance of the extremes of religious imperialism and syncretism and the extremes of violent intolerance and universalism (all-is-one-ness). The tendency toward religious imperialism is somewhat unavoidable for any religion, for religion is precisely an

---

[6]*The Majjhima-Nikaya*, Sutta 63. See Burtt, *Teachings*, p. 36.
[7]Burtt, *Teachings*, pp. 36-37.
[8]Ibid., p. 37.

existential and total commitment to that which is believed to be the ultimate truth. This tendency is evident in monotheistic religions which advance the One Absolute God as the ultimate reality. The tendency toward syncretism or universalism indicates an eclectic approach which attempts to incorporate all teachings into the fold of a given religion, thereby emphasizing the feelings of universality and humanhood. This tendency is evident in pantheistic or polytheistic religions. However, as Phra Khantipalo has stated, the first danger of syncretism is that it is idle to pretend that all religions lead to the same goal: "To try to steamroller every religion into the concept of basic sameness or 'all-is-one-ness' is to ignore facts in favor of a pre-conceived ideal." The second danger of syncretism is that "in trying to believe in everything, one does in fact neither believe anything sincerely nor understand anything thoroughly."[9] Universalists thus lose the essence of both their own religion and that of others.

In Buddhism, which is based on the doctrine of the Middle Way, neither the Buddha nor the great Buddhist sages said, "My teachings alone are true." They did not encourage persecution by religious wars, burning at the stake, massacres, or forced conversions for the sake of their own Dharma, nor did they state that all teachings are the same. In the First Suttanta of the Digha Nikaya, the Buddha said: "Make a trial, find out what leads to your happiness and freedom—and what does not, reject it. What leads on to greater happiness—follow it."

This practical and sure way of distinguishing truth amid falsehood was meant by the Buddha to be applied to his own teachings as well, for he emphasized that one ought not to believe in the authority of any teachers and masters but should believe and practice the religious truth embodied by them. This is the Middle Way in action—as something practiceable, by means of which one can steer a course between blind dogma and vague eclecticism.

Because of this "Middle Way" approach to other religions, when Buddhism was introduced to South Asia, China, Tibet, Korea, and Japan it did not eliminate or drive out native religions but sought to co-exist with them. Of course, when Buddhism was introduced to China and Japan, for instance, there were conflicts between Indian-born Buddhism and such native religions as Confucianism and Taoism in China and Shintoism in Japan. Those conflicts were not necessarily purely religious but rather were caused by the nationalistic feelings of political leaders and their followers against the newly introduced foreign religion. In China, from the fifth to tenth centuries, Buddhism was seriously persecuted four times by pro-Confucian or pro-Taoist emperors. In those persecutions Buddhism was always passive; yet it survived serious damage to its temples and priesthood. There were even those who advocated the unity of Confucianism, Taoism, and Buddhism; thus, Buddhism came to be firmly rooted in Chinese soil. In Japan there was no serious Buddhist persecution except that of the Shogun Oda Nobu-

---

[9]Phra Khantipolo, *Tolerance: A Study from Buddhist Sources* (London: Rider, 1964), pp. 35-37. The author is indebted to this book especially for the discussion of the Middle Way.

naga, who destroyed Buddhist centers at Mt. Hiei and Negoro and the persecution during the early years of the Meiji Restoration in the mid-nineteenth century when the government tried both to revive Shintoism as the state religion
and to destroy the affinity between Buddhism and Shintoism. Most of the four-
teen-century history of Buddhism in Japan, however, proves the harmonious
co-existence of Buddhism with the native Japanese religion of Shintoism. In
short, in spite of its universal character and profound and systematic doctrine,
Buddhism did not eliminate the native religions of the countries into which it
was introduced.

The Buddhist attitude toward other religions stands in marked contrast with
its counterpart in monotheistic religion. When Islam moved into India, it sought
to destroy Hinduism and Buddhism. When Christianity entered into the Germanic world early in the medieval ages, it overwhelmed and absorbed the native
religions of the Germanic peoples. Today, in Christian Europe and England, it is
scarcely possible to find native religions or folklore beliefs in their living forms as
they originally existed among the Teutonic and Anglo-Saxon races.

IV

The Buddhist view of "human rights" is significantly different from that
found in the Western tradition. Strictly speaking, the exact equivalent of the
phrase "human rights" in the Western sense cannot be found anywhere in Buddhist literature. In the Western notion of "human rights," "rights" are understood as pertaining only to humans; nonhuman creatures are either excluded or
at most regarded as peripheral and secondary. "Human rights" are understood
not from the nonhuman or wider-than-human point of view but only from the
human point of view—an anthropocentric view of human rights. By marked contrast, in Buddhism a human being is not grasped only from the human point of
view, that is, not simply on an anthropocentric basis, but on a much broader
trans-homocentric, cosmological basis. More concretely, in Buddhism human
beings are grasped as a part of all sentient beings or even as a part of all beings,
sentient and nonsentient, because both human and nonhuman beings are equally
subject to transiency or impermanency. (That nothing is permanent is a basic
Buddhist principle.) If this universal impermanency that is common to both
human and nonhuman beings is done away with, the problem of life and death
peculiar to human existence cannot be properly resolved. Both the Buddhist
understanding of human suffering and its way of salvation are rooted in this
trans-anthropocentric, cosmological dimension.

This is in sharp contrast to Judaism, Christianity, and Islam, in which the
understanding of human suffering and its way of salvation are based primarily on
the personal relationship between the human being and God which Martin Buber
rightly described in terms of the "I-Thou relationship." That the Buddhist understanding of human suffering and its way of salvation are based on the trans-

anthropocentric, cosmological dimension, however, does not indicate that Buddhism disregards the special significance of human beings in the universe. On the contrary, Buddhism clearly esteems the special distinctiveness of human beings in the universe, as seen in the following verse, which is usually recited by Buddhists as a preamble to the Gatha, "The Threefold Refuge":

> Hard is it to be born into human life.
> We now live it.
> Difficult is it to hear the teaching of the Buddha.
> We now hear it.
> If we do not deliver ourselves in this present life,
> No hope is there ever to cross the sea of birth and death,
> Let us all together, with the truest heart,
> Take refuge in the three treasures!

On this verse, I have made the following comments elsewhere:

> The first and second lines express the joy of being born in human form during the infinite series of varied transmigrations. The third and fourth lines reveal gratitude for being blessed with the opportunity of meeting with the teaching of the Buddha—something which very rarely happens even among men. Finally the fifth and sixth lines confess to a realization that so long as one exists as a man one can and must awaken to one's own Buddha-nature by practicing the teachings of the Buddha; otherwise one may transmigrate on through *samsara* endlessly. Herein it can be seen that Buddhism takes human existence in its positive and unique aspect most seriously into consideration.[10]

As a religion, Buddhism naturally is primarily concerned with human salvation. In this sense Buddhism is not different from Semitic religions. Both Buddhism and Semitic religions are anthropocentric in that they are equally concerned with human salvation. The difference between them lies in the fact that while the basis for human salvation in Semitic religions is the personalistic relationship between the human and God, that basis in Buddhism is the transpersonal, cosmological dimension common to the human and nature: the *Dharma* or suchness (as-it-is-ness) of everything in the universe. In Buddhism, the human problem is grasped not only from the human point of view within the human realm but also from the much wider trans-human, cosmological point of view far beyond the human dimension. Yet it is only human beings who, alone in the universe, have self-consciousness and can thus transcend their own realm and reach the universal, cosmological dimension.

In Buddhism, "human rights" is to be understood in this trans-anthropocentric, universal dimension. If "human rights" is understood to indicate human

---

[10]Masao Abe, "Man and Nature in Christianity and Buddhism," in Frederick Franck, ed., *The Buddha Eye: An Anthology of the Kyoto School* (New York: Crossroad, 1982), p. 152.

rights as grasped only from an anthropocentric point of view—as is the case in the West—we cannot find its counterpart in Buddhist literature. In order to understand the Buddhist view of "human rights" properly we should return to the problem of "self," since in any religion, particularly in Buddhism, human rights and human freedom cannot be legitimately grasped without a proper understanding of the problem of self. Self is not an absolute but a relative entity. As soon as one talks about self one already presupposes the existence of the other. There can be no self apart from the other, and vice versa. Self and the other are entirely interdependent and relational.

Self is not an independent, self-existing, enduring, substantial entity. Nevertheless, because we human beings have self-consciousness and a strong disposition toward self-love and self-attachment, we often reify it as if it were an independent, enduring, substantial entity. Self-centeredness is simply an outcome of this reification or substantialization of the self. Buddhism emphasizes that this reification of the self and its resultant self-centeredness are the root-source of evil and human suffering. Accordingly, as a way of salvation, Buddhism teaches the necessity of realizing the nonsubstantiality of the self, that is, of realizing no-self or *anatman*.

The Buddhist notion of no-self, however, does not preclude human selfhood in the *relative* sense. It is undeniable that we come to a realization of the "self-identity" of ourselves through memories from our childhood and through interaction with friends and other fellow beings. I am I and not you; you are you and not me. Hence, there is a clear distinction between self and other and, thereby, a clear realization of self-identity or selfhood. The question in this regard, however, is whether this self-identity or selfhood is *absolutely* independent, enduring, and substantial. The answer must be "no." For there is no "I" apart from "you," just as there is no "you" apart from "I." As soon as we talk about "I," we already and categorically presuppose the existence of "you," and vice versa. Accordingly, although we have self-identity in a relative sense, we do not have it in the absolute sense. I am I in the relative sense, but I am not I in the absolute sense. The notion of absolute self-identity or substantial, enduring selfhood is an unreal, conceptual construction created by human self-consciousness. Buddhism calls it *maya*, or illusion, and emphasizes the importance of awakening to no-self by doing away with this illusory understanding of the self.

Once we awaken to our own no-selfhood, we also awaken to the no-selfhood of everything and everyone in the universe. In other words, we awaken to the fact that, just like ourselves, nothing in the universe has any fixed, substantial selfhood, even while maintaining relative selfhood. So, on the relative level, all have our own distinctive selfhood; yet, on the absolute level, we have no fixed, substantial selfhood but, rather, equality and solidarity in terms of the realization of no-self. Accordingly, from an absolute standpoint, we can say that, because of the absence of substantial selfhood, I am not I, and you are not you; thereby, I am you, and you are me. We are different relatively but equal absolutely, interfusing with one another, even while retaining our distinct identity.

The same is true with the self and nature, and with the self and the divine. The self and nature are different from one another on the relative level, but on the absolute level they are equal and interfuse with one another because of the lack of any fixed, substantial selfhood. Consequently, nature is not merely a resource for the human self; it is grasped in sympathetic relationship with the self. Finally, and most importantly, the self and the divine—whether one calls it God, *das Heilige*, *Brahman*, or *Nirvana*—are, relatively speaking, essentially different from one another; yet, absolutely speaking, the self and the divine are not different but equal, interfusing and interpenetrating with one another. This is the case because even the divine is understood here without independent, enduring, substantial selfhood.

Clearly, on this point Buddhism and monotheistic religions are radically different, and this difference has important ramifications when we come to the crucial point of the problem of religious tolerance. In Judaism, Christianity, and Islam the divine is the One Absolute God who, being the ruler of the universe, is free-willed and self-affirmative and essentially transcendent to human beings and nature. The self-affirmative character of Yahweh God is clearly seen when Yahweh's "Self" is revealed to Moses on Mount Sinai by saying, "I am that I am" (Ex. 24:12, 34) (the original Hebrew of this phrase, *'ehyeh 'asher 'ehyeh*, means "I will be what I will be"). Further, in the Ten Commandments that Yahweh gave to Moses it was emphasized that, "You shall have no other gods before me" (Ex. 20:3).

In Israelite religions this strongly monotheistic commandment comes first among the Ten Commandments. Buddhism has a Decalogue very similar to that of the Israelite religion, emphasizing that, "You shall not kill, shall not steal, shall not lie, shall not commit adultery," and so forth. In the Buddhist Ten Commandments, however, there is no equivalent to the first commandment of the Decalogue—"You shall have no other gods before me." Instead, the first of the Buddhist Ten Commandments is "Not to destroy life," and this commandment refers not only to human life but also to the life of all sentient beings. In the Judeo-Christian tradition the problem of human rights and human duty to other people must be considered in relation to the exclusive commandment of the supreme God, whereas in Buddhism the same problem should be grasped in relation to all living beings in the universe. This difference entails that in Buddhism conflict between human rights and religious freedom becomes much less serious than in Israelite religions. It also leads to a different attitude toward the problem of the environment, another burning issue of our time. Under the commandment "Not to destroy any life," the rights of animals and plants are as equally recognized as are human rights. Not only is nature subordinate to human beings, but human beings are also subordinate to nature.

V

How can Buddhism contribute to the issue of "religious tolerance and human rights"? I would like to offer Buddhist solutions to this problem in three ways.

1. Elimination of the attachment to doctrine and dogma: No religion is without doctrine, but the attitudes toward doctrine are not the same. When doctrine is regarded as authoritative and binding upon all the faithful, it turns into "dogma." "Dogma" is a fixed form of belief formulated in creeds and articles by religious institutional authority for acceptance by its followers. Within Christianity, the Roman Catholic Church still promulgates dogmas, while Protestant churches have "confessions" in which the faithful confess what they believe from the heart rather than submit to an imposed, external doctrinal statement (dogma)—though the Protestant "confessions" are also interpreted "dogmatically" by some. When dogma is emphasized, schism often takes place within a religion, and opposition occurs among other religions. Conflict—even religious war—erupts. Religions which are based on divine revelation and which emphasize exclusive faith in the revealed truth are frequently liable to the intolerance generated by fixed forms of belief.

By contrast, Buddhism, which is not based on divine revelation but on self-awakening, has no dogma. Although Buddhism has various forms of doctrine—such as the Four Noble Truths, the Eightfold Path, and the twelve-link chain of causation—doctrines are not regarded in Buddhism as something essential. The Buddha himself said: "My teaching is like a raft to cross the stream of life and death so as to reach the other shore of enlightenment. Once you reach the other shore there is no need to carry the raft."[11] From the Buddhist standpoint, what is important for religion is not doctrine—to say nothing of dogma—but one's existential commitment to the religious truth underlying the doctrinal formulation. If we eliminate attachment to dogma and return to the religious truth as the root-source of doctrine, we can largely overcome schisms and religious wars and become more tolerant not only within our own religion but also toward other religions.

2. Emphasis on wisdom rather than justice: In the Judeo-Christian tradition, God is believed to have the attributes of justice or righteousness as the judge, as well as love or mercy as the forgiver. God is the fountain of justice, so everything God does may be relied upon as just. Since God's verdict is absolutely just, human righteousness may be defined in terms of God's judgment.

The notion of justice or righteousness is a double-edged sword. On the one hand it aids in keeping everything in the right order, but on the other hand it establishes clear-cut distinctions between the righteous and the unrighteous,

---

[11]*The Dhammapada: The Path of Perfection*, tr. Juan Mascaro (Harmondsworth: Penguin, 1973).

promising the former eternal bliss but condemning the latter to eternal punishment. Accordingly, if justice or righteousness is the sole principle of judgment or is too strongly emphasized, it creates serious disunion and schism among people. This disunion is unrestorable because it is a result of divine judgment.

Although his religious background was Jewish, Jesus went beyond such a strong emphasis on divine justice and preached the indifference of God's love. Speaking of God the Father he said: "He makes his sun rise on the evil and on the good, and sends rain on the just and on the unjust" (Mt. 5:45). Thus, he emphasized, "Love your enemies and pray for those who persecute you, so that you may be sons of your Father who is in heaven" (Mt. 5:44). Nevertheless, in the Judeo-Christian tradition the notion of divine election is persistently evident. The Old Testament preaches God's choice of Israel from among all the nations of the earth to be God's people in the possession of a covenant of privilege and blessing (Dt. 4:37, 7:6; 1 Kgs. 3:8; Is. 44:1-2). In the New Testament, divine election is a gracious and merciful election. Nevertheless, this election is rather restricted, for, as the New Testament clearly states, "Many are called, but few are chosen" (Mt. 22:14). Thus "the terms [election or elect] always imply differentiation whether viewed on God's part or as privilege on the part of men."[12] In Christianity the notion of the "Elect of God" often overshadows the "indifference of God's love." If I am not mistaken, this is largely related to the emphasis on justice or righteousness.

While Christianity talks much about love, Buddhism stresses compassion. In Christianity, however, love is accompanied by justice. Love without justice is not regarded as true love. In Buddhism, compassion always goes with wisdom. Compassion without wisdom is not understood to be true compassion. Like the Christian notion of righteousness, the Buddhist notion of wisdom indicates the clarification of the distinction or differentiation of things in the universe. Unlike the Christian notion of justice, however, the Buddhist notion of wisdom does not entail judgment or election. Buddhist wisdom implies the affirmation or recognition of everything and everyone in their distinctiveness or in their suchness. Further, as noted above, the notion of justice creates an irreparable split between the just and the unjust, the righteous and the unrighteous, whereas the notion of wisdom evokes the sense of equality and solidarity. Again, justice, when carried to its final conclusion, often results in punishment, conflict, revenge, and even war, whereas wisdom entails rapprochement, conciliation, harmony, and peace. Love and justice are like water and fire: although both are necessary, they go together with difficulty. Compassion and wisdom are like heat and light: although different, they work together complementarily.

The Judeo-Christian tradition does not lack the notion of wisdom. In the Hebrew Bible, wisdom literature such as Job, Proverbs, and Ecclesiastes occupies

---

[12]"Elect, Election," in Everett F. Harrison, ed.-in-chief, *Baker's Dictionary of Theology* (Grand Rapids, MI: Baker Book House, 1960), p. 179.

an important portion in which *hokma* (wisdom) frequently appears. This term refers to both human knowledge and divine wisdom. In the latter case, as a wisdom given by God it enables the human to lead a good, true, and satisfying life through keeping God's commandments. In the New Testament, *sophia* is understood to be an attribute of God (Lk. 11:49), the revelation of the divine will to people (1 Cor. 2:4-7). But, most remarkably, Jesus as the Christ is identified with the wisdom of God because he is believed in as the ultimate source of all Christian wisdom (1 Cor. 1:30). Nevertheless, in the Judeo-Christian tradition as a whole, the wisdom aspect of God has been neglected in favor of the justice aspect of God. Is it not important and terribly necessary now to emphasize the wisdom aspect of God rather than the justice aspect of God, in order to solve the conflict within a religion as well as among religions?

3. A new understanding of monotheism: Above, I criticized monotheistic religion in that, due to its strong emphasis on the One Absolute God, it is apt to be exclusive and intolerant. To any religion, however, the realization of the oneness of ultimate reality is important, because religion is expected to offer an integral and total—rather than fragmental or partial—salvation from human suffering. Even so-called polytheistic religion does not believe in various deities without order, but it often worships a certain supreme deity as a ruler over a hierarchy of innumerable gods. Further, the three major deities often constitute a trinity—as exemplified by the Hindu notion of *trimurti*, the threefold deity of *Brahman*, *Visnu*, and *Siva*. Such a notion of trinity in polytheism also implies a tendency toward a unity of diversity—a tendency toward oneness.

This means that in any religion, especially in higher religion, the realization of the Oneness of ultimate reality is crucial. Yet, the realization of Oneness necessarily entails exclusiveness, intolerance, and religious imperialism, which cause conflict and schism within a given religion and among the various religions. This is a very serious dilemma which no higher religion can escape. How can we believe in the Oneness of the ultimate reality in our own religion without falling into exclusive intolerance and religious imperialism toward other faiths? What kind of Oneness of ultimate reality can solve that dilemma and open up a dimension in which positive tolerance and peaceful coexistence are possible among religions, each of which is based on One Absolute reality?

In this connection I would like to distinguish two kinds of oneness: the first monistic; the second, nondualistic. It is my contention that not the former but the latter kind of oneness may solve this dilemma. How are monistic and nondualistic oneness different from one another? I would like to clarify their differences by making the following four points:

First, monistic oneness is realized by distinguishing itself and setting itself apart from dualistic twoness and pluralistic manyness; it is thus still dualistically related to dualistic twoness and pluralistic manyness. Monism excludes dualism and pluralism and, therefore, stands in opposition to them. Accordingly, monistic oneness is neither truly monistic nor true oneness. In order to realize true oneness we must go not only beyond dualism and pluralism but also beyond monistic oneness itself. *Then* we can realize nondualistic oneness, because at that point we are completely free from any form of duality, including both the duality between monism and dualism and the duality between monism and pluralism.

Second, monistic oneness is realized as the goal or end to be reached from the side of duality or plurality. It is somewhat "over there," not right here. It is conceived and objectified from the outside. Contrary to this, nondualistic oneness is the ground or root-source realized here and now, from which our life and activities can properly begin. When we overcome monistic oneness we come to a point which is neither one nor two nor many but which is appropriately referred to as "zero." Since the "zero" is free from any form of duality, true oneness can be realized through the realization of "zero." Monistic oneness is a kind of oneness which lacks the realization of "zero," whereas nondualistic oneness is a kind of oneness which is based on the realization of "zero."

Third, the true oneness which can be realized through the realization of "zero" should not be objectively conceived. If it is objectified or conceptualized in any way, it is not the real oneness. An objectified oneness is merely something named "oneness." To reach and fully realize the true Oneness, it is necessary completely to overcome conceptualization and objectification. True Oneness is realized only in a nonobjective way by overcoming even "zero" objectified as the end. Accordingly, overcoming "zero" as the end is a turning point from the objective, aim-seeking approach to the nonobjective, im-mediate approach, from monistic oneness to nondualistic oneness. Monistic oneness is oneness before the realization of "zero," whereas nondualistic oneness is oneness through and beyond the realization of "zero."

Fourth, monistic oneness, being somewhat "over there," does not immediately include two, many, and the whole. Even though it can be all-inclusive, it is more or less separated from the particularity and multiplicity of actual entities in the world. This is because monistic oneness is usually substantial. Nondualistic oneness, however, which is based on the realization of "zero," includes all individual things, just as they are, without any modification. This is because in nondualistic oneness conceptualization and objectification are completely overcome. There is no separation between nondualistic oneness and individual things. At this point the one and the many are nondual.

Though we should not confuse monism with monotheism, problems involved in monistic oneness in relation to dualistic twoness and pluralistic manyness may be applied to monotheism as well.

Buddhism often emphasizes the oneness of body and mind, the oneness of life and death, the oneness of good and evil, and the identity of *samsara* and *nirvana*, Buddha and sentient beings. It also talks about *ekacitta* (one dharma Mind), *ekalapsana* (one Nature), *ekayana* (one Vehicle), and the like. It appears to be quite monistic or "mono-theistic" from a surface perspective. In view of the difference between monistic oneness and nondualistic oneness as described in the above four points, however, it is clear that the Buddhist notion of oneness is not monistic, but nondualistic. As stated before, Gautama Buddha rejected the age-old Vedantic notion of *Brahman* as the sole and enduring reality underlying the universe. Instead, he advocated the law of "dependent co-origination" and no-selfhood and the nonsubstantiality of everything in the universe, including the divine and the human. Even the notion of Buddha is nonsubstantial without enduring, fixed selfhood. Rather, one who awakens to the nonsubstantiality and no-selfhood of everything is called a Buddha.

Nirvana, which is often regarded as the goal of Buddhist life, is not really the goal to be reached as the end of life. Mahayana Buddhism emphasizes, "Do not abide in *samsara* or *nirvana*." One should not abide in *samsara*, the endless process of transmigration, but, through the realization of wisdom, should attain *nirvana*, the blissful freedom from transmigration. However, if one remains in *nirvana*, one may enjoy the bliss but forget the suffering of his or her fellow beings who are still involved in the process of *samsara*. Thus it is necessary "not to abide in *nirvana*" by overcoming the attachment to *nirvana*. *Nirvana* should not be attached to as if it were a substantial, fixed, enduring entity. In order to fulfill compassion toward one's fellow beings, one should not abide in *nirvana* but return to *samsara*. This means that true *nirvana* in Mahayana Buddhism does not lie either in *samsara* or in *nirvana* in a fixed sense of the terms but in a dynamic movement between *samsara* and *nirvana* without any attachment to either, without any reification of either. Accordingly, Mahayana Sutras, particularly the *Prajnaparamita Sutra*, emphasize detachment from the sacred realm. In a sense this *Sutra* places greater emphasis on the harmfulness of attachment to the sacred realm than that of attachment to the secular realm. It stresses the necessity of detachment from the "religious" life. This is simply because the attachment to the divine as something substantial is a hindrance for true salvation and because the divine which is substantialized and objectified cannot be the true divine. Yet, Buddhism talks about one Mind, one Nature, and one Dharma. This oneness, however, is not oneness before the realization of "zero" but oneness beyond or through the realization of "zero." In short, it is not monistic oneness but nondualistic oneness. In the long history of Buddhism we have had troubles from time to time when we deviated from this nondualistic oneness in our faith.

When the divine, God or Buddha, is believed to be self-affirmative, self-existing, enduring, and substantial, the divine becomes authoritative, commanding, and intolerant. On the contrary, when the divine, God or Buddha, is believed to be self-negating, relational, and nonsubstantial, the divine becomes compassionate, all-loving, and tolerant. I believe all three monotheistic religions (Judaism, Christianity, and Islam) preach the love of God while emphasizing the Absolute Oneness of God. If our friends of these three religions place more emphasis on the self-negating, nonsubstantial aspect of their "God" than on God's self-affirmative authoritative aspect, that is, if the Oneness of God in these monotheistic religions is grasped not as one before the realization of "zero," but as one beyond the realization of "zero," while thoroughly maintaining their faith in the One absolute God, they may then overcome serious conflicts with other faiths. In this case, as a correlative attribute of God's love and mercy, the wisdom aspect of God must be more emphasized than the justice aspect of God.

This is my humble proposal to this conference as a Buddhist remedy to the problem of the religious intolerance and human rights. In conclusion, I quote the following words of Buddha:

> Not by hatred is hatred appeased:
> Hatred is appeased by the renouncing of hatred.
> It is so conquered only by love
> This is a law eternal.[13]

---

[13]*Maha-Vagga*. See Burtt, *Teachings*, p. 40.

TWO FACES OF HINDUISM
AND THE SEARCH FOR UNIFYING SPIRITUAL PRINCIPLES

D. Scott Korn

Hinduism, like many of the gods in its rich mythological heritage, has many faces. In this essay I will examine two of the most prominent of those faces, one bright with tolerance, spirituality, and meaning; the other, marred with the dark, archaic lines of superstition, intolerance, and exploitation. The first face, which I call "higher Hinduism," expresses the heritage of free philosophical and religious inquiry in the quest for truth. This "truth," however, is not merely a theoretical construct or apprehension; rather it is a power which, when lived and valued, leads to a liberating and blissful realization of the Self and its relation to Ultimate Reality. The second face of Hinduism, which I call "popular Hinduism," often exists as if it were disconnected from the same body as higher Hinduism. Popular Hinduism concerns the caste system, complex ritualism, and an obsession with purity and pollution, along with nobler forms of devotionalism. Mahatma Gandhi, writing in 1946, described Hinduism in this way:

> There are two aspects of Hinduism. There is, on the one hand, the historical Hinduism with its untouchability, superstitious worship of stocks [sic] and stones, animal sacrifices, and so on. On the other hand, we have the Hinduism of the *Gita*, the *Upanishads*, and Patanjali's *Yoga Sutras* which is the acme of *Ahimsa* [nonviolence] and oneness of all creation, pure worship of one immanent, formless, imperishable God.[1]

Mirroring the compartmentalization of academic disciplines in the West, most studies of Hinduism have concentrated on defining Hinduism by one of these two faces. Those disciplines aligned with the philosophy and phenomenology of religions have tended to emphasize the quest for liberation and the search for God as the overriding feature of Hinduism, while sociological and anthropological studies have emphasized religion as one element in the power struggles behind the caste system. Exemplifying the latter type of approach, the pioneering sociologist Max Weber wrote that, "Caste . . . is the fundamental institution of Hinduism. Before everything else, without caste there is no Hinduism."[2] Nevertheless, hosts of Hindu reformers past and present have not seen caste as an

---

[1]Gandhi quoted in Troy Wilson Organ, *Hinduism: Its Historical Development* (Woodbury, NY: Barron's Educational Series, Inc., 1974), p. 368.

[2]Max Weber, *The Religion of India: The Sociology of Hinduism and Buddhism*, tr. and ed., Hans H. Gerth and Don Martindale (Glencoe, IL: The Free Press, 1958), p. 29. Similarly, Victor S. D'Souza holds that, "The notions of purity and pollution as they are manifested in the caste system form the basis of Hindu religious ideology" ("The Religious Factor and the Scheduled Castes," *Social Action* 32 [July-September, 1982]: 283).

essential feature of Hinduism. Sarasvati Chennakesavan, for example, holds that:

> The fundamental characteristic of Hinduism is the belief that man
> should attain freedom from sorrow and suffering incident on life in
> this world and attain *mokṣa* [spiritual liberation]. Since even our
> scriptures have not laid down membership of any caste as a prerequi-
> site for the attainment of *mokṣa*, giving up caste is not going to
> adversely affect a Hindu in the practice of his religion.[3]

My sympathies lie with this reforming and spiritualizing understanding of
Hinduism. What I will attempt in this study, however, is to draw some intercon-
nections between the legacies of both higher Hinduism and popular Hinduism.
Both faces will be put under the lens of critical historical, philosophical, and
sociological scrutiny to expose obvious as well as hidden blemishes. But this
"clinical" type of procedure will not be done with any bias to uphold another
world religion as more worthy of admiration. Rather the intent will be threefold:
(1) on a scholarly level, to understand better the Hindu religion and the relations
between Hinduism and the other world religions, as well as (2) to articulate and
defend some normative principles for evaluating Hinduism and all other religious
traditions; and (3) on a humanitarian level, to encourage a reforming spirit so
that, eventually, Hinduism will be purged of some of its morally questionable
features—features which are at variance not only with international standards of
human rights but also with its own highest sources of scriptural authority and
with the progressive development of its own philosophical tradition. After such
purgation, Hinduism will be even more effective in aiding its own members as
well as the world at large in the desperate battle against the forces of nihilism,
hedonistic materialism, intolerance, and fanaticism.

Hindu apologists of the twentieth century have by and large attempted to
uphold Hinduism to the world as the shining example of a pure form of spirituality free of the dogmatism, intolerance, and exclusivism which have characterized many other religions. Swami Abhedananda of the Ramakrishna Mission
asked:

> . . . is there a common platform on which all these revealed and un-
> revealed religions can meet and unite? The answer is to be found no-
> where except in Vedanta [the philosophy of Hinduism]. . . . First we
> must realize that all these different creeds, doctrines, ceremonies,
> rituals, and beliefs in some particular form or name of divinity, in
> a revealed book, or in any great personality, are like the husks of
> grain which hide the kernel. They are the non-essentials of religion.[4]

From an even more radical perspective on the superiority of the Vedanta,

---

[3]Sarasvati Chennakesavan, *A Critical Study of Hinduism* (New York: Asia Publishing
House, 1974), p. 129.
[4]Swami Abhedananda, *Attitude of Vedanta toward Religion* (Calcutta: Ramakrishna
Vedanta Math, 1947), pp. 124-125.

Sri Krishna Prem believes that, in fact, despite subsequent distortions by others, the founders of the great religions, the *Avataras*, Messiahs, great Prophets, etc., all witnessed to the truth of higher Hinduism: "It is not as separate individuals that they speak, but as the unborn, beginningless Eternal, the *Brahman* in which all abide, 'by which all this is pervaded.' "[5]

What is implicit in these types of evaluation of the relationship of Hinduism to the world religions—besides the ignoring of "popular Hinduism" as a superficial outward form, and besides the genuineness and sincerity of a search for some universal spiritual principle which when realized will foster harmony between the religions of the world—is the exaltation of a particular form of Hindu Vedanta philosophy called "Advaitism" or "Nondualism" as the pinnacle of the world religions: the "top of the mountain," to use a popular apologetic metaphor. S. Radhakrishnan succinctly expressed this hierarchical understanding: "The worshippers of the Absolute [Brahman] are the highest in rank, second to them are the worshippers of the personal God; then come worshippers of incarnation like Rama, Krishna, Buddha." In another work a similar idea is expressed: "Identity with the Supreme is the highest and the stage of meditation is the next, lower still is the stage of repeated hymns and mantras, and lowest of all is external worship."[6]

Now the search for unifying spiritual principles that will foster harmony among diverse religious and quasi-religious communities may indeed be a crying need in our time, but these principles do not necessarily imply either that the essence of religion is one or that the forms that differentiate one religion from another are relatively unimportant. Certainly a religion which encourages human sacrifice is fundamentally different from a religion which holds that nonviolent renunciation of the world is the *summum bonum*, just as both religious forms are fundamentally different from, for example, the religion of the service of humanity which guided Gandhi throughout his adult years. Because the metaphysical view of Advaitism is that all forms belonging to the empirical world of dualities are ultimately unreal (*Maya*) in relation to the Absolute, the unchanging nondual Brahman, the tendency of this particular Vedantic perspective is naturally to see the forms of the world religions as all relatively unimportant. However, we have just seen that the types of these different forms are fundamentally important in the influence they have on how we live our lives. Furthermore, it can be argued that the *form* of explanation and argument presented by the Advaitin position is also relative. It, too, is just one more religious philosophy among other Hindu and non-Hindu explanations of this world in relation to the

---

[5]Sri Krishna Prem, *The Yoga of the Bhagavadgītā* (London: Stuart Watkins, 1969), p. 96. Cf. Swami Prabhavananda: "We know that Jesus, Krishna, and Buddha, when they say 'I' or 'me', are not asserting the ego, as ordinary embodied souls do. They are asserting their divinity, their identity with the universal self [the equivalent of Brahman]" (*The Sermon on the Mount according to Vedanta* [Madras: Sri Ramakrishna Math, 1964], p. 35).

[6]Sarvepalli Radhakrishnan, *The Hindu View of Life* (New York: Allen and Unwin, 1974), p. 32; *Religion and Society* (London: Allen and Unwin, 1947), p. 122.

Ultimate Reality which has the power to help liberate us from our sorrows and troubles.

M. M. Thomas, a past leader of the World Council of Churches, complained of the Advaitin approach to the world religions: ". . . structurally speaking, this idea of inter-religious relation on the basis of elevating Advaitin mysticism to the crown of Christianity, is not different from that based on elevating Jesus Christ to the crown of Hinduism."[7] Thomas is here referring to the Roman Catholic and liberal Protestant perspective of seeing all religions as partial manifestations of God's grace leading their adherents to the fullest manifestation of God for humanity in Jesus Christ. On one side, we have all religions really witnessing to the Absolute Brahman; on the other, we have all religions implicitly seeking Christ. The structure is parallel. Continuing Thomas's line of reasoning, we can see that alternate metaphysical, scientific, or religious models would not necessarily be less adequate for uniting disparate worldviews, that is, for providing a unifying principle of explanation and for providing an ultimate goal of life for all people. For example, Hazel Barnes, in her attempt to explain religion from the perspective of Sartrian atheistic humanism, warned against interpreting Sartre as an Advaitin:

> The dangerous step here is to conclude that Sartre's refusal to ascribe original differentiation and significance to Being-in-itself [the analogue here to the Absolute Brahman] is equivalent to saying that Being-in-itself is all one and the same [or nondual]. To introduce concepts of unity and sameness is to do violence to what Being-in-itself is, fully as much as notions of multiplicity and variation do.[8]

We see a comparable type of resistance toward the absolutizing of the Advaitin perspective among dialectical metaphysicians such as Hegel and Tillich in the West and Ramanuja and Sri Aurobindo in the Hindu tradition. Here, the emphasis is on seeing a dialectical relation between the world of changing forms and the world of unchanging Being-itself. While Sartre, as explained above, would not want to ascribe unity and rest to the Absolute, as the Advaitins do, these dialectical metaphysicians wish to conclude that when we rise to a higher form of understanding than is compatible with empirically inspired laws of formal logic—where Being-itself and becoming, rest and motion, unity and differentiation (nonduality and duality), eternity and time, for example, contradict one another—then we will see that the world of manifold forms and the formless world of Being-itself are both expressions of Ultimate Reality. Neither this world nor the "Wholly Other" transcendent world of the Absolute (or of God) is more real than the other. In Hindu terms, then, this world is not "Maya" in the sense

---

[7]M. M. Thomas, *The Acknowledged Christ of the Indian Rennaisance* (Madras: Christian Literature Society, 1970), p. 194.

[8]Hazel E. Barnes, *An Existentialist Ethics* (New York: Alfred Knopf, 1969), p. 237. Prof. Barnes is here comparing Sartrian Existentialism with Advaitin mysticism. See her chapter: "The Temptation of Eastern Philosophy," pp. 210-277.

of illusion or misapprehension of an undifferentiated Absolute, as in Advaitism; rather, "Maya" means the suprarational way Brahman becomes the world without ceasing to be One. In this pan-en-theistic view, the world is Divine, for those with eyes to see. As Krishna says in the Bhagavadgita (henceforth, the Gita):[9]

> Though (I am) unborn, and My self is imperishable, though (I am) the Lord of all creatures, yet establishing Myself in My own nature, I come into being through My power [*Maya*]. . . . I am the origin of all; from Me (the whole creation) proceeds. Knowing this, the wise worship Me, endowed with conviction. . . . For I am the foundation of Brahman, the Immortal and the Imperishable, of eternal law and of absolute bliss. (4:6; 10:8; 14:27)

This dialectical, metaphysical model, which Aurobindo comprehends as "The Logic of the Infinite,"[10] when applied to the religions of the world, does more justice to the significance and reality of the various forms that each religion embodies—for qualitative distinctions are real, not illusory. But were we to elevate this particular Hindu view as the "crown of the world religions," then once again we would be excluding other worldviews which also can claim to be inclusive. What are we then to conclude about this search: Are there no unifying spiritual principles underlying the world religions? Must the scientific empiricists have the last say when they focus on the obvious distinctions between different religious forms without participating in any spiritual depth which may be common to them all? Or must the religious dogmatists have the last say when they conclude that they "have the truth in their pocket," that their religion—usually the one they inherited—is based on the only true revelation of the Ultimate Reality? Is divisiveness more real than unity?

The first conclusion is that Advaitism offers no satisfactory solution to the problem of disparate religious forms. It, too, we have seen, is just another religio-philosophical form, commendable though it is for its broad catholicity and absence of the spirit of violent proselytization and chauvinism. Second, metaphysics itself, divided as it is into a variety of conceptual forms, offers no satisfactory solution. The third conclusion is that, having exhausted metaphysics, we must then turn to empirical realms, but not to the realm investigated by the

---

[9]*The Bhagavadgītā*, tr. S. Radhakrishnan (London: George Allen and Unwin, 1970). Though he reads the Gita in an Advaitin-like manner, I have chosen to use Radhakrishnan's translation in this study. I depart from his translation in 14:27 where he has "abode" for *pratistha*; in his gloss, however, he agrees with my translation as "foundation." Radhakrishnan also unnecessarily has "(empiric)" before "being" in 4:6.

[10]Contrary to Kierkegaard in his attack on Hegel, reality cannot always be approached with "Either-Or" types of expectations. In terms of contemporary logic, reality is more "fuzzy" than can be apprehended by a love of conceptual precision. Radhakrishnan, however, prefers the either-or precision of traditional Advaitism: "The forms we impose on the Formless are due to our limitations. We turn away from the contemplation of Ultimate Reality to concentrate upon imaginative constructions" (*Bhagavadgītā*, p. 233). For Aurobindo's reformulation of this tradition, see his magnum opus, *The Life Divine* (Pondicherry: Sri Aurobindo Ashram, 1949), especially vol. 2, pt. 1.

purely external types of objective science, for objective science is incapable of uncovering the depth of involvement and personal transformation which characterizes religious experience; rather we must turn to an empiricism of involvement, of being true to all the aspects of our experience, including our experience of participating empathetically in the religious life of our neighbors.

Since all religions, we find, are concerned about what is ultimately most real and valuable for their adherents, it can be asked whether the symbolic forms which characterize a particular religion adequately reveal what is ultimate, or whether the practitioners of a particular religion take as the Ultimate Reality what may be, or what in fact is, limited and tainted with human finitude and cultural disposition. Since this question can be asked of all religious and quasi-religious traditions, without implicitly proselytizing one of those traditions, it can serve as a normative principle for evaluating the world religions. This first principle I call the "Principle of the Ultimate."[11] (For an elaboration of this principle and two others, see my Appendix.)

When the Principle of the Ultimate is applied to higher Hinduism, it highlights the fact that the Advaitin understanding of Ultimate Reality appears to be a human construct and thus is relative to other constructs. Hence, to revere the Advaitin construct as the final, ultimate perspective is to violate the principle of ultimacy. Analogously, on the level of popular Hinduism, the principle supports a critique of the hereditary caste system. Because, as I will argue, this caste system is a humanly constructed social form, it cannot represent the eternal law of truth. In Hindu terminology, the system cannot be an aspect of the *Sanatana Dharma*, for it is shot through with finitude: It had its birth in time, relative to the historical needs of a culture, and its death knell has sounded in the distance.

The fourth conclusion, then, which has arisen from our examination of the Advaitin search for the essence of religion is that there indeed is an underlying principle to the world religions, a principle which is also paradoxically (but like life itself) divisive: Within each religious tradition are found orthodox literalists who commend their religious forms as Absolute, as there are in each religious tradition those who see the relativity of all religious forms (not the relative equality or unimportance of these forms as in Advaitism) and are open to the

---

[11]It will be seen that Paul Tillich's theology has been especially helpful here in articulating this principle. Tillich, however, distorted this principle to uphold Christianity as the "final revelation." E.g., in his *Dynamics of Faith* (New York: Harper and Row, 1958), he wrote: "That symbol is most adequate which expresses not only the ultimate but also its own lack of ultimacy. Christianity expresses itself in such a symbol in contrast to all other religions" (p. 98). Very few Christians, however, would understand the symbol of the cross the way Tillich does. Furthermore, as Walter Kaufmann has pointed out: ". . . symbols that express not only the ultimate but their own lack of ultimacy are found in Judaism and Buddhism as well as Hinduism—quite especially in the Vedānta of Shankara [the foremost Advaitin]" (*Religion in Four Dimensions* [New York: Reader's Digest Press, 1976], p. 246). Also, I am currently nearing completion of a book to be entitled: "The Logic of Exclusivism: A Comparison of Christianity and Hinduism from the Perspective of Paul Tillich's Systematic Theology and the Bhagavadgītā," in which the concept of "final revelation" will be examined in some detail.

possibility of growth and reform of their tradition. Specifically, this means that in each religious tradition are found adherents to either truths of the letter or truths of the Spirit. Gandhi would be a good example of this latter type. He wrote of his own tradition: "If I discovered that the Vedas clearly showed that they claimed divine authority for untouchability, then nothing on this earth would hold me to Hinduism. I would throw it overboard like a rotten apple."[12] And in another context he said in an interview in 1936:

> "And where do you find the seat of authority?" he was asked.
> "It lies here," he said, pointing to his breast. "I exercise my judgement about every scripture including the *Gītā*. I cannot let a scriptural text supersede my reason. . . . I cannot surrender my reason while I subscribe to divine revelation. And above all, 'the letter killeth but the spirit giveth life.' "[13]

Gandhi's attitude toward his own religious tradition not only expresses the Principle of the Ultimate, but it also implicitly expresses a second principle which I call the "Principle of Freedom." Let me elaborate. Since all of us are members of a global community, the thoughtful are all exposed to a multitude of "final" answers in the form of religious and secular philosophies. To claim that one answer is truly final or the true revelation is implicitly to claim that the *choice* we have made to accept this answer is absolutely valid. We are absolutizing our judgment, thereby violating the Principle of the Ultimate. We can express this principle more subtly in light of numerous theological subtleties: The choice we make to accept our *experience* of God's will, election, or revelation as truly genuine—that is, not the will of the devil or the subconscious, or both—is still our choice. While I am not sympathetic with Sartre's understanding of religion, with regard to the second principle of interreligious understanding, his conclusion, experientially, is indisputable: "We are condemned to be free." The choice to believe or not to believe in determinism or fatalism always belies the comprehensiveness of these two doctrines. Thus, the Principle of Freedom, besides being a unifying norm, is also, like the first principle, a dividing line between those in any tradition who take responsibility for their choices with authentic humility and openness to possible error and those who deceive themselves in "bad faith" and claim to have the absolute truth. In this way we can say that Gandhi attempted to embody the Principle of Freedom in an exemplary manner. His lifelong commitment to be open to new truth and to discipline himself in order to sharpen his powers of discernment remains an incomparably valuable gift which higher Hinduism has bequeathed to the world.

There is another significant corollary to the Principle of Freedom which,

---

[12]Quoted in Organ, *Hinduism*, p. 365.
[13]M. K. Gandhi, interview in *Harijan*, vol. 5 (1936), quoted in Arun Shourie, *Hinduism: Essence and Consequence* (Ghaziabad: Vikas Pub. House, 1979), p. 378. Gandhi cited 2 Cor. 3:6. Also note, as is common in Asia, Gandhi pointed here to his heart when referring to the source of his reason.

while applicable to all religions, has special application to Hinduism. If we choose to believe that our fate and the world's fate are predetermined, then we attribute to the powers which determine destiny characteristics of the greatest tyrant and usurper of human rights which history has ever seen. If humanity has no freedom, then the responsibility for the atrocities of world wars, concentration camps, and environmental collapse, for example, must rest with the Creator or the creative forces of nature. How could such creative authority then be loved or respected? Human dignity would lie only in persistent and rebellious scorn—the last hold-out of conscious freedom.[14] In respect to Hinduism, this means that we can never hold *karma* fully responsible for our actions or for the life situation of our neighbors. *Karma* refers only to the sum-total of past actions and present and future tendencies. Due to an overdeterminism of conflicting causes and tendencies, no one cause must of necessity be actualized over another, unless we will it. The act of willing it makes one particular karmic cause the predominant one. Of course the determinist will be quick to say that the action of the will is but the ripening of the predominant karmic seed. However, such a determination is illogically arbitrary (a free choice of the determiner) and experientially unfounded and reductionistic—why consider the conscious decision as less real or causative than the impulse? Thus neither the doctrine of absolute freedom nor the doctrine of absolute necessity taken in isolation from one another does justice to all the facts of our experience. Concretely, this means that Hindu fatalists who, in bad faith and based upon their scriptural revelations, held that this is the darkest age of humanity, the *Kali Yuga*—and that consequently there is no stopping the further degeneration of the world—miss the wisdom of their karma doctrine. The book of life may have been written, but it undergoes continuous revision based upon the Principle of Freedom: we are responsible for our lives, for the future of the world, and for the welfare of our neighbors. This latter responsibility implies that, though our neighbor may have been born into a low, impoverished caste, the choices we actualize in relation to a system which serves to exploit our neighbor determine not only the future of that system, but also our own future. Our karmic destiny depends upon whether we choose to sow seeds of narrow self-interest or seeds of enlightened compassion. The first choice yields the weeds of hell; the second, the garden of God. Let us then look at these choices more closely in relation to the caste system and popular Hinduism.

From the perspective of the United Nations-approved "Universal Declaration of Human Rights,"[15] one of the institutions which most glaringly sanctions

---

[14]See especially A. Camus's story of Sisyphus in *The Myth of Sisyphus, and other Essays*, tr. Justin O'Brien (New York: Vintage Books, 1960); and F. Dostoevsky, *Notes from the Underground*, tr. Ralph Matlaw (New York: E. P. Dutton and Co., 1960)—for the most graphic depictions of this last possible resistance to deterministic tyrannies.

[15]See the U.N. Chronicle *Perspective* 21 (February, 1984), which contains both the declaration itself and a description of the arduous process that was needed to bring it to completion.

the violation of human rights is the caste system of traditional Hinduism. D. N. Trivedi has said of the system that it is the

> . . . most thorough-going attempt in the history of [humankind] to institutionalize inequality. The caste status is ascribed at birth and remains unchanged during [a person's] lifetime, exertion of the individual notwithstanding. Ideally, the caste is a hereditary, endogamous, usually localized group, having traditional association with an occupation and a particular prestigious position in the local hierarchy or castes. Relations between castes are governed, among other things, by the conception of pollution and purity, and generally maximum commensality [inter-dining] occurs within caste.[16]

Before we begin our study of the relation of the caste system to popular and higher Hinduism, it is necessary to note that in principle the worst abuses of the caste system, particularly with regard to untouchability, have been outlawed by the Indian constitution and subsequent judicial decisions. As M. L. Jha has written:

> The Indian Constitution pledges Justice, Liberty, and Equality to all. Any discrimination in public life merely on grounds of religion, race, caste, sex, and birth is prohibited. It favours promotion of education and economic interest of the Scheduled Castes [lower, deprived castes scheduled for upliftment] by the State besides their protection from social injustice and all forms of exploitation. The practice of untouchability in any form is declared a cognizable offence under [the] "Untouchability Offence Act, 1955."[17]

Yet, we know that, despite legislation, many of the worst abuses of the caste system do indeed continue in India, abuses which lead to socioeconomic stratification, a climate of divisiveness and exploitation of others, and often debilitating, humiliating, and impoverishing work and living conditions for many of the lower castes.[18] When we speak of these lower Scheduled and "untouchable" castes, it should be understood that we are speaking of approximately fifteen

---

[16]D. N. Trivedi, "Caste Modernisation and Institutionalisation of Change," *Eastern Anthropologist* 26 (July-September, 1973): 235.

[17]M. L. Jha, *Untouchability and Education (A Socio-psychological Study of Attitudes)* (Meerut, India: Namita Pub., 1973), p. 2. See also Marc Galanter, "Changing Legal Conceptions of Caste," in Milton Singer and Bernard Cohen, eds., *Structure and Change in Indian Society* (Chicago: Aldine Publishing Co., 1968), pp. 299-336. Westerners can temper their shock at the perdurance of the caste system by recalling both how recently slavery was abolished in the U.S.A. and how in the 1950's segregation of Blacks in public places was routine in the Southern states. Furthermore, India's economy of scarcity makes reform even more complex and difficult.

[18]As recently as 1976, I. P. Desai reported: "One thing that our research shows is the limitation of the effectiveness of laws. . . . According to law nobody can practice untouchability anywhere. Yet in the domestic sphere and in religious matters it is as strong as it was" (*Untouchability in Rural Gujerat* [Bombay: Popular Prakashan, 1976], p. 122). Cf.

percent of the Indian population, over 100,000,000 people.[19] Dr. Jose Kananaikil, from his perspective as the Director of the Programme of Scheduled
Castes for the Indian Social Institute (New Delhi), wrote in 1982 that:

> the term "Scheduled Castes" brings different images to the minds of
> different people. To a rural landlord or to an urban contractor the
> term evokes the idea of cheap labour, to a politician it suggests an
> assured vote-bank during election time. To an orthodox Hindu
> "Scheduled Castes" signifies a polluting nuisance; to a zealous social
> reformer or to a religious propagandist it connotes an easy field for
> experiment or proselytization.[20]

In short and quite simply, from the perspective of democracy and compassion for one's neighbor, there is a general climate of unfairness in Hindu society
based upon the caste system. In relation to the "Universal Declaration of Human
Rights," it can be seen that the traditional caste system specifically violates
Articles 1, 2, 16, 20, 23, and 25: because the system holds that human beings
are *not* born free and equal (contra 1); because discrimination is based upon
social origin and birth (contra 2); because restrictions on caste intermarriage
are severe (contra 16); because one is compelled to associate with the caste of
one's birth (contra 20); because types of employment available are traditionally
restricted to one's caste position (contra 23); and, finally, because the lower
castes, particularly the so called "untouchables" (renamed by Gandhi as the
"Harijans" or "Children of God"), are often deprived of the right to a decent
standard of living simply by the fact of being a member of a caste (contra 25).[21]
With regard to these *Harijans*, those most victimized by the system, Dr. Kananaikil noted that, "The practice of untouchability . . . continues in the countryside unabated. Atrocities against Harijans are a common phenomenon in the
feudal countryside. Jobs and scholarships reserved for them seldom reach them,

---

Trevor Fishlock's recent sobering report: "The labourers, many of them untouchables, are
serfs in a feudal system, cowed, effectively disfranchised by a ruling class determined to
maintain the upper hand. Much of Bihar's bloodshed and brutality springs from the efforts
of high caste masters to keep the lower caste helots beneath the hatches" (*Gandhi's Children*
[London: John Murray Ltd., 1983], p. 110). Anyone pursuing the classified marriage sections of any Indian newspaper, whether in India or abroad, is immediately struck by the
tenaciousness of caste considerations in the Hindu community. Even when an ad stipulates
"caste no bar," it usually means the subcaste or *jati* is no bar.
    [19]Cf. Bagwan Das: "The Untouchables account for 15 per cent of the Indian population.
Eighty per cent of them are divided into more than 900 [sub] castes and are spread out in
600,000 villages in India" ("Untouchability, Scheduled Castes, and Nation Building," *Social
Action* 32 [July-September, 1982]: 272). This issue of the Indian journal *Social Action* is
devoted to the theme, "Scheduled Castes and the Struggle against Inequality."
    [20]Jose Kananaikil, "Marginalisation of the Scheduled Castes: A Sociological Perspec-
tive," *Social Action*, ibid., p. 247.
    [21]See *Perspective* 21 (February, 1984): 5, 7, 14, 16. Note that these scheduled castes
currently prefer the name *Dalit* or "the Oppressed."

or when they do, they reach only a few."[22] Consequently, with these types of abuses in mind, Jagjivan Ram could state emphatically:

> There can be no two opinions that the theory [of caste] has ceased to have any validity either in the context of democratic theory and belief or in the context of India's socio-economic needs. The thinking section of the community is united in holding that the sooner this tenacious relic of the past is given a decent burial the better it would be for Indian society.[23]

What is the source of the *religious* sanctions for such a system?[24] Basically, there are five religious sources for this sanction: (1) The consequences of the prevailing Advaitin metaphysics have provided an atmosphere in society resistant to change. (2) In the history of popular Hinduism, the concept of holiness has been inordinately transferred from a quality of consciousness and being to a fixation on preestablished magical notions of purity. Outward forms rather than inner quality or character have been determinate for a hierarchical notion of holiness. (3) Authentication of the caste system has been sought in the *Rig Veda* and the Gita (two of the most prestigious scriptures in Hinduism) along with (4) the legal treatises (the *Dharmasastras*, particularly *Manu Smrti*). Finally, (5) the system has been maintained and "infallibly" sanctified through the strenuous efforts of the Brahmanic priesthood to maintain power and status while securing Hindu culture against manifold threats of ideological subversion.[25]

In questioning the validity of the caste system and supporting social change which will encourage its eradication, the above religious sanctions must be challenged: (1) Alternate Hindu metaphysical models can be encouraged. (2) With the weakening of the other sanctions and with the widespread propagation of higher Hinduism (concomitant with and dependent upon improved socioeconomic conditions), the concept of holiness among the orthodox traditionalists can slowly be transformed. (3) It can be shown through the scientific tools of literary criticism that neither the Rig Veda nor the Gita does in fact sanction the traditional system. (4) Furthermore, it can be shown that the legal treatises,

---

[22]Kananaikil, "Marginalisation," p. 260. It should be noted, however, contrary to Kananaikil, that resistance to reservations when they promote the less qualified can be based as much upon democracy as upon caste prejudice; cf. minority hiring quotas in the U.S. and prejudice against the more qualified.

[23]Jagjivan Ram, *Caste Challenge in India* (New Delhi: Vision, 1980), p. 17.

[24]Of course, there are numerous theories as to the origins of the caste system, particularly in its Indian context. I have here simply presented my theory from a religious and metaphysical perspective. Among the most thorough studies of the sociological aspects caste are Weber, *Hinduism*; Singer and Cohen, *Structure and Change*; and Louis Dumont, *Homo Hierarchicus*, tr. George Weidenfeld (Chicago: University of Chicago Press, 1970).

[25]Cf. Joseph Kitagawa: "Despite the disadvantages and inequalities of the caste structure, no one can deny the historic role played by the caste system in welding into one community the various groups of diverse background in India" (*Religions of the East* [Philadelphia: Westminster Press, 1960], p. 135). See also J. H. Hutton, *Caste in India* (Cambridge: Cambridge University Press, 1946), pp. 97-106.

which do not carry as much prestige as the Vedas and the Gita, are filled with numerous contradictions displaying multiple authorship; consequently, new *Dharmasastras* can either be written or "discovered," as tradition would have it. (5) With the waning of the above sanctions, traditionalists among the priesthood (and other castes) will be unable to garner the popular support necessary for maintaining their hegemony. Because, to the best of my knowledge, no work has been done linking the first three sanctions, and because so little work has been done on examining the Gita as a developing whole in relation to caste, the rest of this essay will be devoted to filling out this gap in scholarship.

From the metaphysical perspective, then, I suggest that when the Absolute, the object of our ultimate concern, is conceived to be immobile, eternally non-dual, and so formlessly itself, then it naturally follows that there will be a love for the static, for the unchanging, when it comes to this world—in short, the perpetuation of the status quo is most suitable as the "moving image of eternity."[26] The ideal of the immovable sage in meditation thus impresses itself upon society in a manner tantamount to the fixation of social hierarchy.[27] Similarly, the Advaitin view which emphasizes the relativity of all forms, resulting in an indifference to a variety of religious forms, also inspires an indifference toward the hierarchical social forms present in Hindu culture. When this philosophical milieu is combined with that aspect of the doctrine of Maya which stresses the relatively illusory, dream-like character of this world in relation to the absolute Brahman, plus the view of karma-reincarnation whereby one is born into the situation one deserves in life based upon past deeds, it is hardly surprising that the method recommended for dealing with frustration with the forms of social life was to leave the world and become a monk—a renunciate of all social forms including caste and karmic-ritual obligations. This is hardly a model for social reformation.[28]

---

[26]This is not to say that there have not been many "enlightened" activists for social reform among the Advaitins—specifically, Ramakrishna Paramahansa, Swami Vivekananda, Radhakrishnan, and Gandhi come to mind—but only to suggest the possible pragmatic and metaphysical (integrally comprehensive) advantages of a different model of the relationship of Being-itself to Becoming. It should be noted, however, that Gandhi's veneration of the Unchanging Nonduality may have had some connection with his conservate support for such traditions as cow worship and the hereditary system of caste. Much to the chagrin of the leaders of the Untouchables, Gandhi wished them to become members of the lowest "touchable" caste: they were to be sudras for life. In protest, tens of thousands became Buddhists.

[27]In a different context, but in support of my approach, Dumont wrote: "That is the essential 'function' of hierarchy: it expresses the unity of such a society whilst connecting it to what appears to it to be universal, namely a conception of the cosmic order, whether or not it includes a God, or a king as mediator. If one likes, hierarchy integrates society by reference to its values" (*Homo Hierarchicus*, p. 252).

[28]Christian missionaries are quick to jump in at this point of a critique of Hinduism with the proposal of Jesus Christ as the indispensable role model for social reformation. There is certainly some truth to this, for the aftereffects of British imperialism coupled with missionary activities was to instigate greater social consciousness among the Hindus themselves. But it must be remembered that for the bulk of Christian history there was hardly present a notion of the "social gospel." Rather, the emphasis was on otherworldly contemplation

The Gita, like the *Mahabharata* epic of which it is a part, may have been rewritten to express the interests of the Brahmanical priestly caste,[29] but it nevertheless has as its essential core a different conception of the Absolute from the static Advaitin ideology; hence, it also has a different conception of the sage or ideal human being and the structure of society in relation to the caste system. The ideal goal of life is to love and imitate the way of activity of the God-human, the Avatara, Lord Krishna himself, who, though one with Brahman and though the creator of all, is still actively involved in the harsh *realities* and ambiguities of this world. The world is real and action in the world is important, according to the Gita, because God's very self is in the world struggling for the triumph of order and higher purpose. This is a real revolution in Hindu religious thought both metaphysically and socially. As to the metaphysics, Aurobindo wrote:

> [T]he Gītā is going to represent the Ishwara [the personal Lord], the Purushottama [the Supreme Person], as higher even than the still and immutable Brahman, and the loss of ego in the impersonal comes in at the beginning as only a great initial and necessary step towards union with the Purushottama. For the Purushottama is the supreme Brahman. It [the Gita] therefore passes boldly beyond the Vedas and the Upanishads as they were taught by their best authorized exponents and affirms a teaching of its own which it has developed from them.[30]

As to the socioreligious revolution, the Gita, as we have intimated, presents a new ideal for society—that love, active service, and knowledge of God are all to be integrated in our daily lives. In traditional Hindu terminology, the ideal life is one that combines *Karma Yoga* (selfless performance of one's responsibilities), *Bhakti Yoga* (devotional participation in the being of God) and *Jnana Yoga*

(imminent eschatology in the early church), sacramentalism, and personal conversion from sin. Even today the latter two categories often overshadow any serious commitment to social reform. Christians might be more helpful and loving by encouraging the acceptance of Christ as an *Avatara* for Hindus rather than encouraging acceptance of Christianity. Furthermore, it should be noted that, "By and large the caste system as a form of social stratification has persisted in all religious categories in India and the ex-Untouchable converts as a whole occupy the lowest socio-economic position in their respective religious communities [Christian, Muslim, Sikh, etc.]" (D'Souza, "The Religious Factor," p. 290).

[29]There is a continuing scholarly controversy over whether the extant Gita has suffered significant recensions over the years. Early Western indologists thought so; more recent scholars such as Zaehner and Minor think not—although A. L. Basham is currently working on the theory (not yet published) that there were three significant recensions of the text. Indian scholars have generally been impressed by religious prejudices against seeing significant interpolations, with the prominent exception of Khair. See R. C. Zaehner, *The Bhagavad-gītā, with a Commentary Based on the Original Sources* (London: Oxford University Press, 1969); Robert Minor, *The Bhagavad-Gītā: An Exegetical Commentary* (New Delhi: Heritage Pub., 1982); and G. S. Khair, *The Quest for the Original Gītā* (Bombay: Somaiya Pub., 1969).

[30]Sri Aurobindo, *Essays on the Gita*, 11th combined ed. (Pondicherry: Sri Aurobindo Ashram, 1980), p. 85.

(liberating knowledge of the Self and the Absolute).[31] Krishna tells us here not to renounce responsible social action but to renounce all egoistic emotionalism which usually accompanies such actions. Toward the end of the Gita he teaches:

> Doing continually all actions whatsoever, taking refuge in Me, he [the yogin] reaches by My grace the eternal, undying abode. Surrendering in thought all actions to Me, regarding Me as the Supreme and resorting to steadfastness in understanding, do Thou fix thy thought constantly on Me. (Gita 18:56-57)

Because the bulk of modern Hindu apologists have expressed their preference for Advaitism, they naturally have tried to read this philosophy into the Gita. Most Western scholars have followed their lead in this, but the vast majority of modern Indian interpreters of the Gita have differed from their Western counterparts in holding that the Gita does not teach the hereditary transmission of caste duties. Both sides of the controversy, however, have by and large used citations out of context to support their respective positions. Having already argued that the Gita departs significantly from the traditional Advaitin metaphysics, I will now show that it also in no way upholds the orthodox Hindu understanding of the caste system. This orthodox position was stated succinctly by Jayadayal Goyandka in his commentary on the Gita:

> If a Śūdra [the lowest of the four castes] . . . though of good conduct and practising self-control as a duty common to all, follows the vocation of a Brāhmin and earns his living by the same, he incurs sin.[32]

Now the vocation of the Brahmins includes, besides the priesthood, teaching in general. Therefore, Goyandka is saying, for example, that today, based upon Krishna's teachings, a low-caste man must ignore his talents and disposition and, even if he is qualified to be a teacher, he should continue to work as a sweeper if that is the vocation of his caste. Albert Schweitzer in his reading of the Gita concurred in this interpretation: "When he [Krishna] speaks of action, he never means more than the exercise of the activity dictated by caste, not subjective action proceeding from the impulses of the heart and self-chosen responsibili-

---

[31]Arun Shourie, the noted social activist, complains that the revolution in social thought instigated by the Gita never got off the ground: "And so it came to pass that the argument for works and deeds that the author of the Gītā tried to graft onto the tradition [which encouraged the ideal of literal renunciation of the world] was quietly set aside" (*Hinduism*, p. 210).

[32]Jayadayal Goyandka, *Śrīmad Bhagavadgītā*, text, tr., and commentary (Gorakhpur: Gita Press, 1978), p. 192. Based upon this type of orthodox interpretation, Prem Nath Bazaz concluded that the Gita presents "a philosophy of the upper classes meant to be utilized by them as a weapon for maintaining a frustrated society in some sort of stability and equilibrium" (*The Role of the Bhagavadgita in Indian History* [New Delhi: Sterling Pub., 1975], p. ix).

ties."[33] My contention, again, is that Goyandka, Schweitzer, and the bulk of Western commentators on the Gita have been wrong in this approach.

The first mistake which inspires what we may call the "hereditary type of interpretation" is that it assumes Arjuna is Everyman. In other words, the plot of the Gita centers around Krishna's convincing Arjuna to fight in the Mahabharata War because it is Arjuna's duty as a member of the warrior caste to fight, especially in a just war. What these interpreters tend to ignore is the fact that Arjuna is told to fight because his nature is warrior-like (Arjuna only objects to *this* war because his relatives are numbered among his opponents; he does not object to all war; see Gita 1:28-46). Thus, Arjuna's caste and his temperament coincide—and this is the substance of Krishna's teaching: Our true caste is our temperament. If our inner disposition coincides with our father's occupation, then we are to follow in his occupational footsteps. In most ancient societies, this coincidence of hereditary and temperament is the rule. Arjuna is never told to fight, however, because his father was a warrior; rather, he is repeatedly told to follow his inner nature (*svabhava*) and his in-born personal law of duty (*svadharma*).[34] Krishna himself does not fight in the war even though he is a member of the warrior caste, and Krishna nowhere censures Dronacharya, a Brahmin, for leading Arjuna's enemies in battle, thereby going against his caste function.[35] As a matter of fact, there is only one stanza in the Gita where Krishna directly links caste with birth (9:32),[36] but the subject matter of this stanza is the democratic nature of liberation, and it would be unreasonable to take one passage out of context of the entire Gita to prove a point. What Krishna does specifically say is that, rather than being based upon heredity, caste is based upon a quite different foundation. Krishna emphatically and unambiguously declares in 4:13: "The four castes were created by Me according to the divisions of quality [*guna*] and work [*karma*]." Radhakrishnan glosses on this:

> The emphasis is on *guṇa* (aptitude) and *karma* (function) and not on *jati* (birth). The *varṇa* or order [of caste] to which we belong is inde-

---

[33]Albert Schweitzer, *Indian Thought and Its Development* (London: Hodder and Stoughton, 1936), p. 43. Many further examples can be given. In the most recent thorough study of the Gita by a Western scholar, Robert Minor wrote that "There is no such idea in the Gītā . . . that one may choose one's caste on the basis of one's talents" (*Bhagavad Gītā*, p. 483. Cf. Douglas Hill, *The Bhagavad-gītā, with a Translation and Commentary*, 2nd ed. (London: Oxford University Press, 1973), p. 61; Franklin Edgarton, *The Bhagavad-gītā, Translated and Interpreted*, rev. repr. ed. (Cambridge, MA: Harvard University Press, 1974), pp. 161-162; and R. C. Zaehner, *The Bhagavad-gītā*, p. 395.

[34]See Gita 5:14; 8:3; 18:41-44, 47, 60; 3:35; and 18:45-47.

[35]P. V. Kane has listed many exceptions in the ancient literature where it was permissible for one to change one's social caste function on the basis of one's talents or disposition. See his *A History of Dharmaśastra*, vol. 5 (Poona: Bhandarkar Oriental Research Institute, 1962), pp. 163 ff.

[36]Arjuna links caste with birth at the beginning of the Gita (1:41-43), not Krishna. Arjuna complains that as a result of the war there will be intermarriages between castes. Krishna seems unconcerned about this, for he never comments on Arjuna's complaint. Similarly, Krishna may only be expressing popular opinion in 9:32 by linking caste with birth.

pendent of sex, birth or breeding. A class determined by temperament and vocation is not a caste determined by birth and heredity.[37]

The key question, then, in determining Krishna's position concerning whether caste must be based upon hereditary principles is to ask whether Krishna as
the Creator and the God-human is depicted in the Gita as being so naive that he
assumes that every person is born in conformity with the aptitude, temperament,
and general psychic disposition of one's parents. This assumption is the basis for
the hereditary theory of caste. In other words, here a Brahmin's inborn nature
(*svabhavaja*) will be best expressed in the "pure" type of work traditional society
expects of one. A "Brahmin" (by society's definition) must do the work one was
created for. There is thus no possible existential conflict between inwardness and
public image—career counseling is never needed. Such social security exacts a
high tax—stability at the price of true spirituality. It is precisely this the Avatara
finds unacceptable. *Ideally*, inwardness and public image coincide (there is no
hypocrisy if there is no repression, just as there is no enlightenment when there
is repression). The Avatara, however, has symbolically "descended" (*ava-tara*,
downgoing) from the Ideal world into the very real existential situation of a
breakdown in social and spiritual values. Krishna is very clear that a person born
into a caste which society might deem Brahmanic, may actually have the inner,
"inborn" nature of the lowest, most "polluted" kind of person (just as a person
born into what society considers to be a low caste may actually have true
Brahmin-like characteristics):

> There are two types of beings in the world—the divine and the de-
> monic. . . . The demonic do not know about the way of action.
> Neither purity, nor good conduct, nor truth is found in them. . . .
> The faith of the embodied is of three kinds, born of their nature
> [*svabhavaja*], good, passionate, and dull [corresponding to the
> *gunas*]. Hear now about it. The faith of every individual, O Arjuna,
> is in accordance with his nature. Man is of the nature of faith; what
> his faith is, that, verily, is he. (16:6-7; 17:2-3)

In the above stanzas there is not the slightest mention of hereditary caste
as the determining factor in one's inborn nature; instead, we are told that all
people, regardless of what caste society says they belong to, are either divine or
demonic. That is, according to Krishna, people are heading for either an eternal
bode of divine consciousness and bliss through acts of love and self-sacrifice, or
they are heading for ever grosser realms of material self-indulgence and competitiveness. In addition, we are told that the faith of all people can be characterized
according to the makeup of the qualitative constituents or *gunas* which comprise
their psychophysical being. Thus, we are told to discern a person's inborn nature

---

[37]S. Radhakrishnan, *The Bhagavadgītā*, pp. 160-161. Note that the Sanskrit compound is
"guṇakarmavibhāgaśaḥ" which could have been written, if that was the author's intention,
as "jātikarmavibhāgaśaḥ."

in terms of certain outward signs; or, as Jesus put it: "By their fruits you will know them" (Mt. 7:16). A person's inborn nature, then, clearly does not depend upon the caste of that person's parents.

Because we are told by Krishna that we should do the kind of work that is in accord with our inner nature, then we should have some guidelines to help us discern just what that nature is. We need to know who we are before we can determine the right path or calling (*svadharma*) to follow. Only when our life work, our *karma*, is in accord with our inner nature can we truly follow in the footsteps of the Avatara, for the Avatara is both the Lord of Dharma overseeing the correct ordering of society and the Lord of Yoga leading his disciples on the path toward self-realization. So does Krishna help us to know "where we are at"? Chapters 16, 17, and the first part of chapter 18 are devoted to just such guidelines for discernment. Furthermore, in 16:5 Arjuna is told by Krishna that he was born with divine-like qualities. Clearly, again, the implication is that just because Arjuna was born to a high-caste family he need not have high-caste qualities. Rather he could have such "demonic" qualities as "ostentation, arrogance, excessive pride, anger, ignorance, etc." (16:7). Chapter 17 discloses that the types of penance and attitudes toward charity are all factors which aid us in discerning a person's inner, qualitative makeup.

Chapter 18, the culminating and therefore the most important chapter in understanding the drift of Krishna's developing argument in the Gita,[38] begins with a continuation of this discernment procedure. Areas that are discussed are the three types of attitude appropriate to the performance of sacrifice, gift-giving, penance, and all duties and actions of any kind (18:1-17). Following this is a discussion of the three kinds of knowledge which accompany action, the three kinds of doers, understanding, steadiness, and happiness (18:18-39). With this background in mind, we come to several verses in the last chapter which, when taken out of context as they often are, can be seriously misunderstood:[39]

> There is no creature either on earth or again among the gods in heaven which is free from the three constituent qualities [*gunas*] born of their nature. Of Brāhmins, Kṣatriyas, Vaiśyas, as also Śūdras [the four castes in classical literature], O Arjuna, the activities are distinguished in accordance with the constituent qualities born of their nature. Serenity, self-control, austerity, purity, forebearance and uprightness, wisdom, knowledge and faith in religion—these are the duties [*karma*] of a Brāhmin born of his nature [*svabhavaja*]. (18: 40-42)

What are we to make of these verses? Is Krishna reversing himself here? Does he not see the trees for the forest, so to speak, as many an idealist? Is he saying

---

[38]Cf. Sri Aurobindo: "The Gītā can only be understood, like any other work of its kind, by studying it in its entirety and as a developing argument" (*Essays on the Gita*, p. 32).

[39]Verses 18:43-44 also recount the qualities born of the nature of the other three castes.

that all Brahmins have divine-like characteristics? Unless we are to make nonsense of the developing argument, the meaning must be more subtle. We know from 18:40 that all people are differentiated according to the kinds of constituent qualities they inherit as their particular psychophysical being. This inheritance, however, is understood to be from a previous lifetime, according to the Gita's doctrine of reincarnation. In other words, there is no mention of inheritance from one's parents, so what one inherits is a bundle of "inherent" tendencies which, when they exhibit themselves in a Brahmin-like way, show that one is to be considered a Brahmin. This is no more complicated than saying of someone who exhibits a great sense of rhythm as a child, "Ah, a born musician," or of saying of someone who relishes some subtle academic point after many long hours of research and indecision: "Ah, a born scholar." Krishna's teaching on the nature of caste is thus, for example, simply a statement that a "Brahmin" without Brahmin-like characteristics is no Brahmin.[40]

Thus, we have shown that one of the two most prestigious sanctions for maintaining the hereditary system of caste is, in fact, no sanction at all. Neither is the Rig Veda. Only one passage, the famous *Purusa Sukta* (X:90), can be found in this oldest of Hindu scriptures seemingly to support the hierarchical structure of the caste system. Here a primordial sacrifice is described such that the dismemberment of the Primal Person occurs in accordance with caste hierarchy, Brahmins come from this Person's head, and the other three original castes come from increasingly lower bodily portions, culminating in the servant caste's coming from the feet. Colebrooke commented on this: "That remarkable hymn is in a language, metre and style, very different from the rest of the prayers with which it is associated. It has a decidedly modern tone." Max Müller also agreed that this stanza is an interpolation: "There is little doubt that it is modern both in its character and its diction." And Benjamin Walker has reminded us that the word "Sudra," the term in the classical literature for the lowest caste, occurs only once in the Rig Veda—in the *Purusa Sukta*.[41]

So we have seen from our examination of basic Hindu source material that

---

[40]I have found only two other similar passages in the Gita which can with some reason—when taken out of the context of the developing argument we have just outlined—be used to show that Krishna supports the caste system as a hereditary source of social stagnation. In 3:35 and 18:47, Krishna warns against doing another person's duty, even if the duty can be performed more perfectly than one's own. This warning can mean nothing more than simply that one who feels a calling to teach should not abandon that for a more lucrative job as, say, a salesperson, even if one could do that better than the average salesperson. Note also that Krishna says again in 18:47 that one will not incur sin if one follows one's nature (*svabhava*)—he does not mention one's parents' caste.

[41]Colebrooke and Müller are cited by Walker in his discussion of "Forgery." See Benjamin Walker, *The Hindu World: An Encyclopedic Survey of Hinduism*, vol. 1 (New York: Frederick A. Praeger, 1968), pp. 362-365. The absence of caste reference in the original Rig Veda makes perfect sense in the context of the Aryan invasion of India. Since this Veda includes references to this invasion, but not later developments, it could not include a description of a system which developed as a socially feasible way to deal with the mixed races settling down in the new society.

the most important scriptural sanctions for the present system of hereditary castes are unreliable and invalid. Another significant sanction, stemming from widespread magical, mechanical, and impersonal notions of purity—where permanent impurity is attached to persons, places, and objects—can be combatted through the slow but sure efforts of enough enlightened individuals sensitive to the substance of Krishna's teaching as outlined above. Only when Krishna's message is understood by enough people in India will popular Hinduism be able to overcome caste prejudice—as well as prejudice against those of different religious persuasions. (Muslims, for example, regardless of their character, are by nature impure according to popular orthodox Hindu ideology.) At that time popular Hinduism will be able to take what Söderblom has described as "The momentous step in the evolution of holiness and purity . . . [when] holiness becomes a personal quality of the deity and of man, instead of being a substance in things."[42]

This discussion of caste has thus led to one final principle underlying the world religions which I would like to propose: The Principle of the Sacred. Since we have found that underlying all religious and quasi-religious beliefs are principles of freedom and ultimacy, and both these principles serve to highlight the finitude of our judgments in the face of the Absolute and the quest for certitude—then it rightfully can be asked: Is there no authentic certitude in religion? The answer is: There is certitude; however, it is found not in doctrine but in the experiences of sacred reality, or holiness. The fact of religious experience is certain. It is a worldwide phenomenon of *homo religiosus*. For some, the experience of the sacred rigidly attaches itself to particular exclusive forms—be it a caste, a holy book, or a religion; for others, the experience of the sacred finds its highest and truest moment in exceptional religious experiences and/or in mystical insight; finally, for yet others, the experience of the sacred finds its highest expression when it is incorporated into a transformed profane existence. As Söderblom wrote: "The holy is apart from ordinary life. Spiritual religion tries to abolish the outwardness of this distinction and to make it a purely personal one. Hence it tries to bring the whole of life under the sway of holiness."[43] Is not this the character of Mahatma Gandhi's religion? In his autobiography he counseled:

> To see the universal and all-pervading Spirit of Truth face to face, one must be able to love the meanest of creation as oneself. And a man who aspires after that cannot afford to keep out of any field of life. That is why my devotion to Truth has drawn me into the field

---

[42]Nathan Söderblom, "Holiness" in James Hastings, ed., *The Encyclopedia of Religion and Ethics*, vol. 6 (New York: Charles Scribner's Sons, n.d.), p. 731. Note that, in the hereditary system, holiness is an *impersonal* quality of human beings; it has nothing to do with character.

[43]Ibid. Good contrasts for these two ways to apprehend the holy would be, e.g., Advaitism versus the religious humanism of Rabindranath Tagore, and in the West in juxtaposing the works of Rudolph Otto and Martin Buber.

of politics; and I can say without the least hesitation, and yet in all humility, that those who say religion has nothing to do with politics do not know what religion means.[44]

APPENDIX:

UNIFYING PRINCIPLES OF THE WORLD RELIGIONS
AND THE BASIS FOR DIALOGUE

I. The Principle of the Ultimate

No religious or cultural form, be it concrete or abstract and conceptual, can fully exhaust the mystery of Ultimate Reality.

A. We see in all religions a tension between the Ultimate Reality, which is the object of faith, and the need to have concrete, tangible representations or symbols of ultimacy. If the object of our ultimate concern is truly to be the reality which transcends all finite and conditioned human limitations, we must achieve a level of self-criticism about the religious and cultural forms we utilize in our spiritual pursuits. Hence, no religious, theological, or metaphysical form is absolute in itself. These forms are symbols of the presence of an Ultimate Reality which cannot be contained in finite receptacles.

B. If a party to interreligious dialogue claims one's own revelation is Absolute while all other revelations are either pure human constructs or genuine revelations distorted by human error and cultural limitations, fruitful dialogue is precluded on the spiritual level. The orthodox literalist or triumphalist can then truly *meet* others (in dialogue rather than in debate or discussion) only in a shared concern for human welfare—until the Principle of the Ultimate is accepted. But in the context where the violation of human rights is the issue (due to intransigent traditionalists committed to maintaining the status quo), dialogue is still impossible until the Principle of the Ultimate can be accepted. Until such time, human rights can only be established by fiat against the will of the intransigent traditionalists.

C. The Principle of the Ultimate allows for growth within religious traditions. Since no historical form is absolute in itself, these forms can be either abandoned or transformed when they no longer serve the purpose of liberating us from temporal constrictions. Adhering to the Principle of the Ultimate thus keeps the faithful alive to the source of inspiration calling for religious and social reforms in the name of truth, tolerance, and compassion.

II. The Principle of Freedom

We are responsible for our beliefs. In a pluralistic world the abundance of belief-systems makes it ever apparent that belief is never "given" in good faith (without self-deception); rather, belief only occurs when *we* choose to accept some doctrine as valid or as coming from an infallible source.

A. We are free to believe in determinism or not. In relation to religion, this means that we can resist the belief that the future is totally in the "hands" of extra-human forces, for such a belief makes a tyranny of those forces responsible for all the atrocities of

---

[44]M. K. Gandhi, *Autobiography: The Story of My Experiments with Truth*, tr. Mahadev Desai (Washington, DC: Public Affairs Press, 1960), p. 383.

history. Therefore, we are responsible for the future of the world. In other words, even if the "Book of Life" has been written, we are free to believe that a merciful author is capable of constant revision of the text in light of our free decisions.

B. The Principle of Freedom is an affirmation of hope: The future is in our hands—if enough of us with goodwill join hands.

C. The Principle of Freedom makes us responsible for the future of our neighbors, for whatever causative factors have led to their present plight, our free actions now contribute to, and so are responsible for, their future.

III. The Principle of the Sacred

There is a fundamental qualitative distinction between *profane* and *sacred* human experience.

A. The Principle of the Sacred establishes the basis for realizing the unity of the world religions. It asserts that the reality which inspires our ultimate concerns and faith commitments is apprehended in a qualitatively distinct way from the events which fill the irreligious, "materialistic" type of life. The latter *profane* events are apprehended in a careless, irreverent, or egotistical manner suitable for exploitative use. On the other hand, *sacred* realities are apprehended most adequately in an atmosphere of reverence, self-lessness, and love.

B. The Principle of the Sacred establishes the meeting ground of the world religions neither in metaphysical nor religious doctrines which invariably and dogmatically contradict one another and exalt one system or religion at the expense of another. Because nonempirical dogmatic systems are incompatible with the scientific temper, it is best that the irrefutable *fact* of religious experience be the basis for the meeting of the world religions in the modern world.

C. Just as the Principle of Freedom established the fact that doctrinal beliefs follow from free choice, so the Principle of the Sacred affirms that doctrinal beliefs presuppose and so follow religious experience or faith. In other words, when doctrines "fall from heaven," there first has to be the religious experience or faith in a transcendent sacred realm, and, secondly, there has to be the free acceptance of those doctrines as genuine articles of revelation. Hence, the Principle of the Sacred is the common meeting ground of the world religions because it is the foundation for all religious phenomena—while the Principle of Freedom is the foundation for the conceptual apprehension of all sacred events, and the Principle of the Ultimate is the foundation for judging the quality of the reception of all sacred events.

D. Scott Korn (Hindu) is a fulltime visiting lecturer in the Depts. of Religion and Philosophy at Rutgers University, New Brunswick, NJ, who has also taught at Northwestern University and in Chicago on the high-school level (world religions). He holds a B.A. in theology and an M.A. in religious education from Loyola University, Chicago; an M.A. in history and literature of religions from Northwestern University, Evanston, IL; and a Ph.D. (1984) in philosophy from Banares Hindu University, Varanasi, India (following four years' study in India). His dissertation was on "The Logic of Exclusivism: A Comparison of Christianity and Hinduism from the Perspective of Paul Tillich's Systematic Theology and the Bhagavadgita." His most recent article appeared in *New Quest* (Aug.-Sept., 1981). He specializes in Eastern religions, existentialism, meditation, and myth and ritual.

HUMAN RIGHTS IN CHRISTIAN AND ISLAMIC THOUGHT: A REPORT ON THE TÜBINGEN "HUMAN RIGHTS PROJECT"

Gerhard Luf

I. Introduction

The Second Vatican Council emphasized the obligation of all Christians to work for greater justice in the whole world, and the German Bishops' Conference has asked people to further the discussion of fundamental values in our society. In response to these challenges, a research project on issues concerning the foundation of human rights was established at the Philosophy Seminar of the University of Tübingen, West Germany. Professor Johannes Schwartländer is the organizer of the project. A number of conferences have already taken place under its auspices since 1980, whose proceedings have been published.[1]

This report is an outline of what has been achieved until now. The first step was to investigate the relationship between the human-rights tradition and the Christian faith and the Christian churches. The title "Human Rights between Theonomy and Autonomy" indicates the orientation of this research project. Our next step was to enlarge the field of our investigations. We began to deal with the further question of "Human Rights in Non-Christian Religions and Cultures," concentrating on Islamic thought till the present. The first conference on this subject took place in 1982, and the next is scheduled for 1986—which shows that these discussions are still underway.

II. Human Rights between Theonomy and Autonomy

A. The Initial Point: Human Rights as Manifestation of the Modern Concept of Freedom

We first considered the fact that human rights are regarded as universal and fundamental principles of political ethics in both the national and the international fields. They have become the central criteria of political legitimacy. It seems most remarkable in this context that their understanding is becoming more and more detached from a specifically occidental point of view. At the same time this brings into the international discussion a multitude of difficulties stemming from different political and cultural backgrounds and from dissenting opinions concerning the concept and interpretation of human rights. In all the many national and international discussions of the subject, one point seems to have

---

[1]Johannes Schwartländer, ed., *Modernes Freiheitsethos und christlicher Glaube* (Munich: Kaiser; Mainz: Grünewald, 1981).

been overlooked or at least neglected: the systematic foundation and integration of human rights in philosophical and theological thought. Therefore, the Tübingen research project places its main emphasis on a sufficient philosophical and theological basis of these rights by confronting them with Christian and Islamic thought.

We have to base our considerations on several premises. Human rights have not been a feature of all periods and all cultures. They are a phenomenon of the modern world, bearing the marks of its experience of reality and its normative ethical notions.[2] They are the result of painful experiences of crises which led under certain socioeconomic, political, and ideological circumstances to the formulation of inalienable human rights. Although these rights are dependent on a multitude of determining factors from a historical-situative point of view, it is still possible to formulate a normative basic principle of all human-rights tendencies from a philosophical perspective; namely, the freedom of human beings and their claim to be accepted and protected in every aspect of their social relations, as subjects called upon to determine themselves. As formulated by Schwartländer:

> In every demand for human rights men and women are ultimately concerned with their freedom, their right to self-determination or their responsible share in decision-making in society. The basic driving force of this new philosophy of freedom is not the subjective freedom of choice but a freedom achieved by rational and responsible self-determination. "Autonomy" . . . seems therefore to be the central content of all demands for human rights. . . . By this autonomy—understood in ethical and legal terms—men and women determine to become members of a free community.[3]

It was pointed out repeatedly in the course of the project that this concept of freedom is not to be equated with the mere possibility of individualistic self-assertion without regard for social responsibilities. Freedom, according to this philosophical understanding, has of necessity a communicative character. It demands in a fundamental and unconditional way (*a priori*) the recognition and respect of each human being as a subject equally entitled to his or her own freedom. This original social relationship is a condition for the realization of freedom. This aspect of responsibility in the concept of human freedom has often been neglected during the development of human rights and still has to be underscored today—a task of central importance for the world religions, as will be shown below.

On this theoretical level, freedom cannot be conceived already as a juridical right. It functions, rather, as a basic—that is, transcendental—principle of uncon-

---

[2]Johannes Schwartländer, "What are Human Rights?" in Johannes Schwartländer, ed., *Menschenrechte—eine Herausforderung der Kirche* (Munich: Kaiser; Mainz: Grünewald, 1976), p. 78.
[3]Schwartländer, *Modernes Freiheitsethos*, p. 79.

ditioned validity which still demands to be transformed into an institutionalized legal form. It implies a permanent demand to which we must respond under certain historical circumstances, when confronted with experiences of suppression and discrimination in their specific historical appearances. According to the variety of these historical conditions, the juridical responses must necessarily be different in order to take into account the historical awareness of human rights.

B. The Confrontation of Christianity with Human Rights, Understood as Fundamental Rights to Freedom

Starting from this normative foundation of the human-rights concept, the project dealt with the question of how far a positive approach to this philosophy of freedom was possible from a Christian point of view, which was long dominated by the natural-law tradition, and what original contribution Christianity can offer to the development of such a concept of human rights. The leading thesis was that there is no contradiction, but an essential correspondence,[4] between theonomy and autonomy, that is, between the goal of the will of God and human self-determination. According to this thesis, the fundamental correlation between the two, it was stressed, has its roots in the Christian message and shows itself in the freedom of the act of faith and in a life according to the precepts of faith.

This view of the relationship between theonomy and autonomy is not self-evident. For a long time autonomy was considered a fundamental threat to the Christian faith and was, therefore, energetically rejected by the church. Because they came from the ideas of the Enlightenment, human rights—especially freedom of religious faith and opinion—were suspect to church authorities. These human rights were, therefore, reproached for leading to relativism, indifferentism, secularism, and "naturalism." Freedom of religious faith meant for the church simply the freedom to leave the fold of the church and to abandon the faith.[5] Thereby, the churches provided a fundamental contribution to a concept of political legitimacy which was based fundamentally on a traditional religious doctrine.

In the papers and discussions of our research, it was argued from a theological viewpoint that this attitude of the church might be understandable in terms of its struggle against a threatened loss of authority, but it nevertheless contradicts Christ's teaching. Christian doctrine addresses itself to the free consent and acceptance of the individual believer and thus relies on the freedom as demanded by the human-rights movement. There is a true correspondence between the concept of freedom inherent in human rights and the concept of freedom authorized by the gospel itself. To support this view Vatican II was quoted in the discussions, especially its Declaration on Religious Freedom. In this declaration a guar-

---

[4]See Walter Kasper, "Theologische Bestimmung der Menschenrechte im neuzeitlichen Bewusstsein von Freiheit und Geschichte," in ibid., pp. 285 ff.

[5]See the article by Charles E. Curran above, in this volume.

antee for religious freedom is demanded, based on the gospel and on human dignity. It was stressed that a paradigm shift has taken place from the "right of truth" to the "right of the person."[6]

Although the theological arguments cannot be retold here in all their variety, it was common to all of them to stress the importance of freedom of human action in all matters of faith.[7] God wants a free creature as a partner, a free person who responds to the divine call in a responsible act of faith: "Those men and women who experience themselves as creators of their 'world' and know they have a responsibility—they in particular can respond to this calling." Christian freedom presupposes human freedom and, at the same time, fulfills itself by free acts of love. This opens a new and more profound view of women's and men's "humanity" and makes us see this humanity clearly in its absolute and inalienable dignity and value. To accept the predominance of human rights does not mean a superficial compromise with the conditions of modern life for the Christian faith, but the realization that it is founded on the Christian message itself. The Bible does not offer a catalogue of legal definitions of human rights, but it demands that we stand up for the freedom of women and men in all social relations and fight for its legal protection.

In what, we asked, does the contribution of Christianity consist in today's situation? Christian faith can make its influence felt in two ways: it can stimulate, and it can criticize, the actual development of human rights. It can stimulate if it concerns itself with all kinds of human misery and sides with the poor and those who are oppressed or discriminated against. This concern should not be limited to acts of charity, but it should fight for the fundamental rights of the oppressed, for an improvement of their legal position, and for an acknowledgement of their fundamental freedom. In this way it could make a considerable contribution to the support of the ethics of human rights in our society by arousing the conscience of the public. These ethics are—beyond all legal guarantees—an essential condition for the realization of human rights.

Christianity's critical function is to wage a permanent war against undesirable developments that are all too common in the actual developments of human rights. What turn this criticism will take depends on the specific matter with which it is concerned. With regard to the narrow, restrictive concept of human freedom stemming from a liberalistic viewpoint, based on the isolated and selfish individual, Christianity has to insist on the social side of fundamental freedoms. However, it also has to turn against all totalitarian trends that tend to make a life of reciprocal acceptance and respect impossible by trying to eliminate all personal responsibility through enforcing absolute sociopolitical dogmas. The

---

[6]E. W. Böckenförde, introduction to the German publication of Vatican II's "Declaration on Religious Freedom" (Münster, 1968), p. 9.

[7]See Schwartländer, *Modernes Freiheitsethos*, especially articles by Kasper, "Theologische Bestimmung," pp. 285 ff., and F. Böckle, "Theonome Autonomie in der Begründung der Menschenrechte," pp. 303 ff.

defense of the "transcendence of the human person" should be the principal aim in this. When Christians take part in the fight for human rights, people will not believe in their good faith if these rights are not sufficiently respected in the law and social order of the churches themselves. This has been pointed out again and again in the course of our project. Yet, many serious difficulties exist in this respect.

The Code of Canon Law of 1917 did not consider the question of fundamental rights at all. Certainly, the new Code, which in a whole section deals with the "duties and rights of all faithful," represents a considerable step toward the recognition of fundamental rights in the church. Nevertheless, there remain many problems. First of all, these rights are severely weakened and limited since they rely upon an intimate and reciprocal link between rights and obligations. Further, this brings about a lack of distinction between moral and legal duties.[8] They risk not fulfilling their purpose of providing effective juridical guarantees of fundamental freedoms.

III. The Dialogue with Representatives of Islam concerning the Foundation of Human Rights

A. Aims, Methods, and Topics of This Dialogue

After dealing with the value of human rights in Christian thought, our second step was to investigate their value in another great world religion—Islam. We were brought to this step by the following basic deliberation. In the present-day world we are all bound together by a common responsibility for the world, and we perceive this feeling to be at the root of the human-rights movement. In this situation it is up to the great world religions to take their stand in a specific way. In a constructive dialogue carried out in a spirit of tolerance and respect, we wanted to learn whether the treatments of these problems in Islam are at least comparable to ours in Christianity, what the fundamental differences were, and how there could be a common approach to these problems by both religions.

From the beginning, this dialogue had to face two difficulties. First, the history of human rights shows them to be a typical product of the Western world. They have been formed by the troubles of European religious wars, by the phenomenon of secularization, by the separation of religion and politics, by the division between law and morality, by the birth of the modern state, by the coming of industrial mass society, etc. Is it really possible to transplant the product of such a development into a different cultural context? Will not human rights remain part of the Western horizon and tradition and provide only a destructive and disintegrating influence within foreign cultural surroundings? Will they not

---

[8]See Gerhard Luf, "Die Autonomie des reliöses Subjekts: Überlegungen zur Begründung von Menschenrechten in der Kirche," in Schwartländer, *Modernes Freiheitsethos*, pp. 322 ff.; and G. Höver, "Die Kirche und die Menschenrechte," in ibid., pp. 344 ff.

be considered elements of an occidental cultural imperialism? At the same time, do they not present universal human values despite their origin in a particular region, and have they not become an inalienable part of universal social and legal progress? Cannot their universal character demand universal recognition regardless of their historical background? What would the substance or form of human rights be like if realized under different cultural conditions?

The second difficulty we faced was whether the specific structure of Islamic thought permits an approach to the fundamental concept of human rights, especially in view of the way Islam regards the relationship between the individual and the community and between religion and politics. This is a complex matter, because an observer cannot be satisfied by a simple enumeration of basic humanitarian values as seen by the Muslim faith. What we look for is an institutionalized structure for the protection of fundamental human rights.

The topics which have already been treated include: possibilities for a Christian-Islamic dialogue, the relationship between the individual and the community in Islamic thought, secularization and its consequences, attempts to find a specific theological reasoning leading to the establishment of human rights, and the difference between "tolerance" and human rights with regard to a legal guarantee of religious freedom. Since we wanted to have the Christians and Muslims understand each other, we arranged for discussions in which Christians tried to explain their viewpoint, and Muslims were to answer and explain theirs. This is one method we used in order to avoid an emotionally charged atmosphere.

B. The Central Problems and Questions regarding the Systematic Integration and Foundation of Human Rights in Islamic Thought (with Emphasis on Religious Freedom)

1. *The Basis of Human Dignity in Islamic Theology.*

The first question we encountered when trying to establish a foundation of human dignity was: Do we have to look for a theological answer which will then lead us to a valid anthropological view? It was pointed out that the Qur'an itself provides, within the context of its anthropological pronouncements, bases for developing a view of humanity which can easily be reconciled with the concept of human rights that has been characteristic of Europe and America. In the Muslim concept, human dignity is based on the fact that the human being has been created as an exceptional being. God placed Adam on earth as *halifa*, as God's representative or delegate, to bring about a moral world order. Another qur'anic passage states that God entrusted Adam with more wisdom than the angels, who had to prostrate themselves before Adam. God breathed into humans something of God's spirit and gave them the ability to respond freely and responsibly to God's call.[9] In this way the Qur'an very clearly emphasizes humanity's quality

---

[9]See Mohamed Talbi's article above, in this volume.

of individual moral responsibility. The words, "No (soul) will carry the burdens of another," mean in the interpretation of modern exegetes that every individual decides on his or her religious conviction individually and must thus be guaranteed the necessary freedom. Similarities and analogies with the Christian ideas on this subject immediately come to mind. With regard to basic anthropological features, we could—and certainly will—continue to find points of consensus.

2. *Foundations of Religious Freedom.*

This characterization of human dignity as bound up with the order of creation enjoins the idea that the act of faith is a free and voluntary act, by which the human being "freely responds to God's call." Therefore, it follows that compulsion is incompatible with religion. Even though the act of faith remains the source of necessary legal consequences, there must be a distinction between the legal adherence to religious (and political) community and the duties that are brought about by it on the one hand, and the pure inner act of religious conviction on the other hand.

3. *The Consequences for a Human Right of Religious Liberty.*

What now are the consequences of this religious approach to religious freedom as a fundamental right, one which in its systematic contents depends in addition on specific political and ideological circumstances? Will it actually lead to an acknowledgement of a fundamental right to religious liberty? The discussion on this point has revealed many problems and difficulties and has resulted in very different answers. Such questions as these were raised: What is the difference between a legal right and mere tolerance as it characterizes the historical attitude of Islam to other "religions of the Book"? How are the non-Islamic minorities treated in Muslim states? What is the significance of the "protective contracts" concerning the *dhimmis*?

Further, what justification can be found for the fact that Muslims demand and use religious liberty when they are a minority in a non-Islamic state, but want —as fundamentalists do—to establish Islam as a state religion in Islamic states? Will it not be necessary to constitute a common rule for minority and majority believers? Has the experience of Islamic minorities influenced the consciousness of Islam as a whole? While some participants in our discussions felt this to be a purely pragmatic problem, others insisted on the need for a fundamentally theological explanation. They argued that no progress could be achieved in the question of universal human rights without such an explanation.

We also discussed the problem of apostasy and the question of the death penalty for this "crime." Further, must leaving the Islamic community be permitted, since punishing a mental attitude may not be allowed in the Islamic religion? Was the death penalty only an act of self-defense in a historical war situation? If the community is based on religion, is not apostasy a breaking of solidarity, which threatens the unity of not only the religious but also the political community?

What does the proclamation of *jihad* mean? Is it, we hope, possible and correct to understand it as a purely ethical ruling based on the persuasive power of religious conviction? These are problems in which the relationship between truth and freedom becomes the focal point of the human-rights discussion. Difficulties arose from the fact that in Islam the individual is much more determined in his or her conviction of ultimate salvation by his or her relation with the community than is the case for a Christian. As an outward token of the believer's allegiance to God, the divine rule gains an eminent position. Adherence to these rules places the believer in a divine order and assures him or her of salvation. Individual and collective salvation of the faithful are closely connected. This makes for difficulties in our concept of religious liberty as a human right, since the latter is necessarily related to an individual.

Following up these concerns, members of our conference formulated the following questions: Can one differentiate between the act of faith and the legal adherence to a religious community? Who is a real member of the *umma*, the community of believers? Can one compare the Christian *communio* and the Islamic *umma*? Has the *umma* any institutional means of claiming religious rights from the political authorities and enforcing them in case of suppression? In short, what is the relationship between state and *umma*? Difficulties became more pronounced at this point, because the Western concept of the right of religious liberty was definitely formed under the doctrine of the separation of church and state and impartiality in the search for religious truth for the sake of peace in political society. The secularization and the neutrality of the state in religious matters are the expression of a development that led to a separation of religion and politics in modern Christian history. Islam cannot follow this development because of different historical and ideological traditions, and it would be a mistake to force this concept of secular freedom of religion upon it immediately. However, it would not be sufficient for Islam to reduce religious freedom to mere tolerance, as the *dhimmi* rules suggest, either. Have we a real dilemma here? The central question for Islam in founding religious liberty seems to be whether it is possible not only to tolerate other religions but also to justify this tolerance by accepting religious freedom as a divinely ordered right. Such a divine right would have to be respected by the state. That leads us back to the relationship of existing Islamic states and the vision of an ideal Islamic "state" or, more generally, state and religion.

Some participants demanded the formulation—analogous to a basic-needs concept of human rights—of a minimal standard of elementary protections for the exercise of religion. The following items have been named: (1) no compulsion, (2) protection of the rights to join and to leave, (3) the right to common divine service, (4) the right to profess one's faith and to give religious instruction, and (5) the right to study one's religion. The intention of the formulation of this minimum standard is to create a substantial basis common to all religions, which can be accepted by everyone.

C. Religion and Politics in Islam

It has repeatedly been affirmed that Islam knows only a necessary union between religion and politics. Therefore, in this view, it is the duty of the Islamic state to reign in the name of religion; dissolving this intimate junction would lead to a radical loss of cultural-religious identity. We found in our discussions that this thesis is *not* self-evident, for it conceals the fact that there is a multitude of different interpretations of the notion of an Islamic state. What is it that makes a state an "Islamic state"? Is it the fact that Islam is the state religion and the *shari'a* the only valid rule of law? Or is it Islamic—as others believe—when the state forces no one to live under the rule of the *shari'a* because such compulsion would contradict the true understanding of the Qur'an?

Since we cannot find simple answers to these questions and problems, I will simply sum them up as follows: What are the criteria of an Islamic state? Has it ever existed in a pure form in history (perhaps in the times of the caliphs?) to which one might have to return, as some suggest? Are there any among the Islamic states of today which deserve this qualification to the full extent? Or does this concept of an Islamic state function only as a guiding utopia for which one must forever strive, without ever reaching it definitively? It became obvious that this notion of state has not been used precisely and unequivocally. Therefore, it is extremely difficult to situate religion and politics in a relationship to each other that would enable us to derive a satisfying foundation of human rights. As a major aim in all these questions, however, we have to postulate that theonomy should be realized in the field of politics without becoming a theocracy, because in a theocracy there is no room for the exercise of freedom as a human right.

D. The Phenomenon of Secularization

As already noted, human rights are a phenomenon of the process of secularization that, along with other developments, came with industrialization and the appearance of an industrial mass society. Christianity has had painful experience with this development, especially in the nineteenth century, and only after a long struggle has it succeeded in establishing conditions which permit a positive approach to these new developments. Even now, there remain several causes of tension. It is quite reasonable, therefore, to pose the following questions: Will not Islam, although belatedly, be confronted with these same difficulties? Will this happen in the near future? Will the change in industrial society influence the Islamic states in their religious, cultural, and political identity? Is it possible to use "Western" achievements in "segments" and still retain the traditional religious and cultural identity? Or are those correct who blame secularization for having abandoned age-old traditions and as being a phenomenon of crisis that has to be overcome by restoring the old traditions? Or is it possible, by way of a more precise differentiation of the relationship between religion and politics, to provide a constructive approach without destroying the cultural roots of faith?

It is remarkable—and, I might add, questionable—that all these problems created by modern secular development have found too little attention in our discussions. These challenges will, I think, be most important for the future development of human rights.

E. Prospects

The discussions in the Tübingen project have convinced me that it is not advantageous to begin the talks about human rights in Western terminology. That will often lead only to misunderstandings. It has proved better to begin with the fundamental human responsibilities and duties and advance from that to fundamental rights. Human suffering and common dangers that threaten all of us are the basic starting points, because they are an experience common to all of us.

Nevertheless, I want to insist on the following observation: In Islam, as well as in Christianity, there is a lack of understanding for the necessity of legal guarantees and an institutionalized defense mechanism for the protection of human rights. There is a widespread inclination to assume that a situation is protected by law, when in truth only ethical ideals have been formulated. To trust exclusively in the effectiveness of moral appeals is to undervalue the importance of legal institutions and the protection they afford. This point should be emphasized in the further discussions.

Gerhard Luf (Roman Catholic) has been an "extraordinary professor" since 1980 at the Institut für Rechtsphilosophie und Rechtstheorie, Vienna (his birthplace), and has credentials to teach legal philosophy and canon law. He previously taught canon law at the Vienna law faculty. He received his doctorate in law from that faculty in 1966. He is also a member of the Research Seminar on Human Rights and Religion of the University of Tübingen in Germany. He has written a book about the relation between freedom and equality in the political thought of Immanuel Kant, and several articles on the foundation of human rights in canon law and methodological research on legal positivism.

FINAL STATEMENT OF THE CONFERENCE
ON RELIGIOUS LIBERTY AND HUMAN RIGHTS

Principles

From November 3 to 8, 1985, we scholars of religion and kindred disciplines from five world religions—Buddhism, Christianity, Hinduism, Islam, Judaism—coming from thirteen countries on four continents, met in Haverford, Pennsylvania, to discuss "Religious Liberty and Human Rights Between Nations, Within Nations, and Within Religions," cosponsored by the *Journal of Ecumenical Studies*, the Religion Department of Temple University, and the Jacob Blaustein Institute for the Advancement of Human Rights, New York. We came to the following agreed understandings:

We are convinced that human society must move beyond mere religious toleration, by which other religious beliefs and practices are grudgingly allowed, to full religious liberty: Wherein both the free choice and practice of religion or belief and the decision to change or leave a religion or belief are held to be fundamental human rights, and members of all religions and beliefs treat each other with full respect as equal fellow human beings. Full religious liberty includes freedom not only from outside coercion or suppression on account of religion or belief, but also from the suppression or restriction of human rights inside each particular religious or belief community. This freedom from coercion within the religious or belief community is as essential as is freedom from outside coercion.

We are convinced that the way each religion and belief teaches its own members to treat fellow members who think differently than they do will tend to carry over in the treatment of members of other religions and beliefs. Hence, it is imperative that all religions and beliefs school their members to accord all others, both within and outside of their ranks, the full human integrity, dignity, and religious liberty they claim for themselves. Moreover, the fundamental integrity of all religions and beliefs demands consistency and reciprocity by extending the same level of religious liberty to adherents of other religions and beliefs that they expect for their own members.

We are convinced that, because religious liberty as a human right is a modern phenomenon which has its origin in the political developments that led to a distinction—not a separation—between religion and the political order, each religion must provide a theological response to this challenge reflecting its own traditions and values. Because we are convinced that in affirming full religious liberty Buddhists, Christians, Hindus, Muslims, and Jews, among others, act in accordance with the central tenets of their respective faiths, where some traditional teachings and practices of religion or belief are inconsistent with the affirmation of full religious liberty for all, scholars of each religion or belief should undertake the necessary research and reflection to resolve them.

Finally, we are convinced that the fundamental mode of approaching members of one's own and other religions and beliefs must be that of dialogue, that is, each speaking with the other primarily to learn from the other. It is only with such a dialogue attitude that we can come to really understand members of our own and other religions and beliefs and live with them as true neighbors, each in full religious freedom.

Recommendations

To promote these principles, we endorse generally the conclusions and recommendations of the U.N. Seminar on the Encouragement of Understanding, Tolerance, and Respect in Matters Relating to Freedom of Religion or Belief (Geneva, Switzerland, December 3-14, 1984). Specifically, we recommend that:

1. The participants in the present Colloquium seek ways to establish a continuing process of consultation and study in regard to questions of religious liberty, such as (a) the role that regional human rights institutions can play in the effort to eliminate intolerance and discrimination based on religion or belief and to promote full religious liberty, and (b) the relationship between religious intolerance, racial or ethnic or sexual discrimination, and political conflict.

2. Nongovernmental organizations should explore the possibility of establishing, individually or cooperatively, an independent center to document and make available to the public information on current violations of religious liberty and manifestations of intolerance in matters of religion or belief, at a minimum as defined in the 1981 U.N. Declaration on this subject. (Declaration on the Elimination of All Forms of Intolerance and of Discrimination Based on Religion or Belief, proclaimed by the United Nations General Assembly, November 25, 1981, in resolution 36/55.)

3. Nongovernmental organizations and independent experts should draft guidelines for a U.N. convention on the elimination of all forms of intolerance and discrimination based on religion or belief and the promotion of full religious liberty, including in the draft, at a minimum, the principles and rules of the 1981 U.N. Declaration.

4. The U.N. General Assembly should declare November 25th "Religious Liberty Day" to mark the day it adopted the 1981 Declaration and to serve as focus and stimulus for educational and promotional activity in support of its principles.

5. The U.N. should urge all governments to disseminate widely in their countries and in their national languages, especially governments whose languages are official languages of the United Nations, the text of the 1981 Declaration, as well as the provisions of the Universal Declaration of Human Rights, the Covenant on Civil and Political Rights, and other international instruments that relate to religious liberty, intolerance, and discrimination. They should draw them to the attention, in particular, of civil servants, including judges, magis-

trates, and lawyers, and any other officials whose duties might involve the protection of religious freedom.

6. States should review their constitutions and laws to ensure that freedom of religion or belief as provided in the aforementioned international documents is adequately safeguarded. In addition, they should examine the possibility of establishing national institutions, or designating existing ones, with the responsibility of promoting religious liberty and of creating training programs for appropriate officials on ways to combat religious discrimination and to promote religious liberty.

7. Educational institutions and the mass media should assume an active role in educating society not only to tolerate others but also to treat them with full respect as equal fellow human beings in a spirit of dialogue, in regard both to interreligious relationships and intergroup relationships generally.

8. Religious bodies at every level—local, national, and international—should foster the spirit of tolerance, respect, and dialogue within their own ranks and between their members and those of other faiths. Activities to this end should include, among others, dissemination of the text of the 1981 Declaration in local languages; participation by clergy and lay leaders in commemorating November 25th as "Religious Liberty Day" through sermons, writings, or public events, and holding interreligious dialogues on the significance of the 1981 Declaration and ways to promote it.

9. The U.N. Centre for Human Rights should continue and should upgrade its Advisory Services in techniques of legislation, education, or information to enable states and other relevant bodies that request them to enhance their efforts to promote religious freedom.

10. The study on the Elimination of All Forms of Intolerance and of Discrimination Based on Religion or Belief mandated by the U.N. Subcommission on Prevention of Discrimination and Protection of Minorities is an important vehicle for achieving progress at the international level toward the goal of religious freedom. Governments and nongovernmental organizations should cooperate fully with the Special Rapporteur designated by the Subcommission to conduct this study by responding in a timely and comprehensive manner to requests to furnish information and ideas in order to assist in its preparation.

DECLARATION ON THE ELIMINATION OF ALL FORMS OF INTOLERANCE AND OF DISCRIMINATION BASED ON RELIGION OR BELIEF
(Adopted by the General Assembly of the United Nations, November 25, 1981)

The General Assembly,

Considering that one of the basic principles of the Charter of the United Nations is that of the dignity and equality inherent in all human beings, and that all Member States have pledged themselves to take joint and separate action in cooperation with the Organization to promote and encourage universal respect for and observance of human rights and fundamental freedoms for all, without distinction as to race, sex, language, or religion,

Considering that the Universal Declaration of Human Rights and the International Covenants on Human Rights proclaim the principles of nondiscrimination and equality before the law and the right to freedom of thought, conscience, religion, and belief,

Considering that the disregard and infringement of human rights and fundamental freedoms, in particular of the right to freedom of thought, conscience, religion, or whatever belief, have brought, directly or indirectly, wars and great suffering to [hu]mankind,* especially where they serve as a means of foreign interference in the internal affairs of other States and amount to kindling hatred between peoples and nations,

Considering that religion or belief, for anyone who professes either, is one of the fundamental elements in [one's] conception of life and that freedom of religion or belief should be fully respected and guaranteed,

Considering that it is essential to promote understanding, tolerance, and respect in matters relating to freedom of religion and belief and to ensure that the use of religion or belief for ends inconsistent with the Charter, other relevant instruments of the United Nations, and the purposes and principles of the present Declaration is inadmissible,

Convinced that freedom of religion and belief should also contribute to the attainment of the goals of world peace, social justice, and friendship among peoples and to the elimination of ideologies or practices of colonialism and racial discrimination,

Noting with satisfaction the adoption of several, and the coming into force of some, conventions, under the aegis of the United Nations and of the specialized agencies, for the elimination of various forms of discrimination,

Concerned by manifestations of intolerance and by the existence of discrimination in matters of religion or belief still in evidence in some areas of the world,

Resolved to adopt all necessary measures for the speedy elimination of such intolerance in all its forms and manifestations and to prevent and combat discrimination on the grounds of religion or belief,

Proclaims this Declaration on the Elimination of All Forms of Intolerance and of Discrimination Based on Religion or Belief:

Article 1

1. Everyone shall have the right to freedom of thought, conscience, and religion. This right shall include freedom to have a religion or whatever belief of [one's] choice, and freedom, either individually or in community with others and in public or private, to manifest [one's] religion or belief in worship, observance, practice, and teaching.

2. No one shall be subject to coercion which would impair [one's] freedom to have a religion or belief of [one's] choice.

3. Freedom to manifest one's religion or beliefs may be subject only to such limitations as are prescribed by law and are necessary to protect public safety, order, health, or morals or the fundamental rights and freedoms of others.

---

*The bracketed inclusive language is added or substituted by the editor.

Article 2

1. No one shall be subject to discrimination by any State, institution, group of persons, or person on the grounds of religion or other beliefs.

2. For the purposes of the present Declaration, the expression "intolerance and discrimination based on religion or belief" means any distinction, exclusion, restriction, or preference based on religion or belief and having as its purpose or as its effect nullification or impairment of the recognition, enjoyment, or exercise of human rights and fundamental freedoms on an equal basis.

Article 3

Discrimination between human beings on the grounds of religion or belief constitutes an affront to human dignity and a disavowal of the principles of the Charter of the United Nations, and shall be condemned as a violation of the human rights and fundamental freedoms proclaimed in the Universal Declaration of Human Rights and enunciated in detail in the International Covenants on Human Rights, and as an obstacle to friendly and peaceful relations between nations.

Article 4

1. All States shall take effective measures to prevent and eliminate discrimination on the grounds of religion or belief in the recognition, exercise, and enjoyment of human rights and fundamental freedoms in all fields of civil, economic, political, social, and cultural life.

2. All States shall make all efforts to enact or rescind legislation where necessary to prohibit any such discrimination, and to take all appropriate measures to combat intolerance on the grounds of religion or other beliefs in this matter.

Article 5

1. The parents or, as the case may be, the legal guardians of the child have the right to organize the life within the family in accordance with their religion or belief and bearing in mind the moral education in which they believe the child should be brought up.

2. Every child shall enjoy the right to have access to education in the matter of religion or belief in accordance with the wishes of his [or her] parents or, as the case may be, legal guardians, and shall not be compelled to receive teaching on religion or belief against the wishes of his [or her] parents or legal guardians, the best interests of the child being the guiding principle.

3. The child shall be protected from any form of discrimination on the grounds of religion or belief. He [or she] shall be brought up in a spirit of understanding, tolerance, friendship among peoples, peace and universal brother[sister]hood, respect for freedom of religion or belief of others, and in full consciousness that his [or her] energy and talents should be devoted to the service of his [or her] fellow [human beings].

4. In the case of a child who is not under the care either of his [or her] parents or legal guardians, due account shall be taken of their expressed wishes or of any other proof of their wishes in the matter of religion or belief, the best interests of the child being the guiding principle.

5. Practices of a religion or beliefs in which a child is brought up must not be injurious to his [or her] physical or mental health or to his [or her] full development, taking into account article 1, paragraph 3, of the present Declaration.

Article 6

In accordance with article 1 of the present Declaration, and subject to the provisions of article 1, paragraph 3, the right to freedom of thought, conscience, religion, or belief shall include, *inter alia*, the following freedoms:

(a) to worship or assemble in connection with a religion or belief, and to establish and maintain places for these purposes;

(b) to establish and maintain appropriate charitable or humanitarian institutions;

(c) to make, acquire, and use to an adequate extent the necessary articles and materials related to the rites or customs of a religion or belief;

(d) to write, issue, and disseminate relevant publications in these areas;

(e) to teach a religion or belief in places suitable for these purposes;

(f) to solicit and receive voluntary financial and other contributions from individuals and institutions;

(g) to train, appoint, elect, or designate by succession appropriate leaders called for by the requirements and standards of any religion or belief;

(h) to observe days of rest and to celebrate holidays and ceremonies in accordance with the precepts of one's religion or belief;

(i) to establish and maintain communications with individuals and communities in matters of religion and belief at the national and international levels.

Article 7

The rights and freedoms set forth in the present Declaration shall be accorded in national legislations in such a manner that everyone shall be able to avail him[or her]self of such rights and freedoms in practice.

Article 8

Nothing in the present Declaration shall be construed as restricting or derogating from any right defined in the Universal Declaration of Human Rights and the International Covenants on Human Rights.

THE DIALOGUE DECALOGUE
Ground Rules for Interreligious, Interideological Dialogue

Leonard Swidler

Dialogue is a conversation on a common subject between two or more persons with differing views, the primary purpose of which is for each participant to learn from the other so that he or she can change and grow. This very definition of dialogue embodies the first commandment of dialogue.

In the religious-ideological sphere in the past, we came together to discuss with those differing with us, for example, Catholics with Protestants, either to defeat an opponent, or to learn about an opponent so as to deal more effectively with him or her, or at best to negotiate with him or her. If we faced each other at all, it was in confrontation—sometimes more openly polemically, sometimes more subtly so, but always with the ultimate goal of defeating the other, because we were convinced that we alone had the absolute truth.

But dialogue is *not* debate. In dialogue each partner must listen to the other as openly and sympathetically as he or she can in an attempt to understand the other's position as precisely and, as it were, as much from within, as possible. Such an attitude automatically includes the assumption that at any point we might find the partner's position so persuasive that, if we would act with integrity, we would have to change, and change can be disturbing.

We are here, of course, speaking of a specific kind of dialogue, an interreligious, interideological dialogue. To have such, it is not sufficient that the dialogue partners discuss a religious-ideological subject, that is, the meaning of life and how to live accordingly. Rather, they must come to the dialogue as persons somehow significantly identified with a religious or ideological community. If I were neither a Christian nor a Marxist, for example, I could not participate as a "partner" in Christian-Marxist dialogue, though I might listen in, ask some questions for information, and make some helpful comments.

It is obvious that interreligious, interideological dialogue is something new under the sun. We could not conceive of it, let alone do it in the past. How, then, can we effectively engage in this new thing? The following are some basic ground rules, or "commandments," of interreligious, interideological dialogue that must be observed if dialogue is actually to take place. These are not theoretical rules, or commandments given from "on high," but ones that have been learned from hard experience.

FIRST COMMANDMENT: *The primary purpose of dialogue is to learn, that is, to change and grow in the perception and understanding of reality, and then to act accordingly*. Minimally, the very fact that I learn that my dialogue partner believes "this" rather than "that" proportionally changes my attitude toward her; and a change in my attitude is a significant change in me. We enter into dialogue so that *we* can learn, change, and grow, not so we can force change on the *other*, as one hopes to do in debate—a hope realized in inverse proportion to the frequency and ferocity with which debate is entered into. On the other hand, because in dialogue *each* partner comes with the intention of learning and changing herself, one's partner in fact will also change. Thus the goal of debate, and much more, is accomplished far more effectively by dialogue.

SECOND COMMANDMENT: *Interreligious, interideological dialogue must be a two-sided project—within each religious or ideological community and between religious or ideological communities.* Because of the "corporate" nature of interreligious dialogue, and since the primary goal of dialogue is that each partner learn and change himself, it is also necessary that each participant enter into dialogue not only with his partner across the faith line—the Lutheran with the Anglican, for example—but also with his coreligionists, with his fellow Lutherans, to share with them the fruits of the interreligious dialogue. Only thus can the whole community eventually learn and change, moving toward an ever more perceptive insight into reality.

THIRD COMMANDMENT: *Each participant must come to the dialogue with complete honesty and sincerity.* It should be made clear in what direction the major and minor thrusts of the tradition move, what the future shifts might be, and, if necessary, where the participant has difficulties with her own tradition. No false fronts have any place in dialogue.

Conversely—each participant must assume a similar complete honesty and sincerity in the other partners. Not only will the absence of sincerity prevent dialogue from happening, but the absence of the assumption of the partner's sincerity will do so as well. In brief: no trust, no dialogue.

FOURTH COMMANDMENT: *In interreligious, interideological dialogue we must not compare our ideals with our partner's practice,* but rather our ideals with our partner's ideals, our practice with our partner's practice.

FIFTH COMMANDMENT: *Each participant must define himself.* Only the Jew, for example, can define what it means to be a Jew. The rest can only describe what it looks like from the outside. Moreover, because dialogue is a dynamic medium, as each participant learns, he will change and hence continually deepen, expand, and modify his self-definition as a Jew—being careful to remain in constant dialogue with fellow Jews. Thus it is mandatory that each dialogue partner define what it means to be an authentic member of his own tradition.

Conversely—the one interpreted must be able to recognize herself in the interpretation. This is the golden rule of interreligious hermeneutics, as has been often reiterated by the "apostle of interreligious dialogue," Raimundo Panikkar. For the sake of understanding, each dialogue participant will naturally attempt to express for herself what she thinks is the meaning of the partner's statement; the partner must be able to recognize herself in that expression. The advocate of "a world theology," Wilfred Cantwell Smith, would add that the expression must also be verifiable by critical observers who are not involved.

SIXTH COMMANDMENT: *Each participant must come to the dialogue with no hard-and-fast assumptions as to where the points of disagreement are.* Rather, each partner should not only listen to the other partner with openness and sympathy but also attempt to agree with the dialogue partner as far as is possible while still maintaining integrity with his own tradition; where he absolutely can agree no further without violating his own integrity, precisely there is the real point of disagreement—which most often turns out to be different from the point of disagreement that was falsely assumed ahead of time.

SEVENTH COMMANDMENT: *Dialogue can take place only between equals*, or as Vatican II put it: *par cum pari*. Both must come to learn from each other. This means, for instance, that there can be no authentic, full dialogue between a learned scholar and a naively informed person, but at most there can be a gathering of information as in a sociological interrogation. Further, if, for example, the Muslim views Hinduism as inferior, or if the Hindu views Islam as inferior, there will be no dialogue. If authentic interreligious, interideological dialogue between Muslims and Hindus is to occur, then both the Muslim and the Hindu must come mainly to learn from each other; only then will it be "equal with equal," *par cum pari*. This rule also indicates that there can be no such thing as a one-way dialogue. For example, Jewish-Christian discussions begun in the 1960's were mainly only prolegomena to interreligious dialogue. Understandably and properly, the Jews came to these exchanges only to teach Christians, although the Christians came mainly to learn. But, if authentic interreligious dialogue between Christians and Jews is to occur, then the Jews must also come mainly to learn; only then will it, too, be *par cum pari*.

EIGHTH COMMANDMENT: *Dialogue can take place only on the basis of mutual trust*. Although interreligious, interideological dialogue must occur with some kind of "corporate" dimension, that is, the participants must be involved as members of a religious or ideological community—for instance, as Marxists or Taoists—it is also fundamentally true that it is only *persons* who can enter into dialogue. But a dialogue among persons can be built only on personal trust. Hence it is wise not to tackle the most difficult problems in the beginning, but rather to approach first those issues most likely to provide some common ground, thereby establishing the basis of human trust. Then, gradually, as this personal trust deepens and expands, the more thorny matters can be undertaken. Thus, as in learning we move from the known to the unknown, so in dialogue we proceed from commonly held matters—which, given our mutual ignorance resulting from centuries of hostility, will take us quite some time to discover fully—to discuss matters of diagreeement.

NINTH COMMANDMENT: *Persons entering into interreligious, interideological dialogue must be at least minimally self-critical of both themselves and their own religious or ideological traditions*. A lack of such self-criticism implies that one's own tradition already has all the correct answers. Such an attitude makes dialogue not only unnecessary, but even impossible, since we enter into dialogue primarily so *we* can learn—which obviously is impossible if our tradition has never made a misstep, if it has all the right answers. To be sure, in interreligious, interideological dialogue one must stand within a religious or ideological tradition with integrity and conviction, but such integrity and conviction must include, not exclude, a healthy self-criticism. Without it there can be no dialogue—and, indeed, no integrity.

TENTH COMMANDMENT: *Each participant eventually must attempt to experience the partner's religion or ideology "from within"*; for a religion or ideology is not merely something of the head, but also of the spirit, heart, and "whole being," individual and communal. John Dunne here speaks of "passing over" into another's religious or ideological experience and then coming back enlightened, broadened, and deepened. As Raimundo Panikkar notes, "To know what a religion says, we must understand what it says, but for this we must somehow believe in what it says": for example, "A Christian will never fully understand Hinduism if he is not, in one way or another, converted to Hinduism. Nor will a Hindu ever fully understand Christianity unless he, in one way or another, becomes Christian."

Interreligious, interideological dialogue operates in three areas: the practical, where we collaborate to help humanity; the depth or "spiritual" dimension where we attempt to experience the partner's religion or ideology "from within"; the cognitive, where we seek understanding and truth. Interreligious, interideological dialogue also has three phases. In the first phase we unlearn misinformation about each other and begin to know each other as we truly are. In phase two we begin to discern values in the partner's tradition and wish to appropriate them into our own tradition. For example, in the Buddhist-Christian dialogue Christians might learn a greater appreciation of the meditative tradition, and Buddhists might learn a greater appreciation of the prophetic, social justice tradition—both values traditionally strongly, though not exclusively, associated with the other's community. If we are serious, persistent, and sensitive enough in the dialogue, we may at times enter into phase three. Here we together begin to explore new areas of reality, of meaning, and of truth, of which neither of us had even been aware before. We are brought face to face with this new, as-yet-unknown-to-us dimension of reality only because of questions, insights, probings produced in the dialogue. We may thus dare to say that patiently pursued dialogue can become an instrument of new "re-velation," a further "un-veiling" of reality—on which we must then act.

There is something radically different about phase one on the one hand and phases two and three on the other. In the latter we do not simply add on quantitatively another "truth" or value from the partner's tradition. Instead, as we assimilate it within our own religious self-understanding, it will proportionately transform our self-understanding. Since our dialogue partner will be in a similar position, we will then be able to witness authentically to those elements of deep value in our own tradition that our partner's tradition may well be able to assimilate with self-transforming profit. All this of course will have to be done with complete integrity on each side, each partner remaining authentically true to the vital core of his/her own religious tradition. However, in significant ways that vital core will be perceived and experienced differently under the influence of the dialogue, but, if the dialogue is carried on with both integrity and openness, the result will be that, for example, the Jew will be authentically Jewish and the Christian will be authentically Christian, not despite the fact that Judaism and/ or Christianity have been profoundly "Buddhized," but because of it. And the same is true of a Judaized and/or Christianized Buddhism. There can be no talk of a syncretism here, for syncretism means amalgamating various elements of different religions into some kind of a (con)fused whole without concern for the integrity of the religions involved—which is not the case with authentic dialogue.